The Zymoglyphic Museum

a guide to the exhibits
third edition

Jim Stewart, Curator

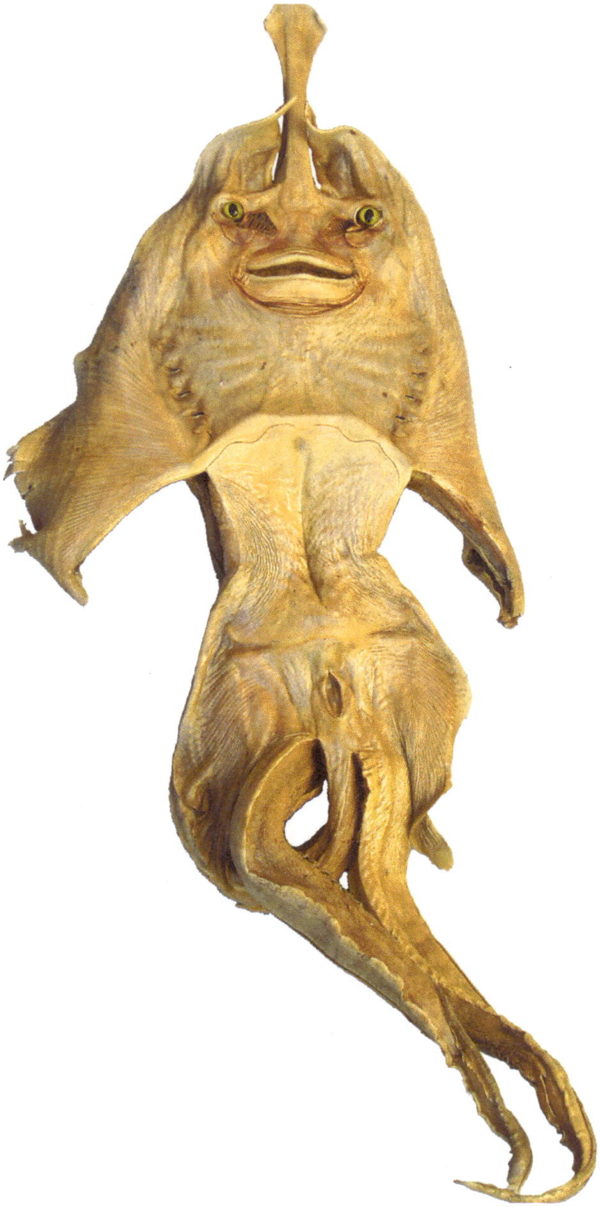

ISBN: 978-1-7332296-8-5

A publication of the **Zymoglyphic Museum Press**

Visit the museum online at **zymoglyphic.org**

zy'-mo-glyph'-ic, adj. [Gr. *zyme* leaven + Gr. *glyphe* carving]

1. Of, or pertaining to, images of fermentation, specifically the solid residue of creative fermentation on natural objects.
2. The collection and arrangement of objects, primarily either natural or weathered by natural forces, for poetic effect

The world as anatomized in conventional encyclopedias is full enough of wonders to slake the thirsty minds of most. But for we desperate few, we who go everywhere and nowhere at once, we who have glimpsed the tacky sideshow machineries behind the scrim of sloppy substance, there's a state of mind that is also a place and, dare I say it, a state of grace, a rich abyss that sings us home as if it's where we come from.

The first fragile notes might reach you through a poem or an accident or an umbrella placed with menace beside a sleek, defenseless sewing machine on a recreational dissecting table.

Any arrangement of objects that seems to obliquely evoke a shaping eye in the mess of things, any shrill synchronicity that burns you with its urgency without overtly disclosing its significance, any moment that makes you wonder which dream you went to sleep in…these are the vectors through which a sophisticated Otherness enthusiast is led from the vaguely mystical and the amorphously occult to the Zymoglyphic.

The museum. The mythology. The way of seeing.

I was barely a person to start with, it's true, but it took this curious cabinet of alien ephemera to mess me up and thrill me forever.

—Jason Squamata, author of *Hotel Zymoglyphic*

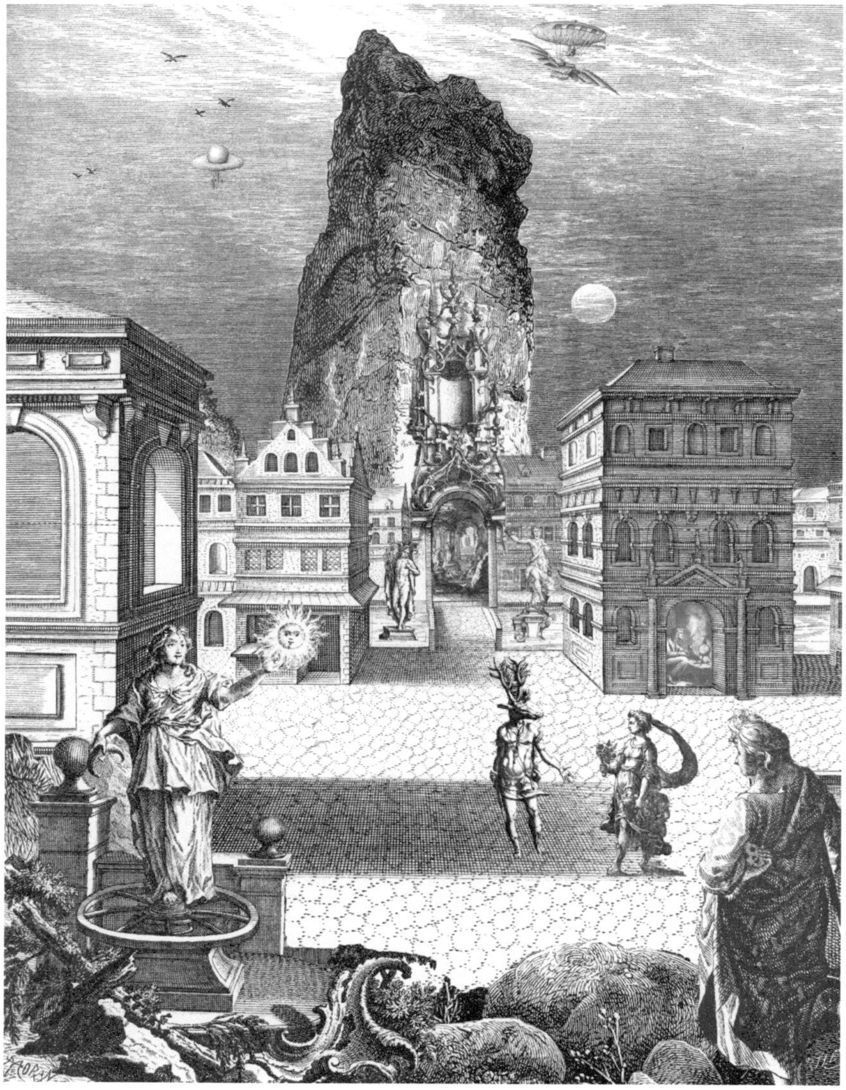

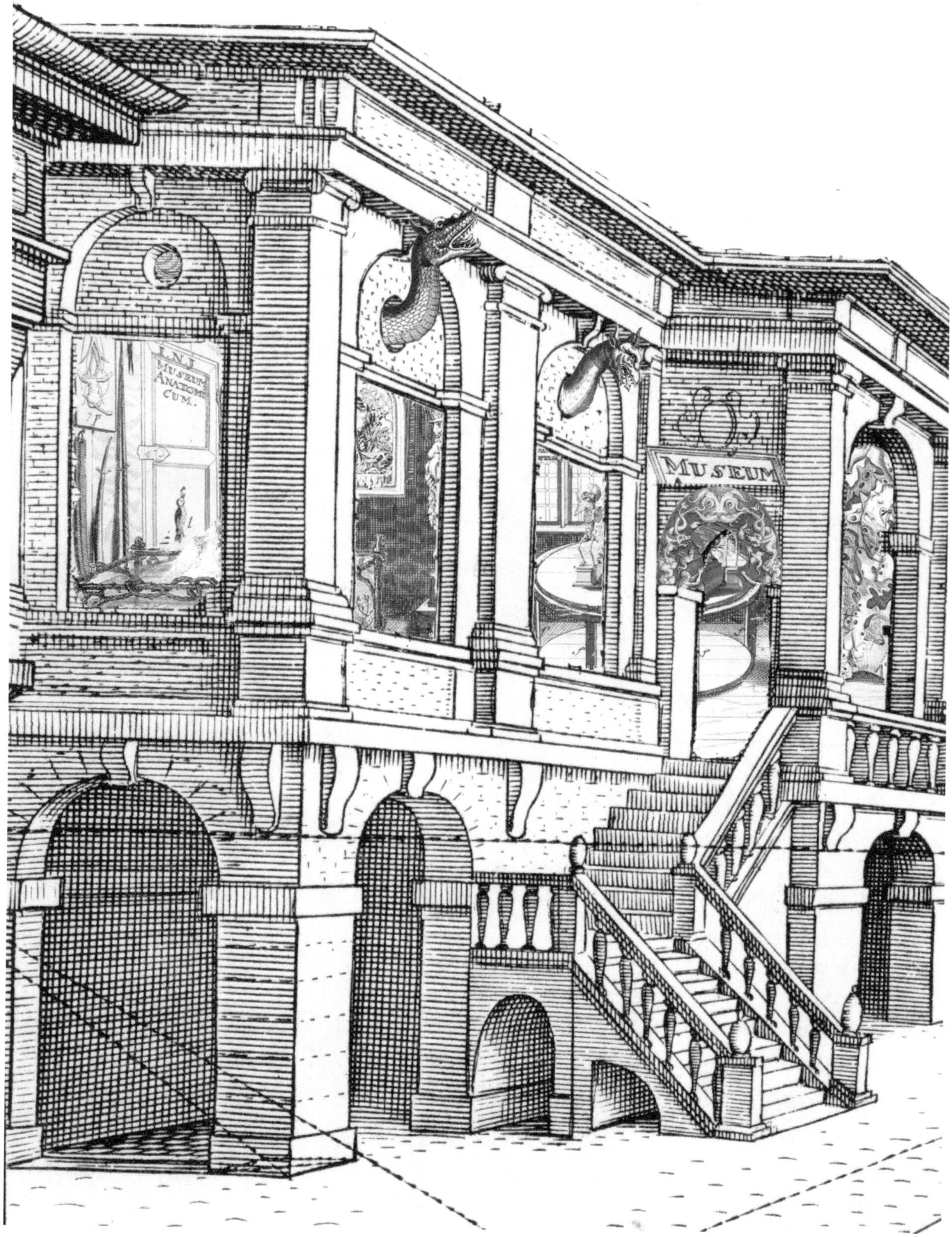
MUSEUM
ANATOMI
CUM.
MUSEUM

INTRODUCTION

The Zymoglyphic Museum is a small but complex and multi-layered institution, the custodian for the world's only collection of the art, artifacts, and natural history specimens of the Zymoglyphic region, a place whose very existence is questioned by many. The museum's mission is to research and document the history and culture of the region, reconstructing artifacts as necessary, and presenting its findings to an interested public. This is a multidisciplinary effort. We rely on mystical anthropology, spontaneous surrealism, literary analysis, esoteric taxonomies, interpretive photography,and other arcane methodologies to illuminate the shadowy undercurrents of the region.

THE EXHIBITS

The exhibits in the museum are organized along the general timeline of the development of the Zymoglyphic region.

The **Natural History Wing** of the museum is the first exhibit one encounters upon entering the museum. This section is a small but carefully curated set of collections of specimens from the natural world including an array of picture rocks (presented as a miniature art gallery), the museum's signature collection of Xenophora (sea snails that collect objects and are billed as "Assemblage Artists of the Deep"), and, most importantly, species endemic to the region.

The **Mud Age** is known in Zymoglyphic mythology as the time before the beginning of time, when no records were kept and no events were recorded. Perpetual dense mists shrouded the tree-fern forests. Mud pots and fumaroles boiled and popped everywhere, caked with colorful minerals, sulphurous yellows, coppery greens and blues. Millions of tiny creatures ate the sulphur and excreted all the colors of the rainbow. Where pools of cool water were able to form, they were covered in pond scum and bacterial mats, known as the "primordial ooze." Frequent lightning strikes on these ponds caused convulsive chain reactions on the organic materials, letting loose aethereal spirits and demons of all kinds. Unfortunately, there are not enough artifacts to warrant a specific exhibit for this era, but its influence oozes everywhere.

The **Rust Age** was a preliterate era for which we have a number of intriguing artifacts, both unearthed and reconstructed. These range from ceremonial pieces, such as masks and figurines, to more functional items such as bioluminescent fungus lamps and pre-literate books. The actual meaning of these objects is speculative at best and based on indigenous cultures that have survived into the modern age. However, even divorced from any original spiritual function and mounted trophy-like on the wall of a museum, these artifacts retain a fascination based on their aesthetics alone.

The **Age of Wonder** was an exuberant time of exploration, invention, and examination of the physical world, rather than the spiritual concerns of the Rust Age. This urge manifested itself in the collection and arrangement objects which were if interest for various reasons. These were organized into eclectic wonder cabinets and themed collections, the latter becoming the collections we have today. This exhibit also contains examples of the alchemy and cosmography studies of the time, as well an extensive set of narrative dioramas.

The **Era of Oriental Influence** was a relatively short-lived reaction to the excesses of the Age of Wonder. Zymoglyphic explorers during the Age of Wonder made contact with a culture whose aesthetic was immediately seized upon. Overly elaborate art works fell out of fashion in the region, and in their stead appeared small, quiet, serene works made for contemplation, perhaps a simple tray landscape or a gnarled rock or stick mounted on a stand. People came to appreciate the aesthetics of simple, ordinary things instead of the exotic and rare, local contemplation in place of exploration and collection.

The **Modern Age** came inevitably to this remote region as it has to rest of the world. Various modernist trends in art became refracted though a zymoglyphic lens, resulting in a plethora of styles and schools, captured on the walls of the museum and in miniature art galleries. The turning inward inspired by the Era of Oriental Influence resulted in the discovery of unconscious wellsprings of creativity that became manifested.

Outreach

In addition to its conservation and exhibition functions, the museum conducts outreach efforts promoting the cultural values and philosophy of the Zymoglyphic region.

The **Zymoglyphic Postal Service** creates postcards for the museum shop and issues postage stamps to bolster the museum's claim to be the last remaining sovereign territory of the Zymoglyphic region.

The **Zymoglyphic Museum Press** issues books and booklets related to the museum and its themes. For a complete list of available titles, see p. 206.

The museum maintains an extensive online presence at **zymoglyphc.org**, The Web site includes additional online-only exhibits.

On the most general level, the museum promotes the Zymoglyphic process of making connections: found objects are assembled to make new objects, objects are organized into collections, collections evolve into a museum, and the museum connects to the world through outreach programs.

The museum's outreach efforts also serve to educate the public on themes that are prominent in Zymoglyphic culture:

- Art that is formed by nature or in partnership with nature
- Art that is formed by assemblage of natural objects
- Art that is formed by the action of weathering and other natural forces
- A sense of wonder in the world through collections of curiosities
- Personal museums as a means of creative expression

NATURAL HISTORY

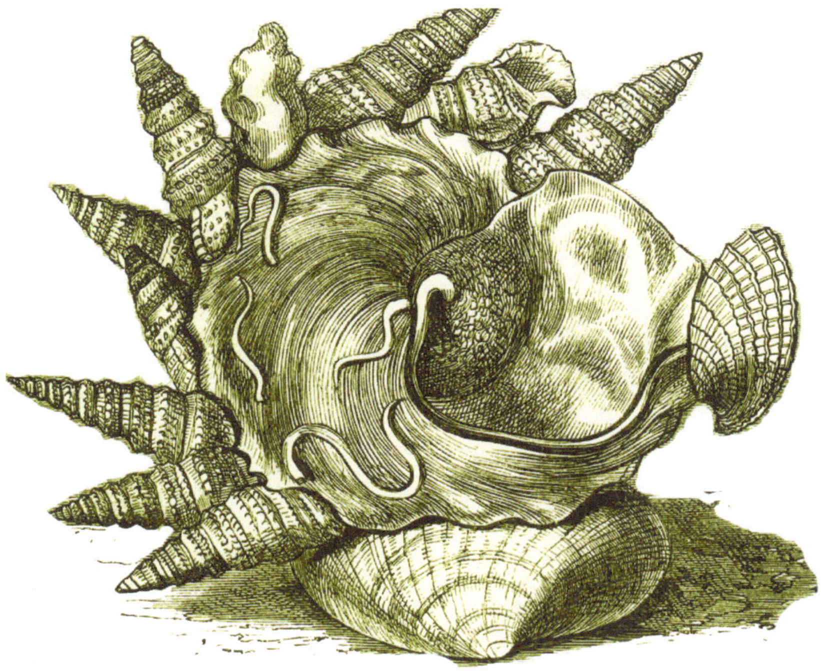

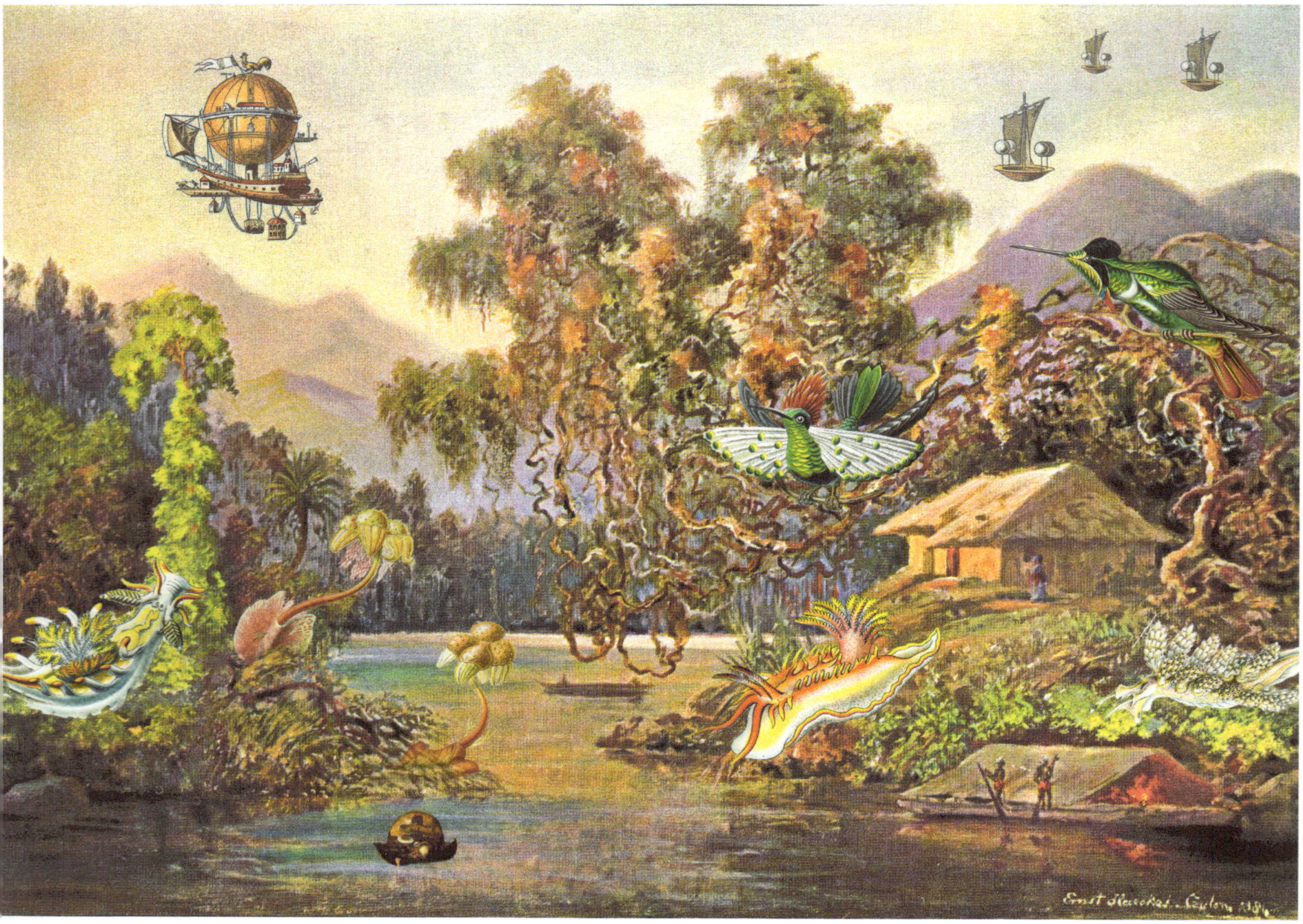

An expedition to a mountain lagoon in the Zymoglyphic region

Natural History

The natural history of a region consists of the study of its rocks and minerals, its geological structures and climate, its panoply of living creatures, and all the ways in which any one of them one affects the others. The historic and biological isolation of the Zymoglyphic region in particular is due in part to the peculiarities of the currents in the surrounding seas, and the dense fogs that sometimes surround the islands. Lacking influence from surrounding areas, some very unusual flora and fauna have evolved in response to evolutionary pressures. The Natural History Wing of the Zymoglyphic Museum showcases these unique life forms, as well as examining the influence that natural forms have had on the artistic expression of the region.

The Zymoglyphic land masses were formed by the upwelling of molten magma from the underworld pushing up through cracks in the Earth's crust, boiling the sea, cooling, hardening, finally poking out of the water and mellowing in the tropical breezes. Once the land settled into shape, its mountainous terrain blocked the breeze, forcing it to rise up and over and drop its contained moisture on the land. The windward side of the island grew dense with jungle, a rich multilayered ecosystem with strange things going on in the undergrowth, rusting anything in its path. The leeward portions of the islands have become parched deserts, being passed over by empty clouds. The sea, lapping persistently at the rough edges of the new land, created ledges and beaches. The fierce storms that occasionally wash over the islands, rusting anything in their path, deposit on the beaches a bounty of intriguing objects churned up from the ocean deeps. These deposits, along with items gathered from the underbrush, form the basis for much of the art of the region.

Hall of Rocks and Minerals

Geological artifacts have held a fascination for the people of the Zymoglyphic region throughout its history, although in many different ways.

During the **Rust Age**, picture stones were prized both as the fossil record of a bygone archetypal era, and a source of natural aesthetics..

In the **Age of Wonder**, rocks and minerals were collected for their stories. While the scientific analysis of the fossil record revealed the epic scope of the evolution of life, individual collectors created small collections of interesting minerals.

In the **Era of Oriental Influence,** the provenance of a rock was not as important as its inherent aesthetic qualities. Collectors simply mounted interesting stones on stands as objects for contemplation.

During the **Modern Age,** stones of a certain type were valued for their sculptural qualities, and, like their Rust Age forebears, valued as natural art.

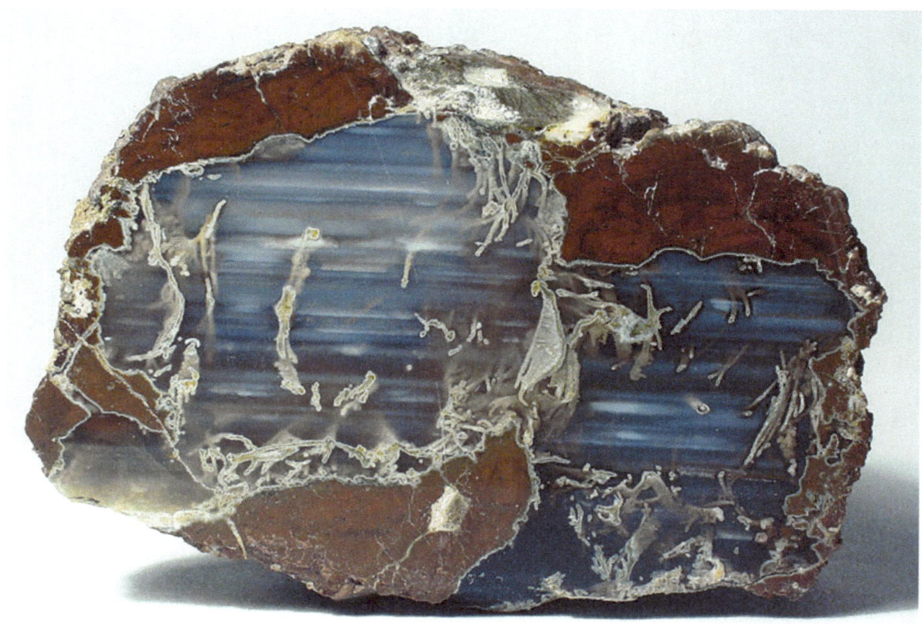

Aquarium stone, Rust Age

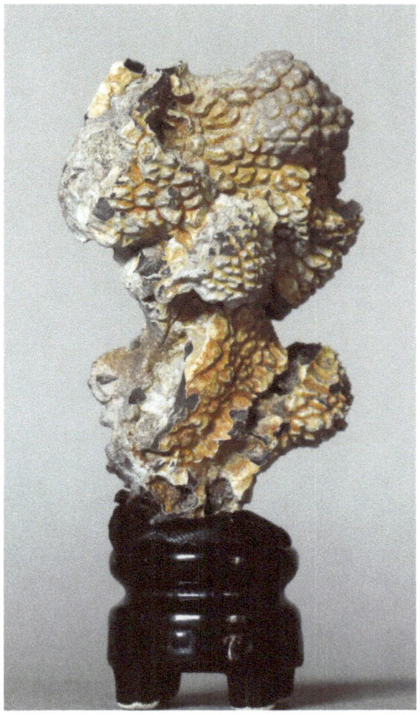 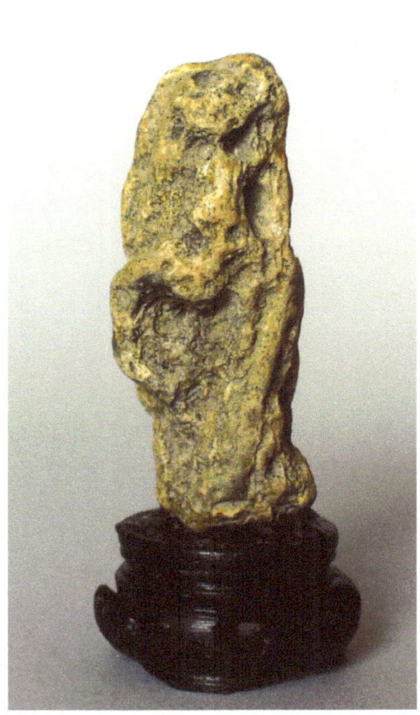

Miniature viewing stones, Era of Oriental Influence

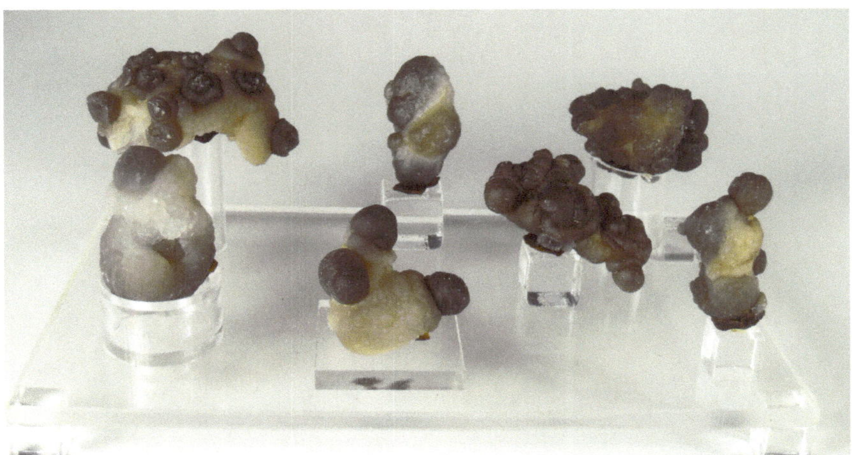

Agates presented as modernist sculpture

Picture Stones

Picture stones were prized during the Rust Age as illustrations of the Mud Age, when no other means of recording was possible. They were believed to have been formed by an impressionist geophotogenic process whose mechanism has not yet been determined. These picture stones served as the oracular equivalent of a crystal ball, helping to induce miasmatic visions of the Mud Age, especially in conjunction with the vapors of the hallucinogenic House Fungus.

During the Age of Wonder, agate slabs were used as "windows" when building miniature grottoes (see p. 128 for an example). In the Era of Oriental Influence, they were mounted as viewing stones for contemplation (see example on p. 20). In the Modern Era, they served as an inspiration for abstract art.

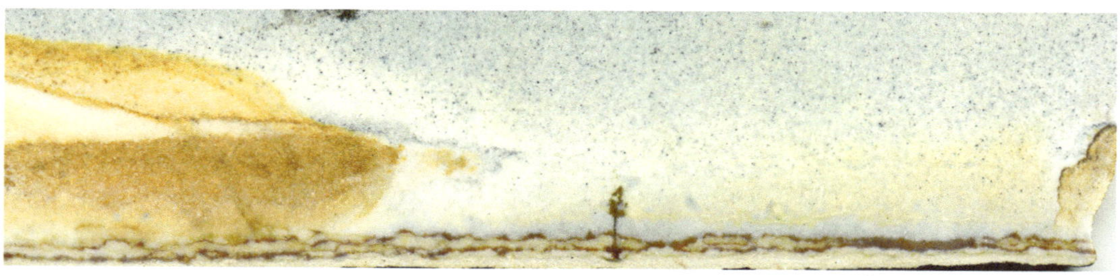

Chicken track jasper

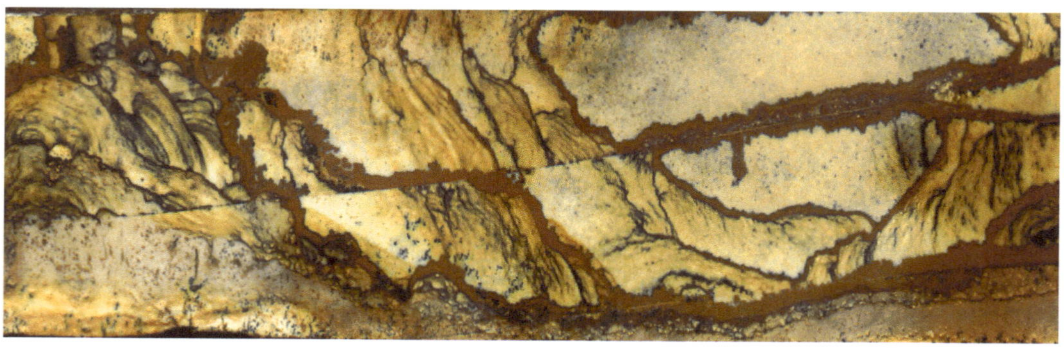

Picture Jasper

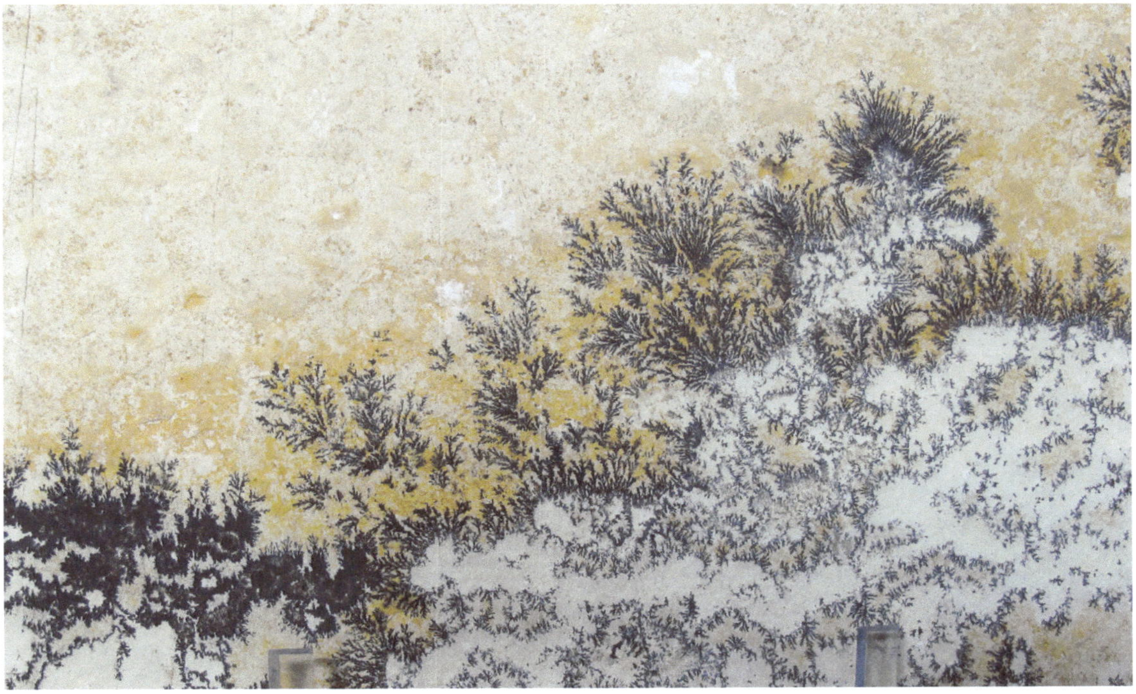

Dendritic sandstone

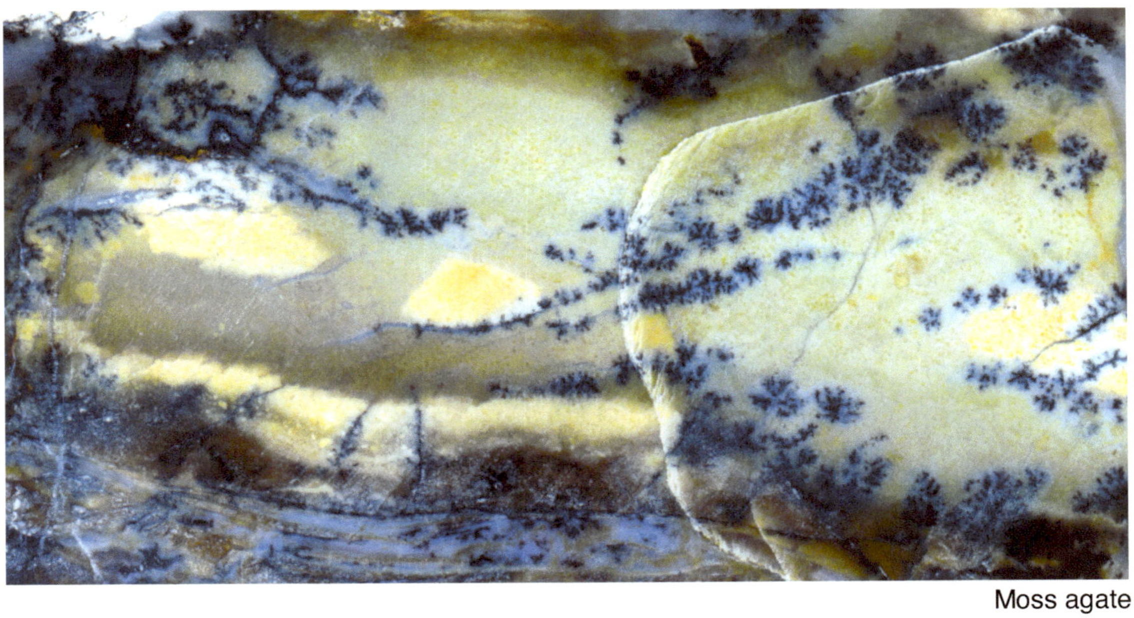

Moss agate

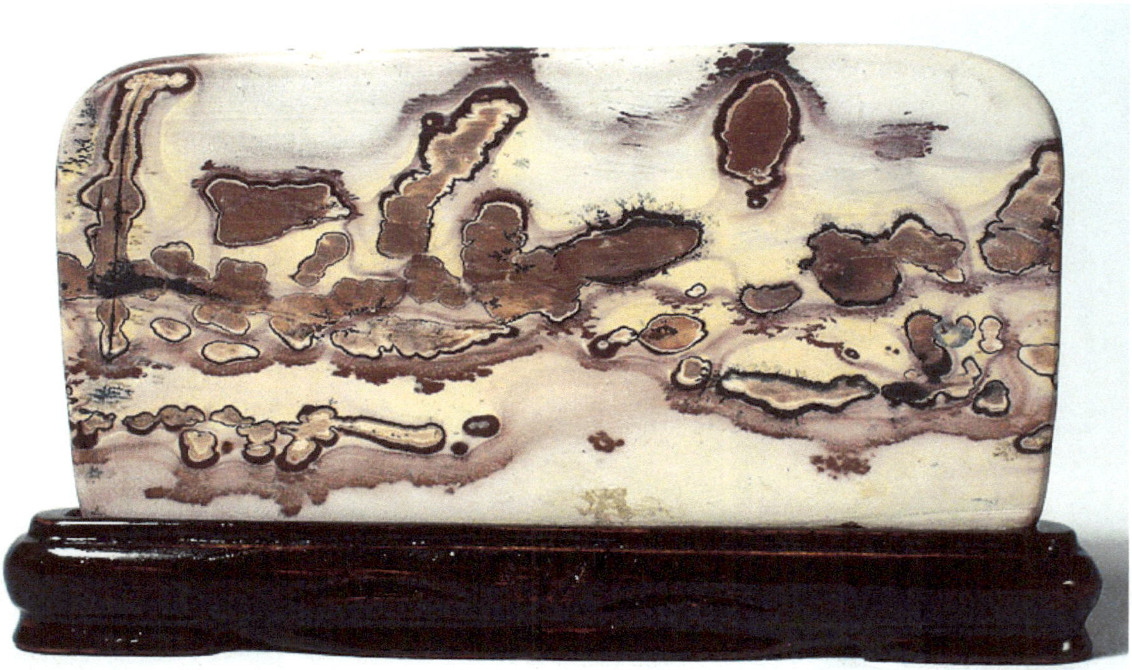

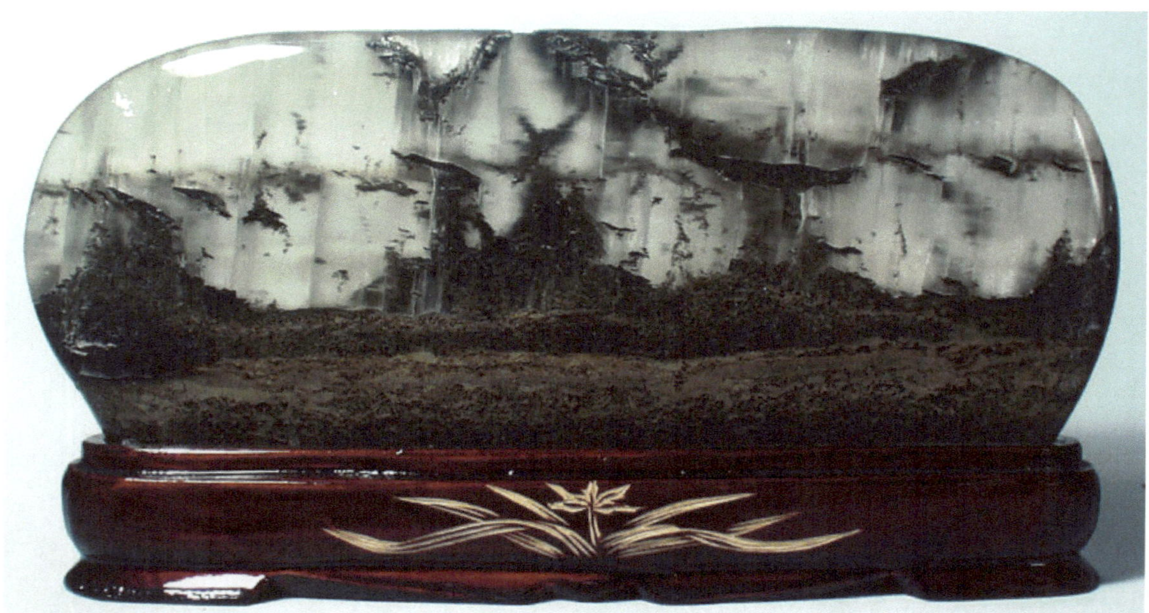

Picture stones from the Era of Oriental Influence, when they were popular as objects of contemplation.

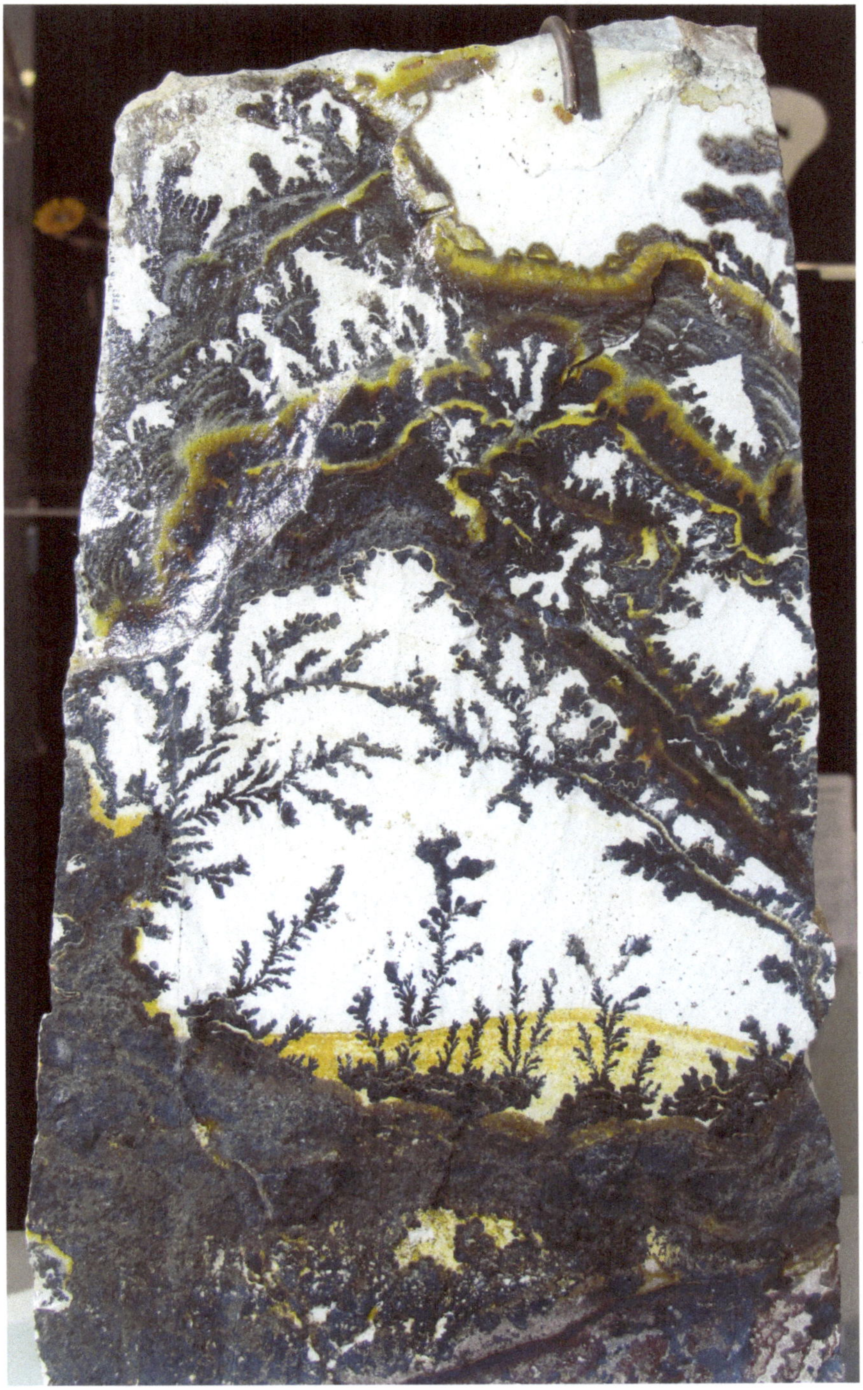

Dendritic sandstone

XENOPHORA

Marine snails of the genus Xenophora collect shells, rocks, and other debris from their environment. They attach these objects to their shells at intervals during the shell's growth. Sometimes it creates a neat radiating pattern; sometimes the effect is more that of a jumble of debris. The result for us in any case is that their collections become little samplings of a variety of faraway underwater realms.

NATURAL HISTORY

It is not known to what extent an artistic sensibility plays a part in this behavior. The snails who live in shallower water (where there is enough light for them to be seen) probably use their collections for camouflage. The ones that live in the deeper, dark waters, such as X. pallidula, are believed to be motivated more by a desire to not to be sucked into the viscous muck in which they live. Attaching extensions to their shells spreads out the shell's surface area and helps prevent the animal from sinking. The additions may also strengthen the snail's relatively thin shell.

> *Characteristically, the shell is covered with other shells, shell fragments, coral pieces, or stones that are attached or cemented with secretions from the animal. The shells are attached dead, although there is one account of a live kitten's paw being attached in an aquarium. All bivalves and bivalve pieces are attached inner side up and gastropods are usually attached with the aperture up. Once an object is selected, it is cleaned (as is the site of intended attachment), and then the object is rotated and fitted to the attachment site. This may take up to 1 1/2 hours. The piece is then held in place with the animal's foot, snout, and tentacle bases and glued into place. The Xenophora may then lay motionless for up to 10 hours, only rocking in place now and then, seemingly a check on the strength of its new attachment.*

—from the (now extinct) Xenophoridae home page (retrieved Aug 30, 2009). The "kitten's paw" referred to is actually a species of bivalve.

Not all of the items on a Xenophora's shell are put there by the creature itself. As a solid substrate in a mucky environment, the shell is an enticing landing spot for tube worms, oysters, and, most spectacularly, glass sponges. Their new home even has the advantage of being mobile, transporting a rooted animal to new feeding grounds.

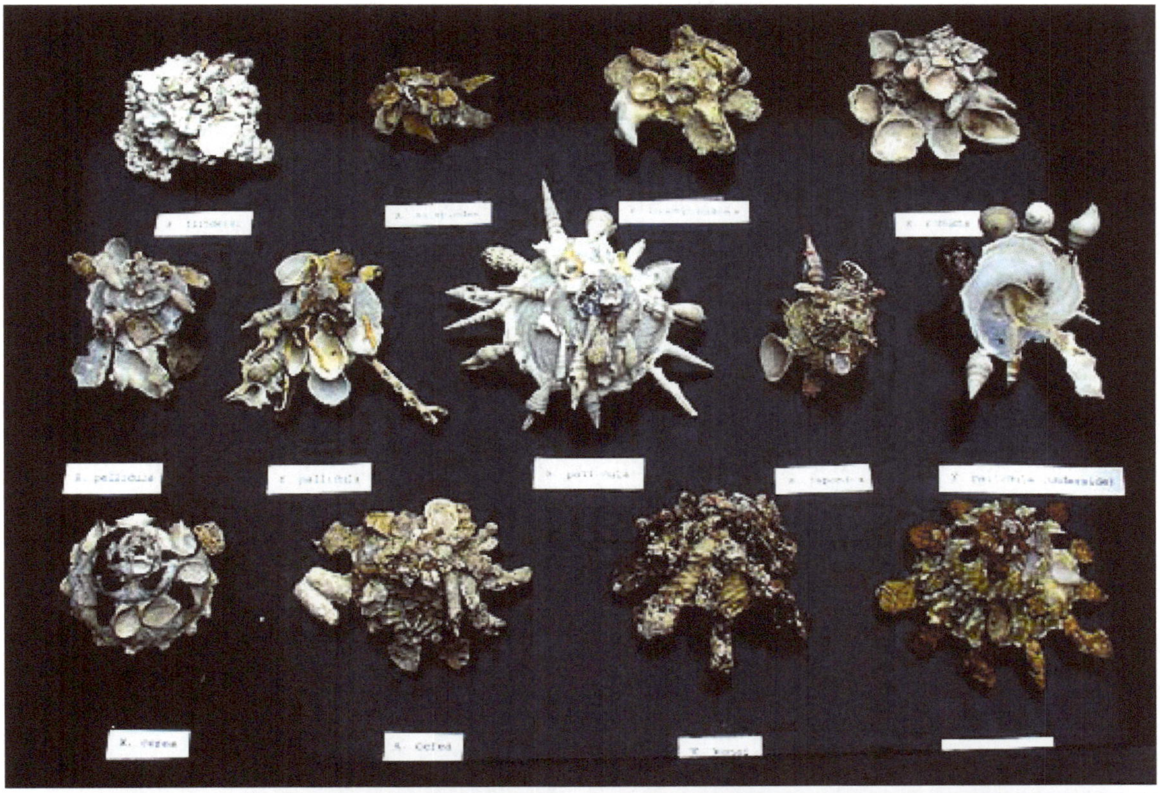

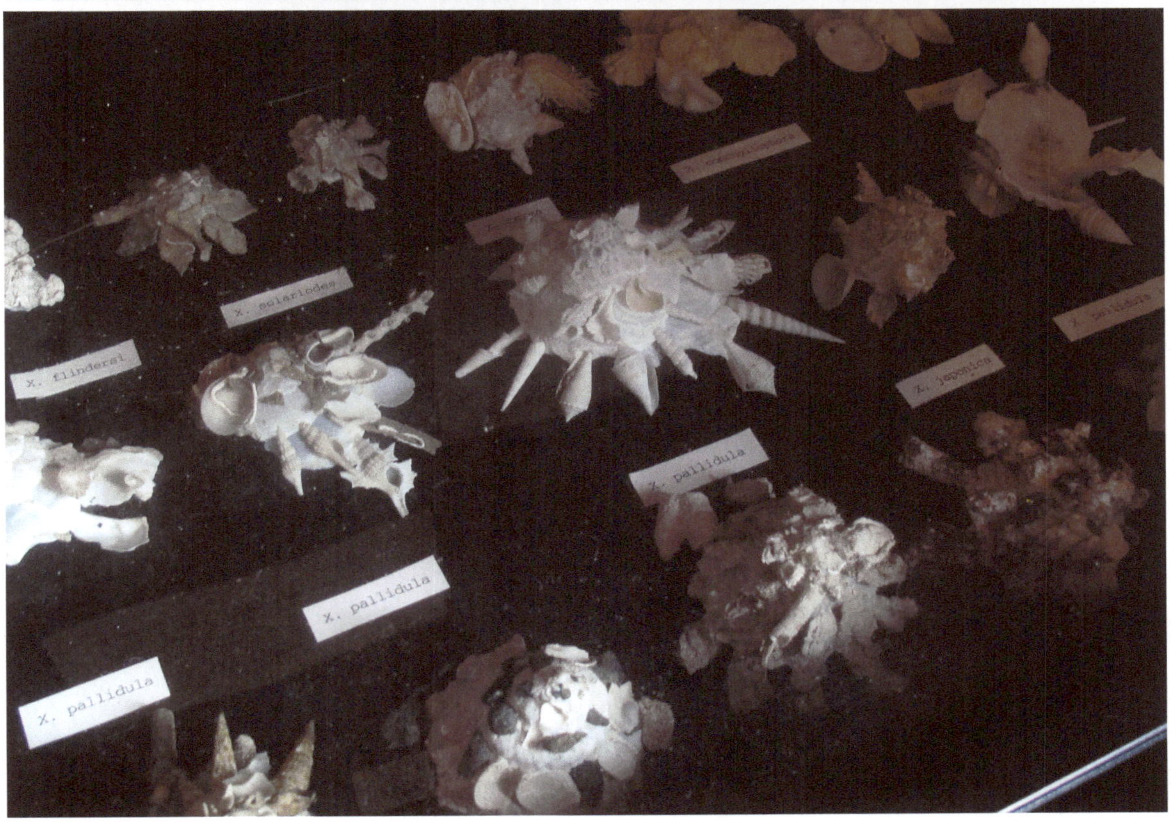
X. solarioides
X. flinderai
X. japonica
X. pallidula
X. pallidula
X. pallidula

Cultural Significance

During the Rust Age, Xenophora were valued for their mystical connections as messengers from a deeper world. During the Age of Wonder, their collections were seen as little samplings of a variety of faraway underwater realms, a sort of natural curiosity cabinet. It was in the Modern Age that they acquired the nickname "assemblage artists of the deep."

Outsiders have doubted the existence of these animals for many years. Visitors to the region often imagined that the shell assemblages were created by bare-breasted native women working in happy little groups on the beaches, who then sold their creations to unwitting tourists.

This collection was on display at the Peninsula Art Museum in San Mateo, California, as part of their "Obsessions" show (on collectors and their collections) as a collection of collectors. It was also featured in the (now extinct) Proceedings of the Athanasius Kircher Society (2006) and on Atlas Obscura (2017)

The Zymoglyphic Postal Service has issued a commemorative stamp to honor these beloved mollusks.

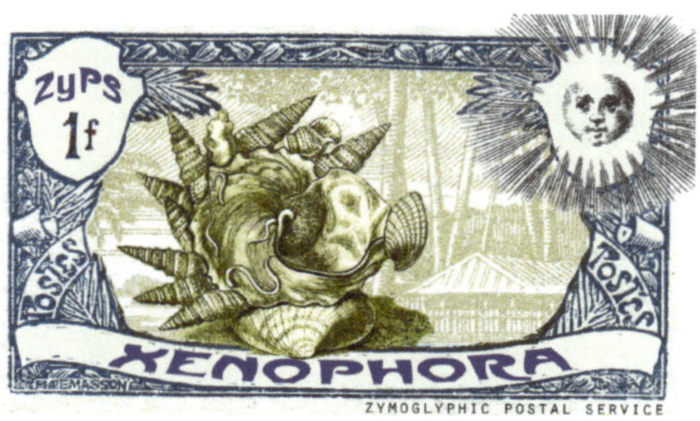

Further reading:

Xenophoridae of the World: A Revision of the Recent Xenophoridae of the World and of the Australian Fossil Species (1983) W.F. Ponder, The Australian Museum. This obscure volume is, as its author states, "the only comprehensive review of the family in 100 years."

Recent Xenophoridae (1999) Kurl Kreipl and Axel Alf, ConchBooks. A somewhat less technically oriented publication for the serious shell collector.

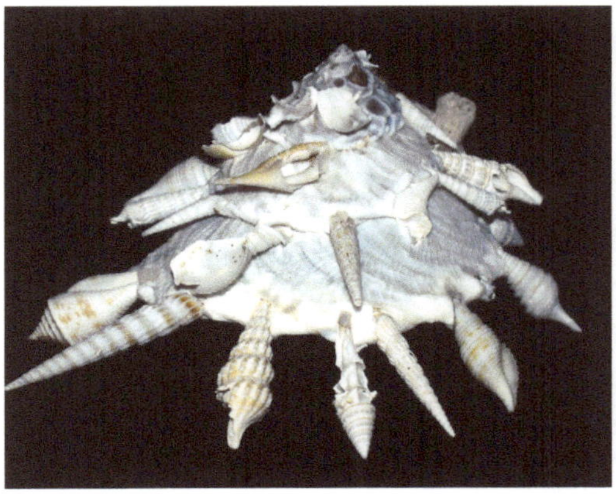

X. pallidula

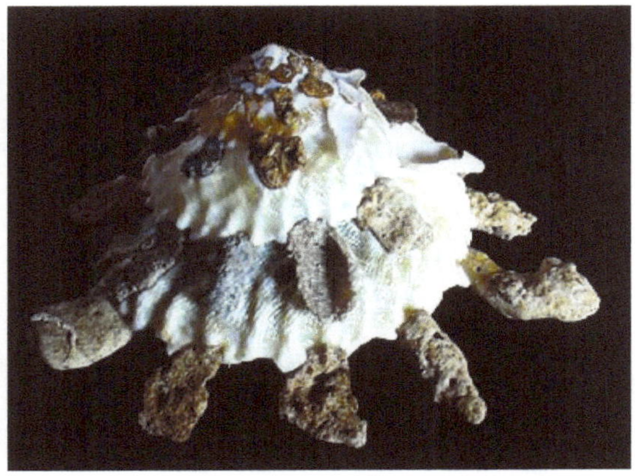

X. corrugata

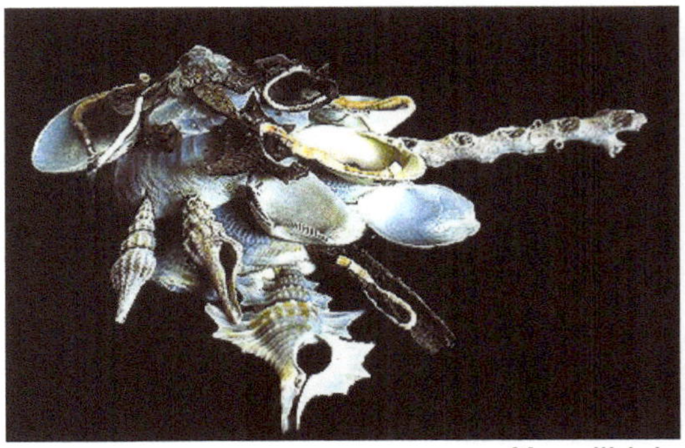

X. pallidula

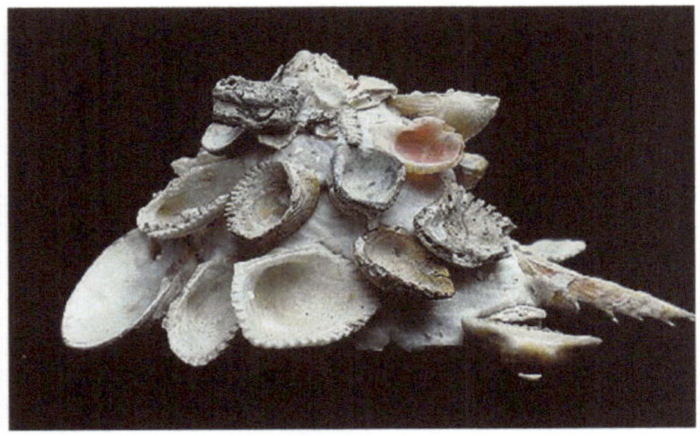

X. robusta

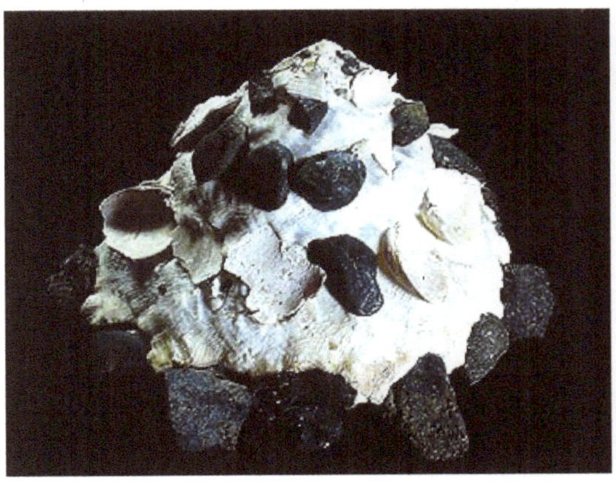

X. cerea

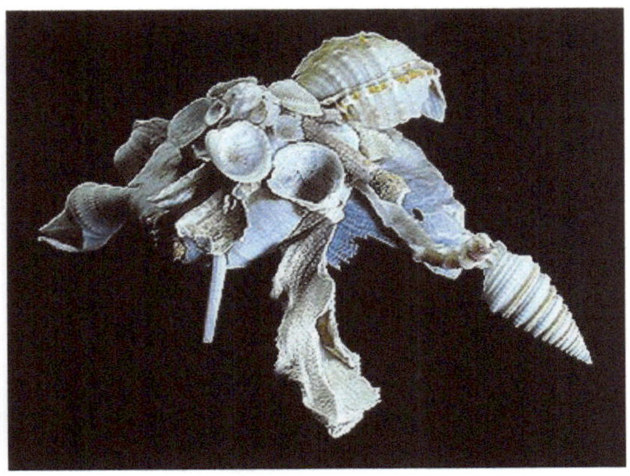

X. pallidula

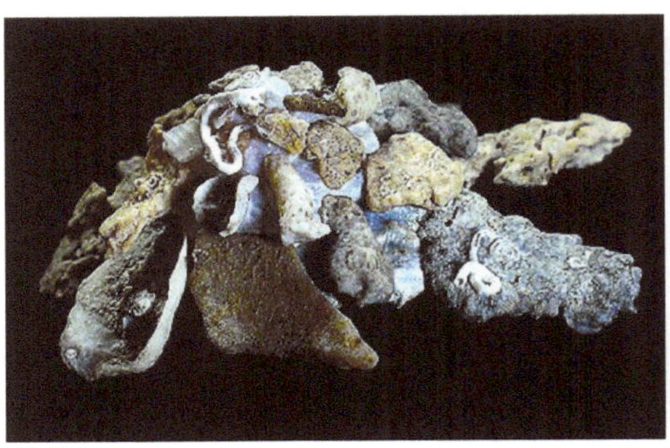

X. solariiodes

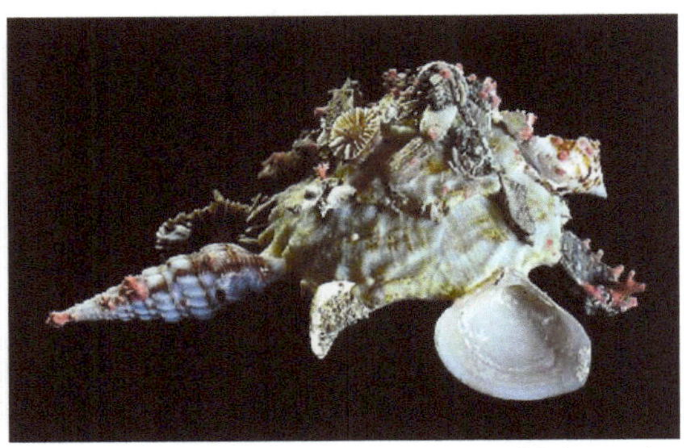

X. japonica

Species endemic to the Zymoglyphic region

The term "endemic" refers to species that are found in a specific ecological context and nowhere else in the world. The relative inaccessibility of the Zymoglyphic region makes collecting genuine specimens extraordinarily difficult, so many of the items in this collection are recreated from rumors and hearsay.

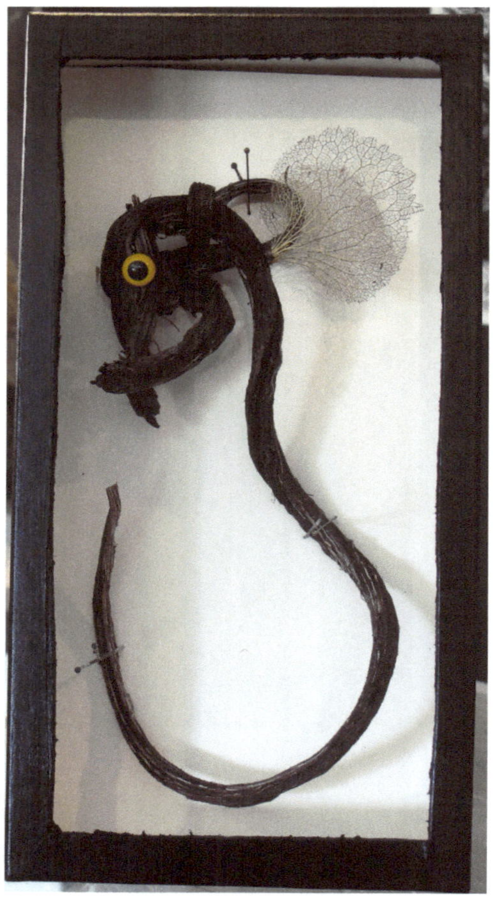

Unidentified beach find, possibly a sentient seaweed

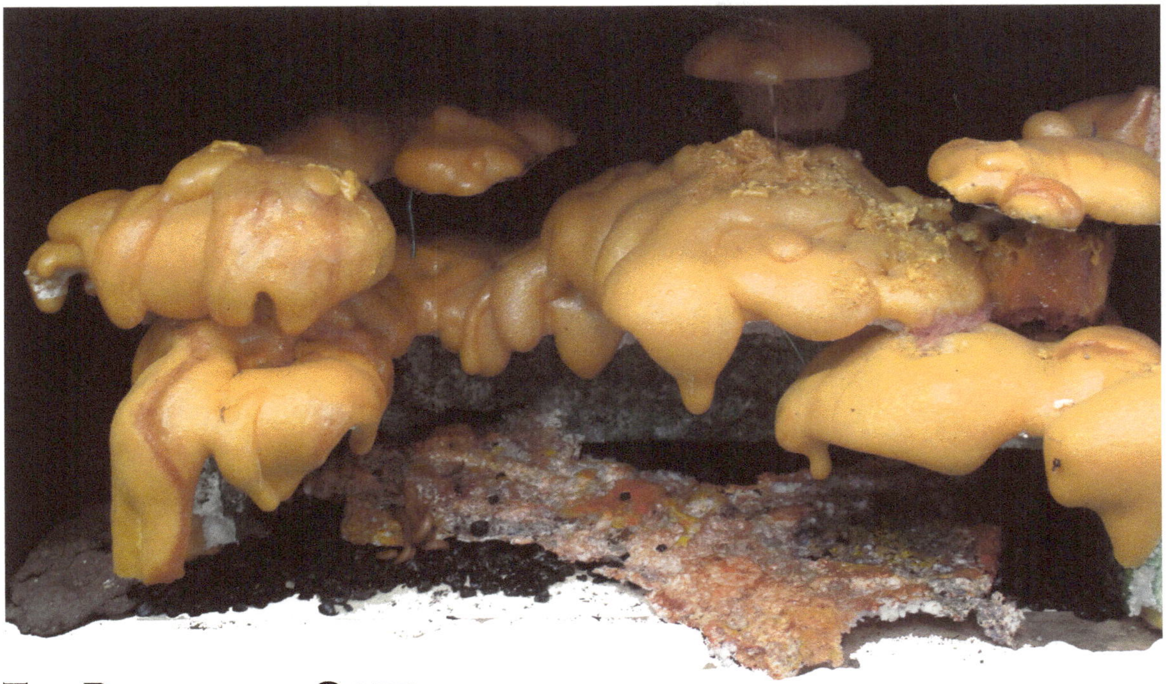

The Primordial Ooze

The primordial ooze is the subject of much speculation and research. It is shown here in a crude reconstruction. It seeped and bubbled in the mudpots of the Mud Age. Also known as the ur-yeast, the ooze was revered during the Rust Age as the ultimate source of creative fermentation. Researchers during the Age of Wonder attempted to determine whether it was material or metaphysical. Early in the Age of Wonder, alchemists equated it with the materia prima, the crawling chaos, void without form, seething with potential. Late in Age of Wonder, a substance discovered on the abyssal plain was thought to be physical origin of organic life. It was named Bathybius haeckelii, in honor of Ernst Haeckel, whose recordings of microscopic life have been so inspiring to Zymoglyphic art. It was later found to be an inorganic chemical precipitate.

In The Modern Age, controversy continues as to whether this concept should be taken literally or metaphorically. The museum's laboratory uses various species of carbon polymers to recreate that magic moment during the Mud Age when carbon chains began to coalesce into slithering forms that reproduced and evolved, eventually becoming conscious. This complex, multi-billion-year process is compacted to a single event in many mythologies as the creation of humans from clay, dirt, or similarly otherwise valueless substance. The most promising research in this direction is the Cybernetic Aquarium project, which attempts to create silicon-based life forms in a purely mathematical environment.

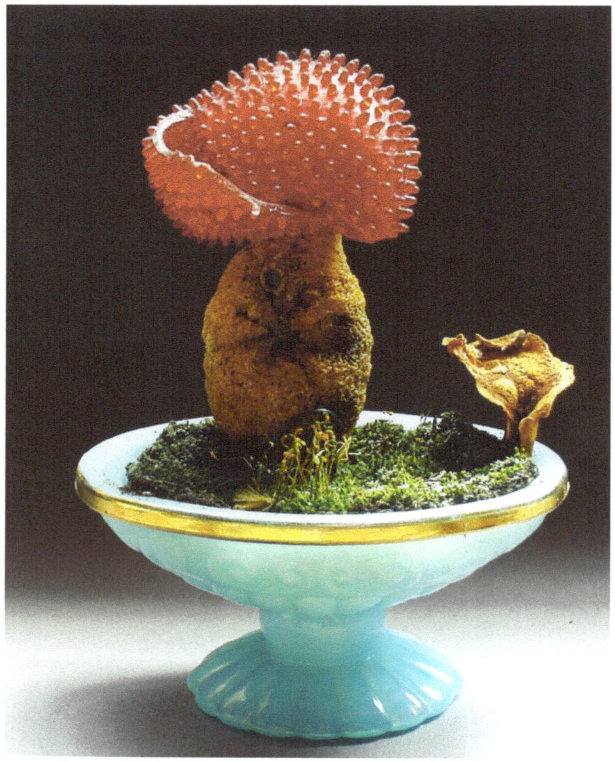

House Fungus

The House Fungus grows natively in the denser tropical forests, and looks for all the world like it is made of plastic and an old orange peel. It is in fact a colorful fungus found in the Zymoglyphic region which is commonly grown there as a house plant. The spiky head fills at certain times of the year with a hallucinogenic gas that is highly prized by the native inhabitants. This particular specimen has already made its atmospheric contribution and collapsed into a stupor.

The House Fungus is one of a number of molds, fungi, and ergots with psychotropic properties. During the Rust Age, these organisms were central to many shamanic rituals and ecstatic dances. In the Modern Age, these properties helped artists focus on the significance and visual properties of objects rather than their functions or literal representations.

It is controversial whether the dreamlike quality in much of Zymoglyphic art is due to the pervasiveness of these gases affecting perception, or inherent in the landscape itself.

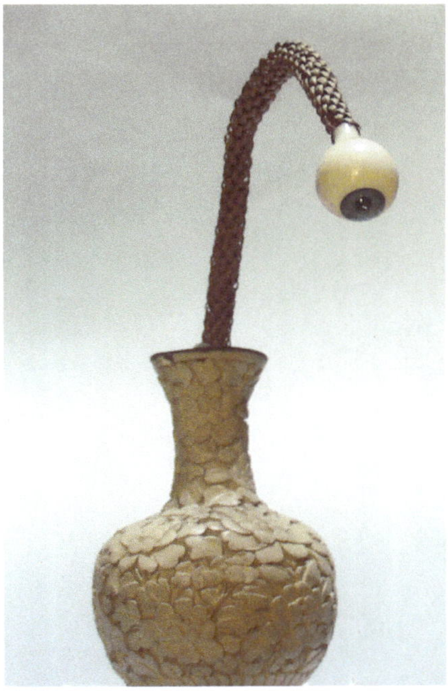

Scaly Eyeball Plant
Ophthalmophytos lepidus

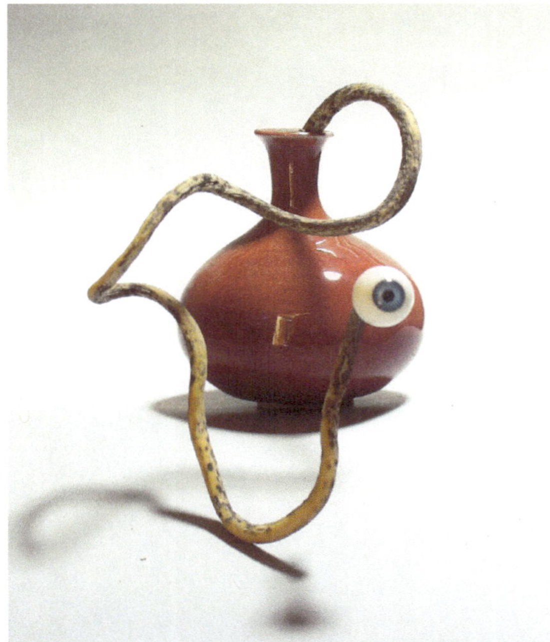

Convoluted Eyeball Plant
Ophthalmophytos tortuosa

EYEBALL PLANTS

Naturalists peering too deeply into the undergrowth may find themselves being observed in return by the "eyes of the forest," as shown in the diorama below. The eyes belong to the scaly eyeball plant and the convoluted eyeball plant. During the Rust Age, these plants were revered for their oracular qualities, in the belief that they could see into the unknown.

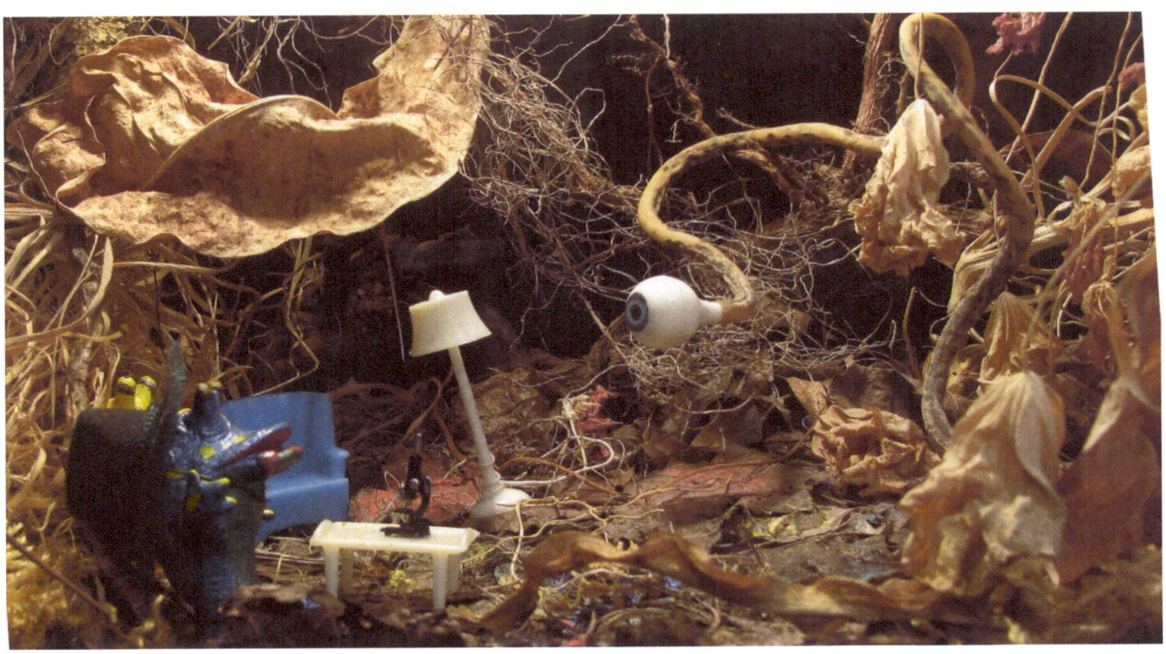

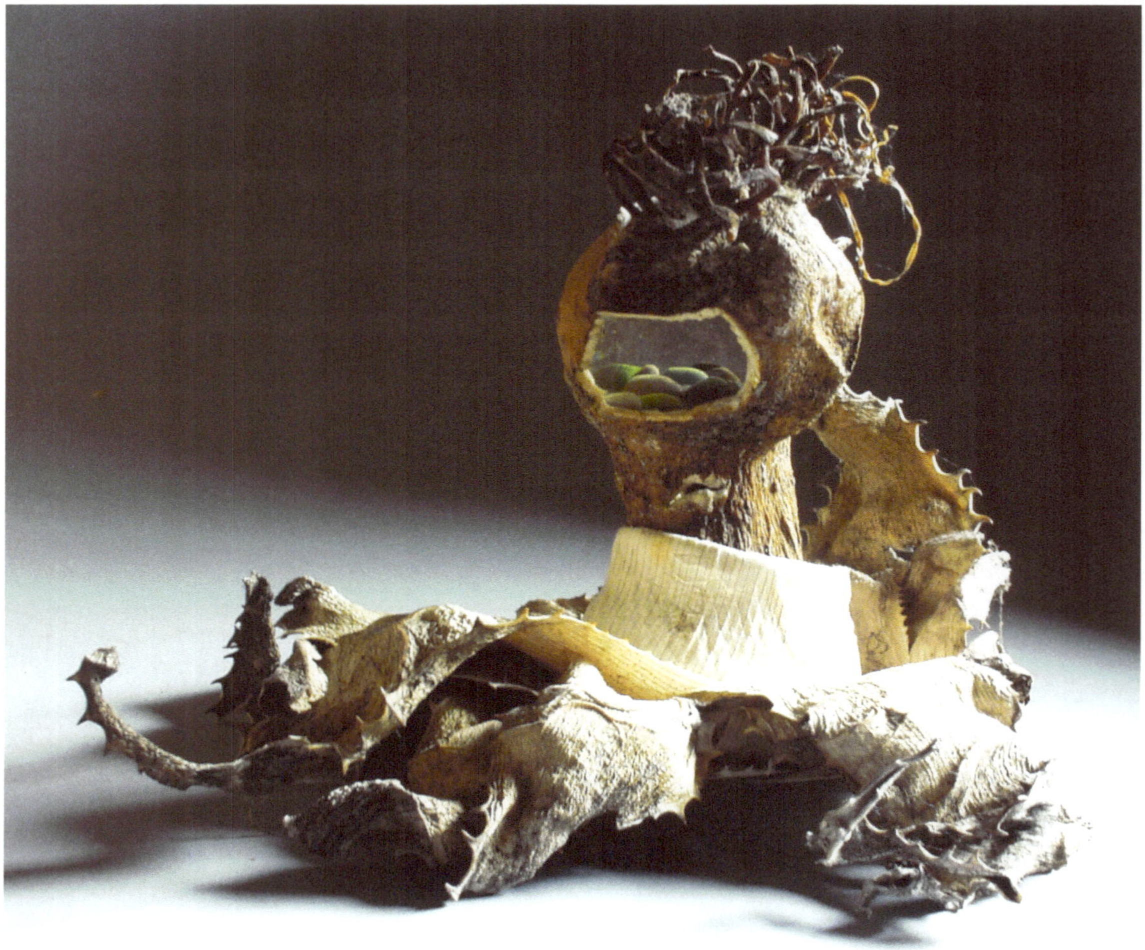

POND-HEADED CACTUS

The mountains of the region produce dense jungles on the windward side of the islands, leaving very little moisture for the leeward side and resulting in deserts. These harsher conditions require some remarkable adaptations for survival.

The pond-headed cactus is a plant species that originated in the ocean as a member of the kelp family and has evolved to become a land based species. It carries within it a little bit of the sea.

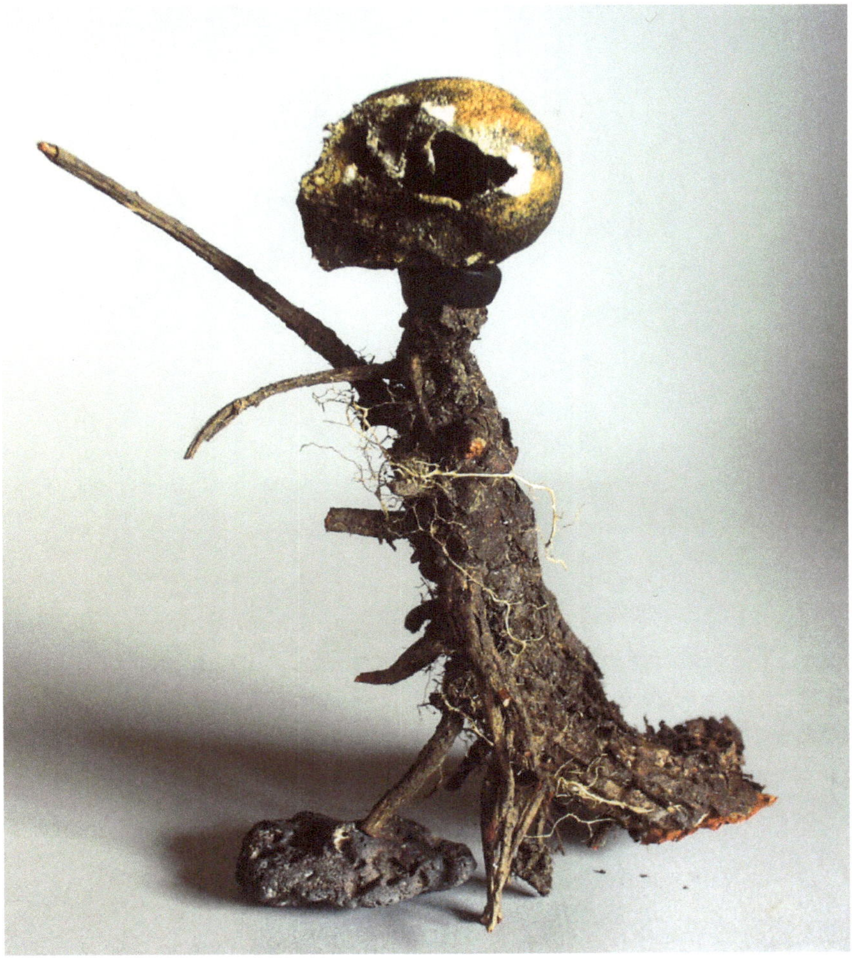

Root Worm

The root worm, in contrast, is often found on the forest floor. Its resemblance to an old root causes it to get stepped on and bumped frequently, resulting in a rather irritable disposition.

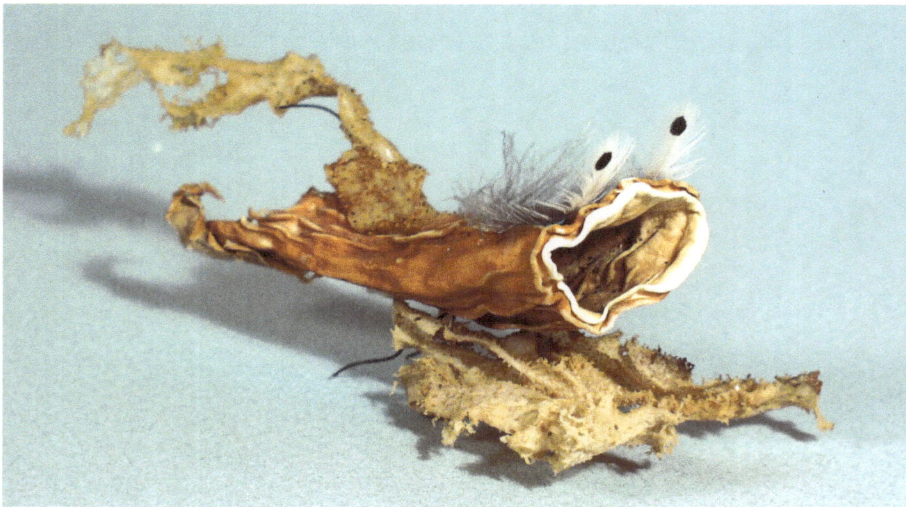

Happy Fish

As the land itself is hidden from outsiders, so many of the inhabitants hide from each other. The Happy Fish (*Piscatonius delitus*) can be found clinging to rocky bottoms in fast-moving waters. Its rough exterior camouflages it well; it might be confused with a random selection of seaweed. Its happy demeanor is thought to be due to its lack of internal organs. Its watery environment just passes right through it.

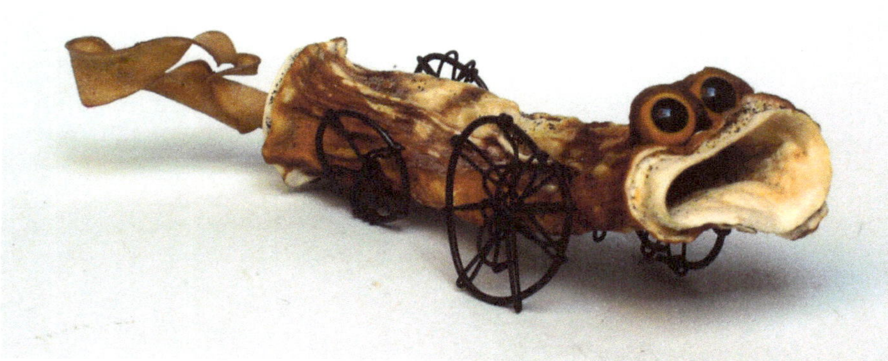

Wheeled Fish

This relative of the Happy Fish is uniquely adapted for its forays onto land.

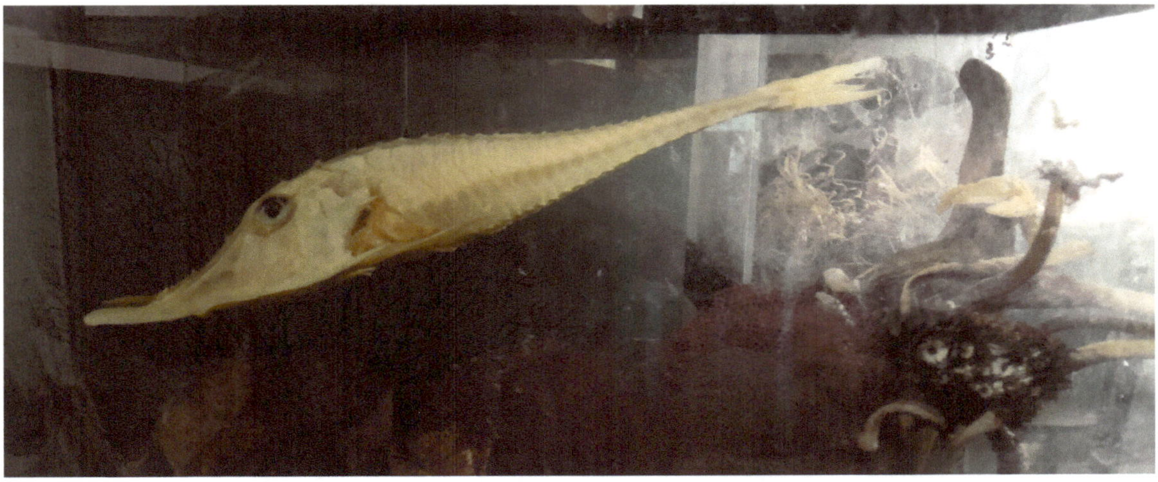

Nautilus Fish

Also known as an armored sea robin, this fish was named for its supposed resemblance to the famous submarine piloted by Captain Nemo, whose voyages were chronicled by Jules Verne in *20,000 Leagues under the Sea*. Nemo and the *Nautilus* are believed to have visited the Zymoglyphic Region during the Age of Wonder. Nemo was revered as a great collector and had an extensive onboard art and oceanographic collection.

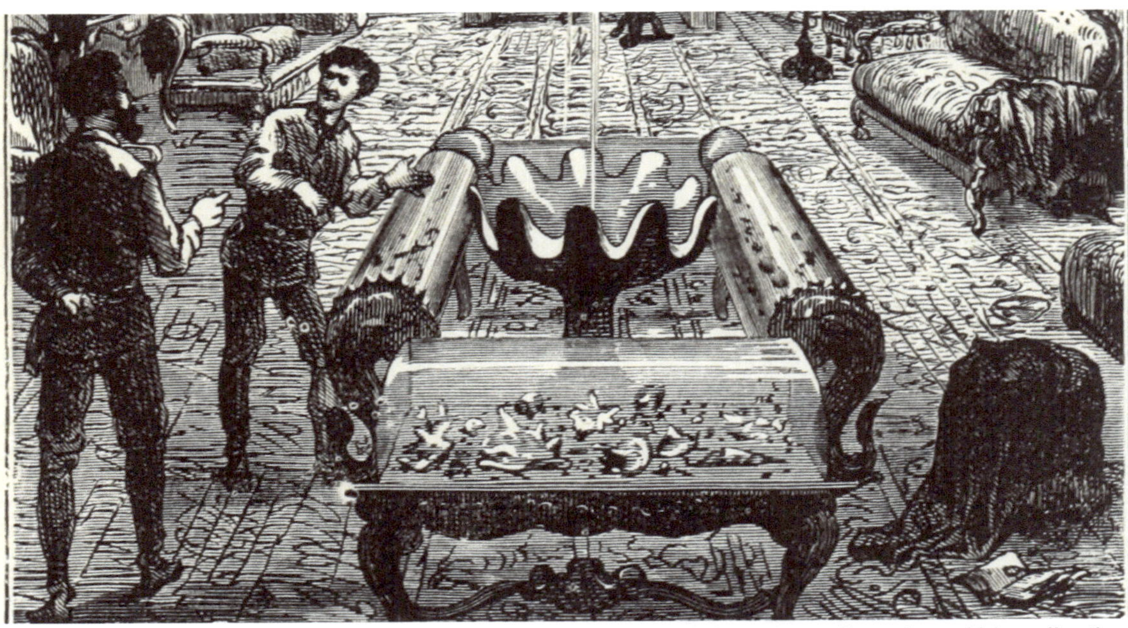

Nemo displays a small portion of his collection

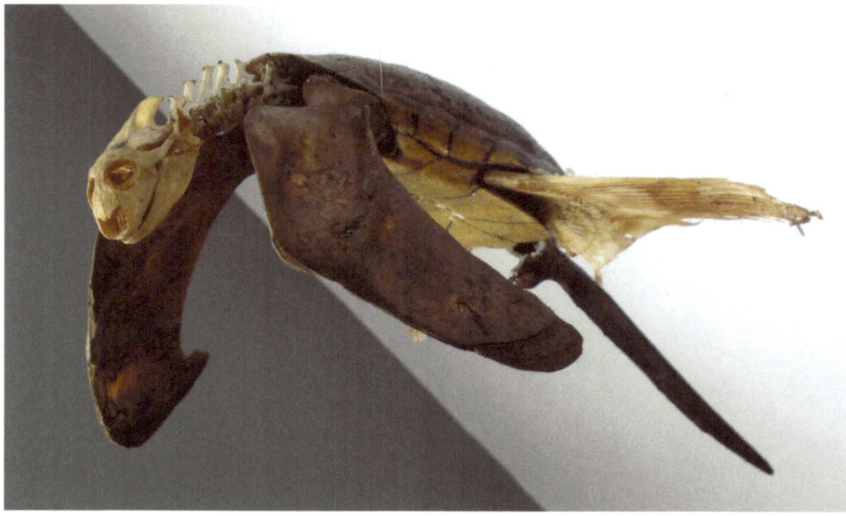

Flying Turtle

Speculative reconstruction of an extinct species of flying turtle found in the Zymoglyphic region. They were more likely a gliding species rather than practitioners of true flight.

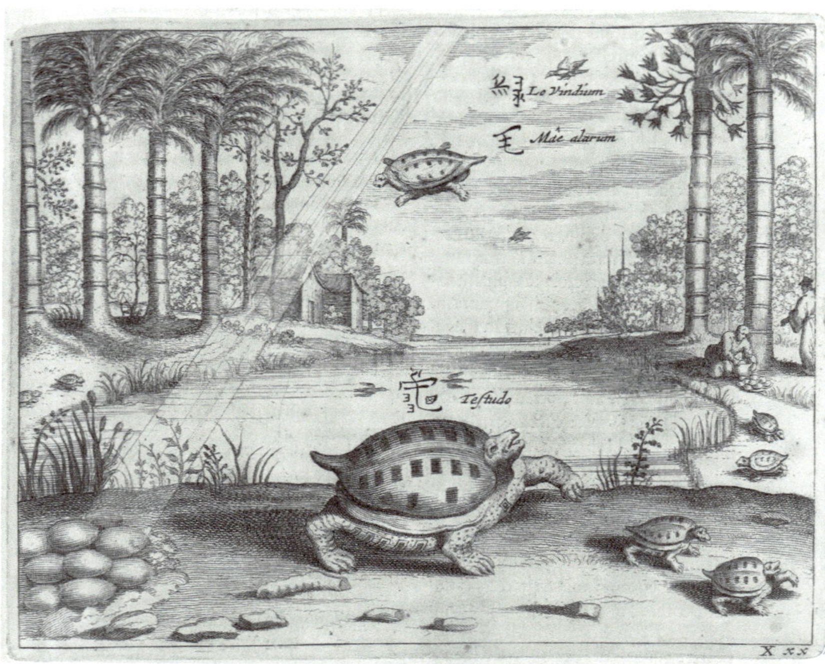

"Flying" turtles were reported at late as 1667 (Athanasius Kircher, *China Illustrata*).

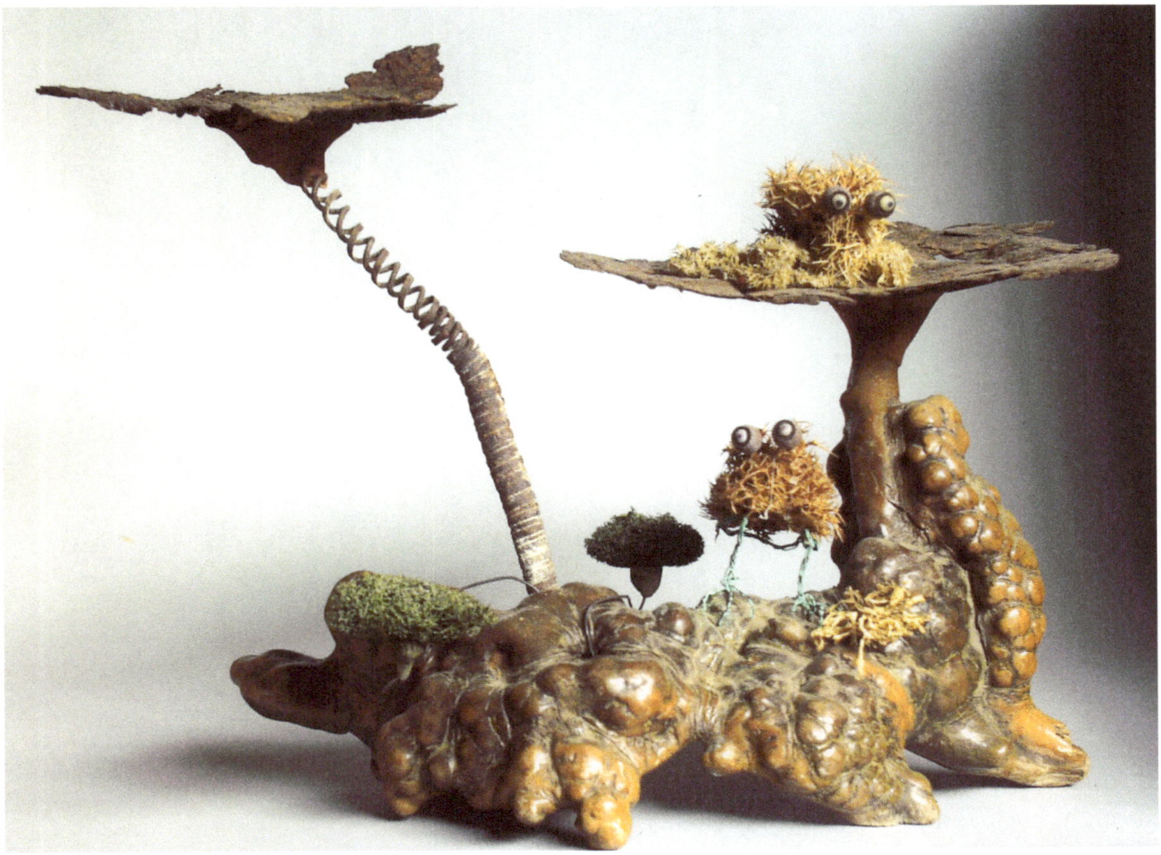

Spinybirds

Spinybirds are small, shy, flightless birds that have evolved a unique cactus-like means of defense against the nocturnal predations of the leatherwings.

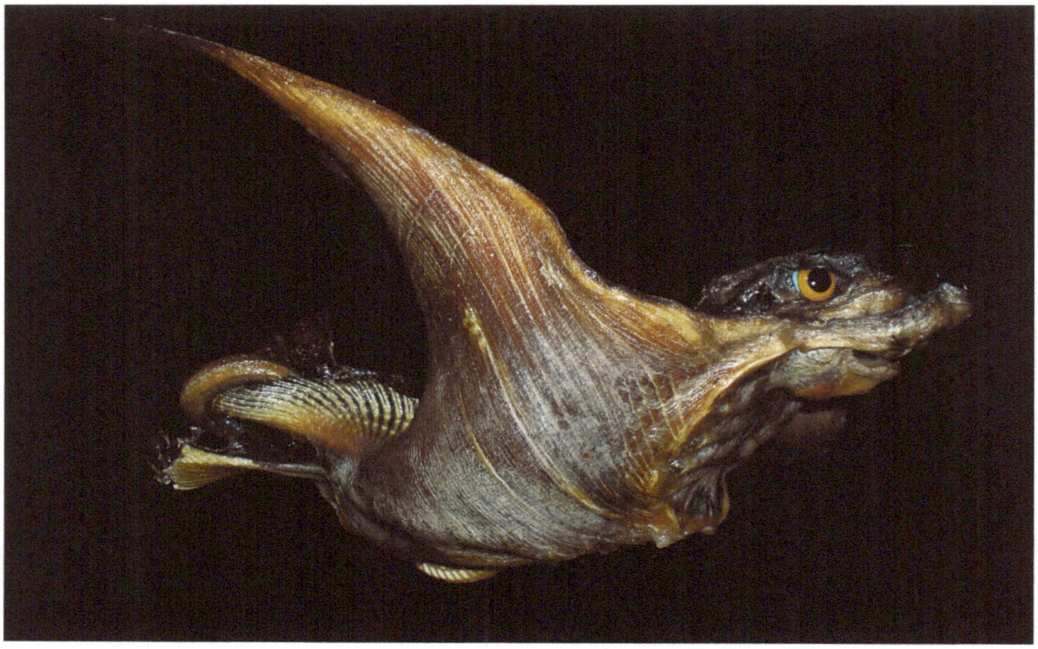

The Leatherwing

The Leatherwing is a silent, nocturnal creature adapted for long flights from the sea through the jungle. Although rare, early European explorers to the region sometimes brought back samples for their curiosity cabinets.

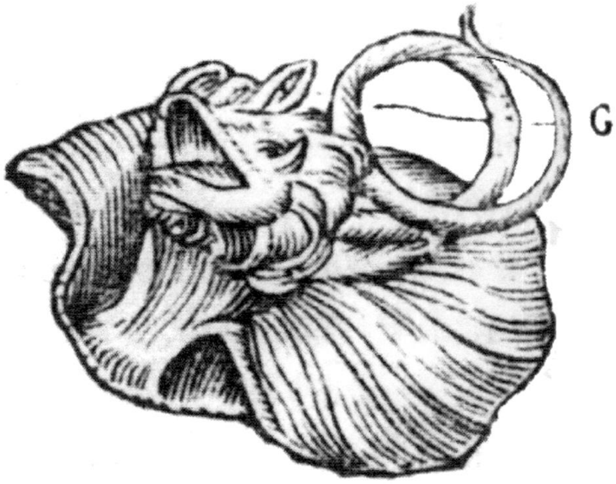

Ulisse Aldrovandi
Monstrorium Historia, 1642

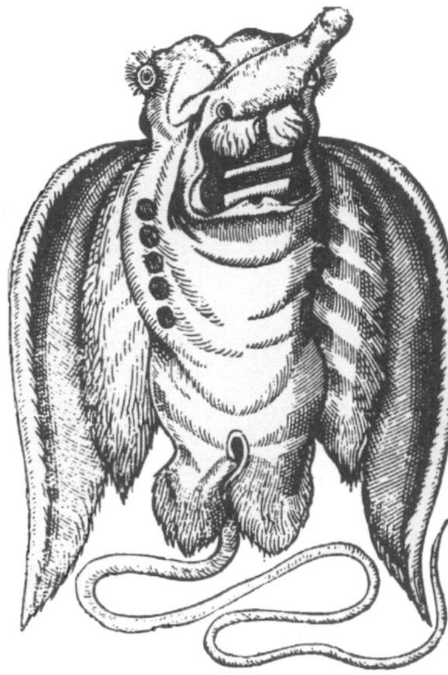

60. Figure of another very monstrous flying fish

] 124 [

Ambroise Pare
On Monsters and Marvels, 1573

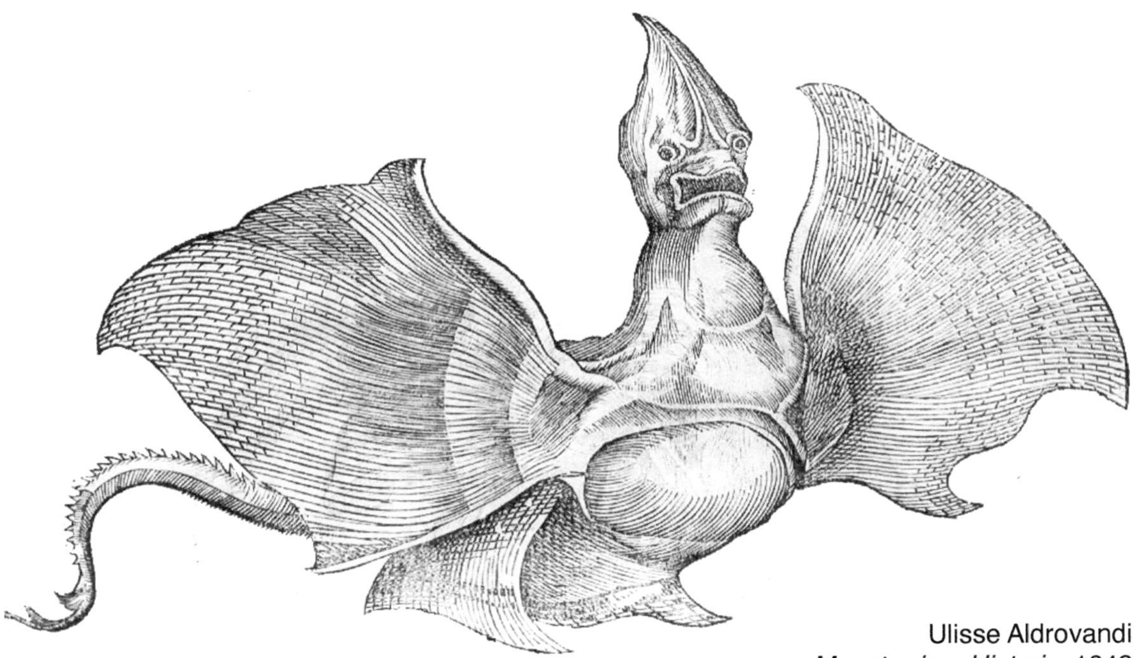

Ulisse Aldrovandi
Monstrorium Historia, 1642

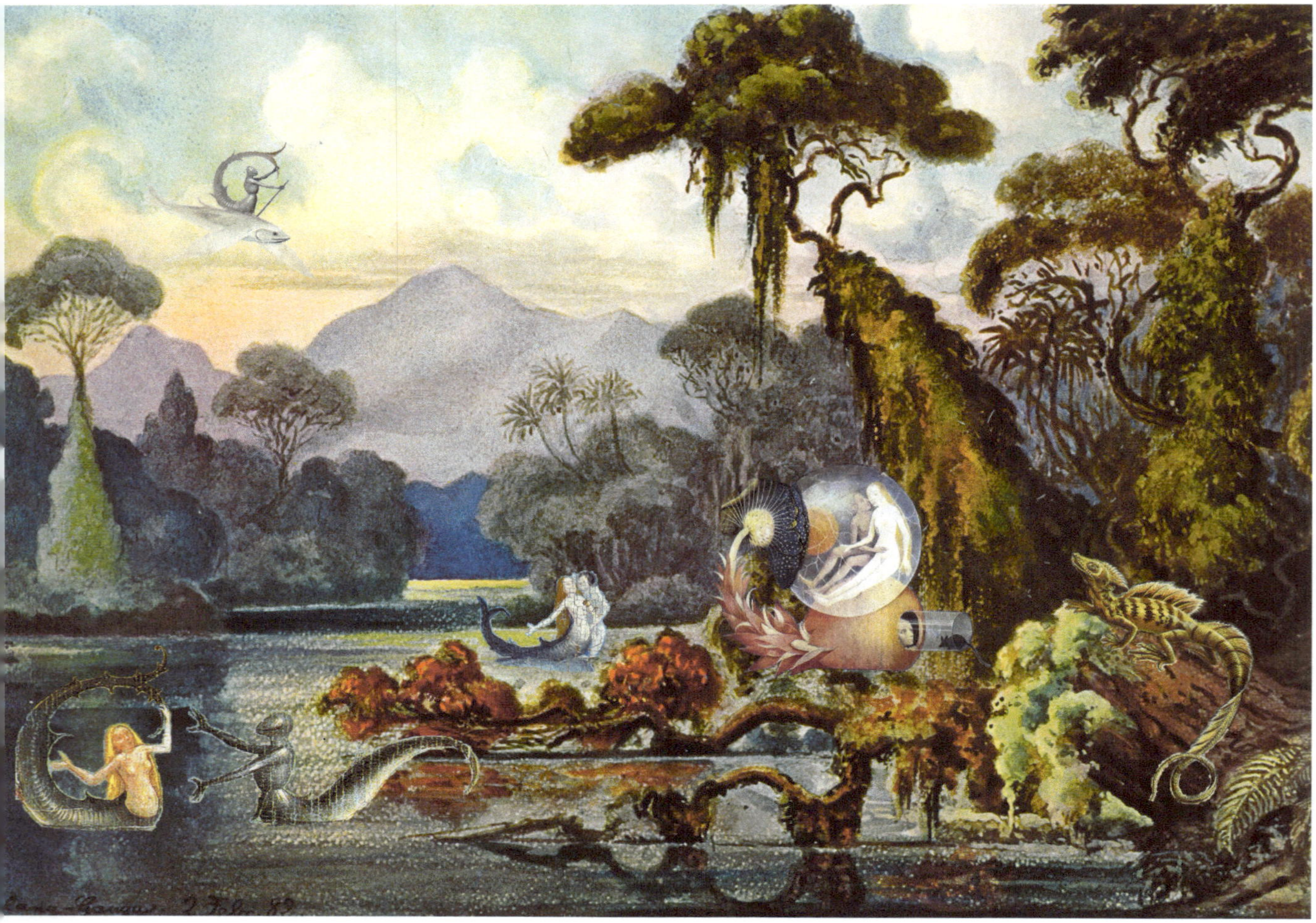

Mermaid lagoon

Mermaids

Tales of mermaids frolicking in the moonlit lagoons of the Zymoglyphic region have spawned much speculation about who these creatures might be. Known as the "fish with a human face" during the Rust Age, they were revered as creatures partially human and equally animal, at home on the surface of the sea but capable of plumbing its depths, learning its secrets, and possibly sharing them with people if only the people could communicate with them.

Expeditions to the region during the Age of Wonder of resulted in tales of glamorous fish-women. They were known for their intelligence, cunning, and apparently consistently happy demeanor.

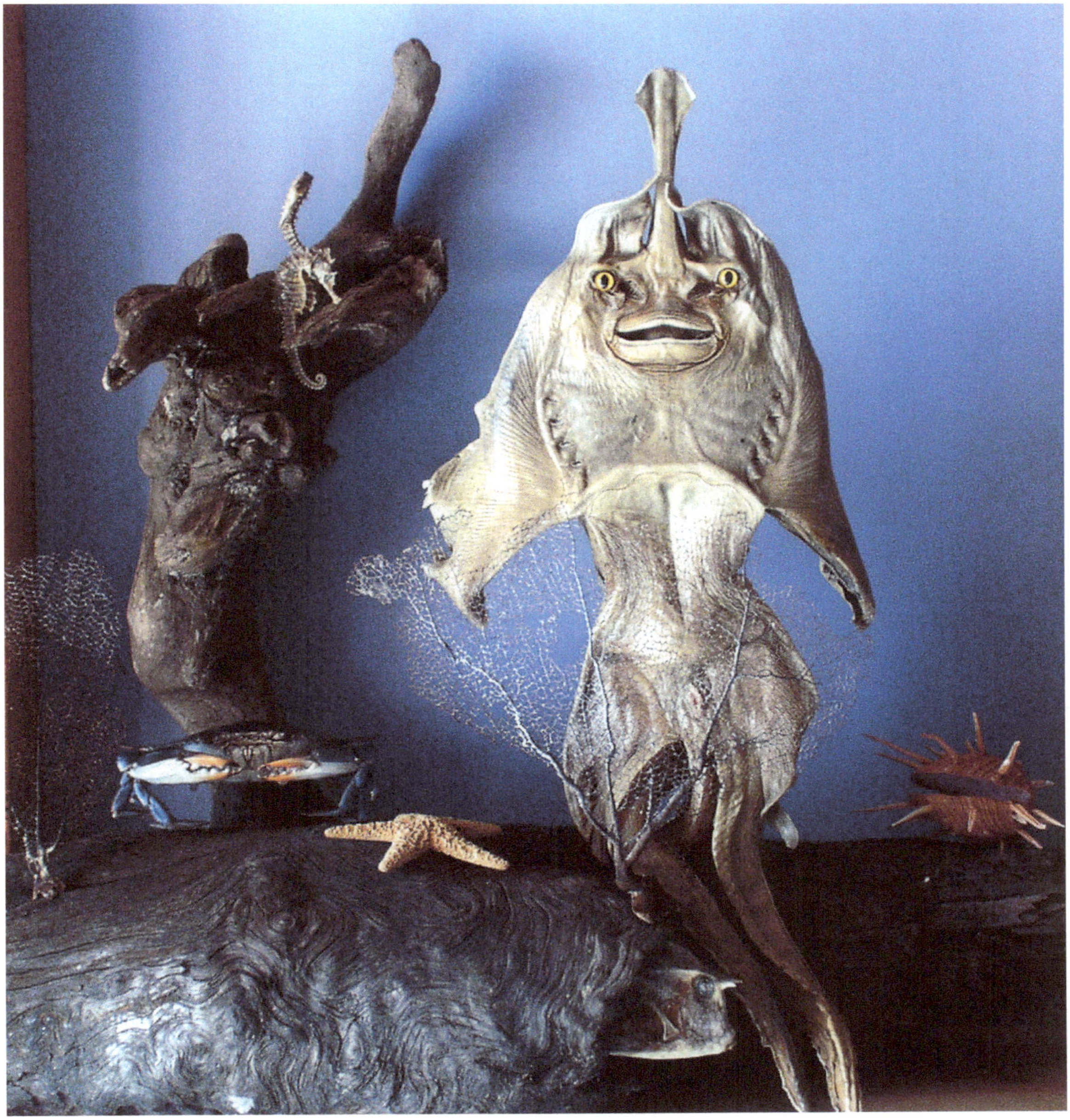

The largest and most primitive mermaid species in the museum's collection is affectionately known as "The Zymoglyphic Mermaid" and has become somewhat of a spokesmodel for the museum, Its sinuous body and delightful smile grace the museum shop's drinkware, clocks, and clothing, as well as the frontispiece of this guide.

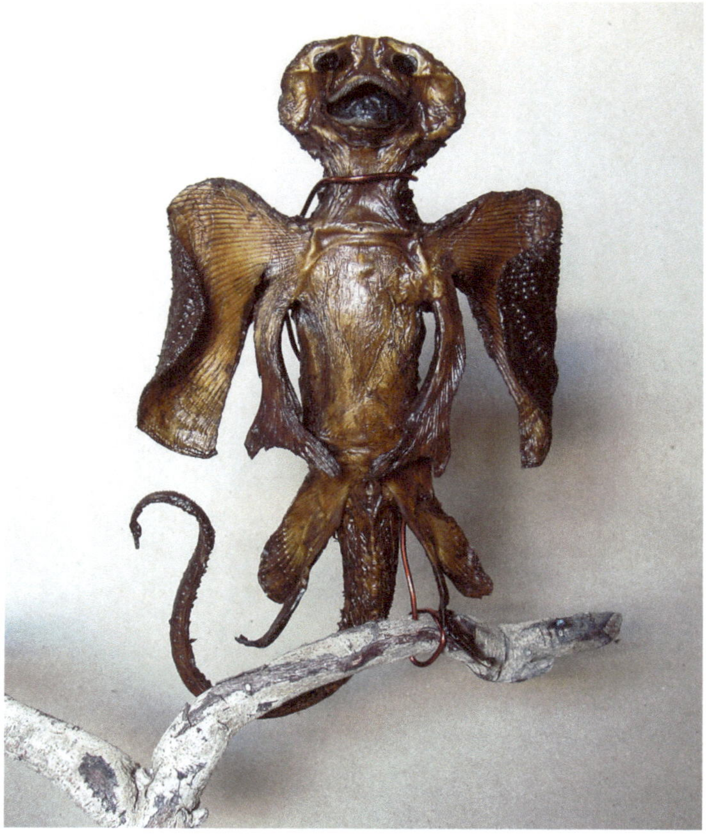

The actual specimens returned by collecting expeditions, however, bear little resemblance to the fanciful illustrations. This is a purported sentient fish creature, apparently also capable of flight.

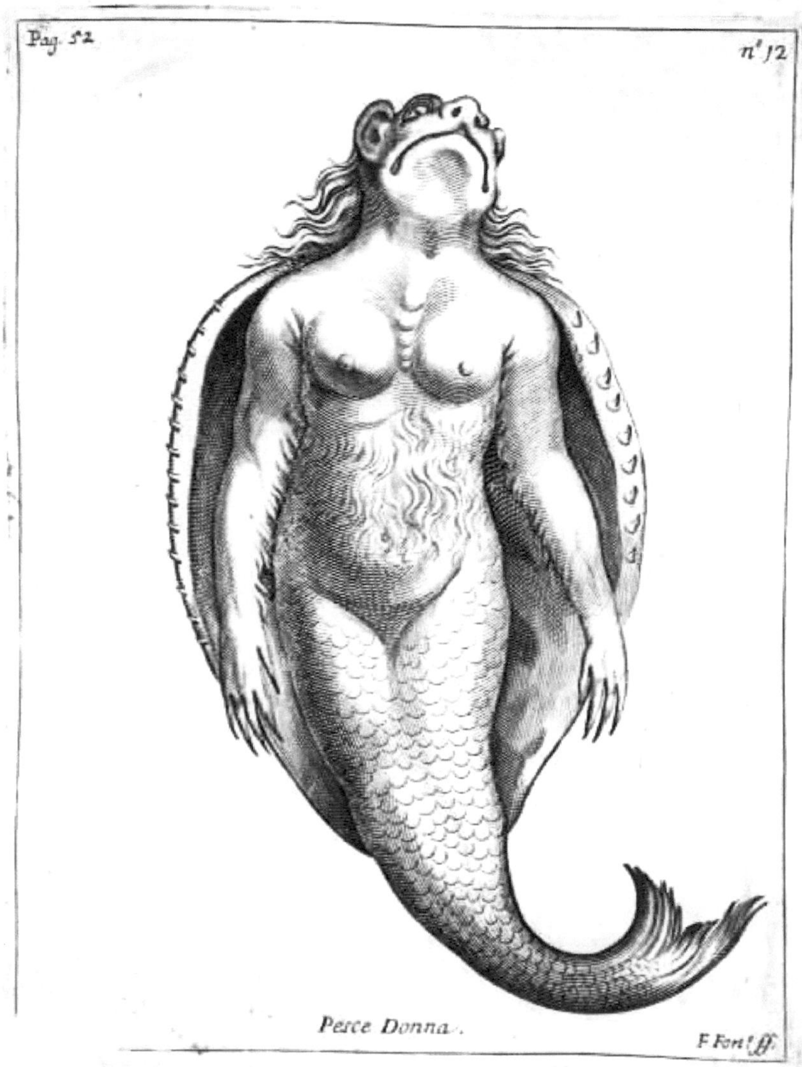

A similar species of mermaid as recorded by G.A. Cavazzi in 1687, possibly under the influence of the House Fungus or simply a natively overactive imagination combined with wishful thinking.

The Rust Age

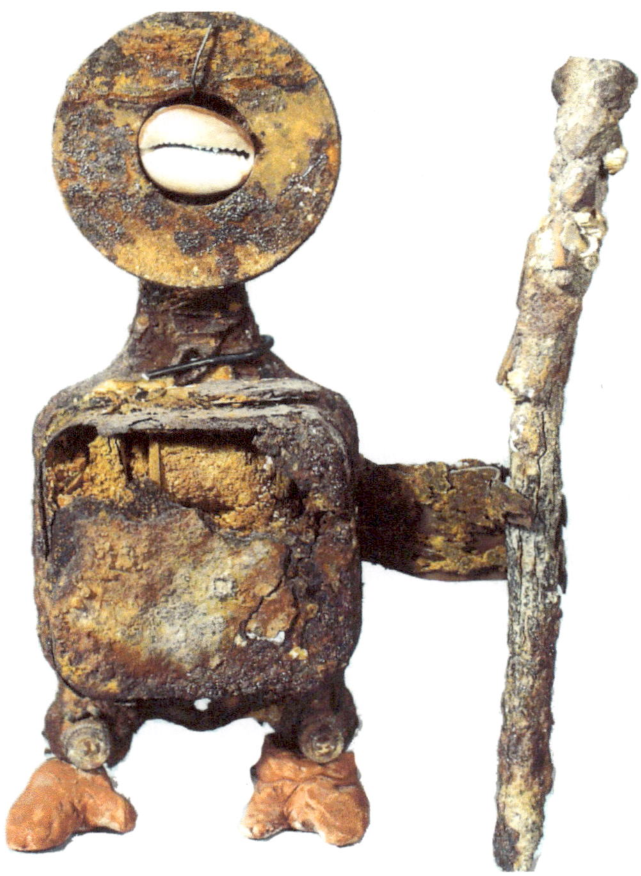

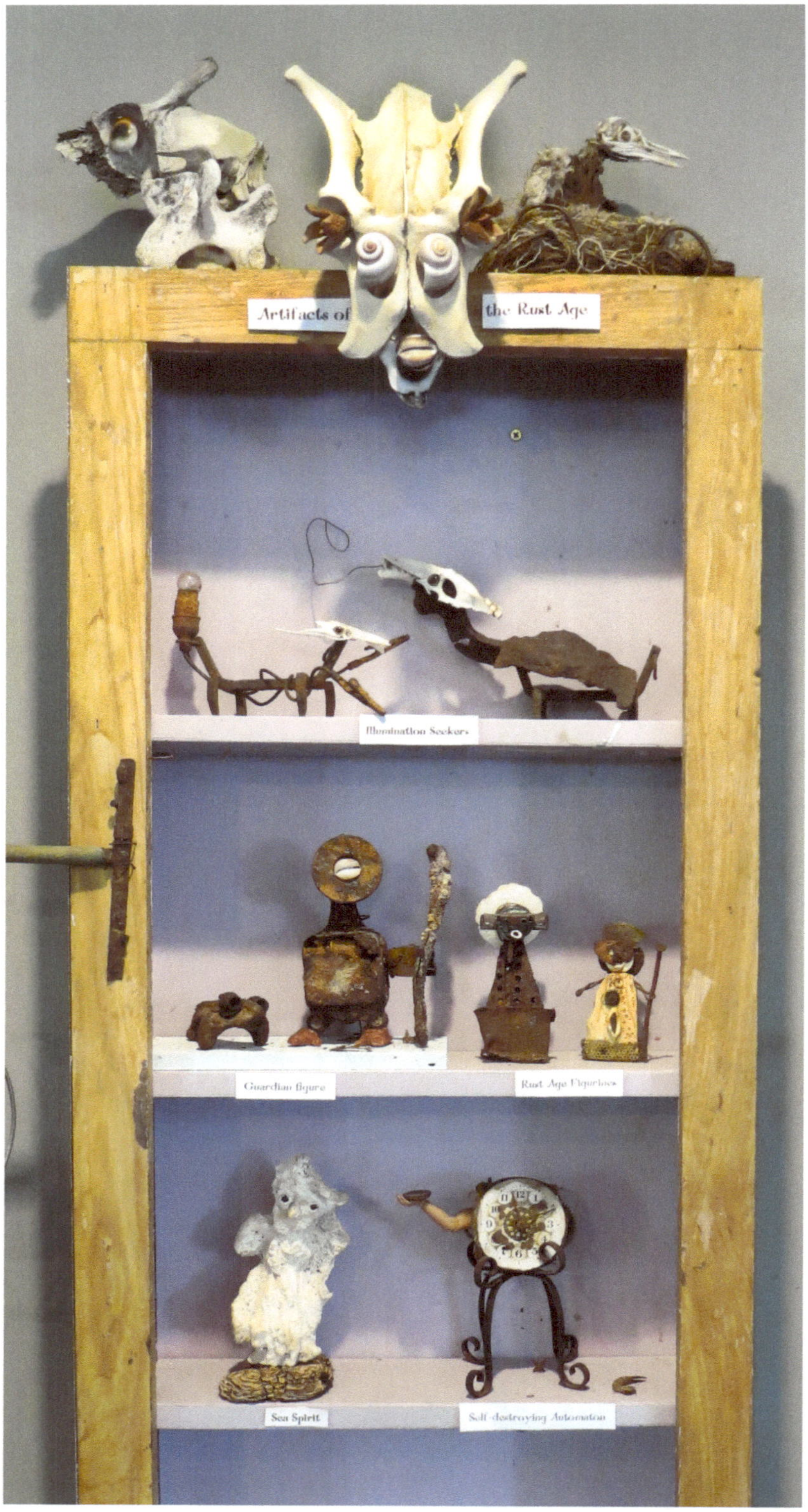

Exhibit of Rust Age artifacts

The Rust Age

The museum's collection of ethnographic artifacts from the Rust Age (formally known as the Oxidocene) provides a glimpse into a long-vanished way of life. We know little of the reality of life in those times and what we imagine is probably idealized to some extent. It was a time of spiritual concerns, centered on various rituals, many of whose details are lost to us today.

The Rust Age is so named because many of the ceremonial artifacts were made of decaying metal, which was thought to have a sublime quality of character and texture of age. In some of the artifacts, the rust continues to decay and eat away at the core of the object. The decaying metal, along with delicate organic material such as feathers and leaves, was intended to create a sense of time passing and of the fleeting nature of life.

One of the beliefs of the Zymoglyphic people during this age was the sense of life being an illusion, that they were in fact the dream of a god, not the serene, all-knowing deity found in some cultures, but the one with a fevered imagination, a fitful god constantly trying out new things, experimenting with the course of their lives, ultimately wiping them clean and trying anew with the next one, never quite getting it right. Their lives were often stories that started out well, lost focus along the way, then needed to be discarded in order to start a new one.

Ceremonial artifacts

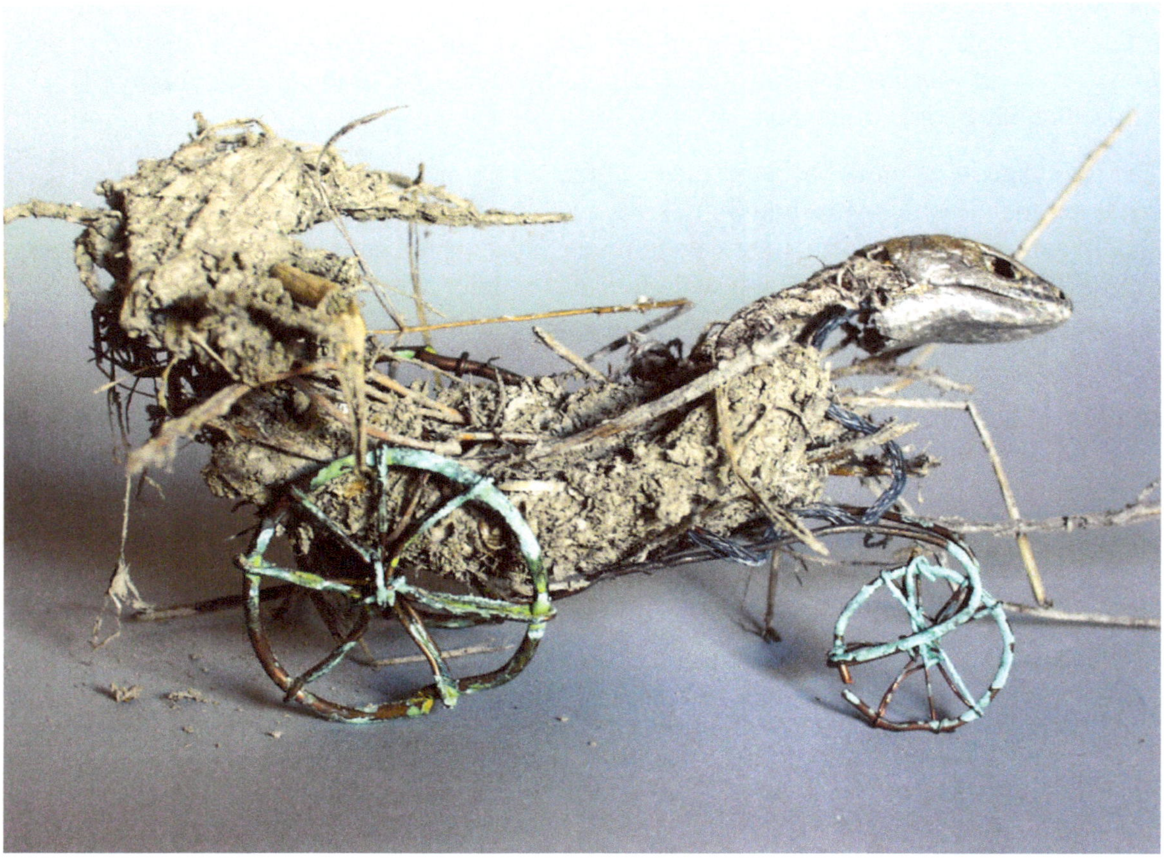

Lizard-headed mud cart

This artifact refers back to the Mud Age. It is a wheeled cart believed to be a magic vehicle for navigating the spirit-infested landscape. It was guided by a reptilian brain and harnessed the generative power of mud.

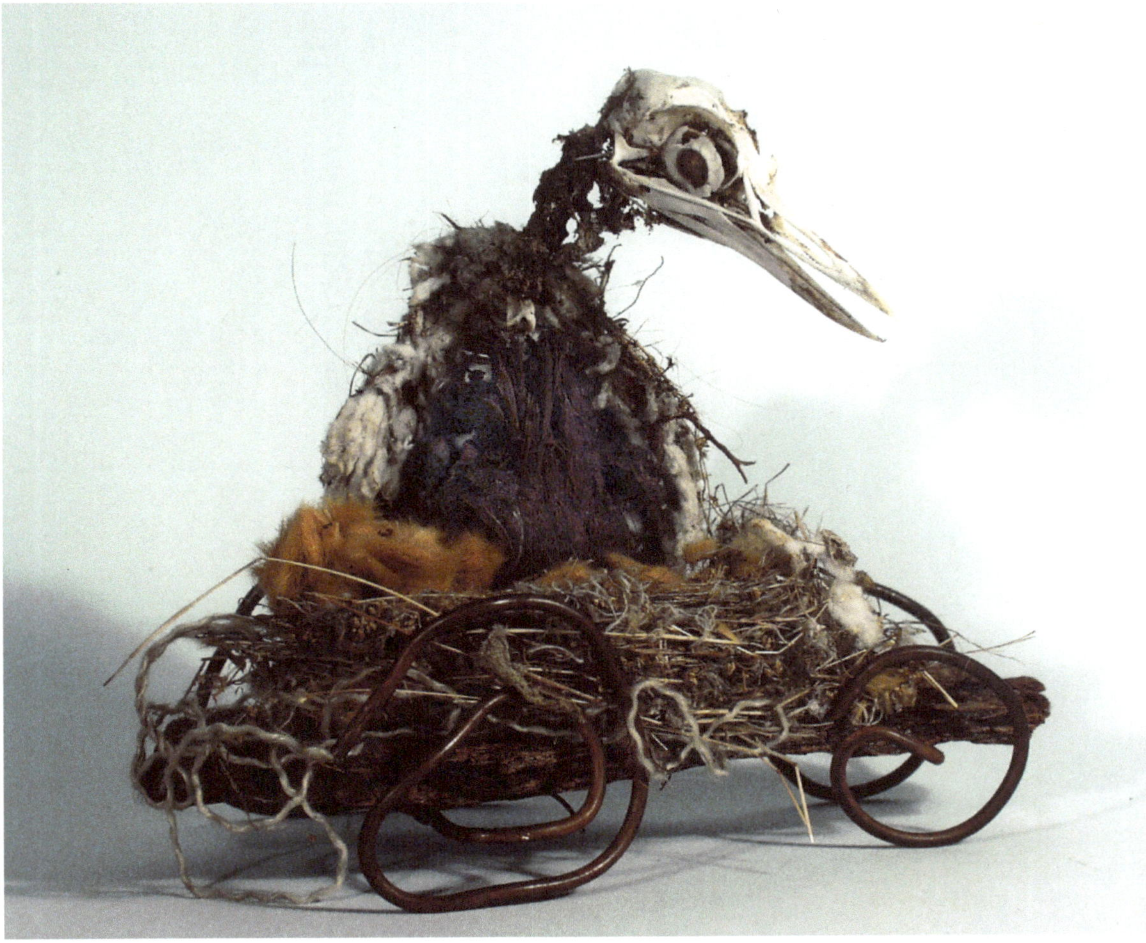

Bird cart

This bird cart is a wheeled vehicle which embodies a full circle of life, as symbolized by the combination of the bird nest and the skull, along with the potential motion of the cart as it traverses life's meandering paths.

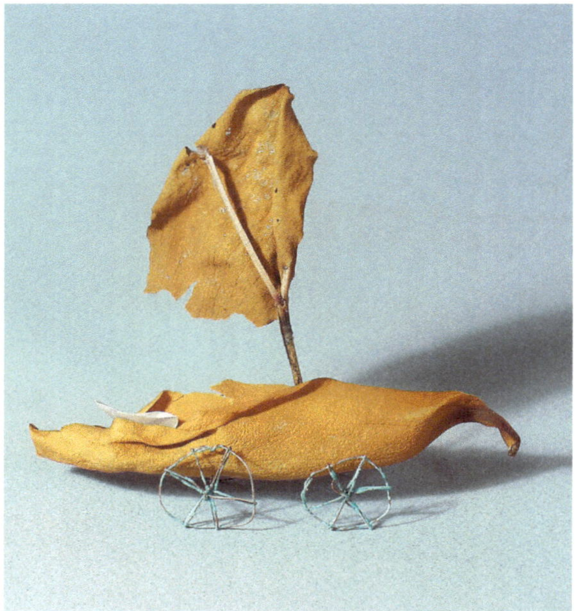

Leaf boat

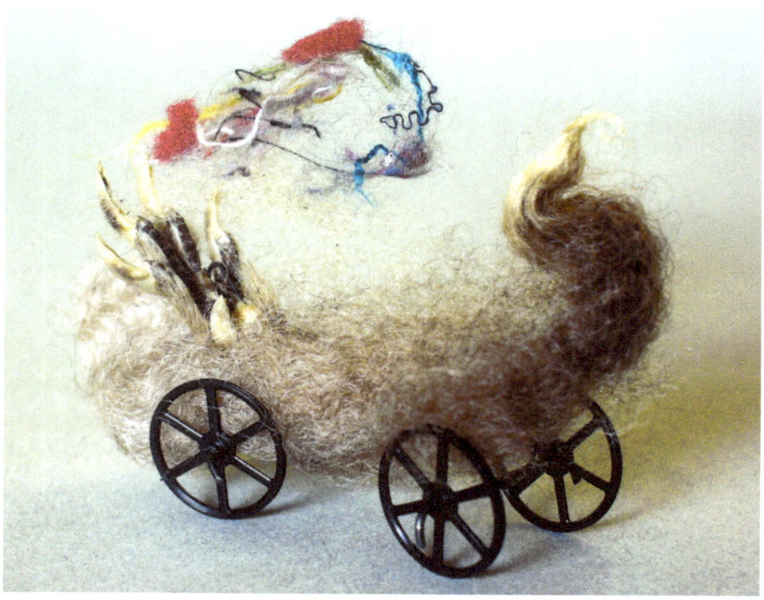

Wool boat

Wheeled boats

Models of wheeled boats that were used to convey the spirits of bygone souls to a watery grave.

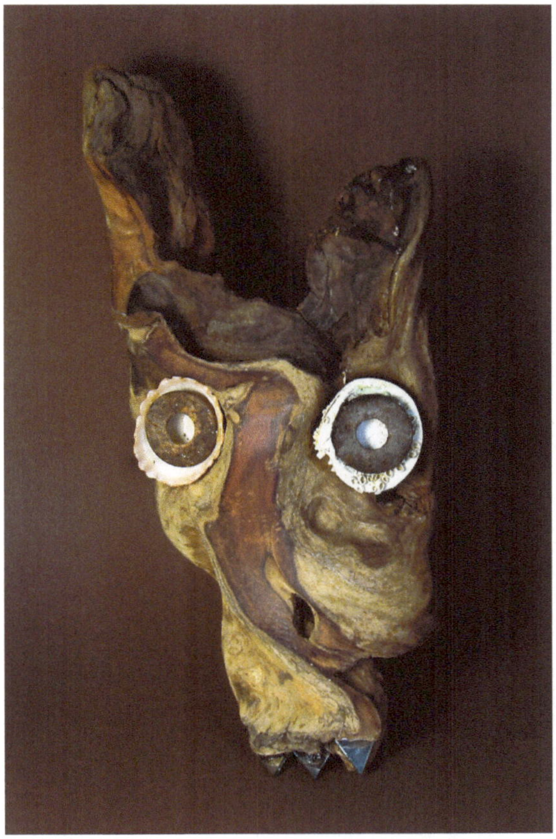

Wooden mask

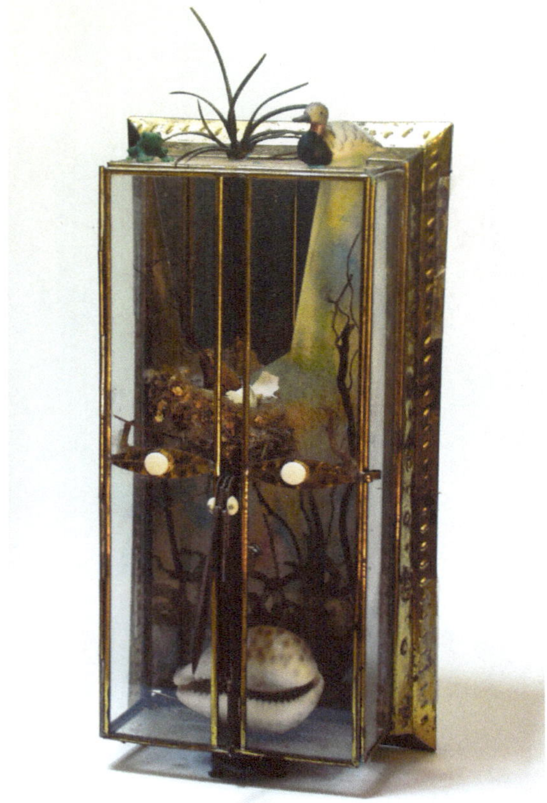

Mirror mask

Masks

As with many tribal cultures, facial images were used in ceremonies. Ritual ecstatic dance was a means of communicating with the spirit world. Dancing with a mask and costume transformed the wearer from an ordinary individual into one participating in a great cosmological unity. The details of these rituals have been lost, and the masks that remain as artifacts were not necessarily wearable.

The wooden mask on the left dates from the early Rust Age and is a simple but expressive depiction of an animal spirit. It is constructed from a minimally modified piece of gnarled wood, shells, rusty circles, and mirrored shards for teeth.

The mirror mask was constructed very late in the Rust Age as baroque complexity became more valued. Its themes are presented as an interplay of visual puns and allusions: a metal "bird" perched on the face doubles as a nose, a topknot of hair is part of a pond scene, and a mirror, where a brain might be, symbolizes "reflection."

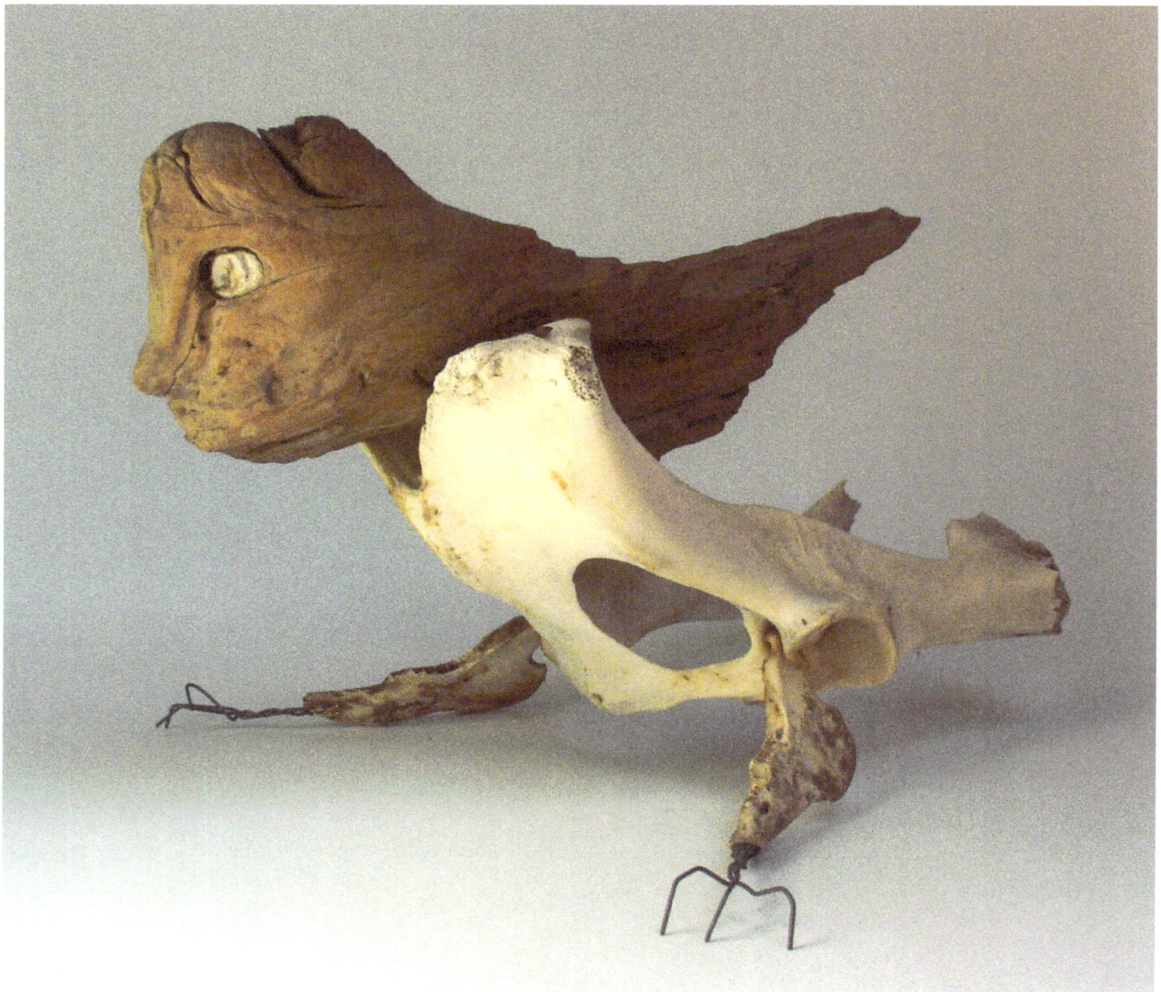

SIMULACRUM

A "simulacrum" is the natural appearance of a face. This wooden profile has been made into an anomalous creature.

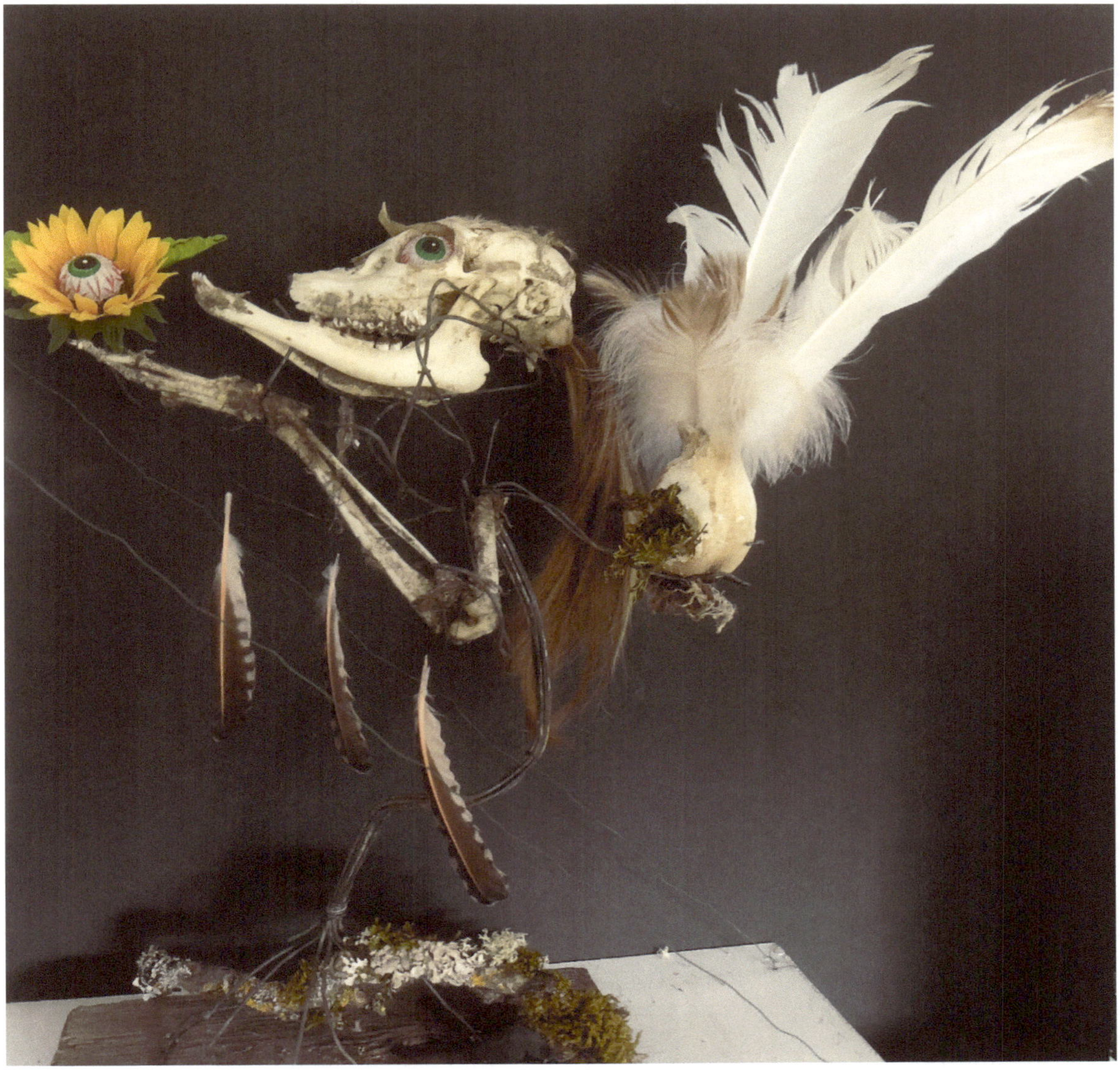

Greeting Figure

A primitive memento mori that might greet a visitor to a Rust Age hut, reminding them to spend their remaining time on the planet well.

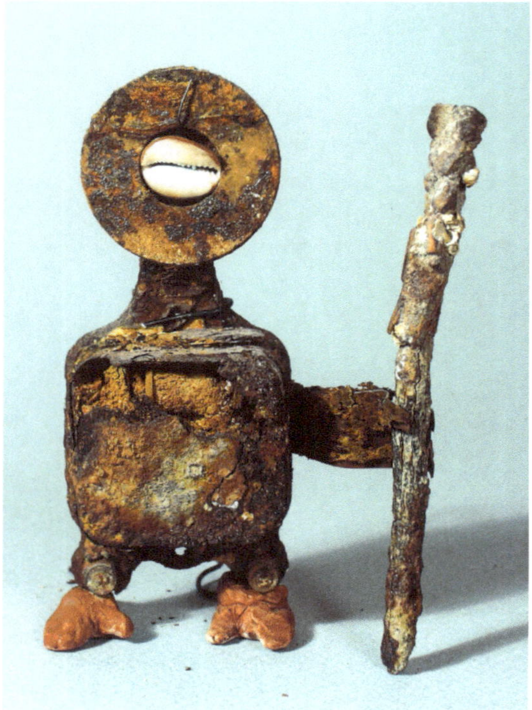

Guardian figure

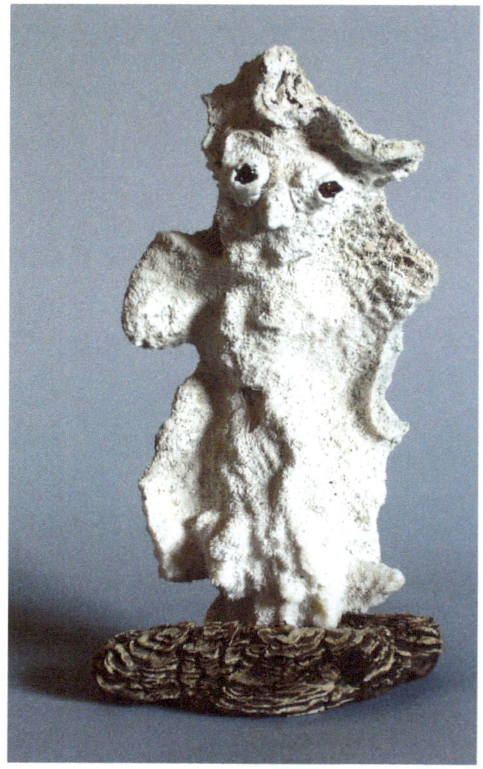

Sea spirit

Figurines

During the Rust Age, shamans attempted to gain control over their lives by developing ways to communicate with the many spirits, some helpful, some not, that inhabited the region. One such method was building figurines imbued with mystical powers.

The **guardian figure** is a figure in a defensive posture who is in fact crumbling and exposing its mechanical innards. The figure was originally supposed to serve as a protector against certain demons, but its fragility and constant state of decay have transformed it into a symbol of the futility of relying on such talismans
The **sea spirit** figure represents a helpful spirit that assisted shamans in finding the significant organic materials for use in constructing their objects. It is itself made from a beach find, a piece of anthropomorphic coral.

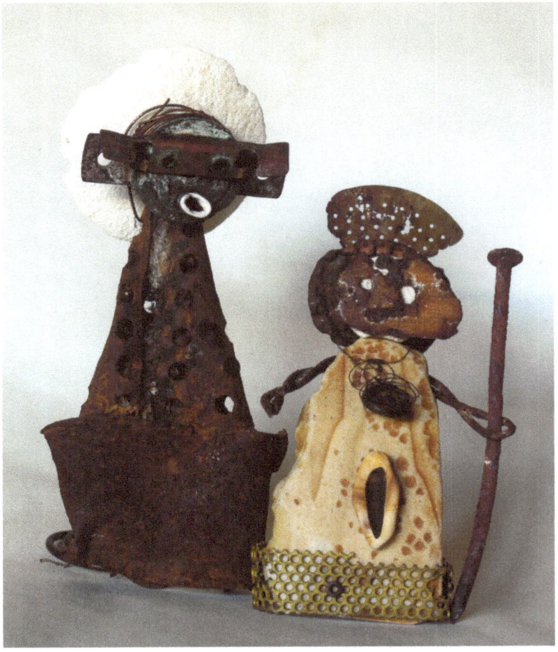

Primordial couple

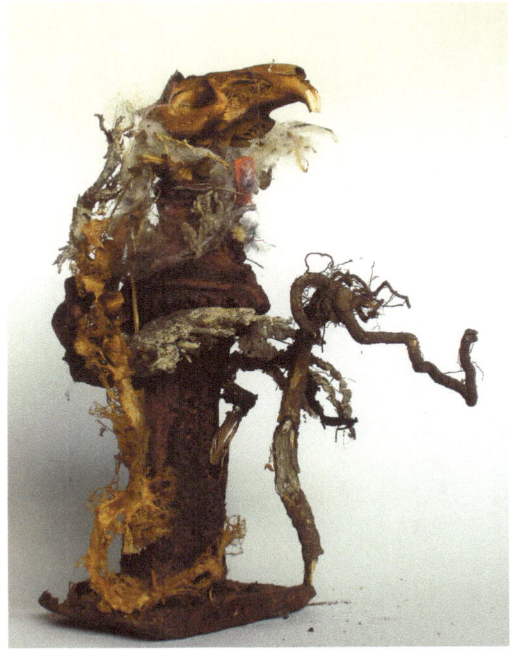

Shamanic figure

The **primordial couple set** represents various aspects of the generative principle, including the mystery of birth and heredity, as well as the disconnect between sexual attraction and procreation..

The **shaman** is represented in spirit form as an intermediary between the human and spirit worlds, with skull headdress, feathered neck ruffle, and traditional gnarled walking stick. The figure is made of bone, rusty metal, wood, lichen, and delicate organic filaments.

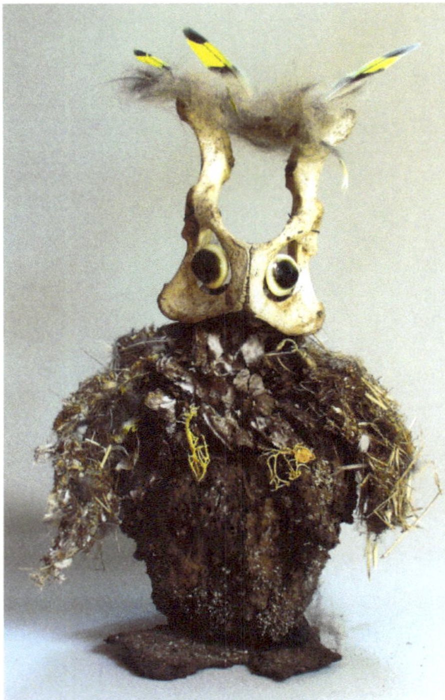
Ancestor figure

Ancestor figures were constructed from various organic materials, symbolizing the reinvestment of deceased ancestors' parts into new forms The figure shown here is made of bone, decaying wood, cat hair, feathers, mica, and tar. It has two mollusk opercula for eyes.

Royal figures were a special type of ancestor figure for those who believed themselves descended from royalty (mortals with divine blood).

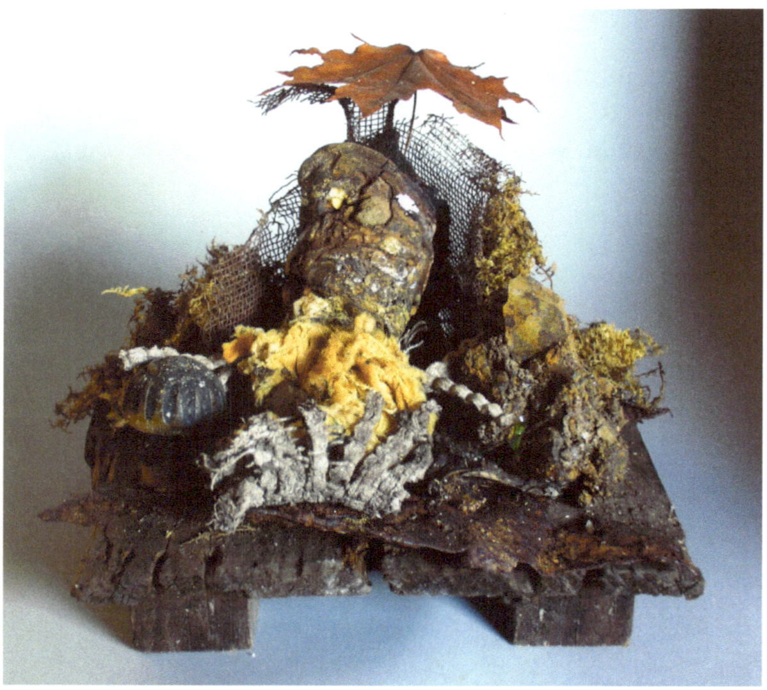
Royal figure

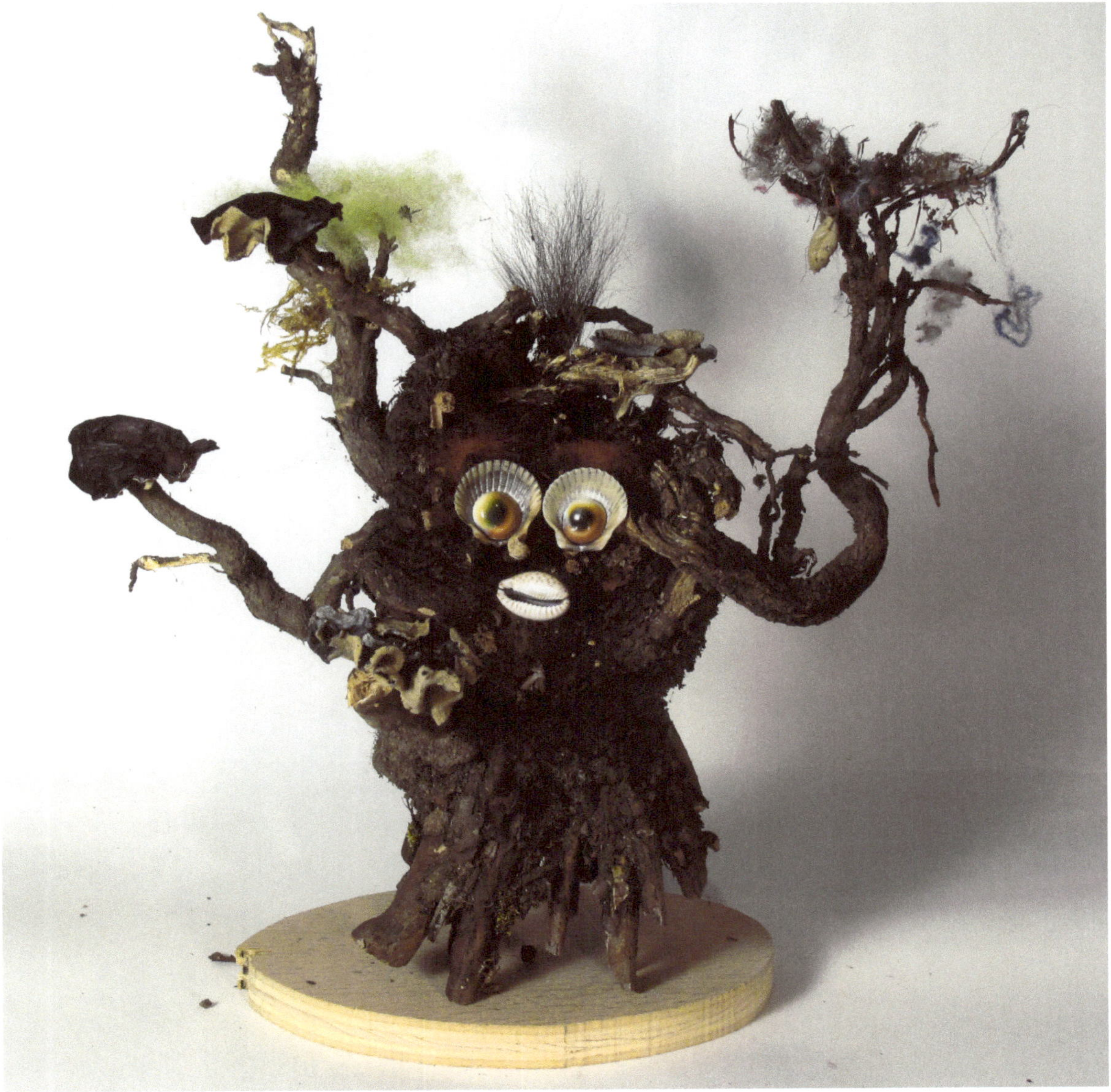

Tree gnome

The **Tree Gnome** represents the spirit of the forest, in recognition of its interconnectedness and diversity.

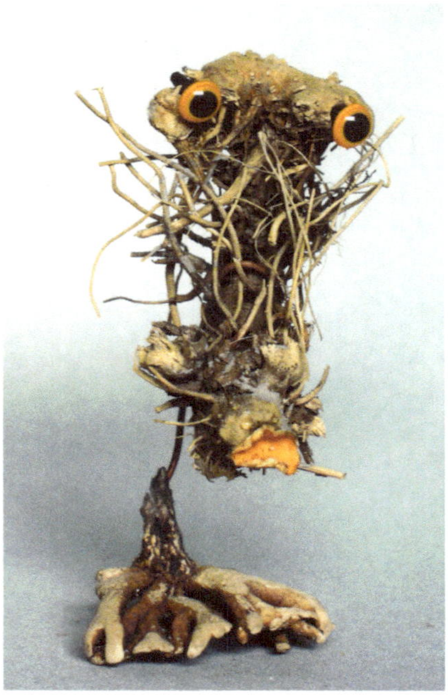

Root spirit

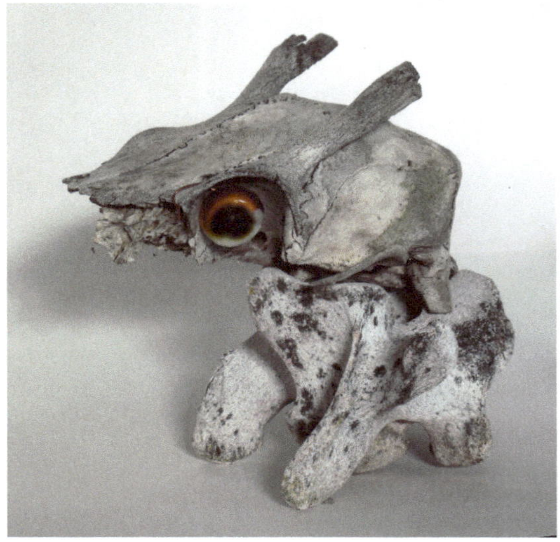

Bone spirit

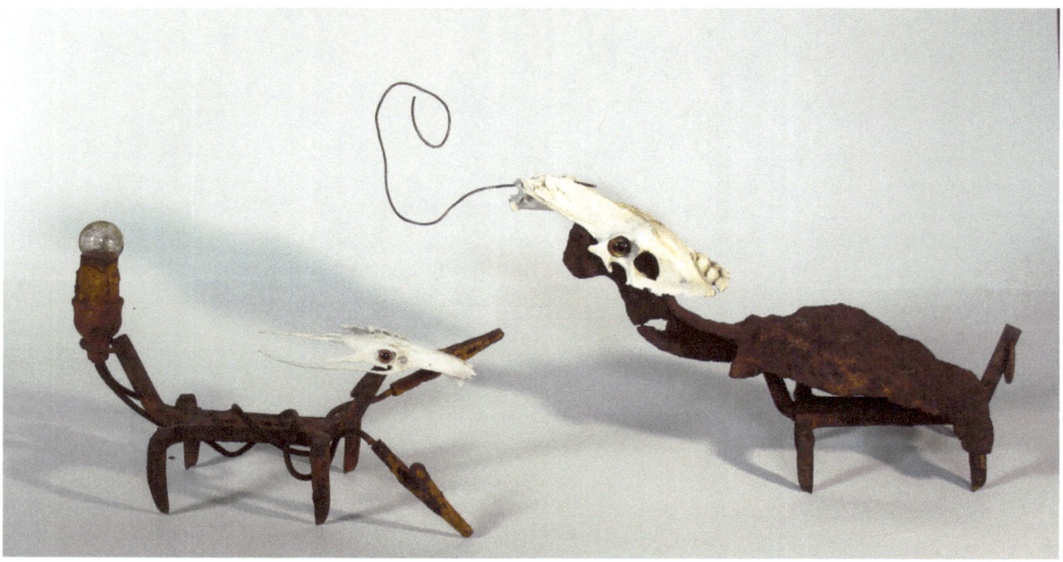

Illumination seekers

While the Tree Gnome champions the cause of the trees in the forest, the **root spirit** looks out for the creatures and organisms of the undergrowth. He is assisted in this task by his faithful **bone spirit**.

The **illumination seekers** wander the forest floor seeking spiritual enlightenment.

Late Rust Age art

For most of the Rust Age, visual art was deeply tied to cultural and spiritual practices and was not considered a separate discipline. However, toward the end of that era, a few "proto-modernists" were fascinated by the purely aesthetic possibilities to be found in assemblage of natural materials such as pond-moss, bones, and feathers.

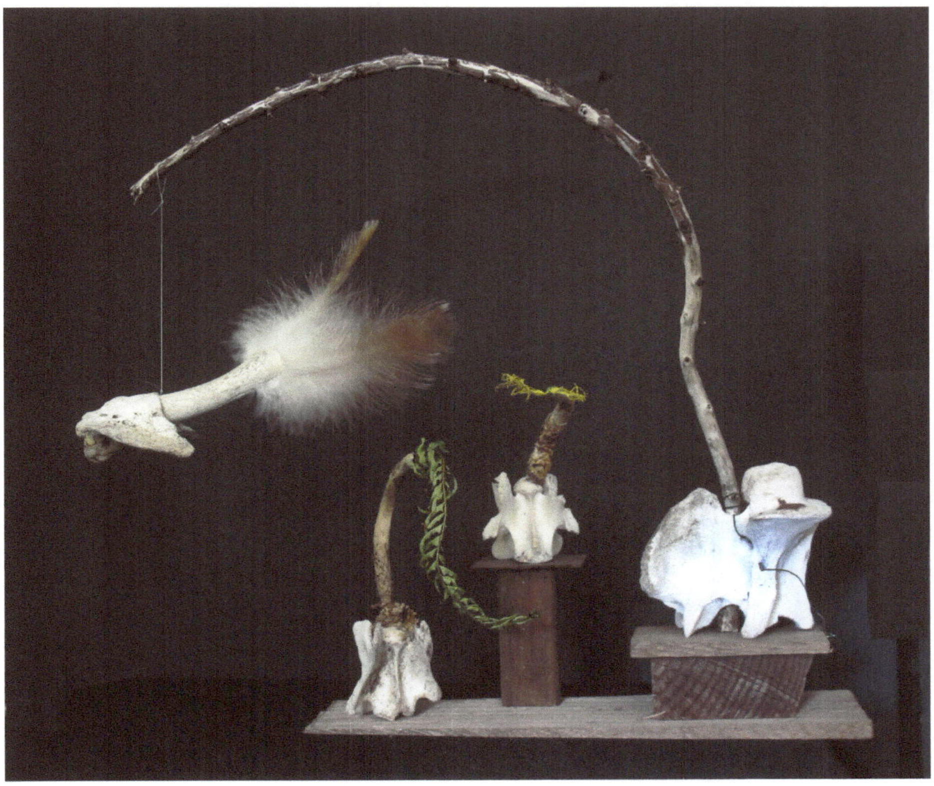

Bone Sculpture

A presciently modernistic piece highlighting the natural sculptural properties of bones and feathers.

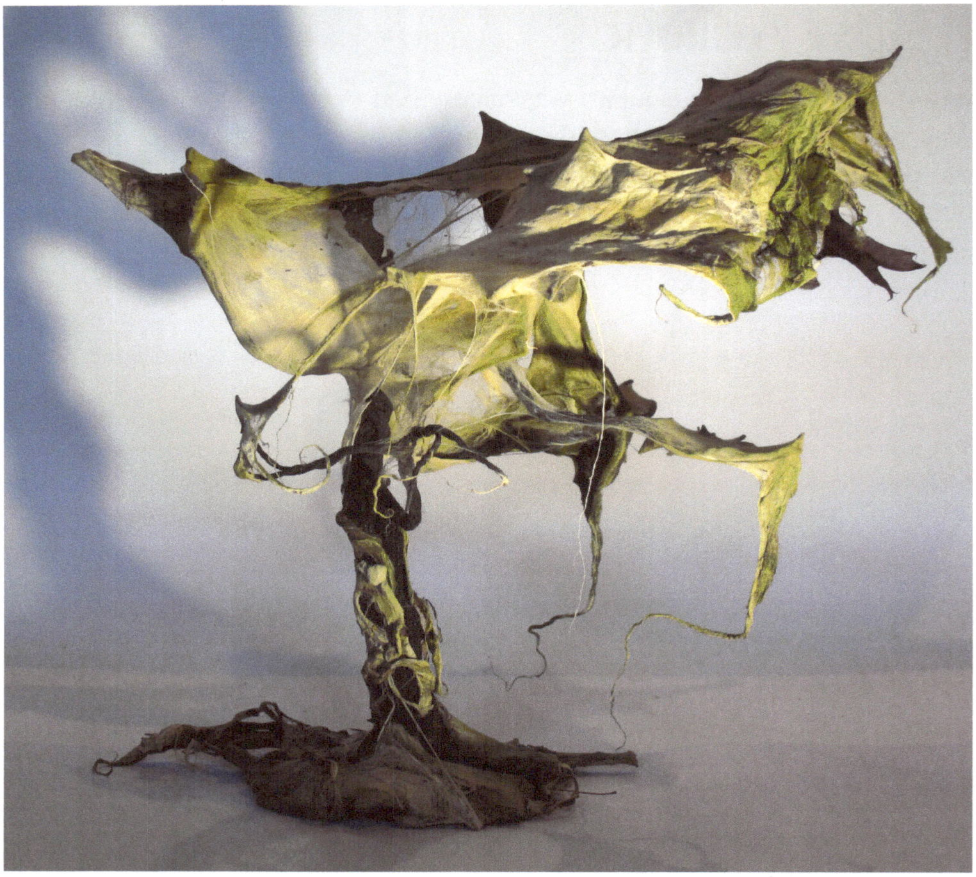

Pond-moss tree

Pond-Moss Sculpture

Proto-minimalist sculpture created by dipping a branched armature into a pond with a vigorous population of filamentous algae, letting it dry in the sun, and perhaps adding some embellishments. This art form was derided by some critics at the time as "scum art" but it is now recognized for its aesthetic qualities.

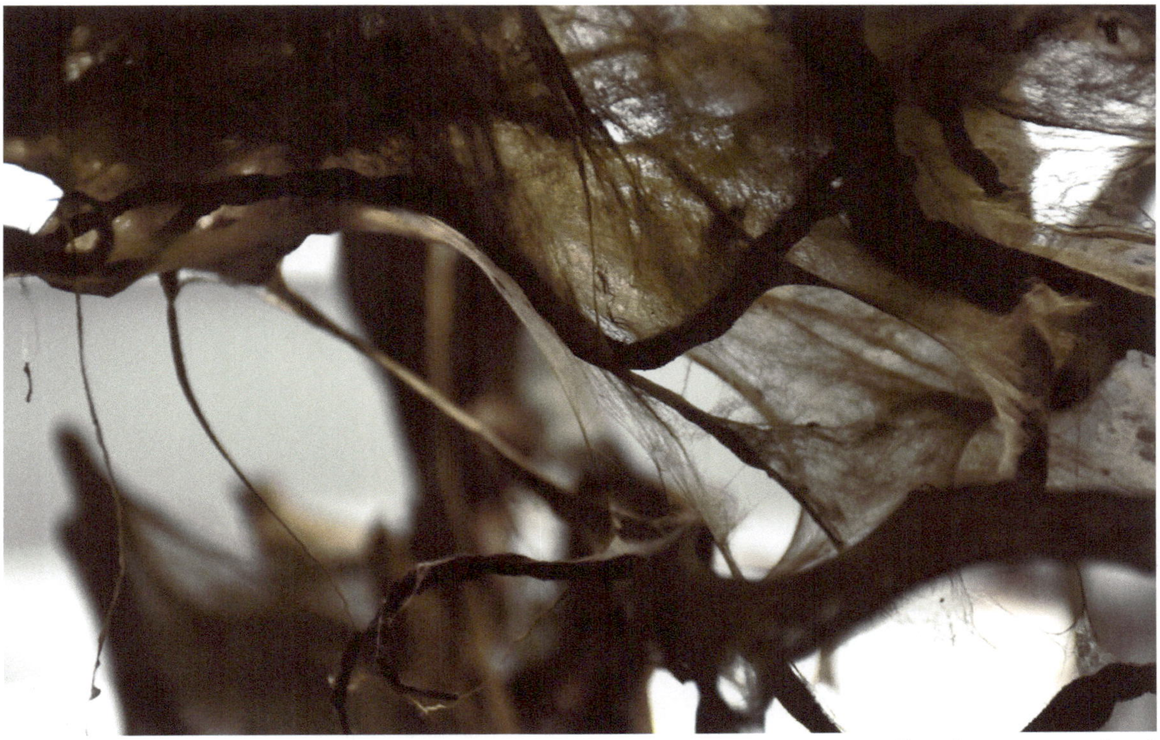

Pond-moss tree detail

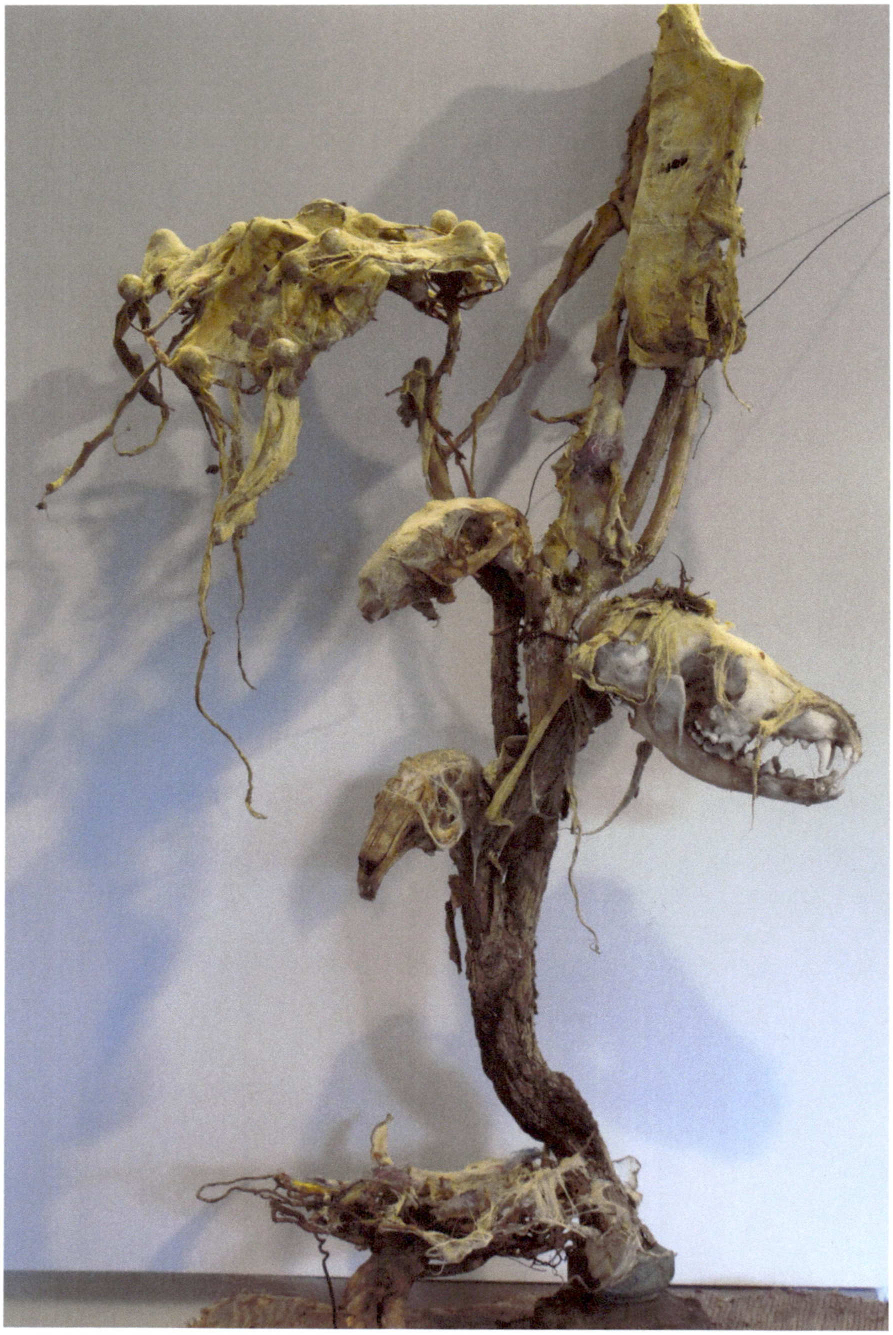

Pond-moss skull totem

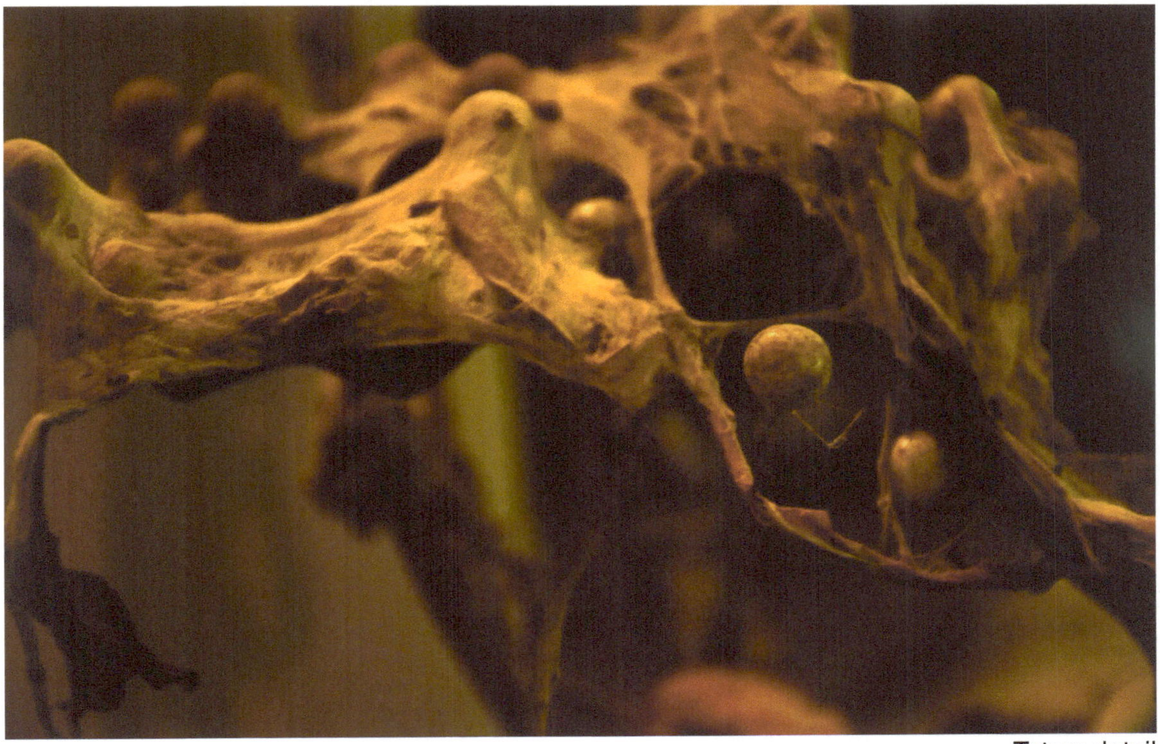

Totem detail

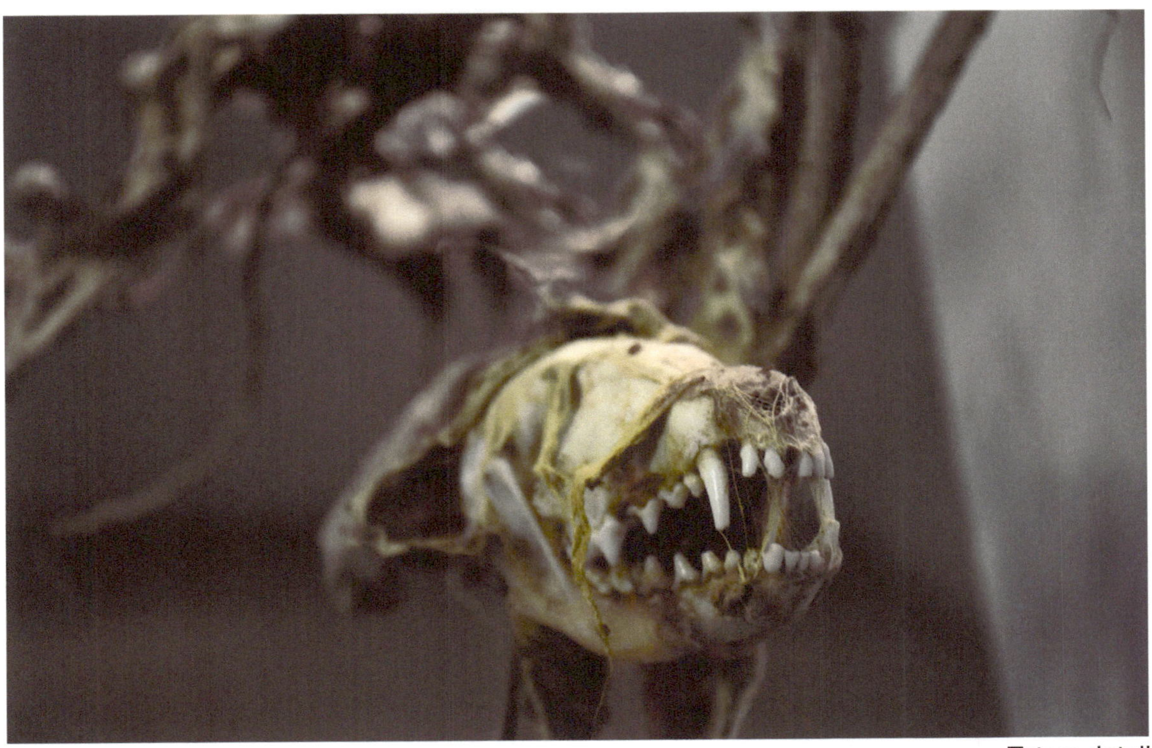

Totem detail

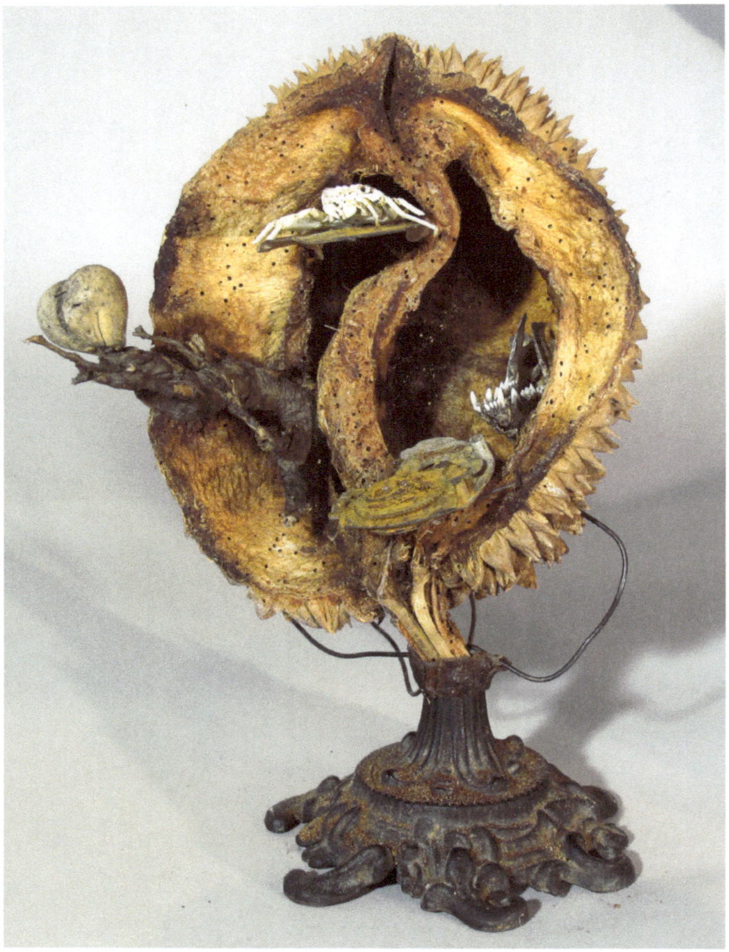

Diorama

Late in the Rust Age, found objects began to be assembled in a somewhat narrative form, foreshadowing the great dioramas of the Age of Wonder.

Rust Age media technology

The more practically-minded developed early media technology, precipitating a split between art and science that continues to this day.

Communication in the pre-literate Rust Age consisted of signs and symbols, both artificial and natural, often with vague non-specific meanings.

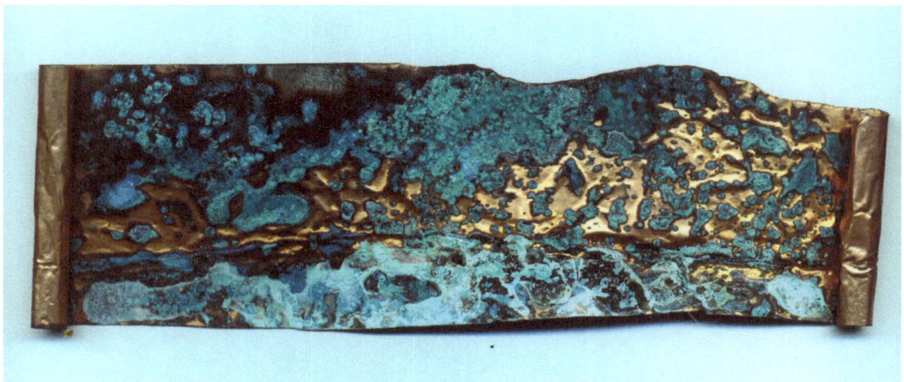

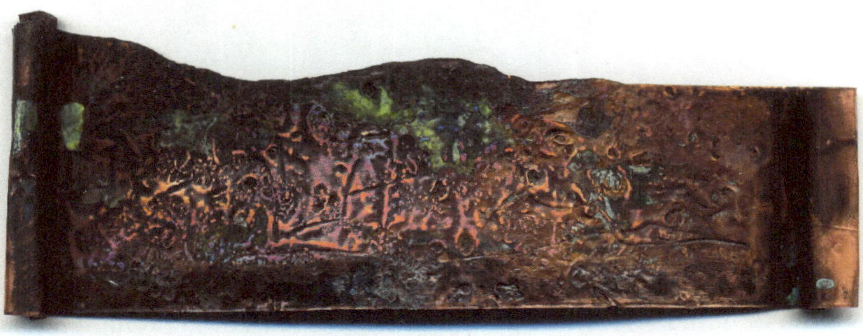

Copper scrolls

Metallic scrolls were primarily made from copper, hammered and subjected to various chemicals to create visions of the primordial ooze. Some of these chemicals were blue vitriol (copper sulfate), sal ammoniac (ammonium chloride), liver of sulfur, and common salt, as well as biologically derived fluids such as vinegar and urine. This was an early attempt to produce artificially the complex natural patinas that were prized by artifact makers. These processes were further developed by the alchemists of the Age of Wonder.

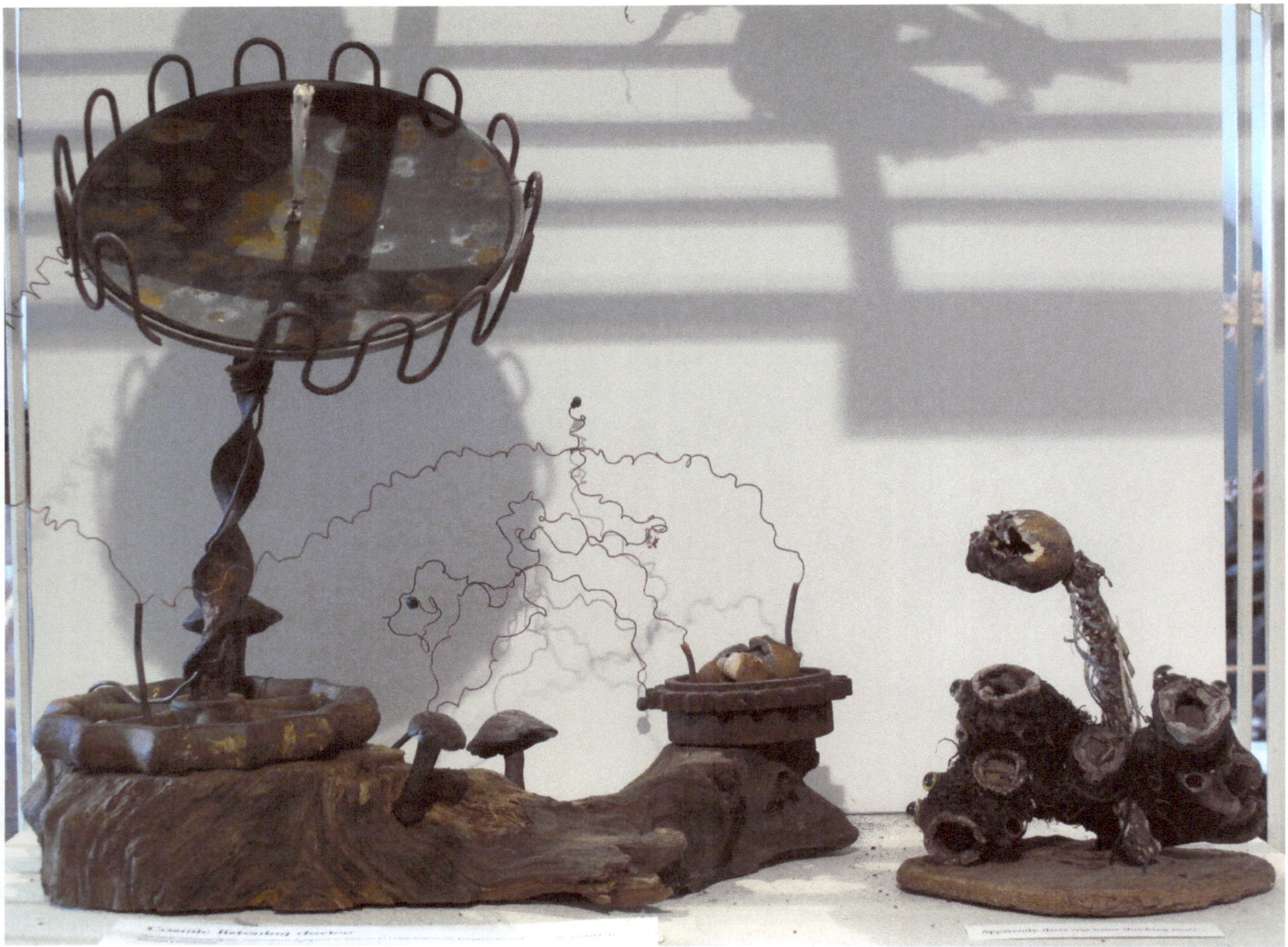

Cosmic Listening Device

An early cosmographic device designed to tune in to information on frequencies not normally available to human perception. The listening audience (facing page) eagerly awaits news.

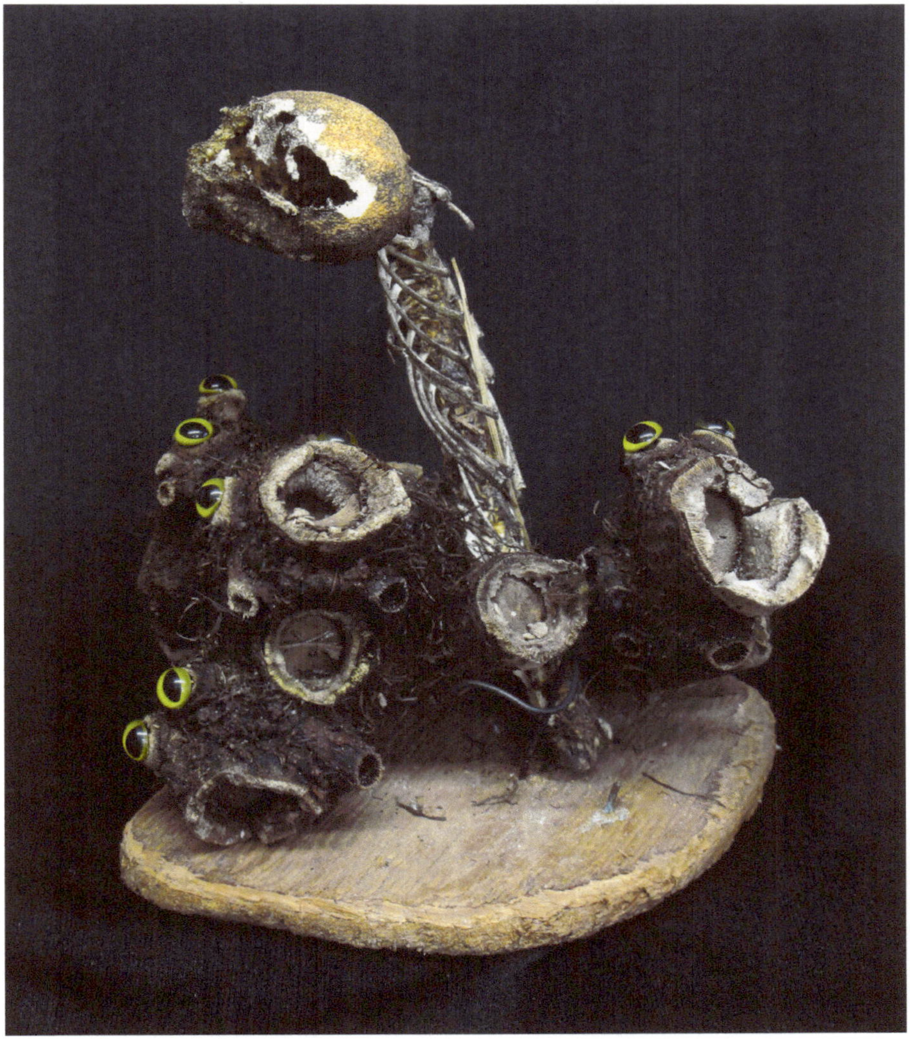

Apparently the news is not good. Perhaps they have detected signs of the imminent end of the Rust Age.

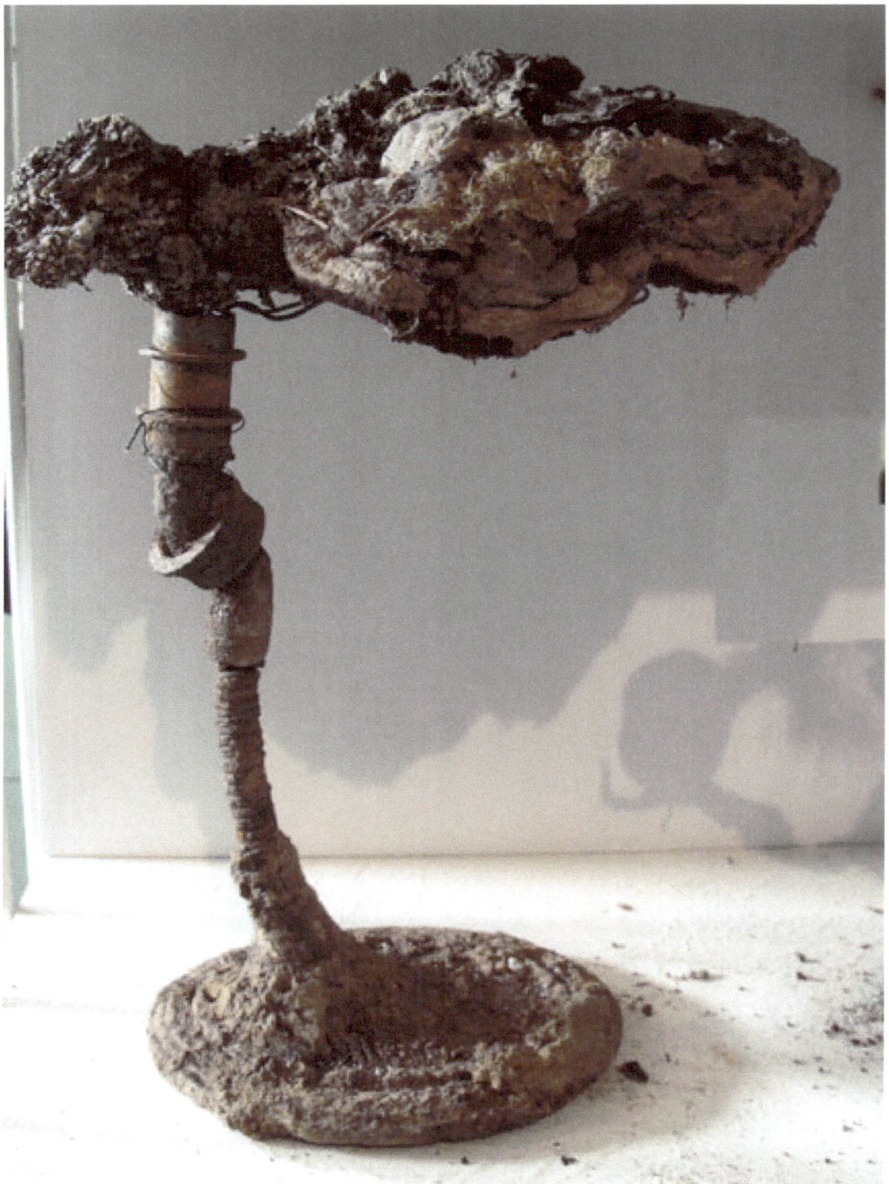

Fungus Lamp

Rust Age fungus lamps provided a soft glow through bioluminescence

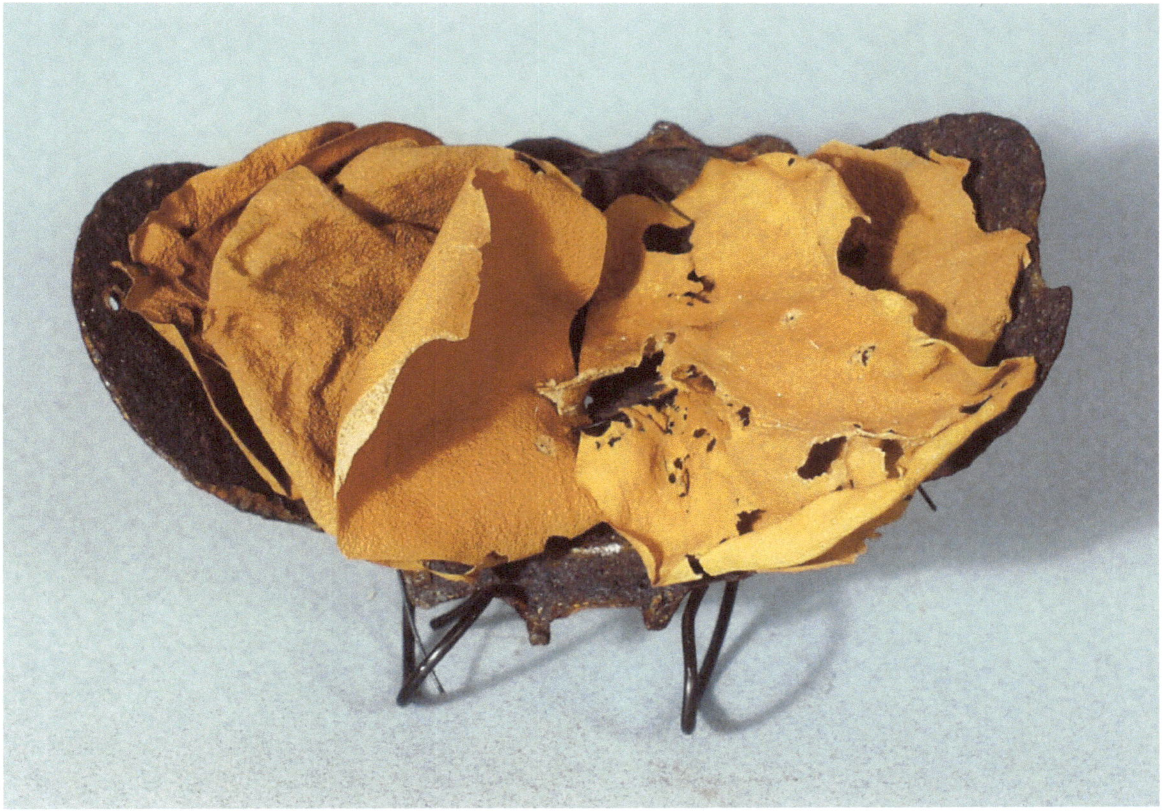

Leaf book

Leaf books were an early attempt to impose a narrative structure on the inchoate ramblings of nature. It was thought that there was a story that could not be expressed in words to be found in the folds, tears, and textures of the book's leaves. This example uses dried magnolia petals in a rusty metal binding.

The Age of Wonder

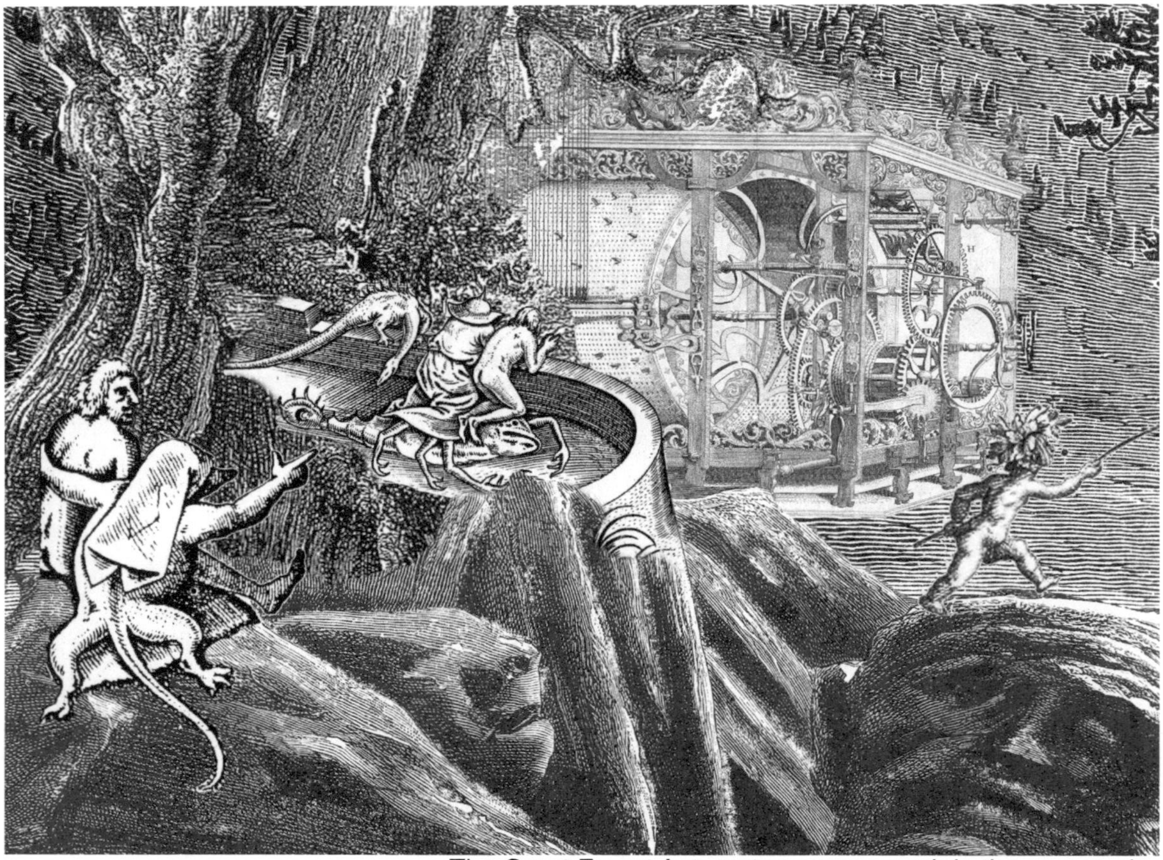

The Great Forest Automaton causes a stir in the community

The Age of Wonder

The combination of contact with European explorers and the discovery of oil in the Zymoglyphic region spelled an end to the Rust Age, freeing up the rusted wheels of progress and ushering in the Age of Wonder. This was a marvelous time of technological innovation, discovery, and exploration. The creative focus shifted from the uncertainties of the next world to the wondrousness of the world around us.

A rising curiosity about how things actually worked led to an empirical approach to the study of the natural world, which displaced the magic and religion of the Rust Age. Some feared that this approach of reductionist analysis and emphasis on identification and classification would lead to the disenchantment of the world. In the end, the epic tale told by the results of these investigations, from the creation of the universe though the evolution of life and development of human consciousness, was sufficiently astounding to qualify as a wonder in itself.

Still, there was a strong need to connect with something not bound by physical laws and rigid taxonomies. The metaphysicians of the age sought out the miraculous exceptions, violations of the established order, a delight in the unexpected. Anything unclassifiable was valued, anything sitting on the border between sensation and thought, between aesthetics and science. These phenomena were the miracles and wonders of the age. Far from being considered disturbances, they were applauded and sought out as welcome exceptions to dreary predictability.

Clockwork marvels

During the Rust Age, events in the world were attributed to the interaction of various sentient spirits, demons, and other mysterious entities. They could be appealed to through ceremonies, but not directly controlled. The Age of Wonder adopted a more materialistic view of the world where an observed effect has a discernible cause, the total being akin to a giant clockwork, constructed and set in motion by some primal force long ago. It was believed that if one knew the location and direction of each particle of which the universe was composed, one could predict all future events.

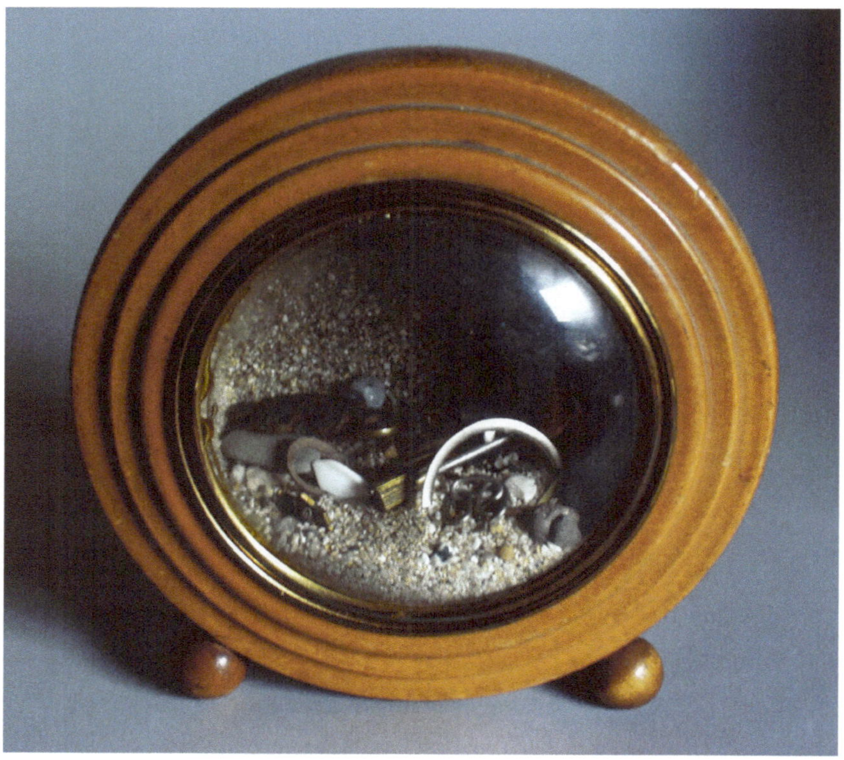

End -of-days clock

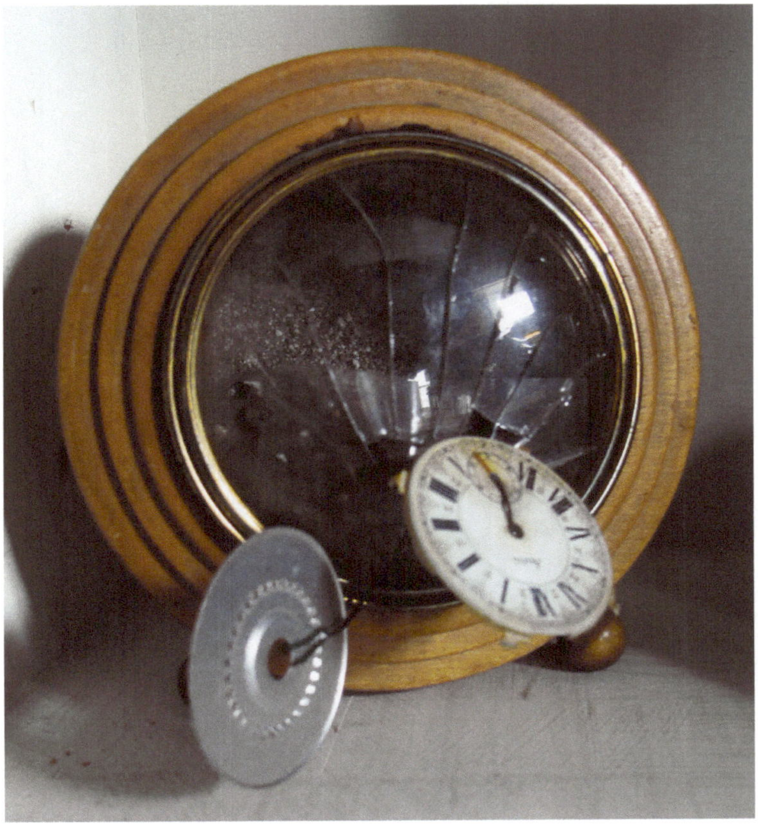

END-OF-DAYS CLOCK

This timepiece was originally conceived as a clock with an eye to eternity with its inner workings melted into the sands of time. however, something seems to have gone horribly wrong as serene timelessness came to and end.

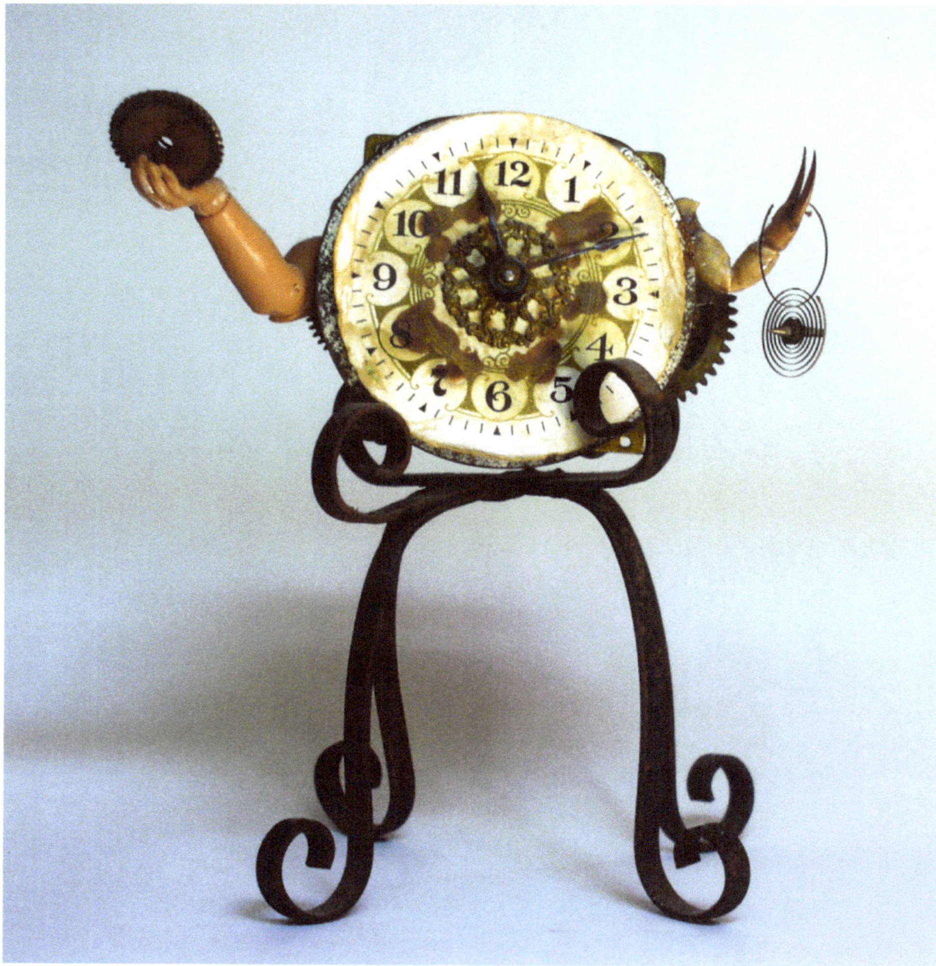

SELF-DESTROYING AUTOMATON

Automata and other mechanical marvels were of particular interest in this time because they occupied a mysterious gray area between life and death. Although clearly made of inanimate parts, they had some semblance of life. They offered the disturbing (for some) possibility that living creatures were at heart themselves merely mechanical devices.

This particular mechanical wonder not only told time but continuously removed pieces of itself and offered them to passers by. How the internal parts were regenerated has yet to be determined despite intensive investigation by the museum staff.

MEMENTO MORI

The coming of the Age of Wonder and its focus on the material world did not diminish the preoccupation with, and bafflement by, the universal sentence of death. A number of artifacts fall into the category of "memento mori," reminders that one's time to enjoy the wonders of the world is limited.

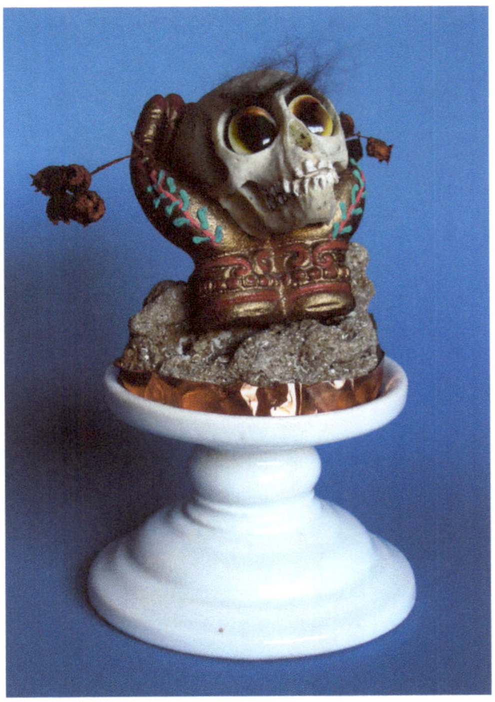

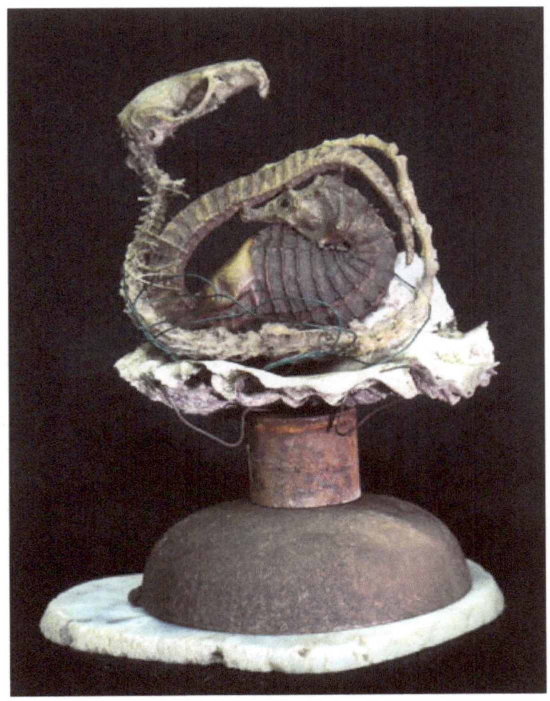

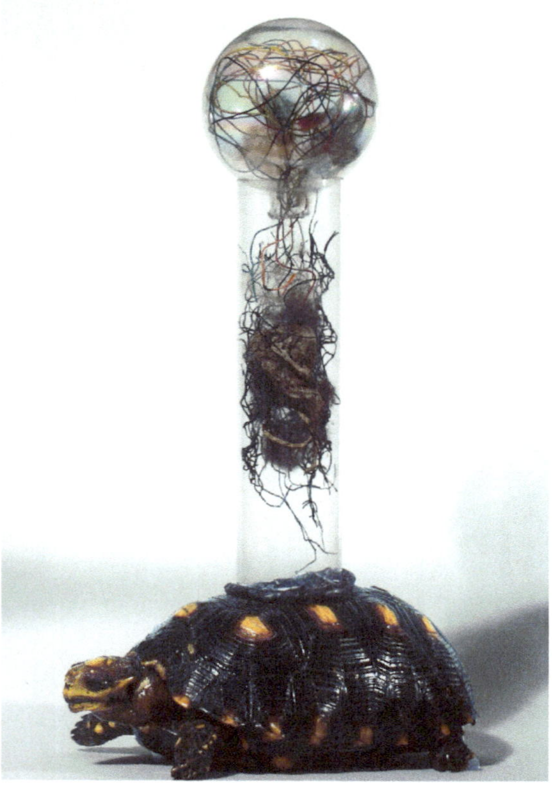

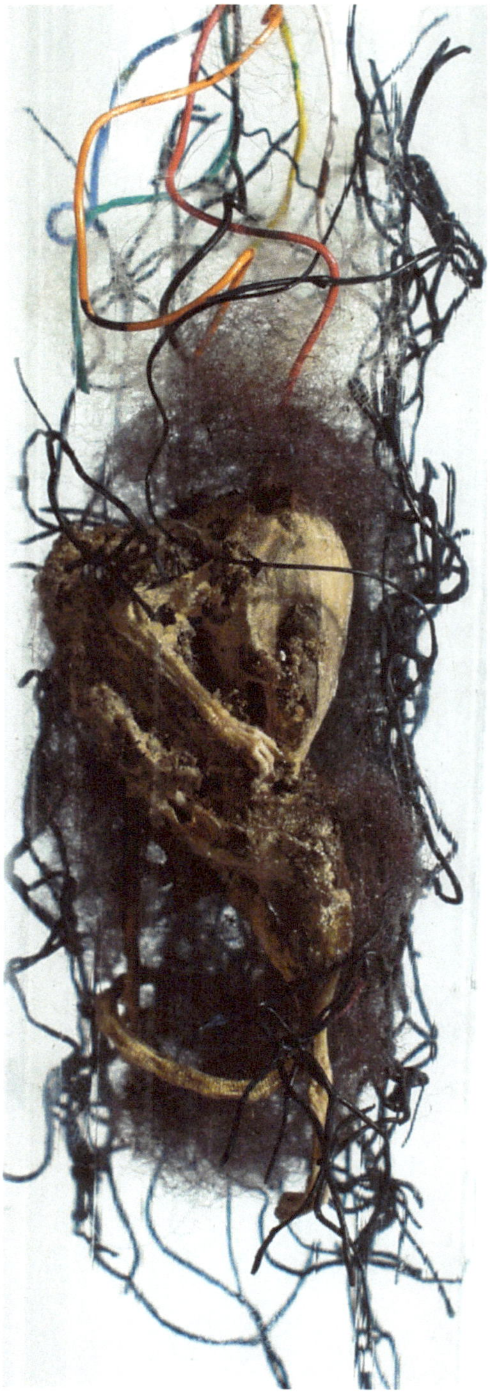

Another example of a memento mori is this symbolic burial urn, in which a transparent column rises out of a wandering turtle and contains the decaying remains of a mouse, swathed in wires and fur.

HAND STONES

The tradition of constructing "hand stones" began early in the Age of Wonder. The term comes from the practice of collecting attractive or unusual rocks and minerals of about the size that could fit in one or two hands. These specimens were placed on a stand, then decorated with figures and other material to create tiny landscapes, thus effecting an ideal synthesis of naturalia and artificialia. A common theme was to have a human or animal observer in the scene. What the observer was observing tended to get more bizarre as the era wore on.

Hand stones are echoed by the viewing stones, or scholar's rocks, of the Era of Oriental Influence. In the viewing stone tradition, there is more emphasis on framing the rock itself, and less on adding to it.

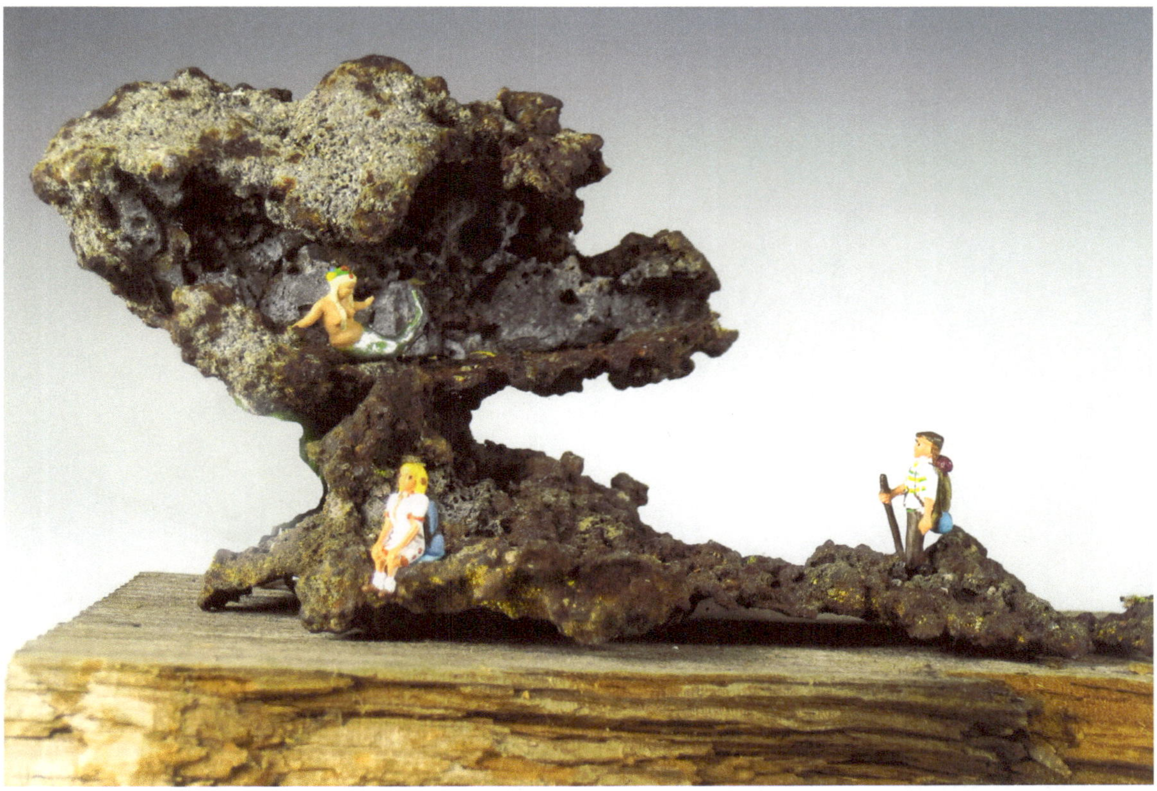

Mermaid Rock

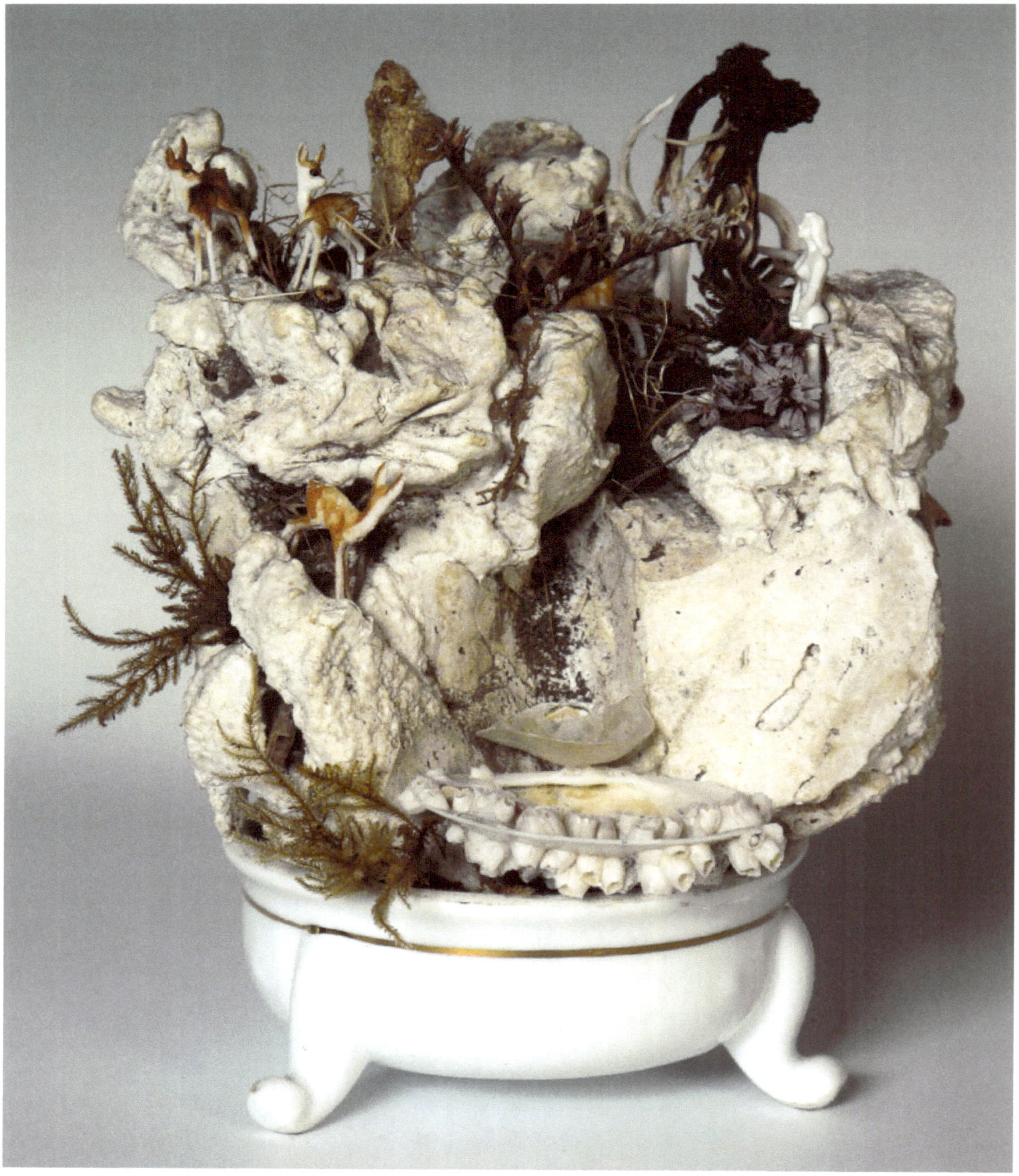

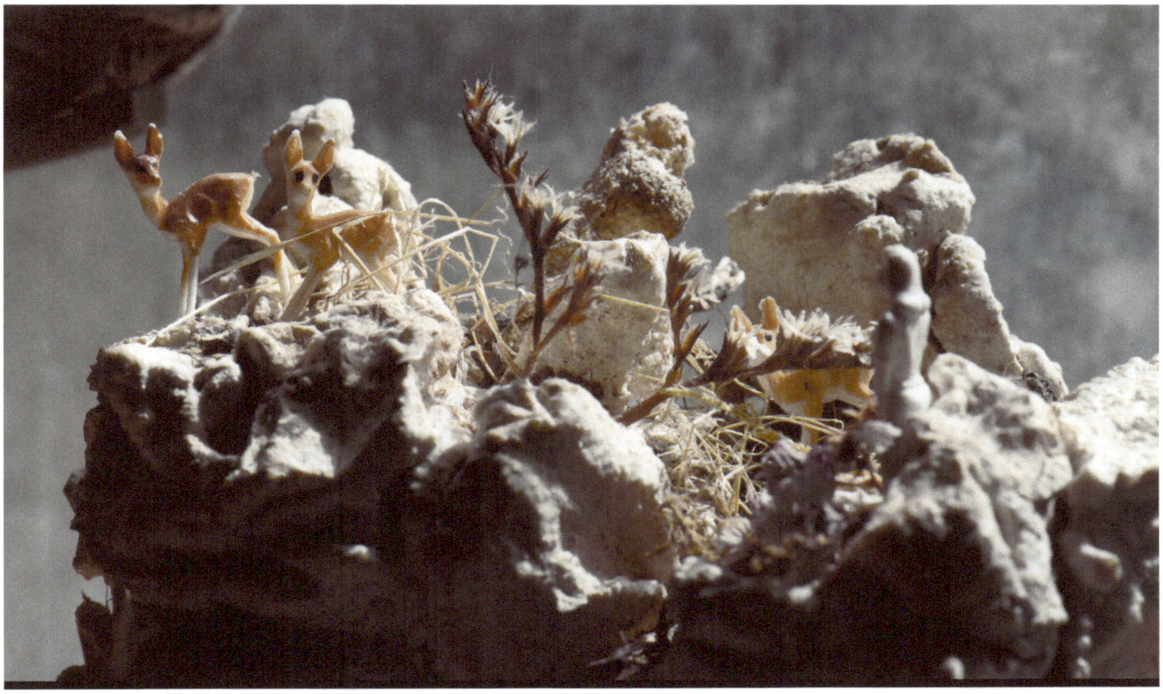

Pastorale - detail

Pastorale

A classic example of a hand stone, decked out with an idyllic pastoral scene (see previous page)

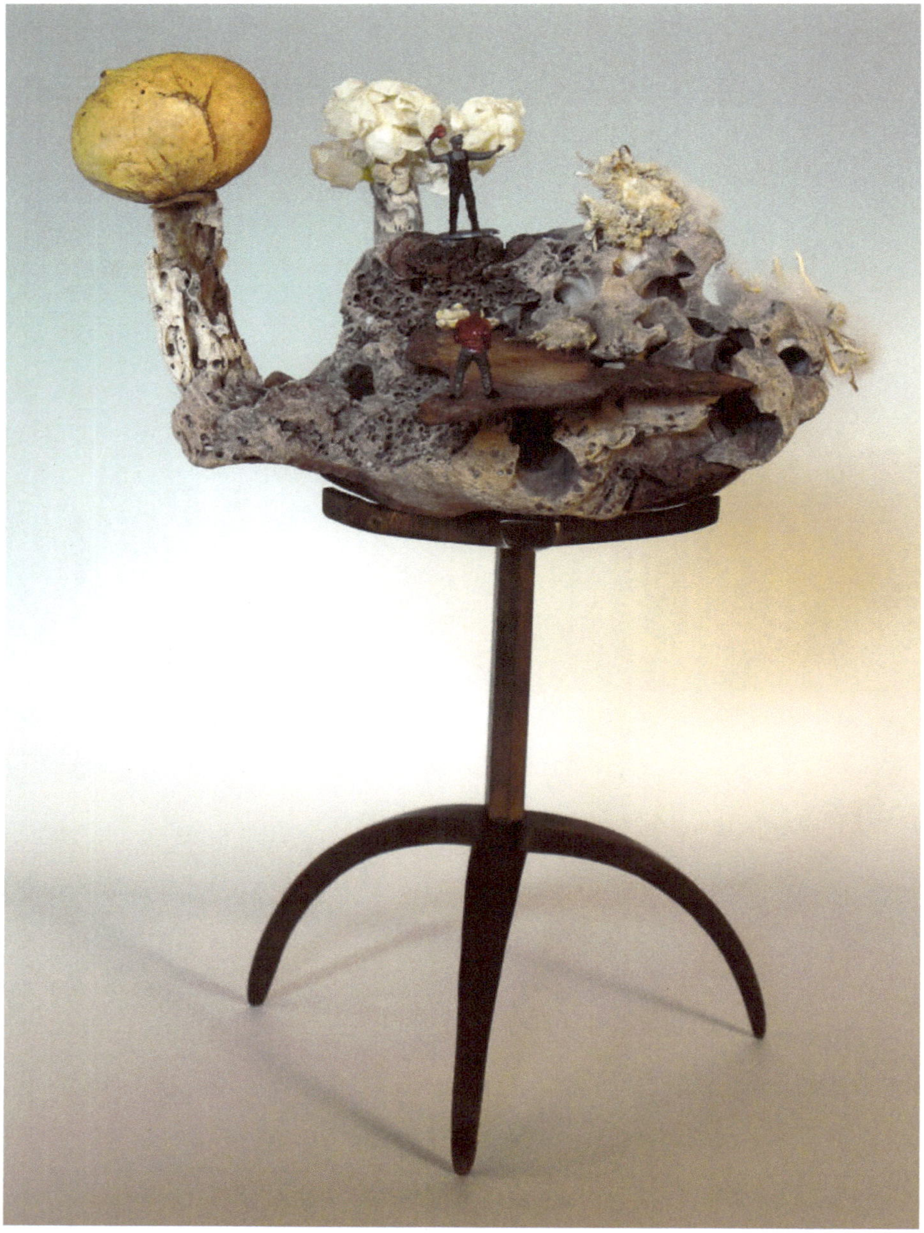

The Rise of the Crustaceans

In the coastal areas, people used driftwood instead of stones. Here, there seems to be a sort of dispute between two men and some wayward crustaceans.

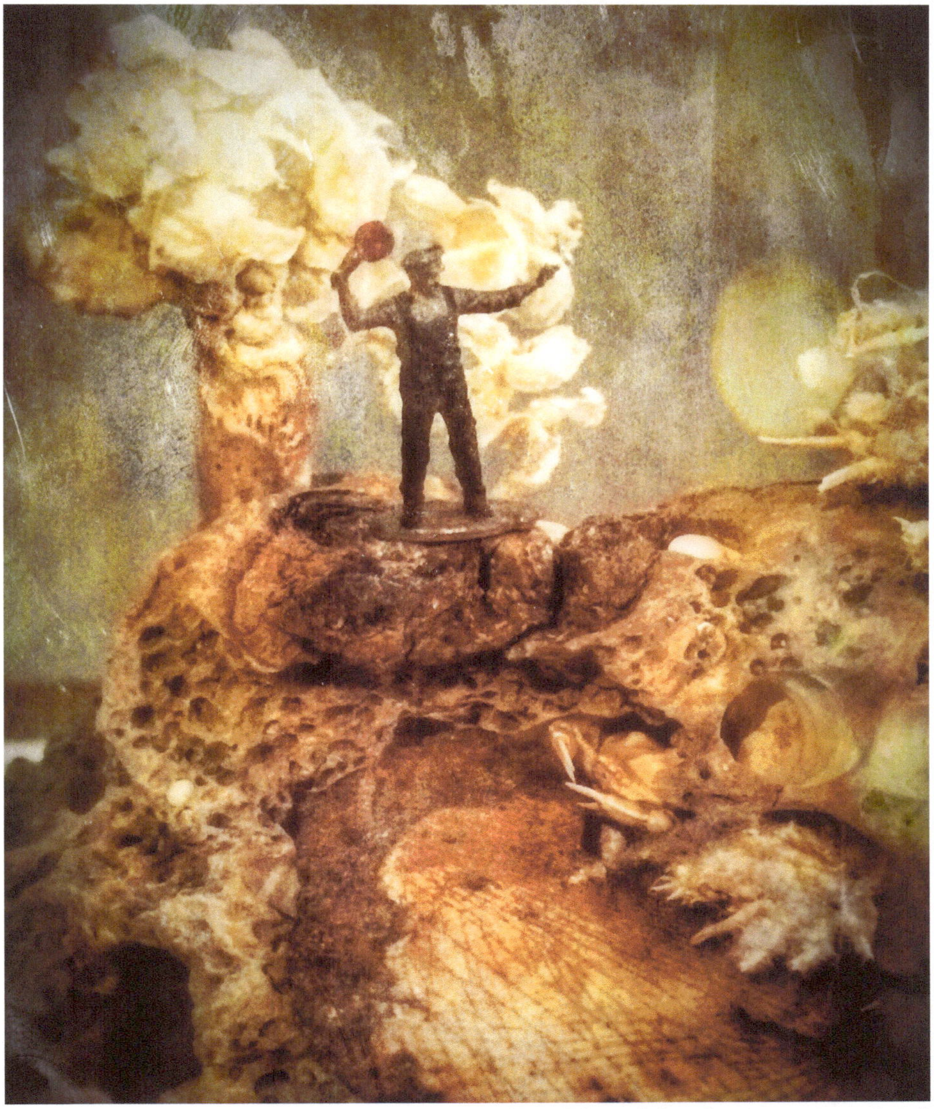

The Rise of the Crustaceans - detail

GOETHITE

Iron ore named after Johann Wolfgang von Goethe, the 18th century writer and natural philosopher.

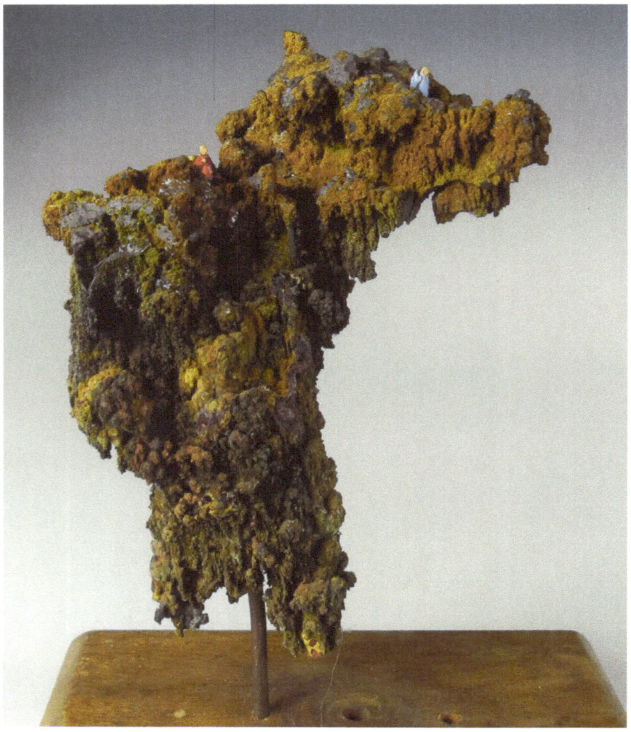

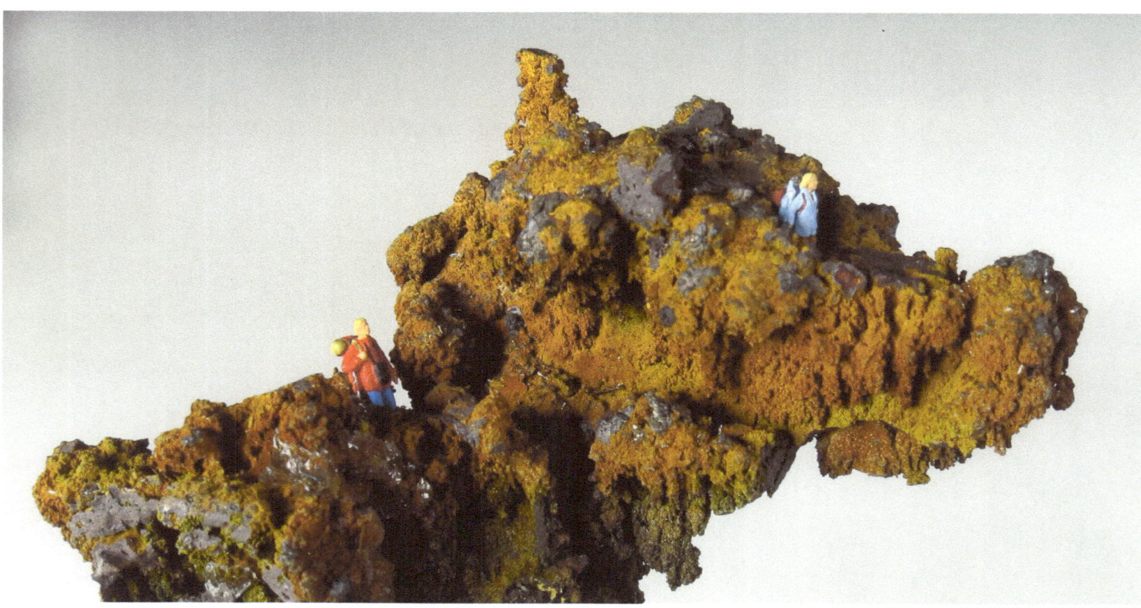

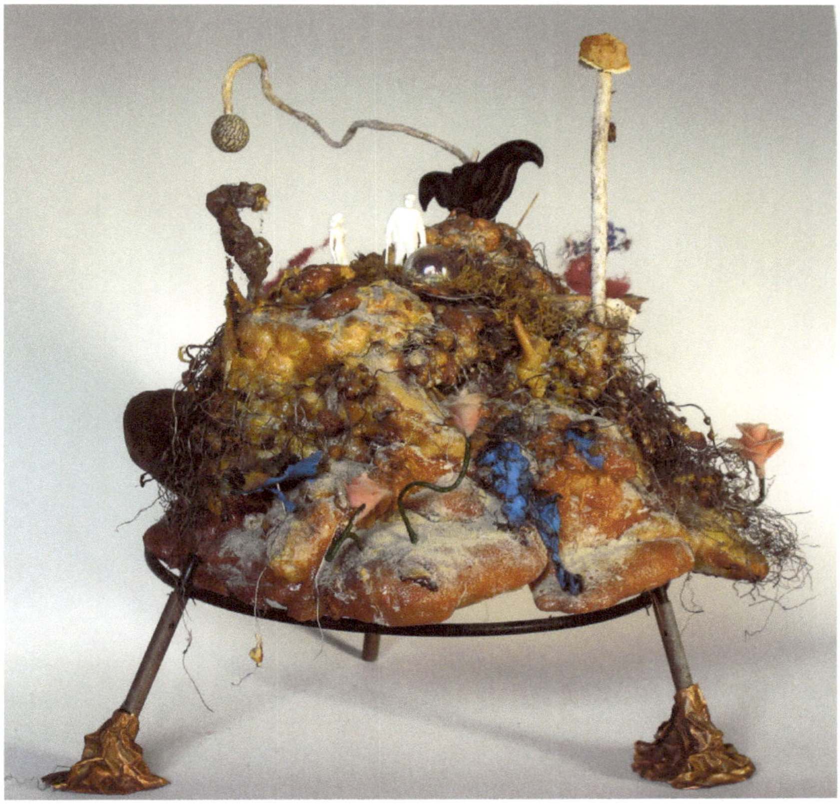

The Enchanted Bubble

In this scene, perched on a mysterious pile of industrial waste, two people discover a fascinating bubble.

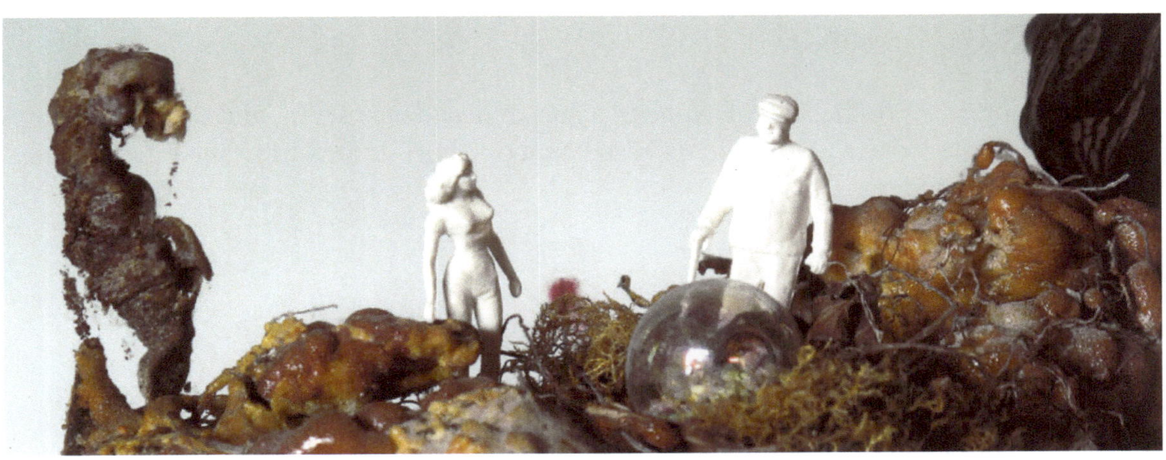

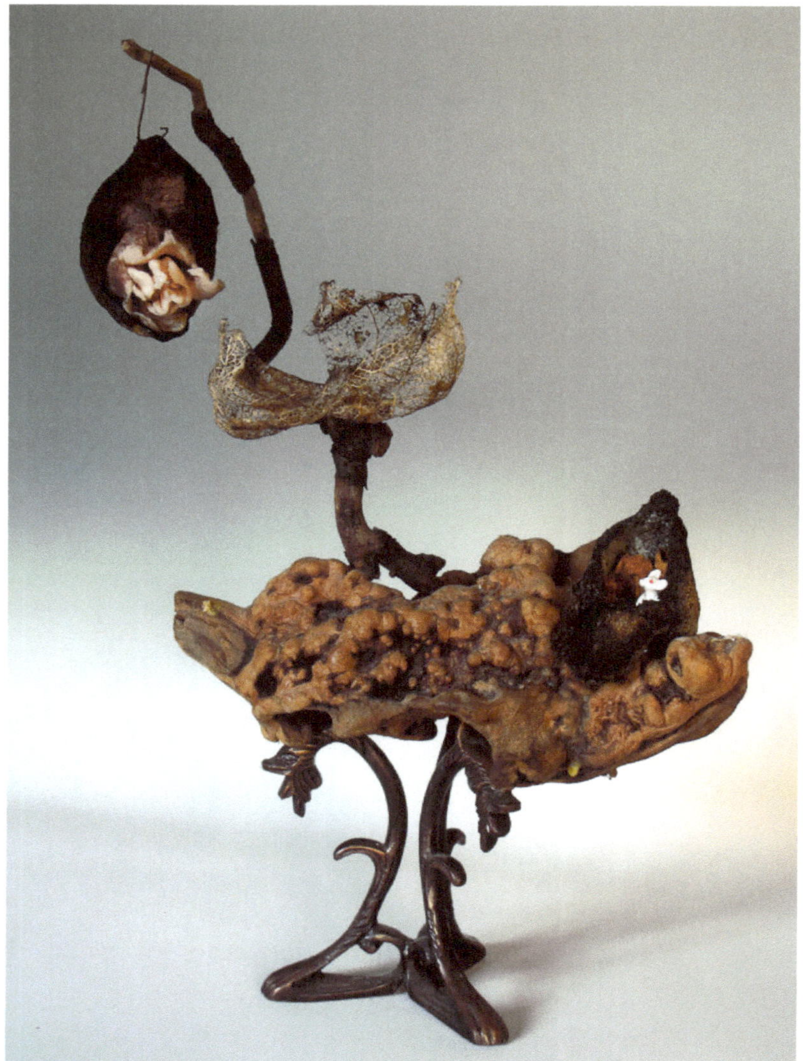

WHAT IS THAT THING?

In the waning years of the Age of Wonder, a sort of decadence set in, and the hand stone tradition became looser. This oddity is based on a tree burl. In it, a tiny, big-eared mouse looks out and wonders.

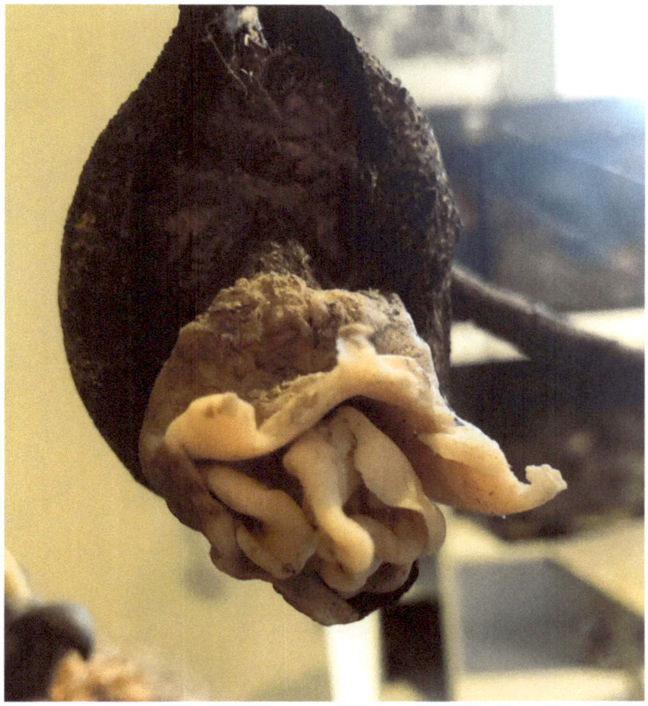

Detail view - the thing

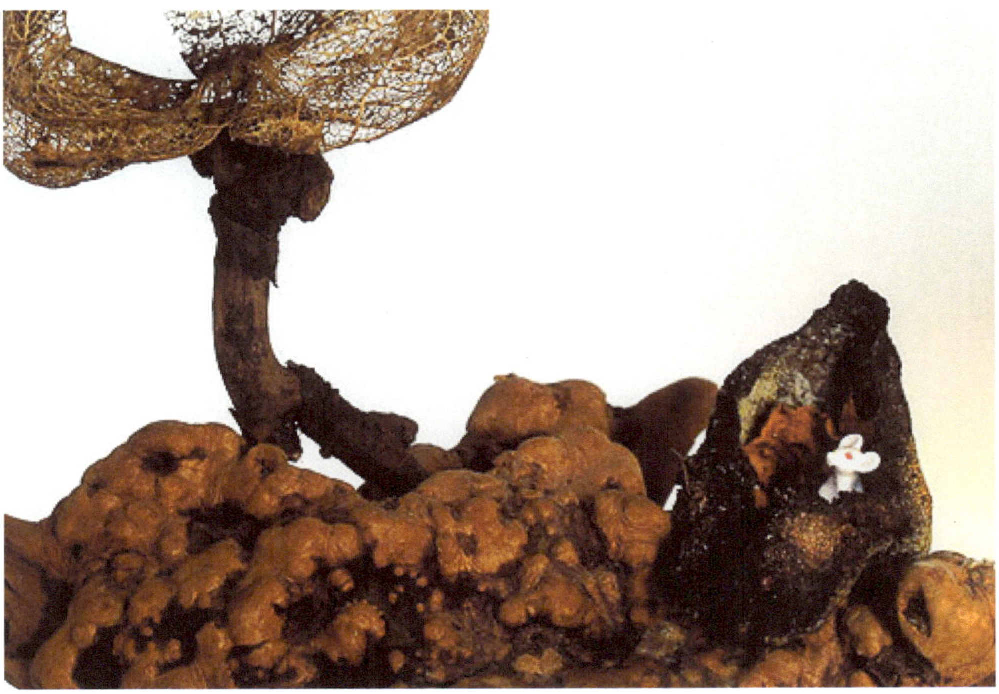

Detail view

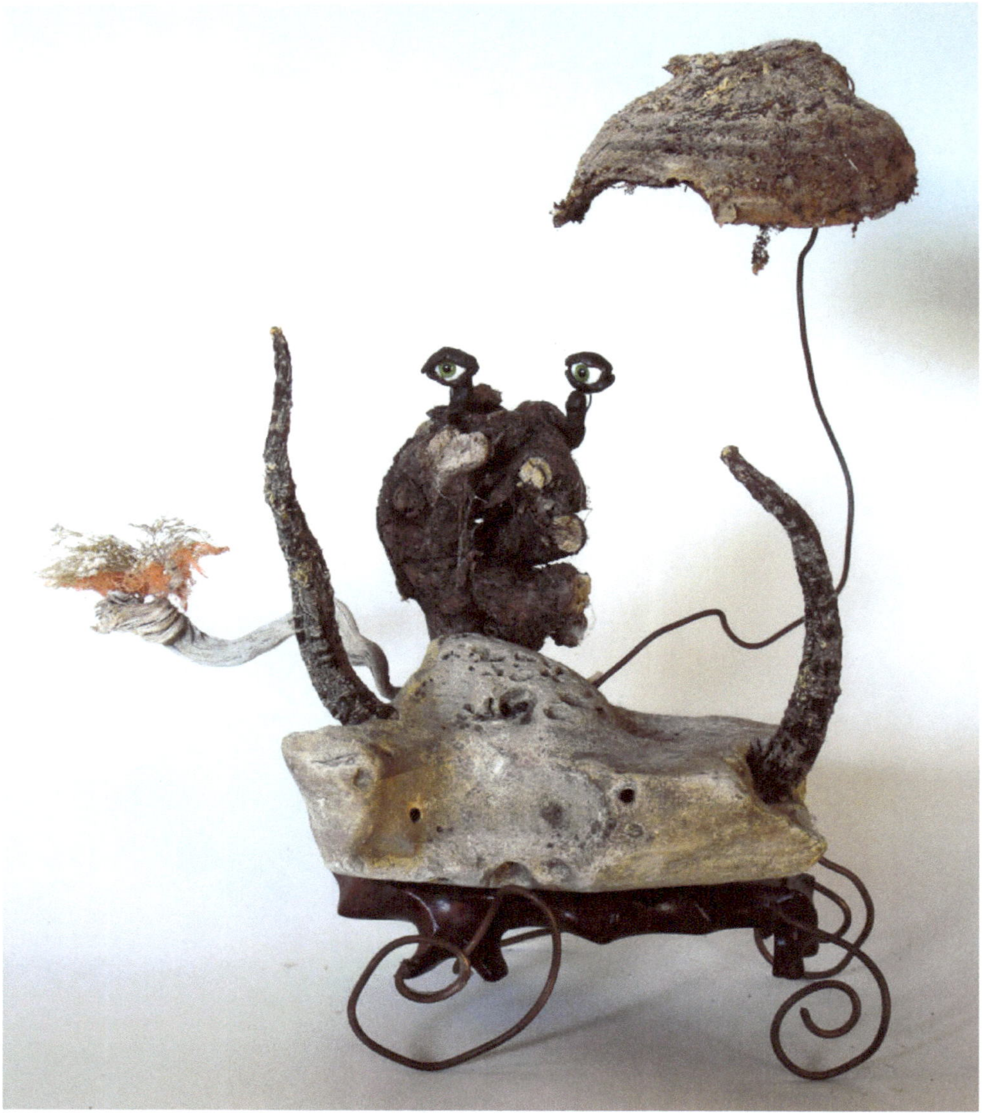

THE EYES HAVE IT

This object, built around a sea rock with convenient holes, anticipates the surrealism of the Modern Age.

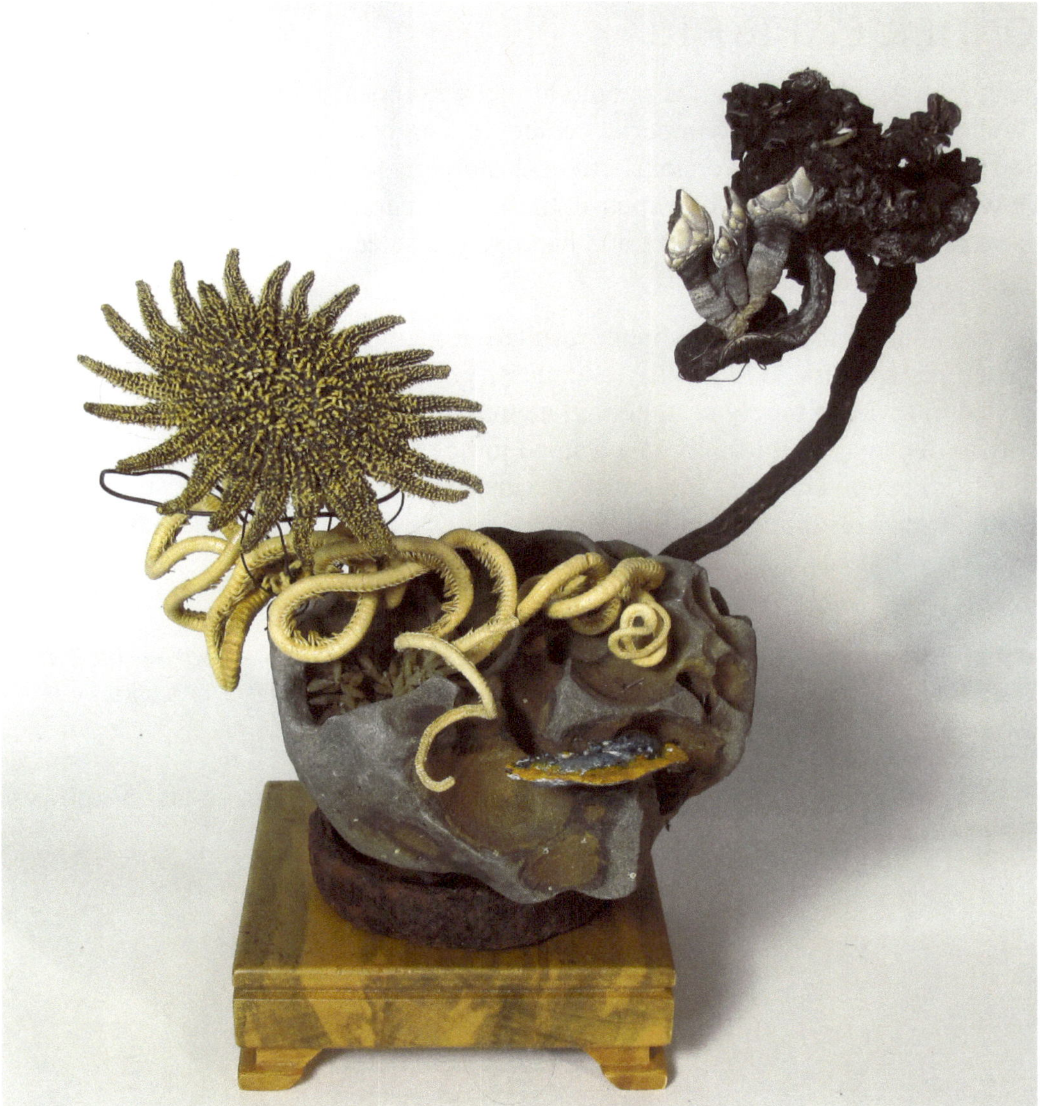

SEASCAPE

Fantasia on marine life

Wonder cabinets

During the Age of Wonder, the people of the region heard fantastic tales of the great Wunderkammeren in the imperial centers of Europe.. The people of the region were inspired to create their own versions, but on a more personal scale. Instead of impressing people with vastness, rarity, and expense, these were carefully curated microcosms that ideally reflected a person's interests and history. The selected objects were not labeled but "arranged for poetic effect."

Exploration during the Age of Wonder resulted in many novel objects coming into view. Early attempts were made to identify and classify them, but these efforts were soon abandoned in favor of purely aesthetic arrangement. Curiosity cabinets became popular as a way to display them, usually in a heaped jumble. A typical cabinet would include artifacts from exotic cultures, antiquities, taxidermied creatures, strange animals, fossils, shells, dried sea life, and mechanical wonders, as well as objects whose function and purpose is mysterious.

> *a conglomeration at any rate of the most heterogeneous and ill-assorted objects, piled higgledy-piggledy...proved that when the shrivelled skin of the ordinary is stuffed out with meaning it satisfies the senses amazingly.*
>
> —Virginia Woolf

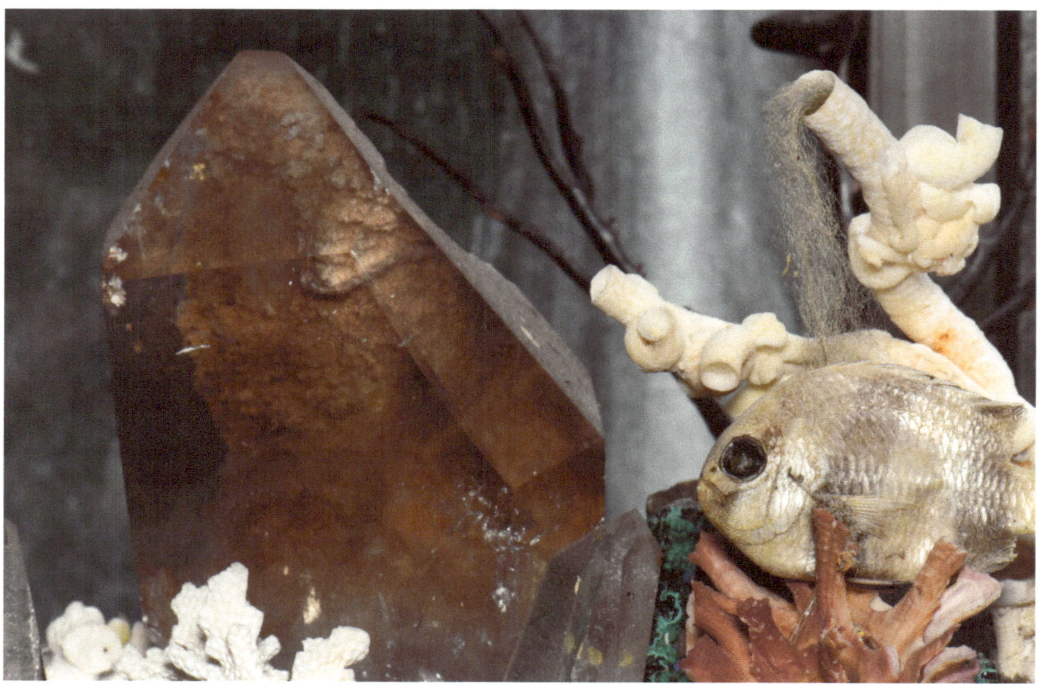

Tabletop wonder cabinet - detail

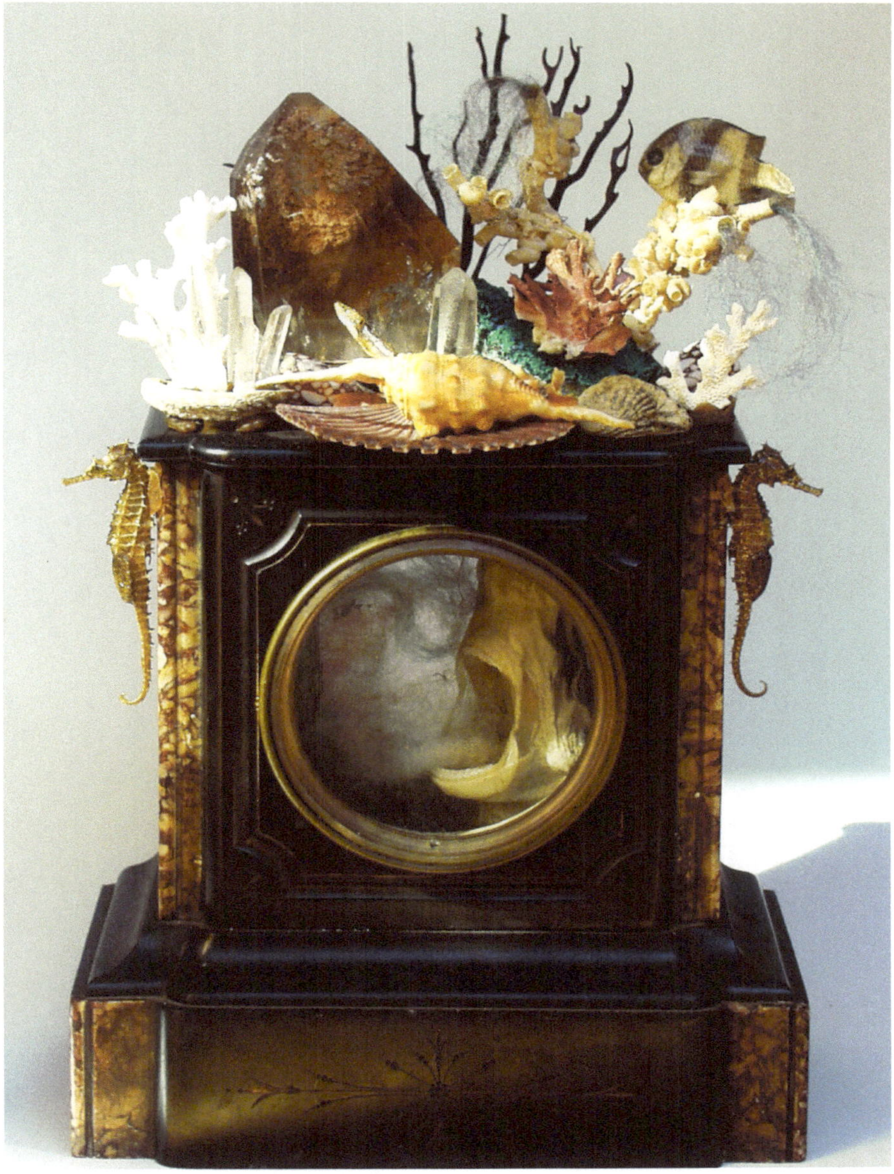

Tabletop Wonder Cabinet

Eclectic collections of marvels were popular during the Age of Wonder. Crystals, shells, minerals, and marine life decorate this tabletop variety. The large crystal is rutilated quartz, a variety which is particularly prized because its inclusions form a microcosm of precipitous cliffs and chasms. The figure inside the cabinet is the generative source for the profusion of objects above.

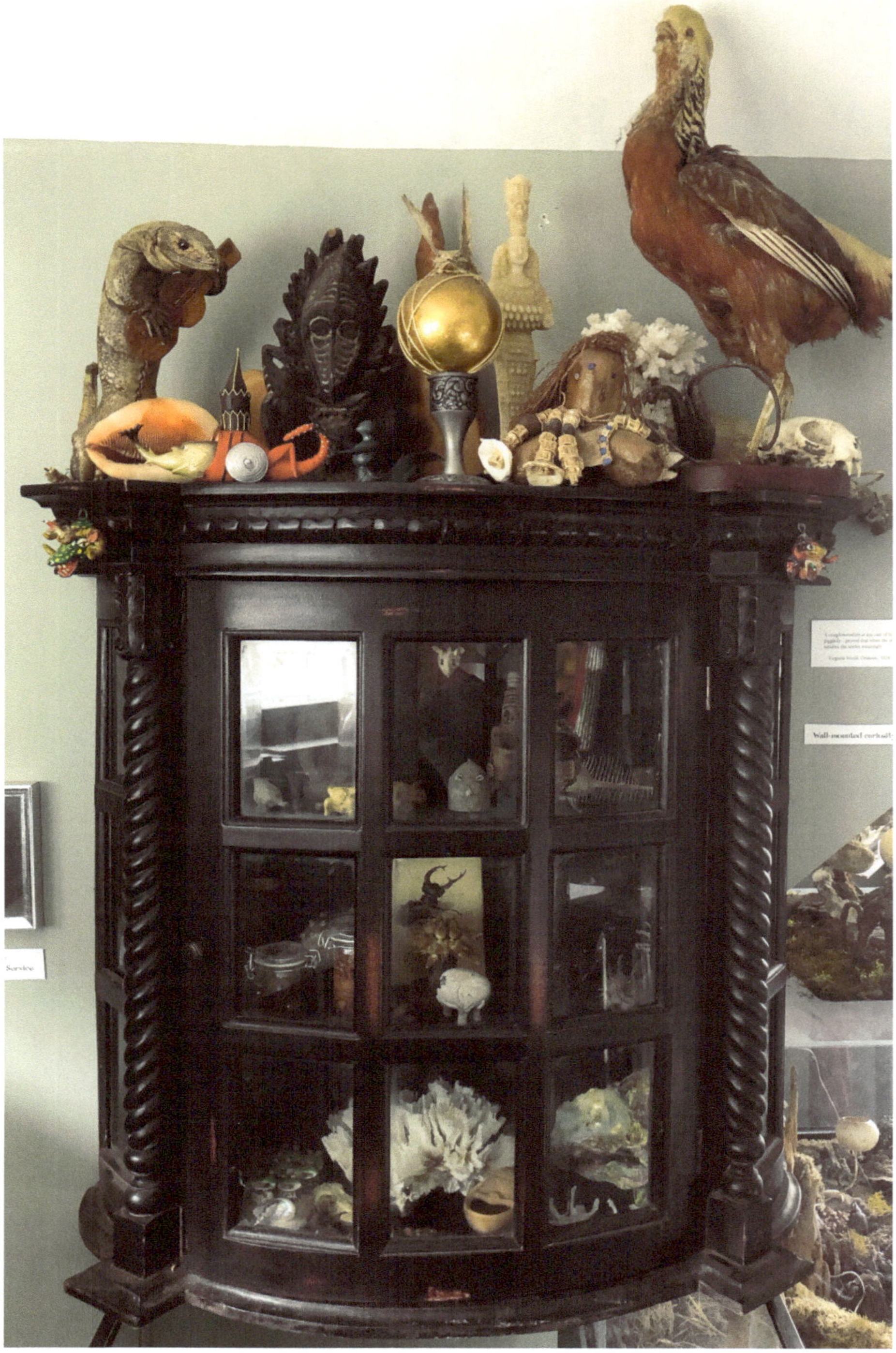

Wall-mounted wonder cabinet

Mid-sized model for small and mid-sized treasures.

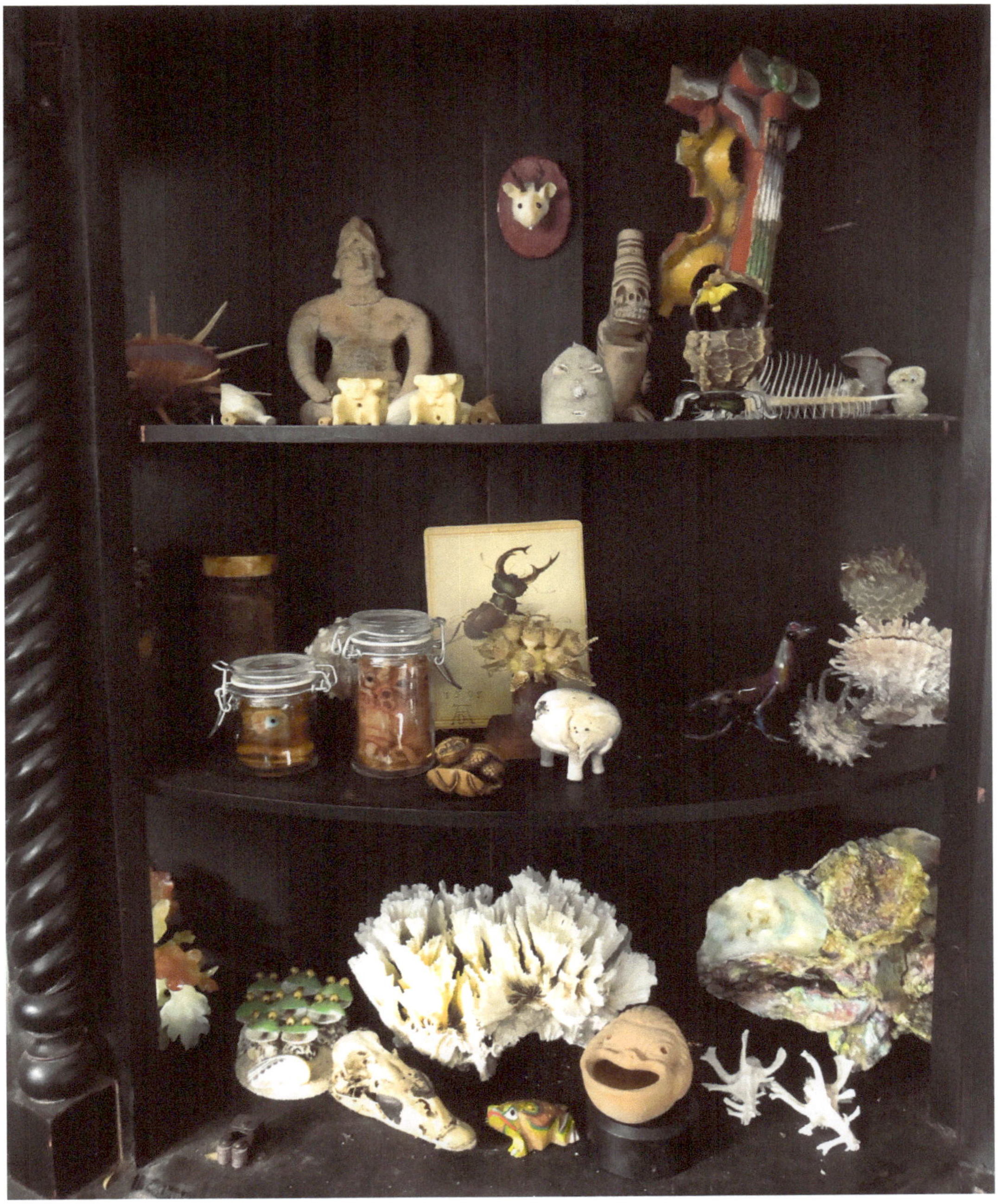

A snapshot of the ever-in-flux contents of the cabinet

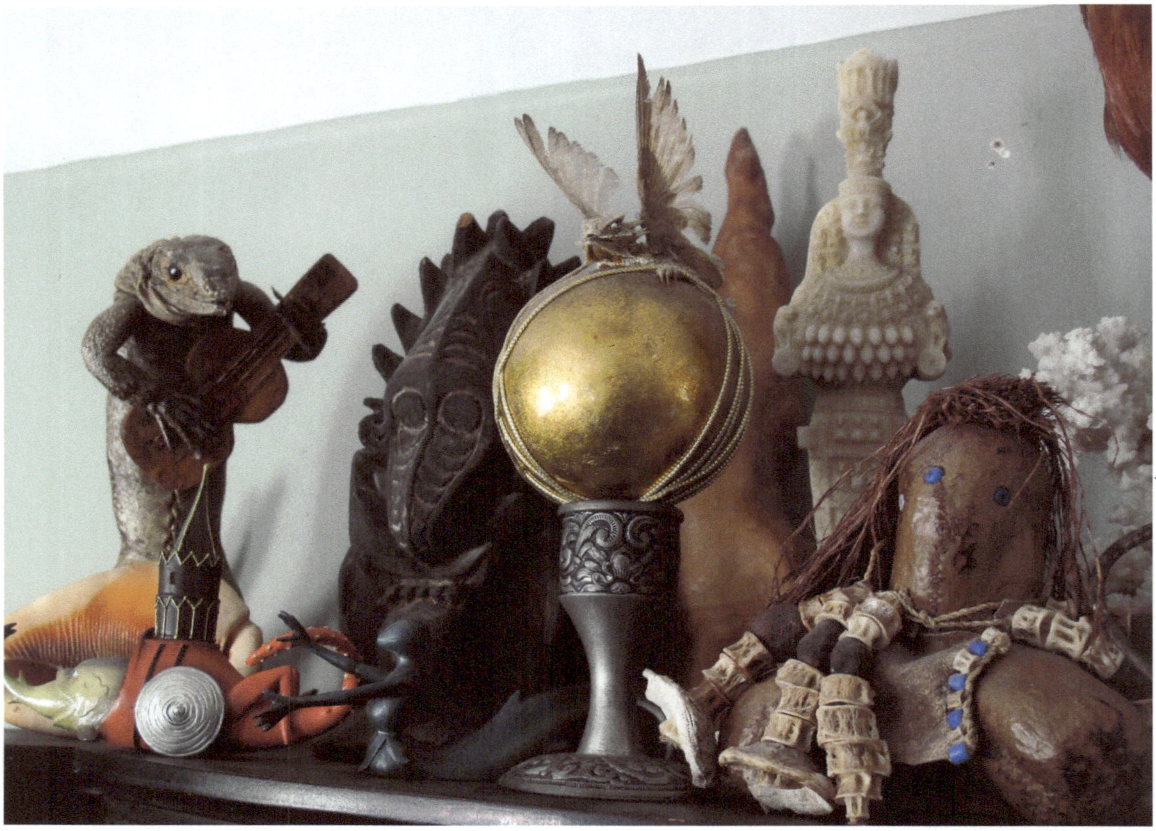

Eclectic objects on top of cabinet

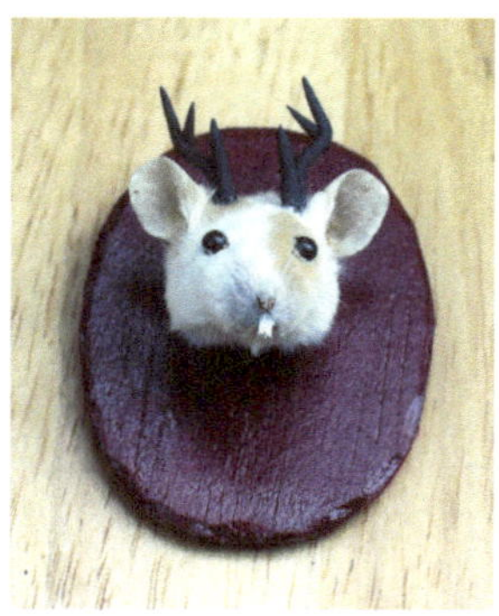

Mousealope

The mousealope is a diminutive relative of the jackalope which flourishes in the nooks and crannies of the urban wilds, rather than the wide open spaces of its larger cousin, the jackalope.

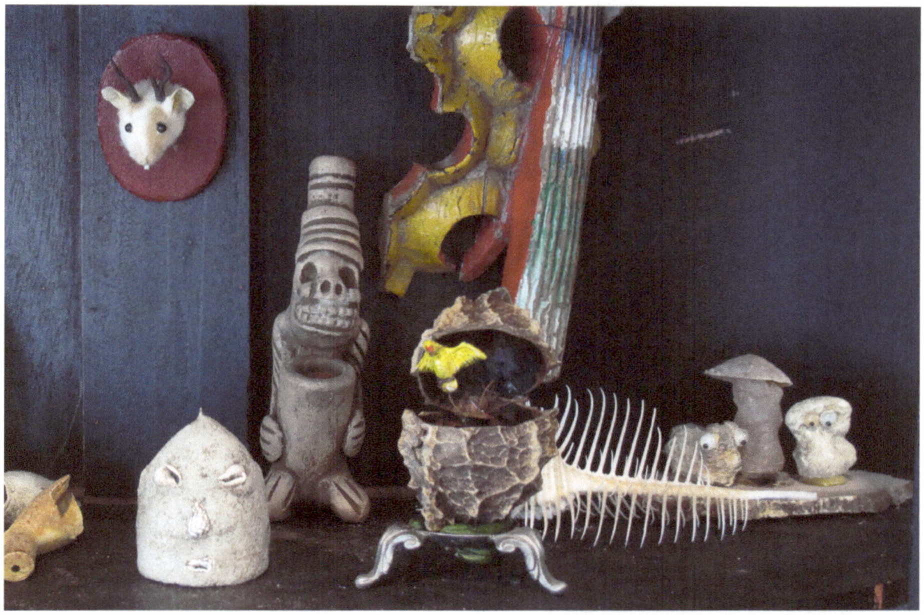

Upper shelf with mousealope

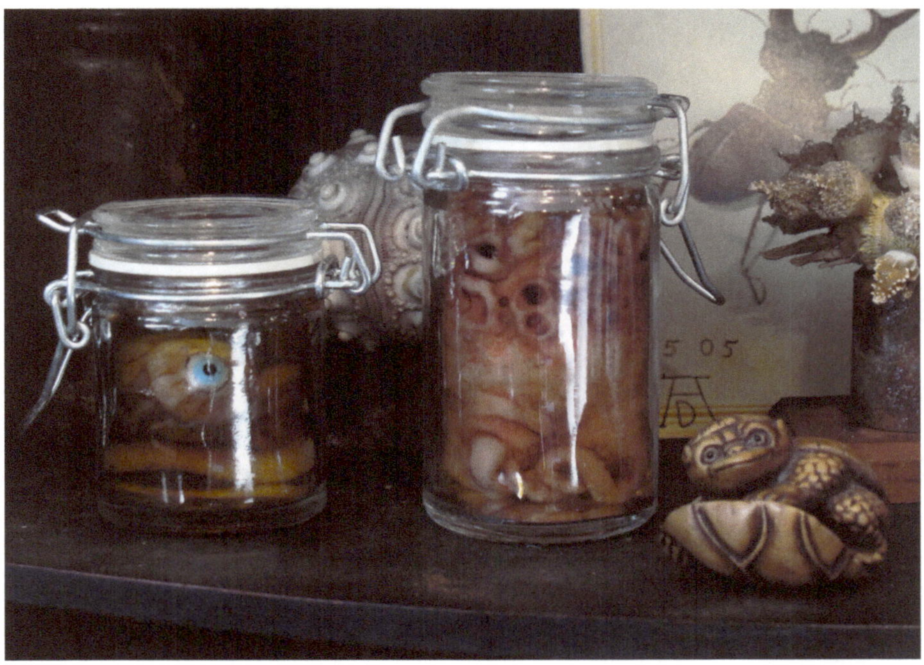

Things in jars

The mineral cabinet

During the Age of Wonder, field taxonomists collected, identified, and classified a wide variety of rocks, minerals, and fossils. A few of these, due to their provenance, became prized items for a type of curiosity cabinet that specialized in the mineral kingdom.

While small in size, this cabinet manages a historic span from the beginning of the solar system through the industrial and atomic ages. The museum's mineral cabinet is a recreation, with items that may have been found in ancient times, as well as modern versions.

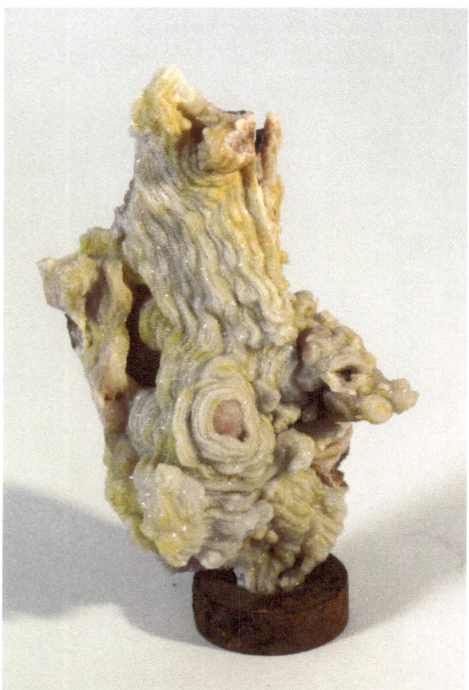

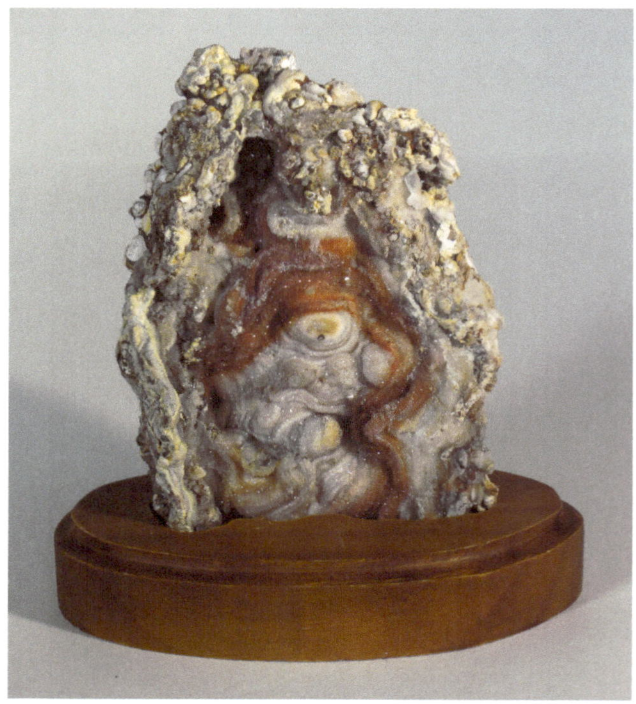

A pair of druzy quartz specimens from the cabinet

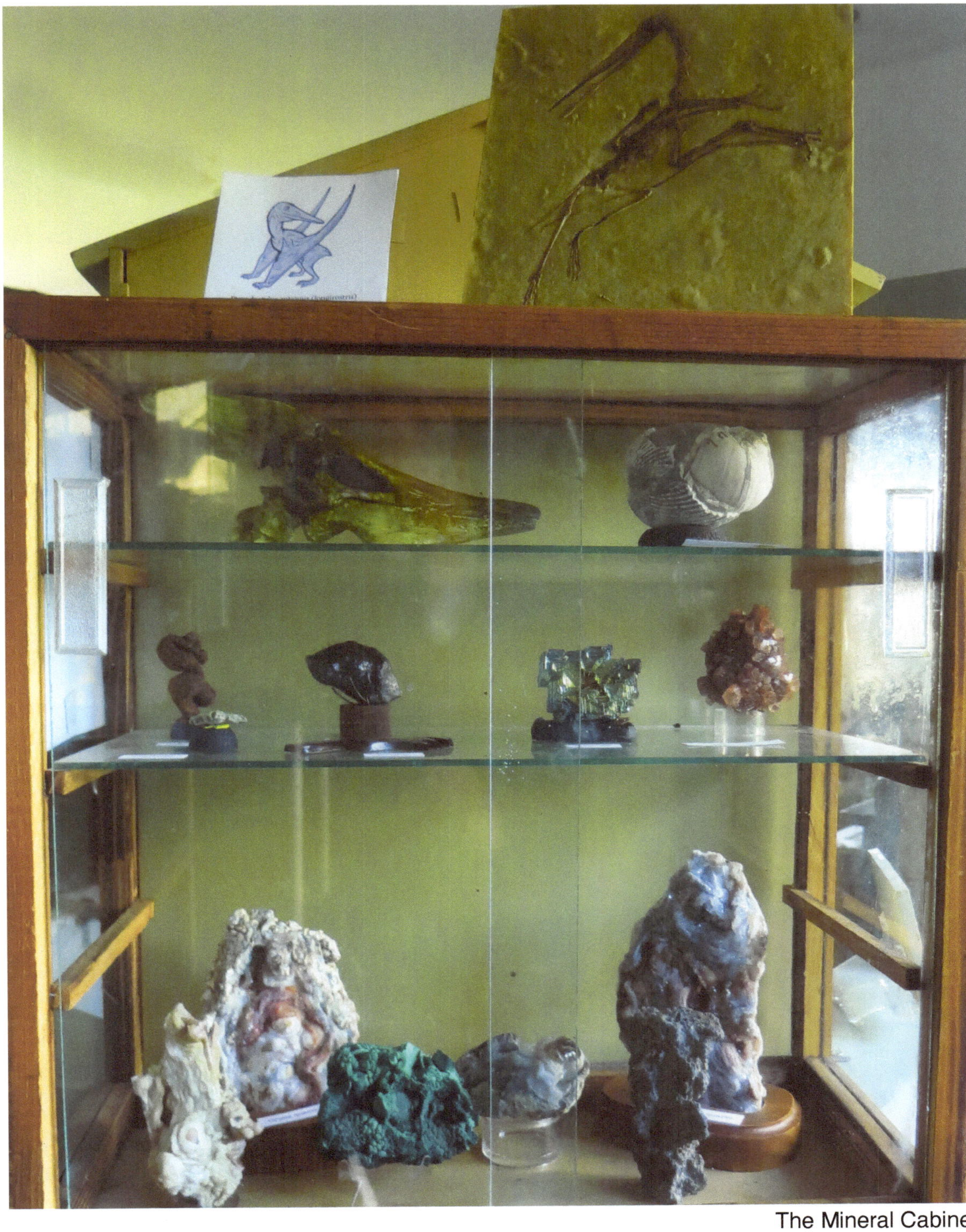

The Mineral Cabinet

Selected specimens from the mineral cabinet

Meteorite
A 4 billion-year-old remnant of the iron core of an asteroid that broke up over Namibia in prehistoric times, seared and pocked from its violent entry into the earth's atmosphere. It was formed during the creation of the solar system and is older than life itself.

Fulgurite
"Fossilized lightning" formed when lightning strikes sand. Lightning is believed to have played a part in the creation of organic molecules.

Dinosaur coprolite
Fossilized dinosaur excrement—scatological remains from the rear end of the Jurassic era. All that remains of a dinosaur's meal consumed some hundreds of millions of years ago. It has been mounted as a viewing stone for quiet contemplation, in the style popular during the Era of Oriental Influence.

Bismuth
Elemental bismuth is a lump of gray metal with a relatively low melting point. It can be coaxed into forming synthetic crystals with an iridescent oxide sheen.

Fordite
Formed from the accumulation of layers of paint in car manufacturing plants when cars were painted by hand, now prized for jewelry

Trinitite
"Trinity" was the code name for the first atomic bomb detonation in New Mexico in 1945. The surrounding desert sands were converted into a glassy mineral.

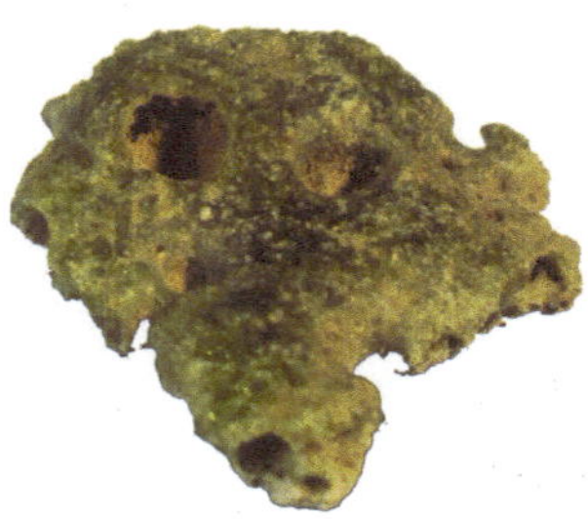

Trinitite

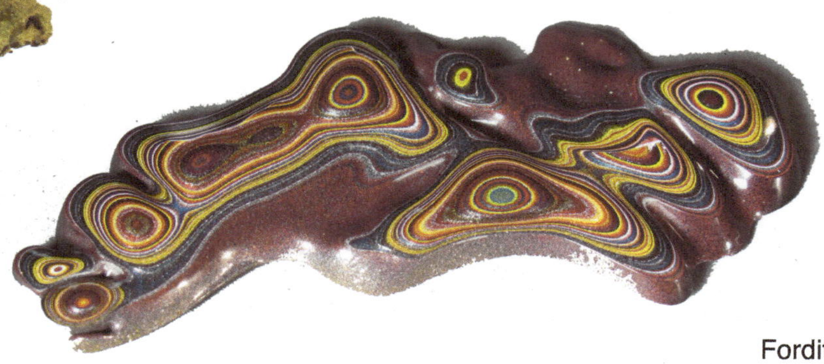

Fordite

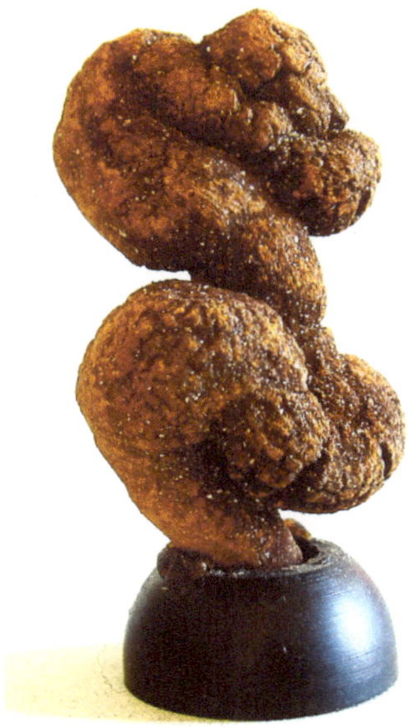

Coprolite

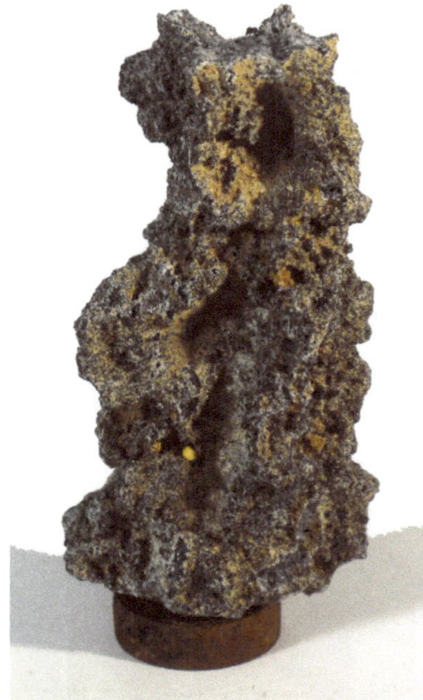

Fulgurite

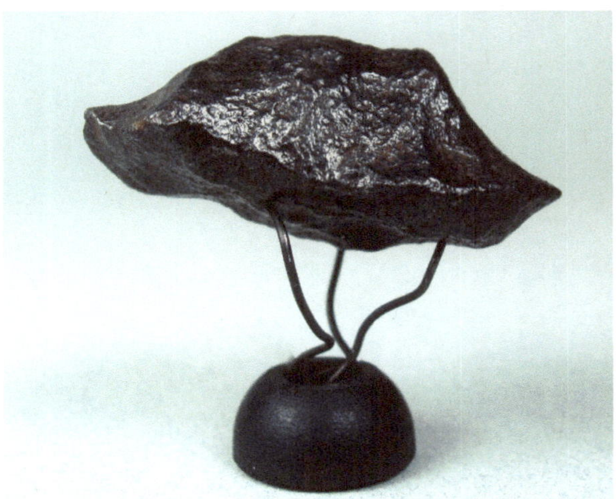

Meteorite

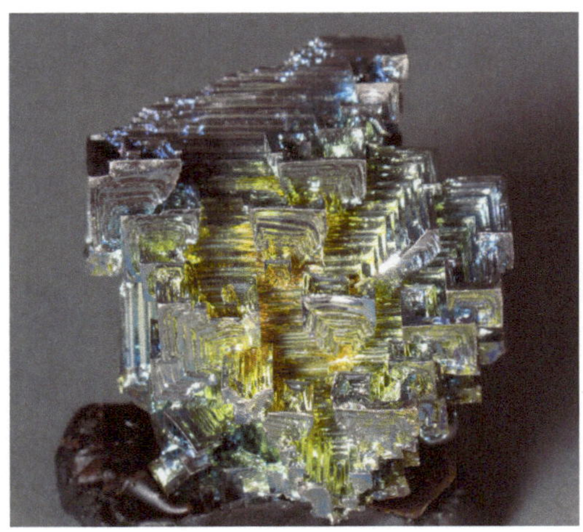

Bismuth

Fossils

Creatures found encased in stone were once thought to be part of some mysterious mythology with a large cast of fanciful creatures.

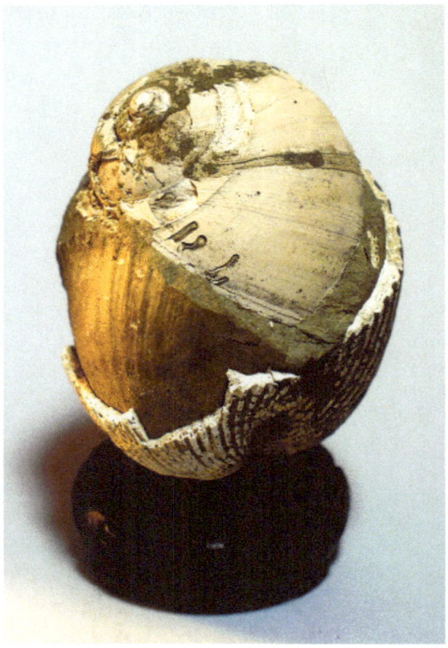

A clam-egg gives birth to a moon snail

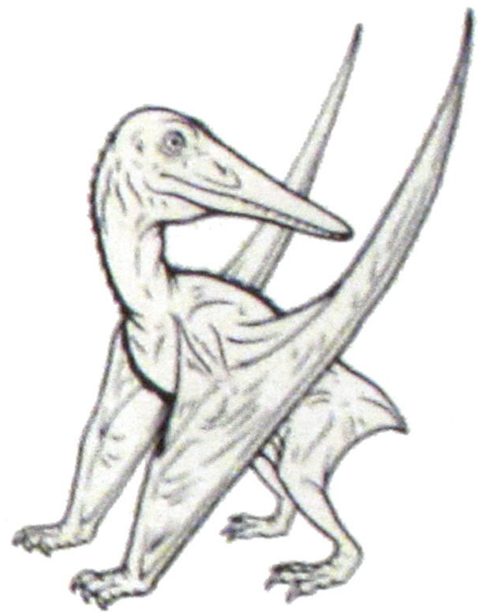

Artist's reconstruction of *Pterodactylus* on facing page

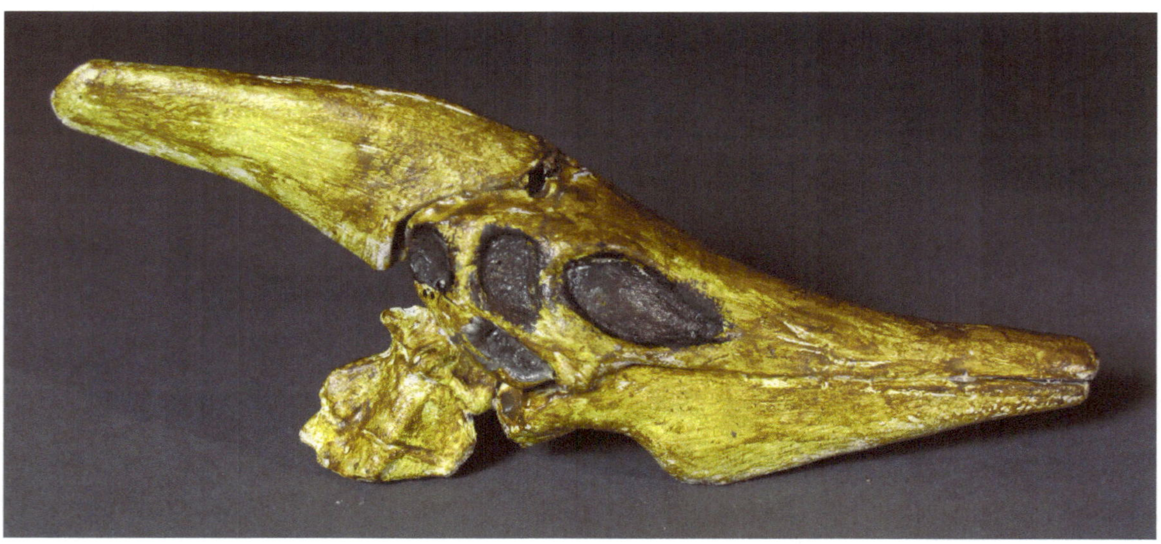

Pteranodon skull

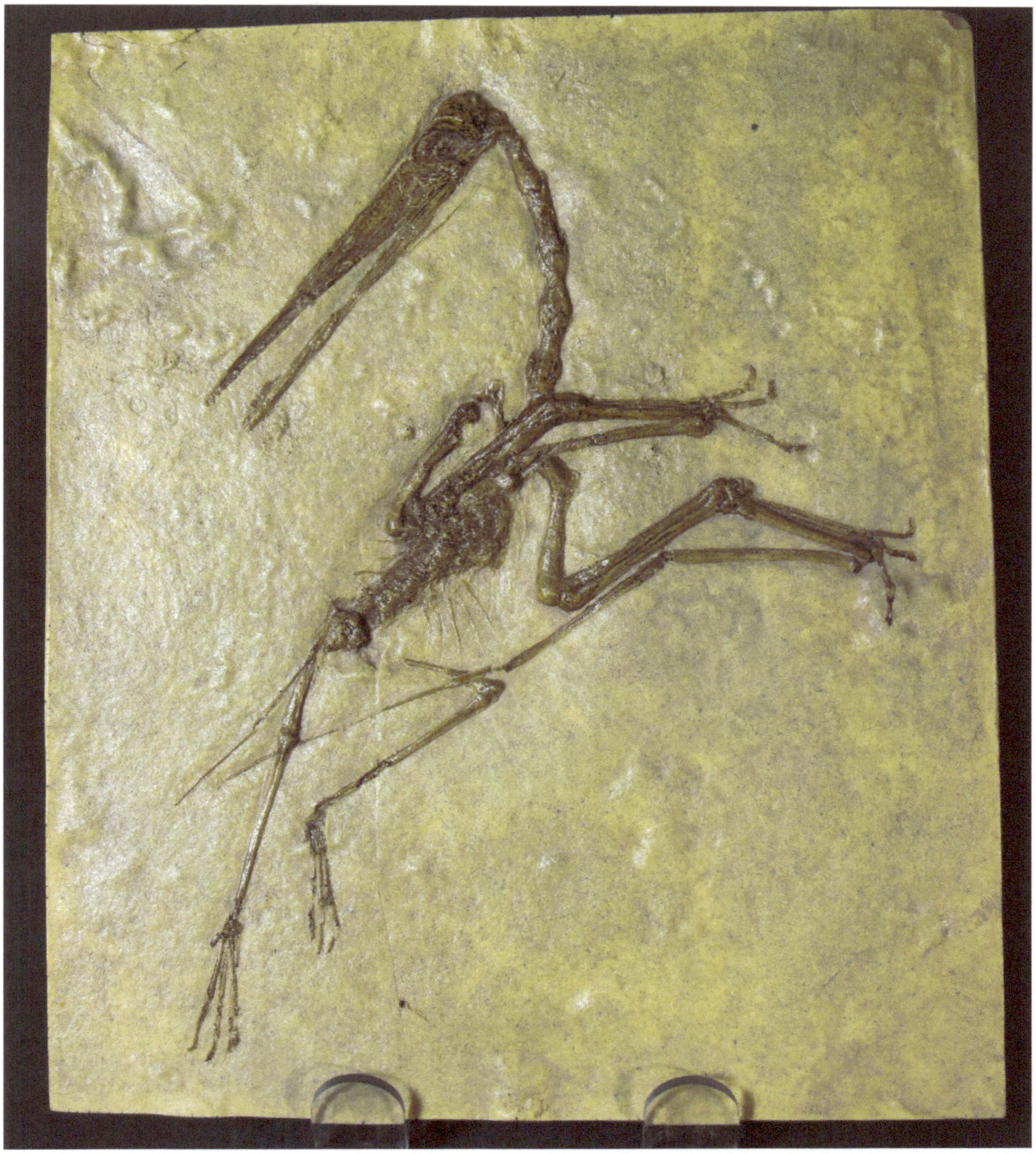

Pterodactylus antiquus (longirostris)

Crab collection

During the Age of Wonder, the ideal collection was an eclectic set of objects, often displayed in a jumble. In the latter years of that era, more systematic collections became popular, appealing to a "theme and variations" aesthetic.

Crabs have an important place in Zymoglyphic culture. When dead, they often look as though they are just holding a long pose, and so make excellent diorama characters. They are nautical mechanical marvels, from the tight, interlocking parts of a box crab to the implausibly leggy spider crabs. Some, such as the fiddler crab, verge on becoming "eccentric contraptions," surreal beings whose very existence seems impossible. Some have great character, such as the leopard crab shown below. The lack of gravitational pull underwater allows the development of unusual forms.

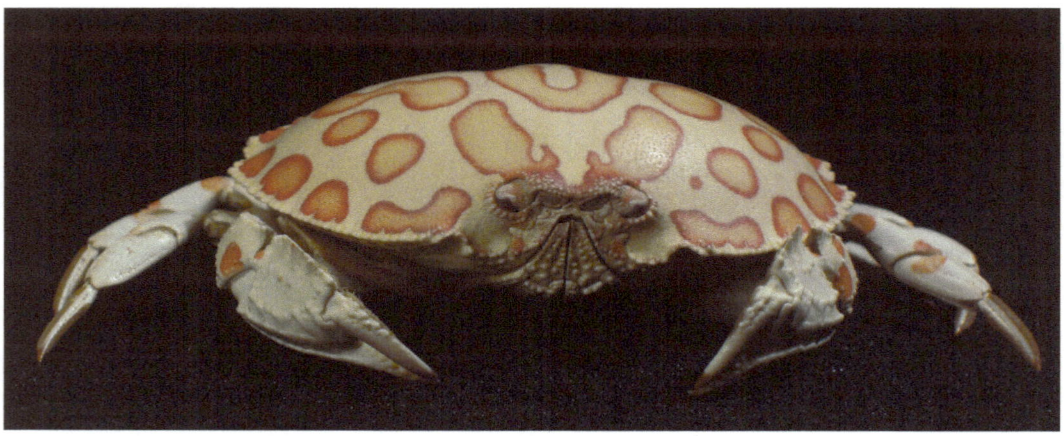

Leopard crab

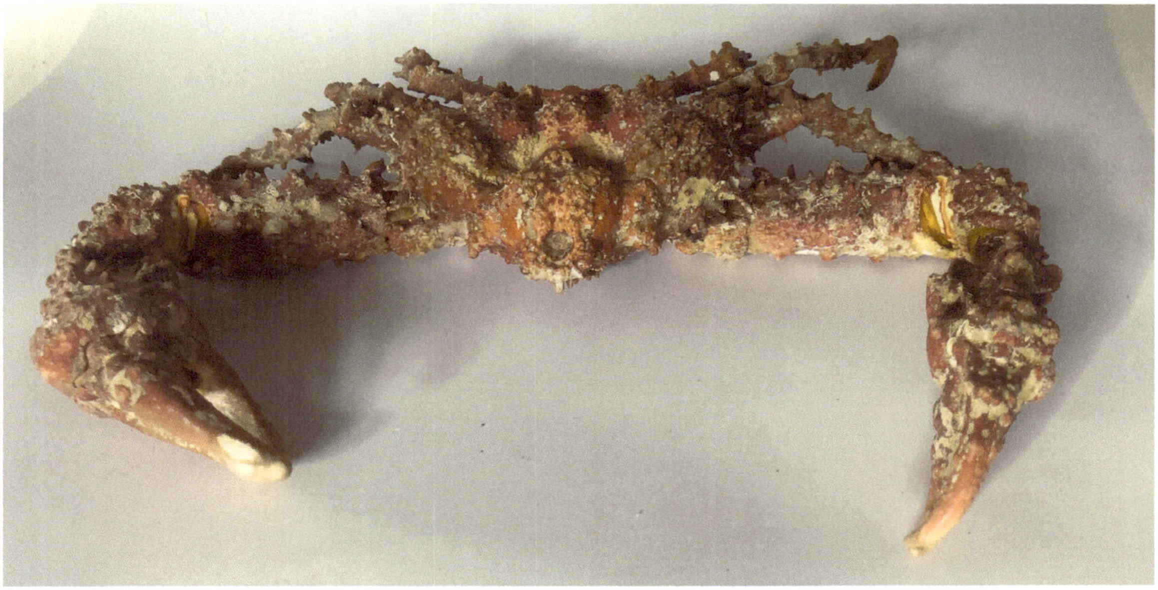

Decorator crabs make themselves into living, walking gardens. They cover themselves with a selection of living seaweed and plant-like animals, such as sponges, corals, and bryozoans. This is not a weed garden in the sense of just allowing things to grow on the carapace; the selections are carefully nipped and placed on specialized projections on the shell. The purpose is both camouflage and protection due to the venomous nature of many of the selections.

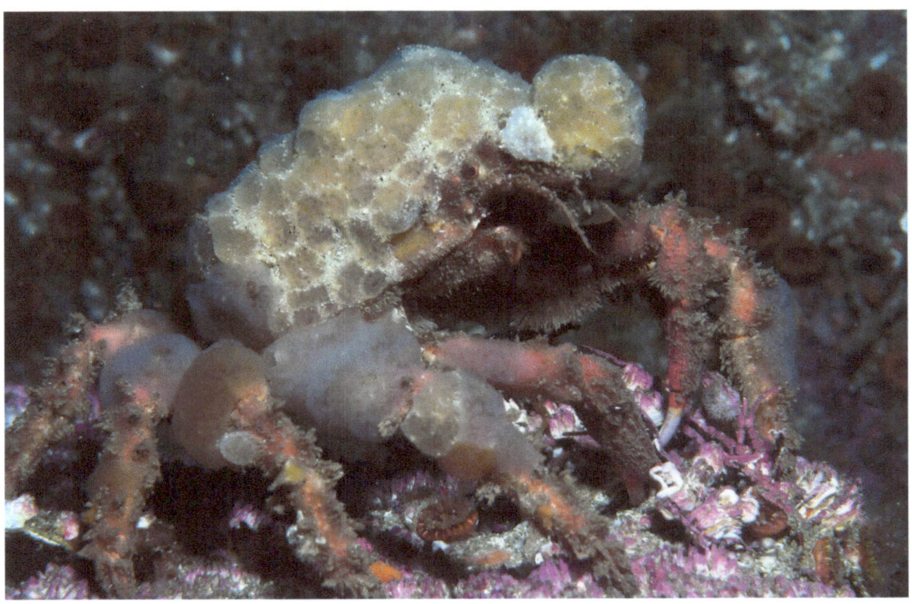

Oregonia gracilis

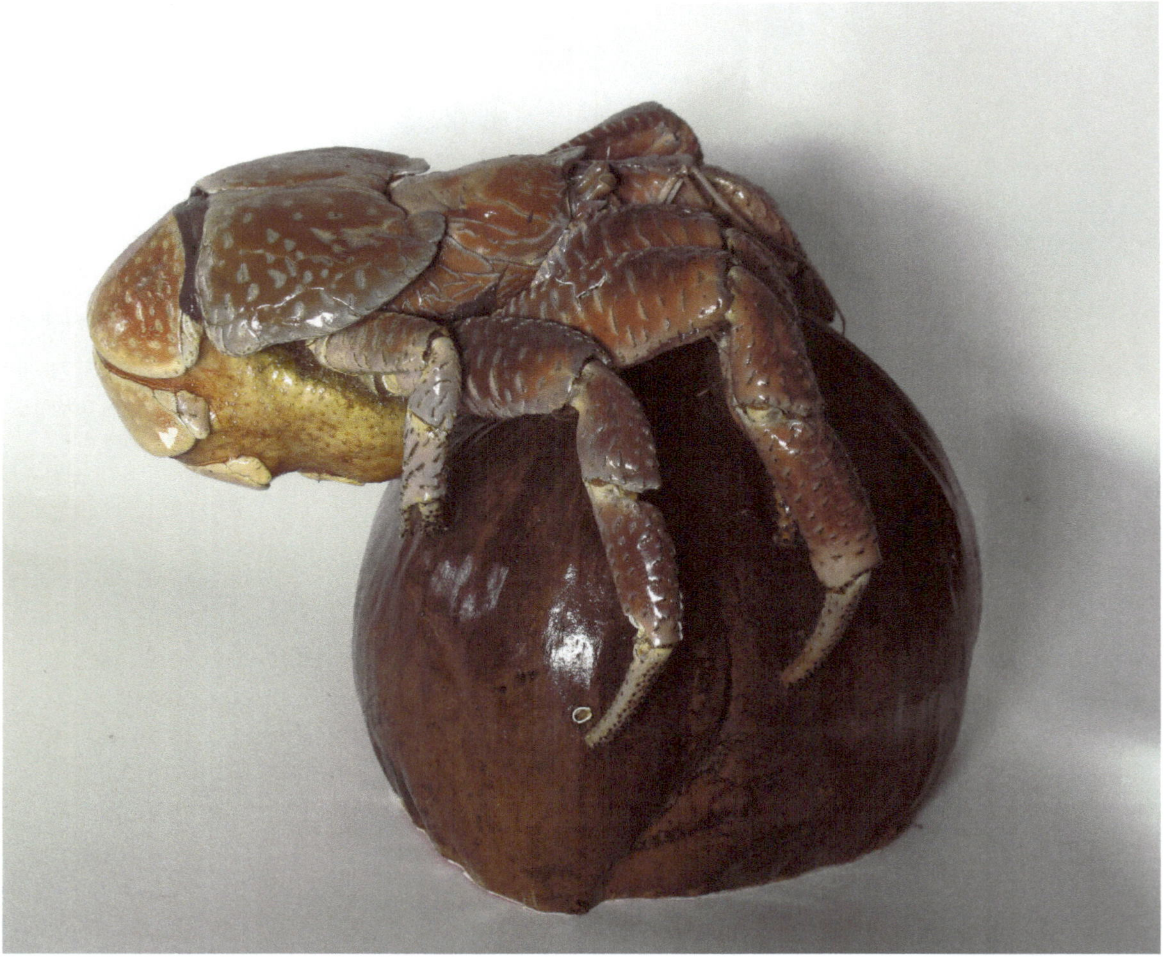

Coconut crab
Birgus latro

Above:

Coconut crabs are, as a species, the largest terrestrial invertebrates. Their stout claws are strong enough to open coconuts. They are a type of hermit crab.

Facing page:

Hermit crabs are well known for their creative re-use of discarded materials, in this case the durable shells of creatures whose flesh has decayed and departed. There are over a thousand species of hermit crab. This individual has chosen a particularly spectacular domicile.

Spannner crabs are interesting because of their unusual shape. They are also known as frog crabs.

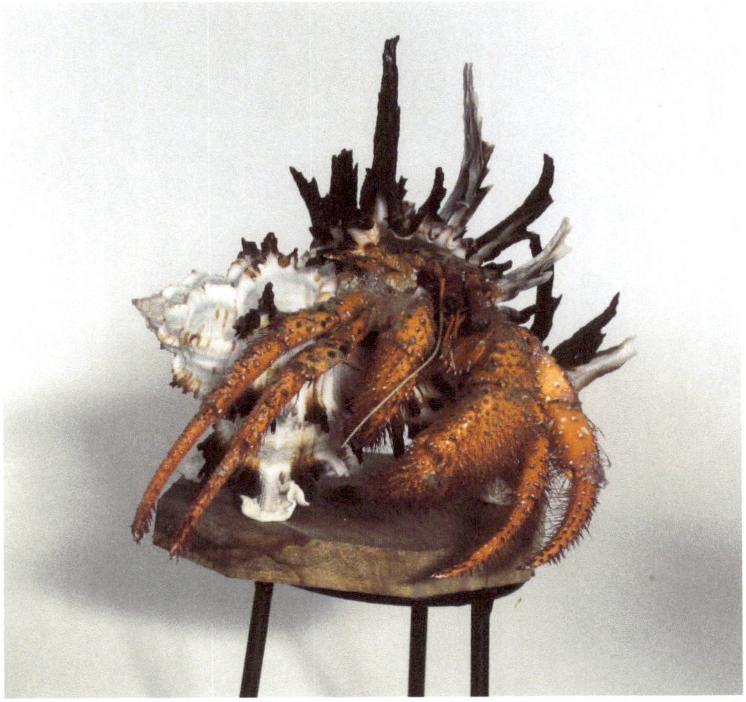

Hermit crab
Paguroidea

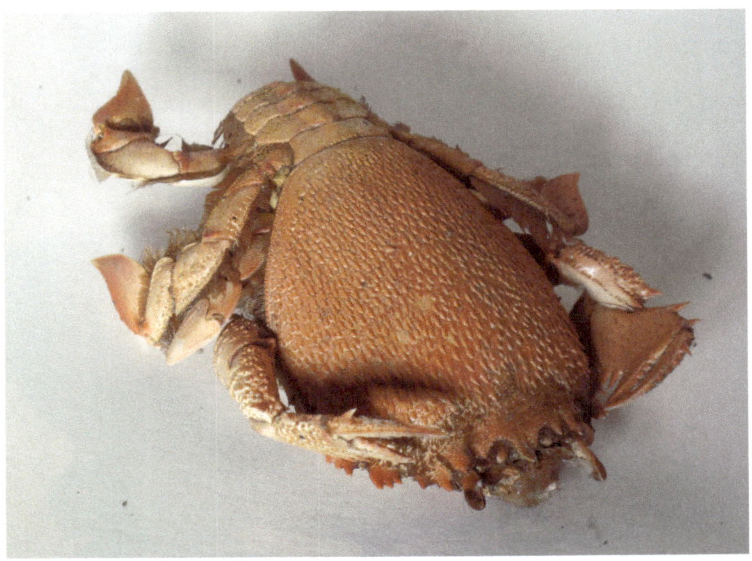

Spanner crab
Ranina ranina

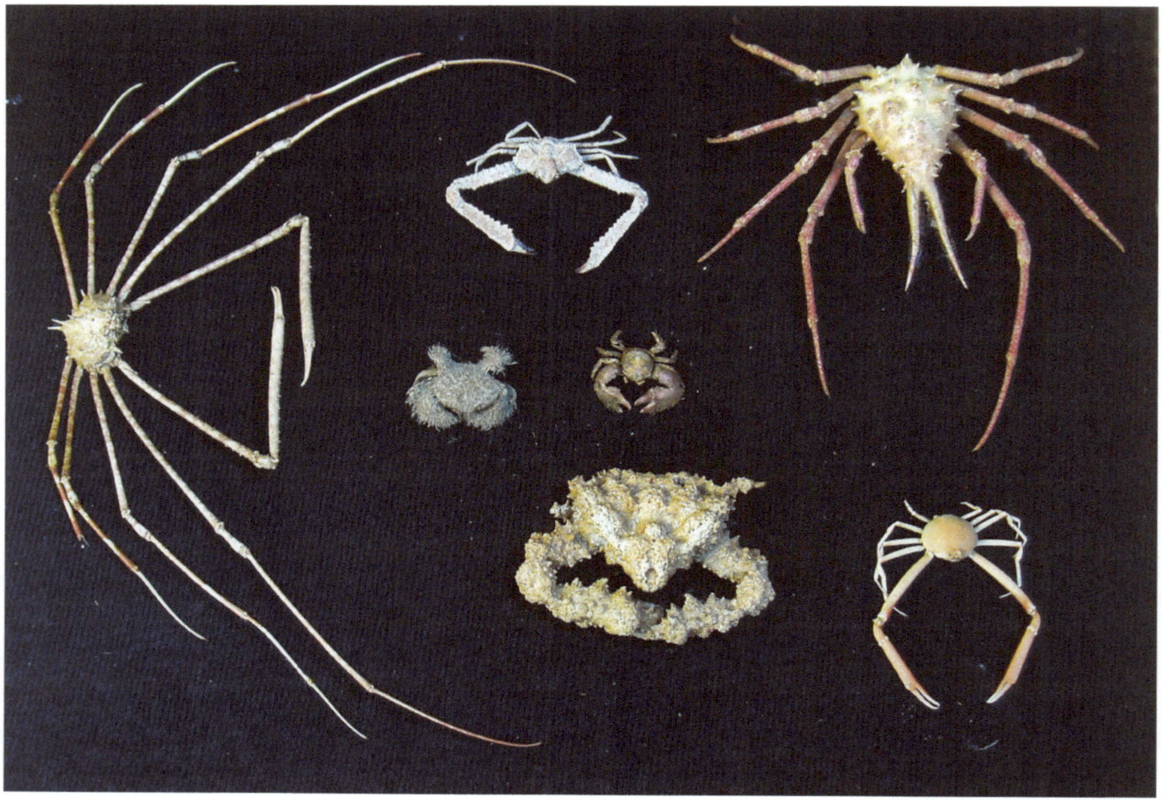

Left: Phalangipus hystrix

Top: Platylambrus validus - Naxoides mammillata

Middle: Pilumnus verspertilo - Porcellana platycheles

Bottom: Daldorfia horrida - Randalia eburnea

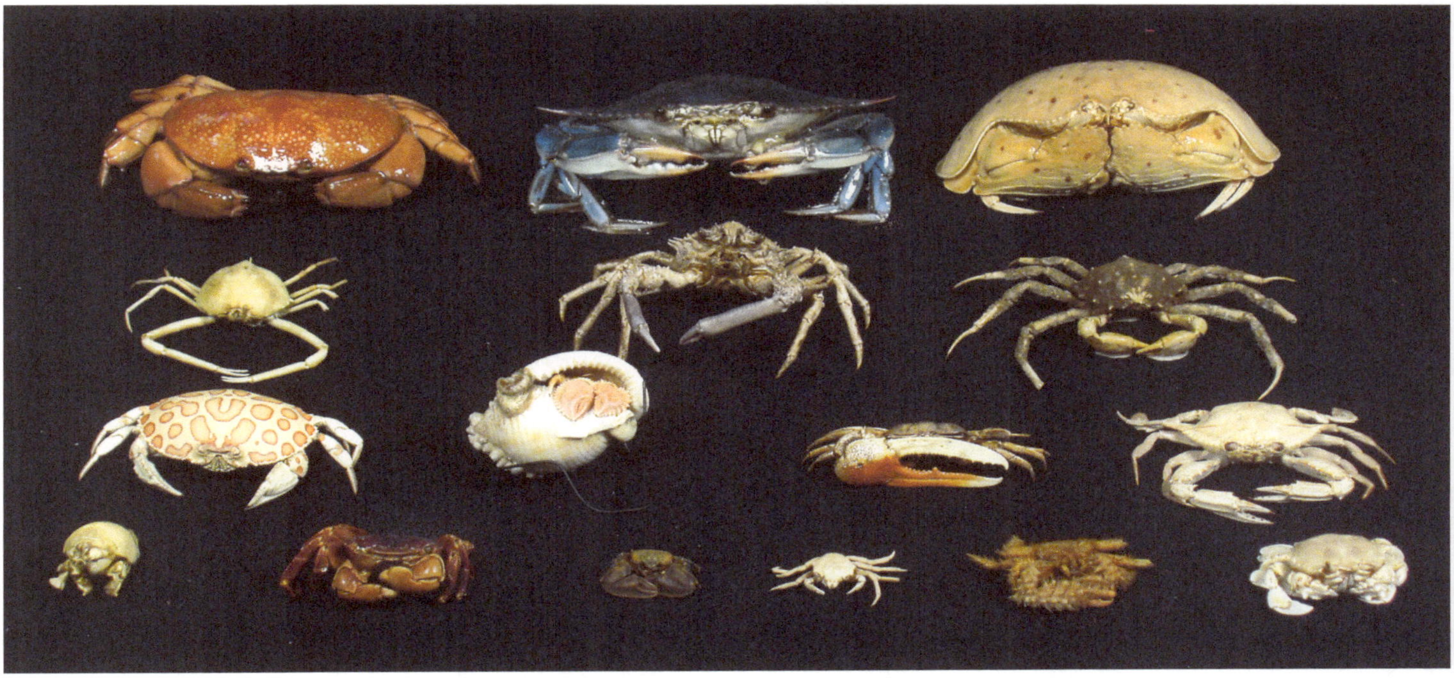

Top row: Red stone crab (Atergatis floridus) - Blue crab (Callinectes sapidus) - Box crab (Calappa calappa)

Row 2: Purse crab (Randalia sp.) -Spider crab (Libinia sp.) - Spider crab (Majidae?)

Row 3: Leopard crab (Hepatus epheliticus) - Hermit crab (Pagurus impressus) - Fiddler crab (Uca sp.) - Swimming crab (Portunus spinimanus)

Row 4: Pacific mole crab (Emerita analoga) - Purple shore crab (Hemigrapsus nudus) - Porcelain crab (Petrolisthes cinctipes) - Kelp crab (Pugettia producta) - Hairy crab (Hapalogaster mertensii) - Matuta banksii

Many years ago I was once, by accident, locked in a museum...I found myself in a lengthy hall containing nothing but Crustacea of all varieties. I used to think they were a rather limited order of life, but as I walked about impatiently in my search for a guard, the sight began to impress, not to say overawe, me...there were crabs built and riveted like Sherman tanks, and there were crabs whose claws had been flattened into plates that clapped over their faces and left them shut up inside with little secrets. There were crabs covered with chitinous thorns that would have made them indigestible; there were crabs drawn out and thin, with delicate elongated pincers like the tools men use to manipulate at a distance in dangerous atomic furnaces.

There were crabs that planted sea growths on their backs and marched about like restless gardens. There were crabs as ragged as waterweed or as smooth as beach pebbles; there were crabs that climbed trees and crabs from beneath the polar ice. But the sea change was on them all...Around us in the museum cases was an old pattern, out of the remote sea depths...It is not the individual that matters; it is the Plan and the incredible potentialities within it. The forms within the Form are endless and their emergence into time is endless... those crabs taught me a lesson really. They reminded me that an order of life is like a diamond of many reflecting surfaces, each with its own pinpoint of light contributing to the total effect.

—Loren Eisely

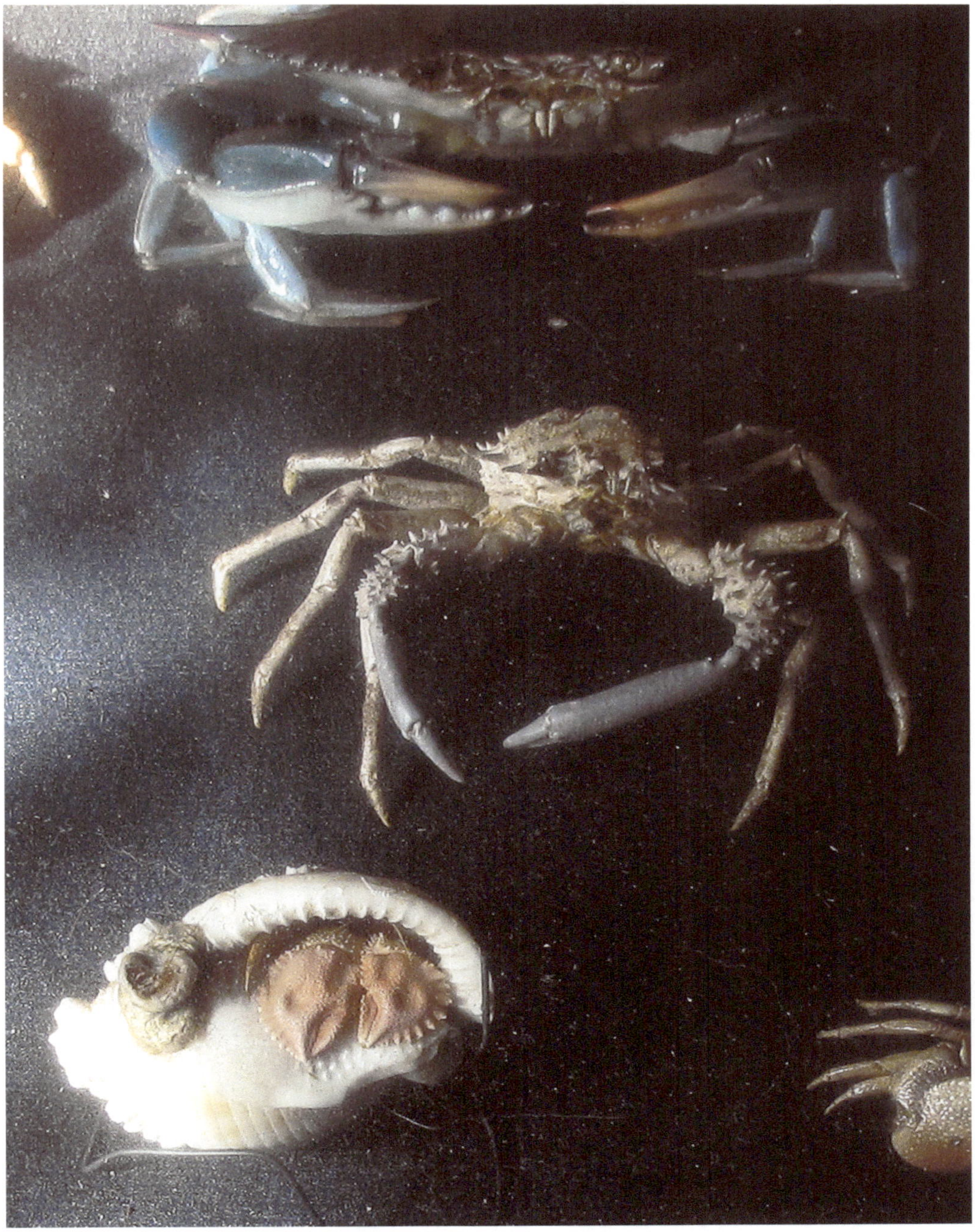

I should have been a pair of ragged claws
Scuttling across the floors of silent seas.

—T.S. Eliot

Dioramas

Collecting various objects in curiosity cabinets was popular; the next stage was to arrange found objects into narratives and create environments for them. Diorama environments and narratives were never intended to be literal or even linear. The Age of Wonder exhibit includes a number of these dioramas, large and small, containing natural objects and figures arranged with some narrative theme. The smallest ones, contained in ten-gallon fish tanks, resemble dessicated terraria and aquaria, often giving the impression that some living creature may yet survive in them. Larger dioramas are unenclosed and spill out somewhat into the visitor space. Unlike literal natural history museums of our region, there was no requirement for the narratives in these scenes to be a literal recreation of events in the natural world, only that they primarily consist of natural objects. This combination gives them a dreamy, mythical air while consisting of undeniably material, often ordinary, components.

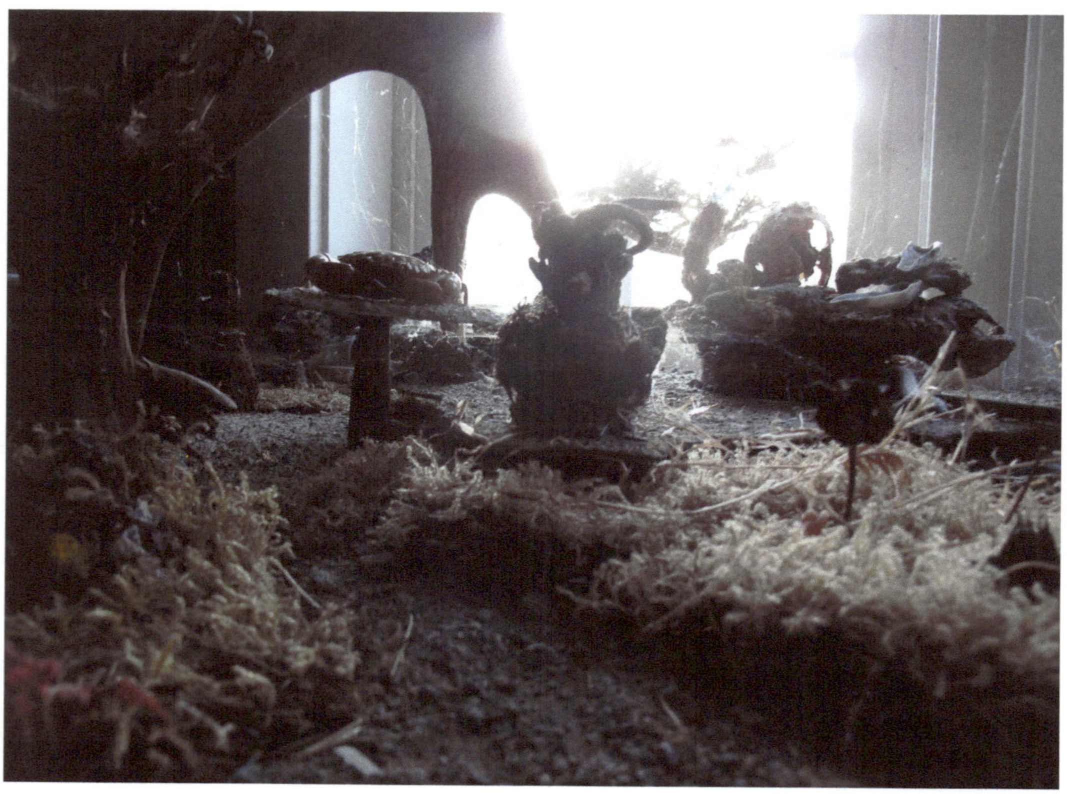

Heading toward the light

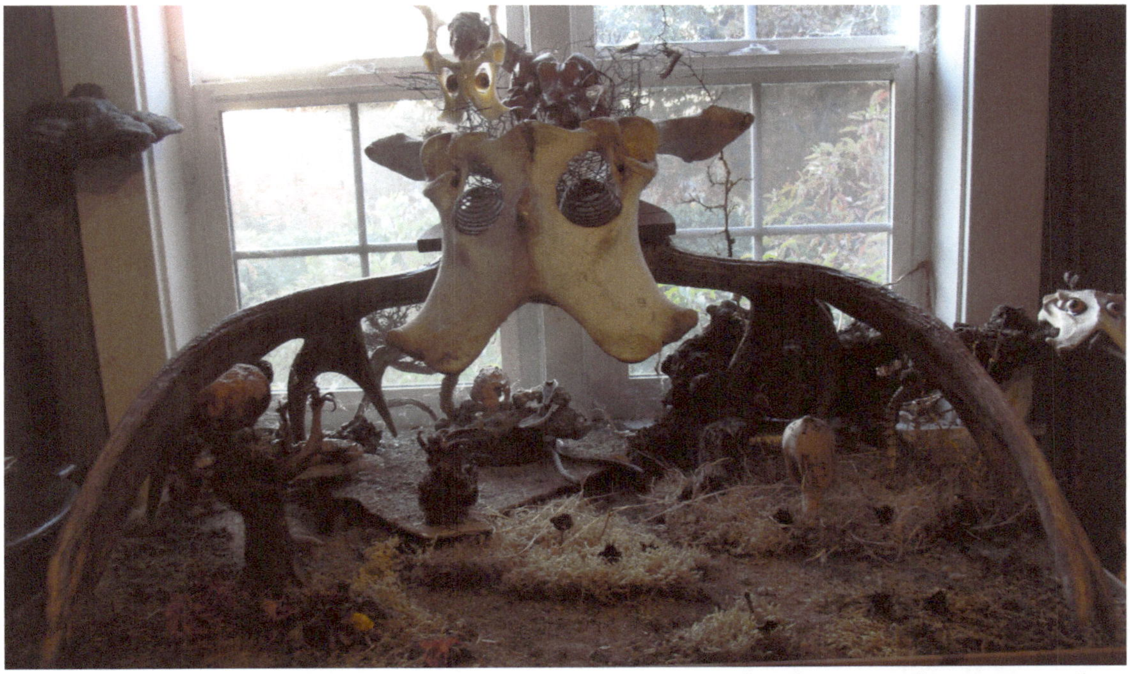

Landscape under moose antlers

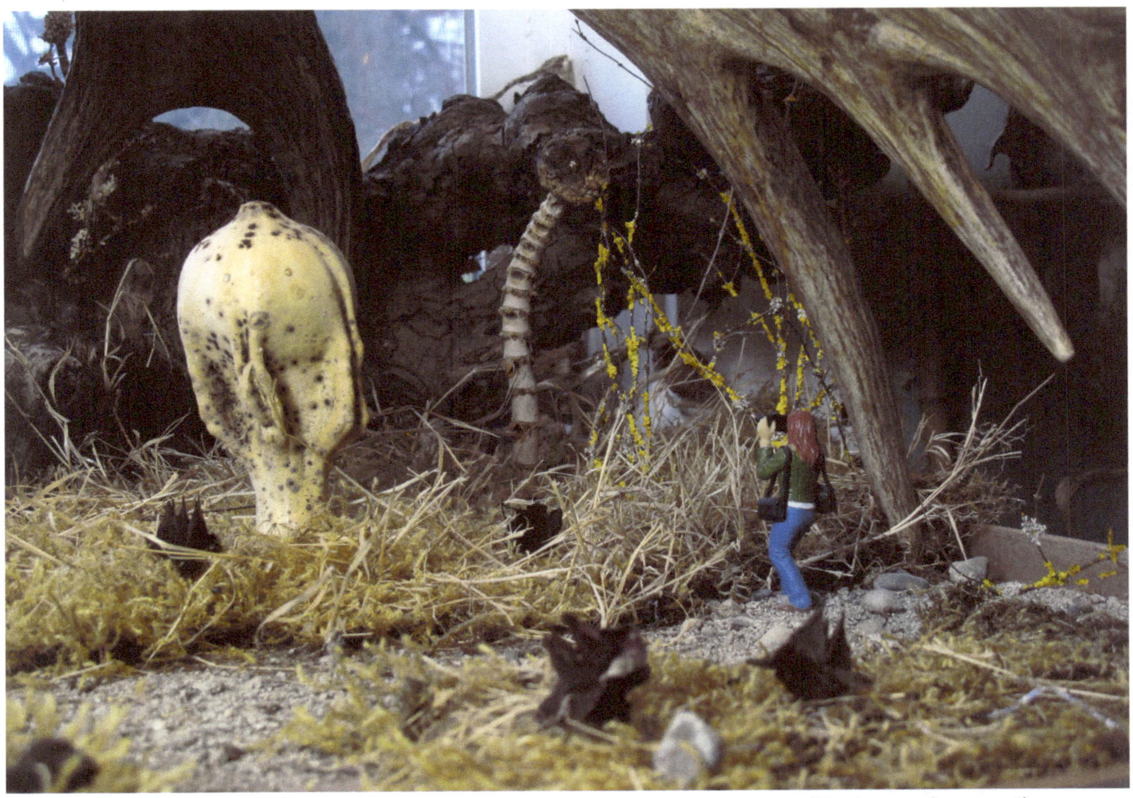

Photographer on the scene

Miniature Dioramas

When space is limited, it's possible to create dioramas in small aquarium tanks. This series demonstrates just that.

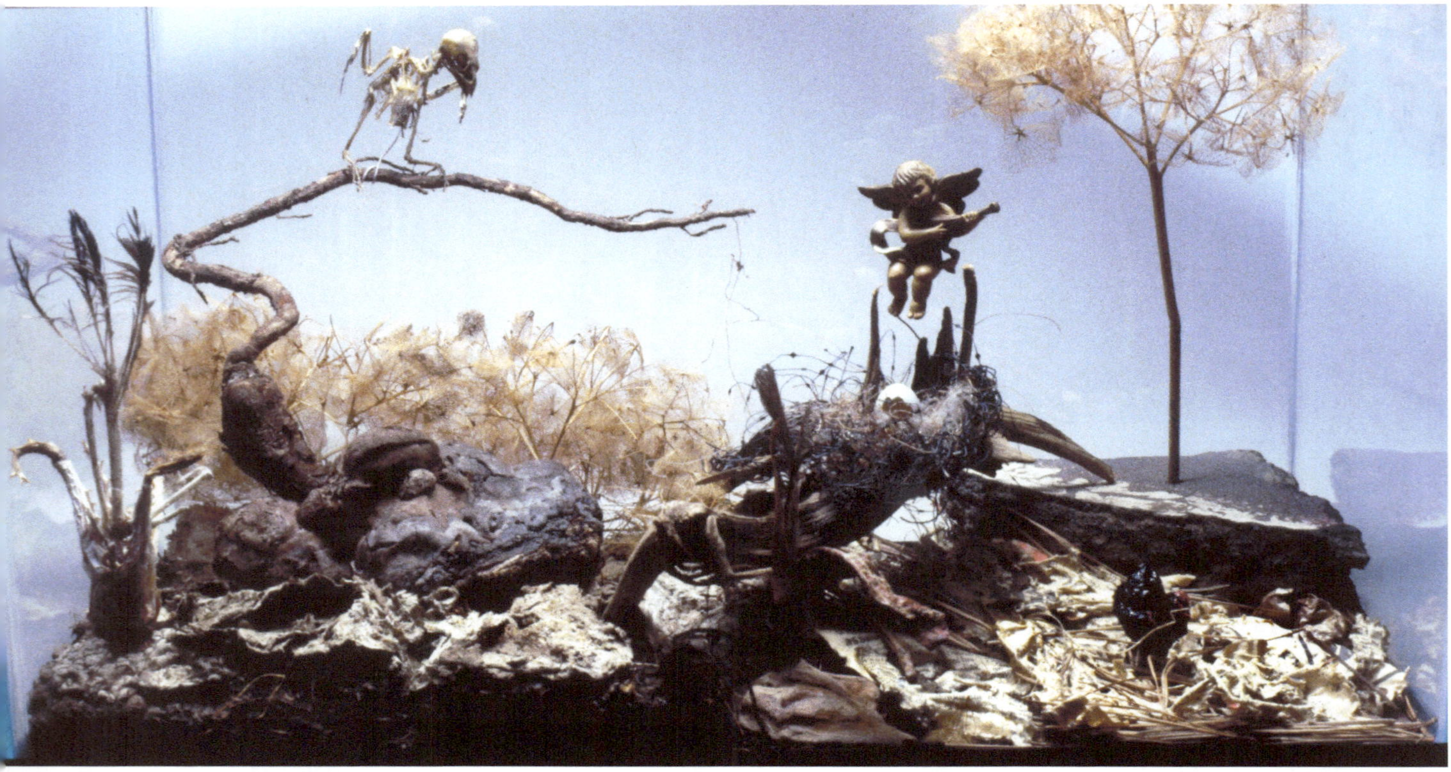

Creation

The collection opens with a scene of two winged creatures and a broken egg in a nest perched perilously on a wooden bridge. One is a skeletal bird with perched on a gnarled branch, its head tilted in such a way as to give it a puzzled expression. The other is a beatific plastic angel, serenely playing its lute for the benefit of the invisible being that has hatched out of the egg and filled the whole diorama with its unseen presence. The landscape is typical of these dioramas: a strange mix of winged creatures, natural materials and castoffs from human civilization—a chunk of roadway, a candy wrapper growing like a fungus, newsprint that has melted onto pine needles.

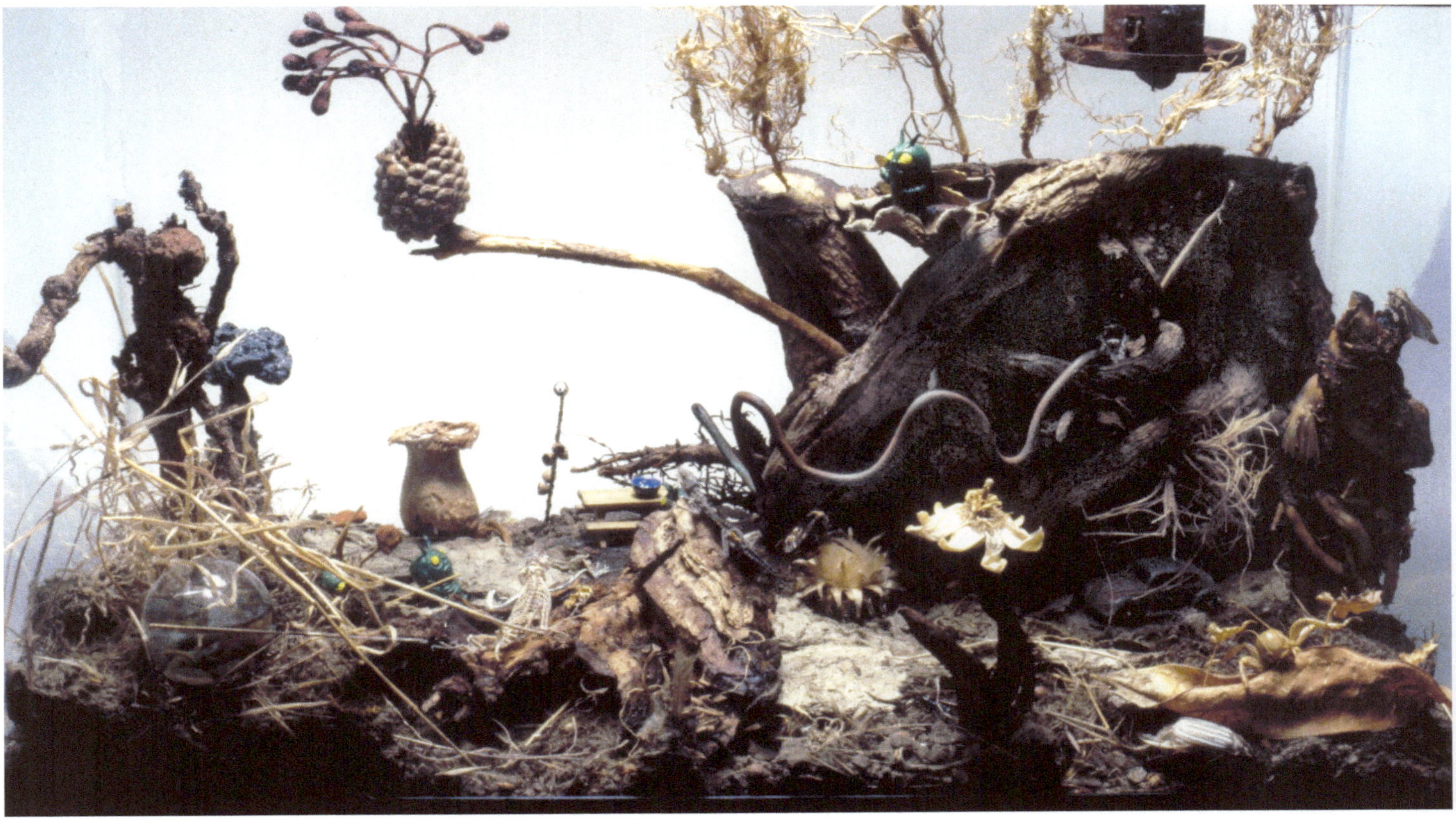

Picnic

As visitors move to the second scene, they see another species of winged creature. This one often reminds them of the "bug-eyed monsters" popularly associated with the evolution of life forms on other planets. In this scene, they have landed their tiny, rusted spacecraft in a desiccated, dreamlike spot in the undergrowth of the Zymoglyphic region. One stands on lookout; two others have hunted down a nice juicy beetle and are preparing to make a meal of it. They are being watched by a skeletal lizard, and a tiny car is approaching from the right side of the scene.

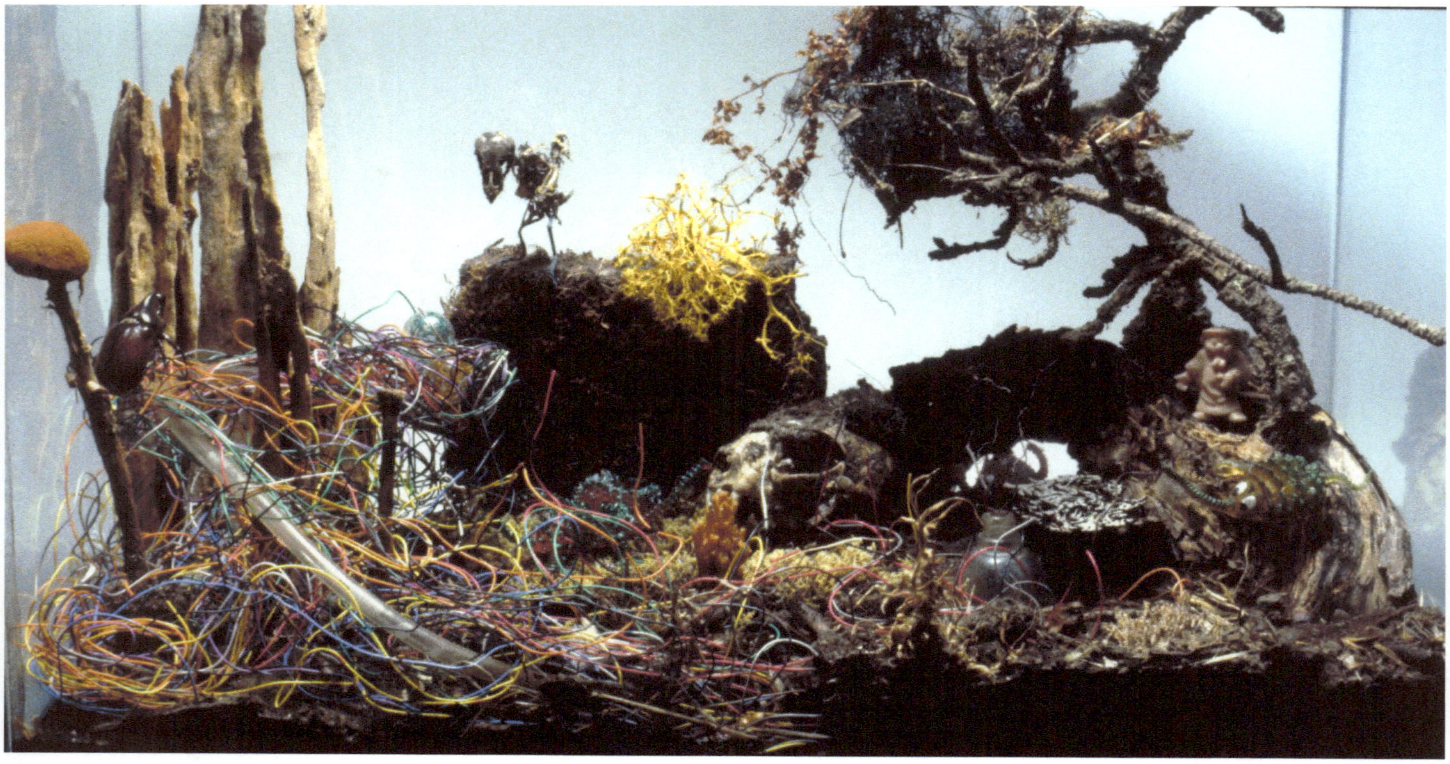

Curiosity

The third diorama of this series moves past the basics of birth and finding food; creatures are now looking around at their environment with curiosity. The central characters are a pair of "nosy" plastic creatures with long snouts ending in peculiar heart-shaped flaps on the end. The are investigating the skull of a cat, an animal that may well have met its demise as a result of its own curiosity. Perched above them, a skeletal bird cocks its head and focuses an eye socket on one of the many peculiar organisms of the Zymoglyphic region, which to the untrained eye resembles nothing so much as a colorful tangle of wires erupting from the earth to form plastic spore clusters.

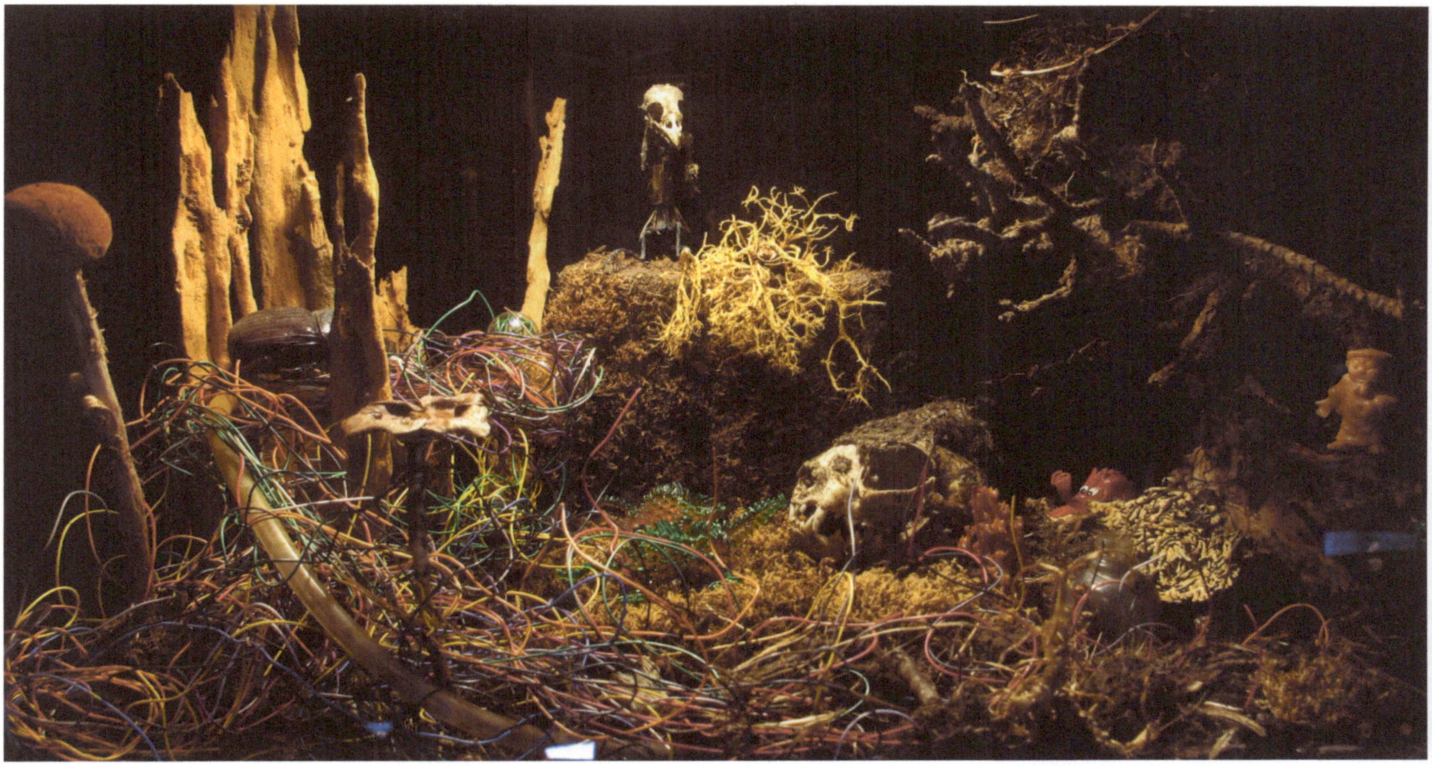

Curiosity -night view

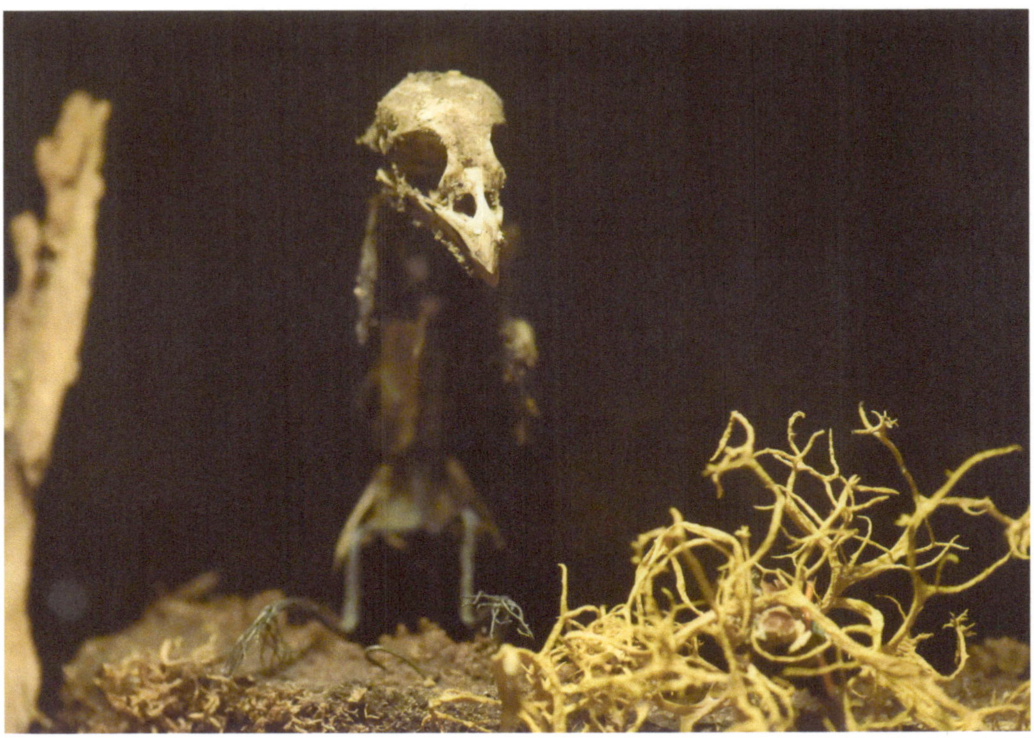

Curiosity - detail

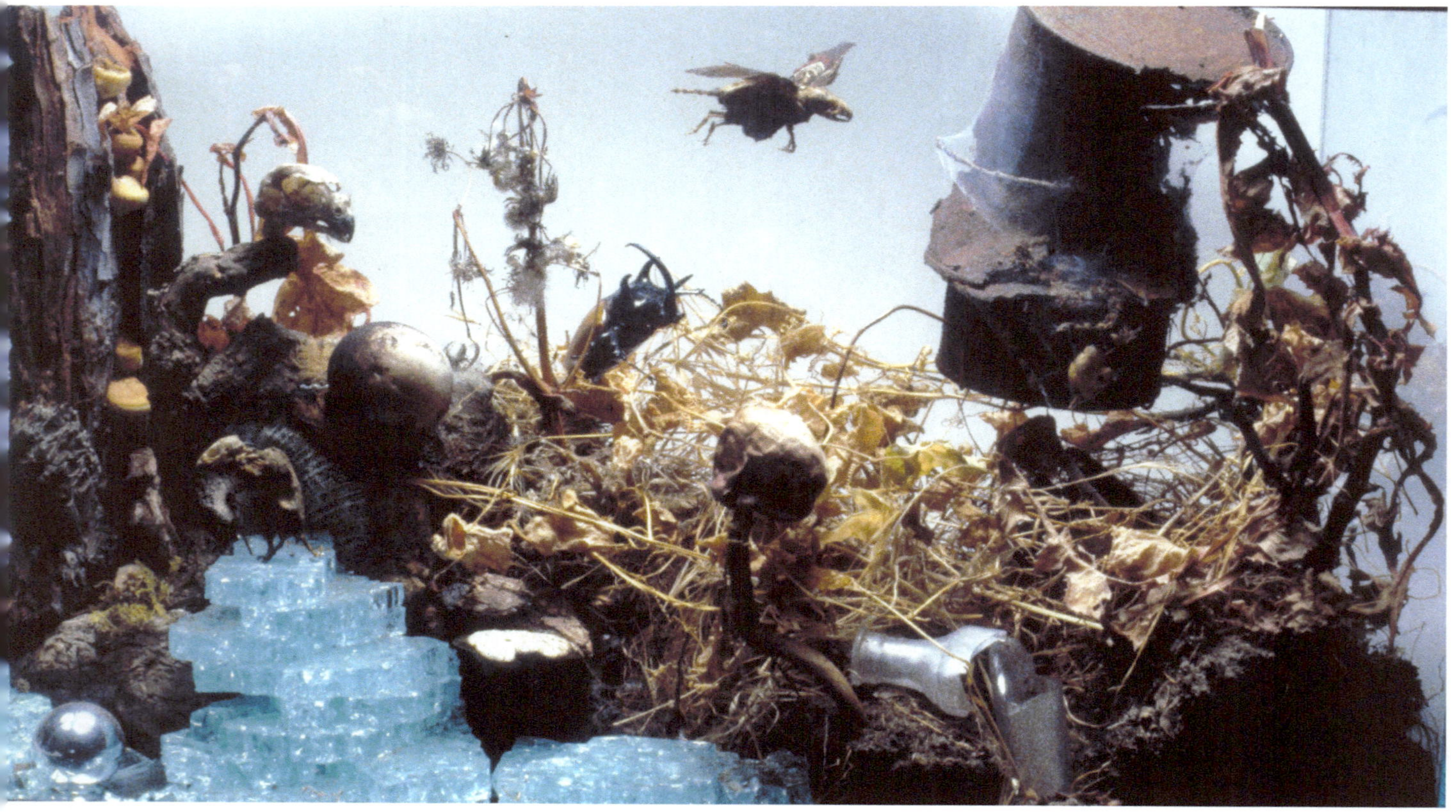

Getting On

In the fourth diorama, we move to the inevitable aging, decay, and death, ever-present themes in Zymoglyphic art. A wizened mouse, bent with age, its skull already emerging from its leathery skin, leans on his cane at the entrance to the underworld, ready to make his final descent. When visitors to this diorama scan the dry weeds, they find other mice at the ends of their lives, one of them near a rusted structure of old can.

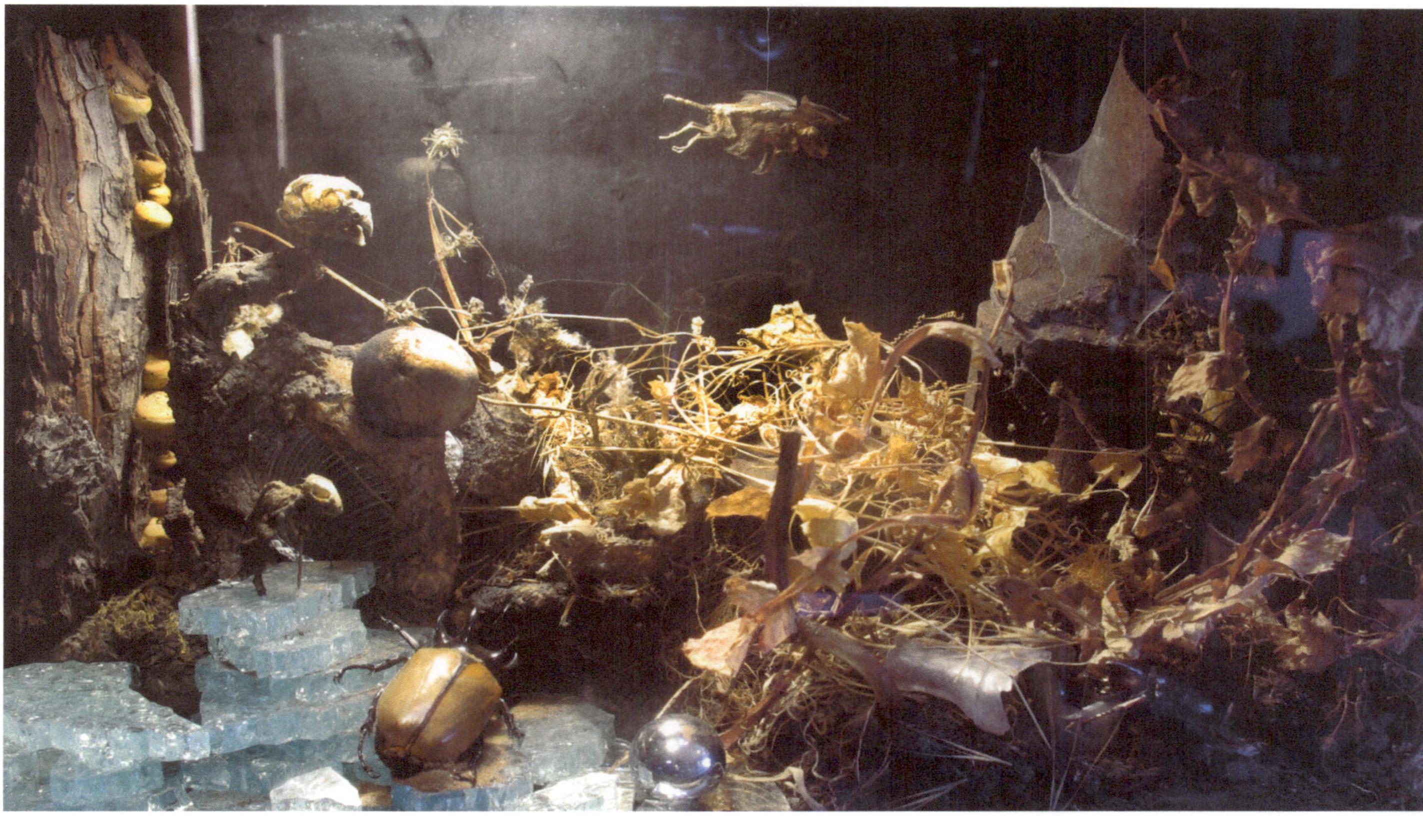

Getting On - night view

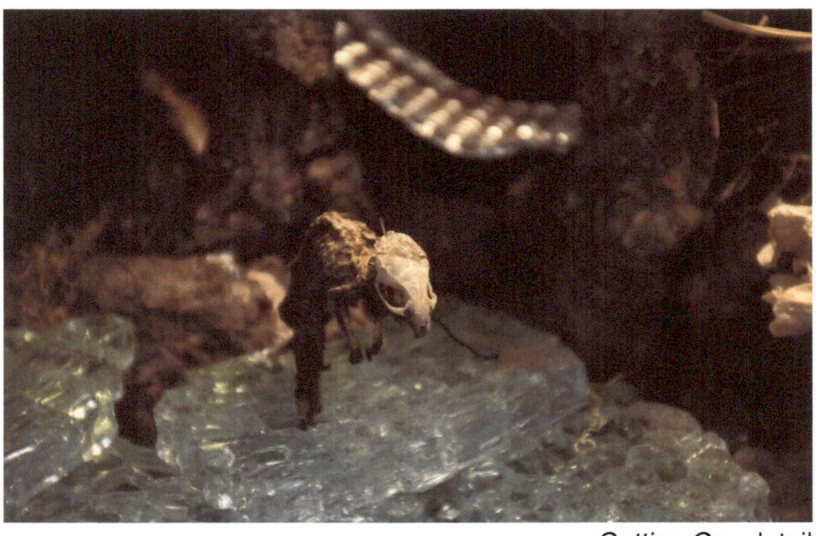

Getting On - detail

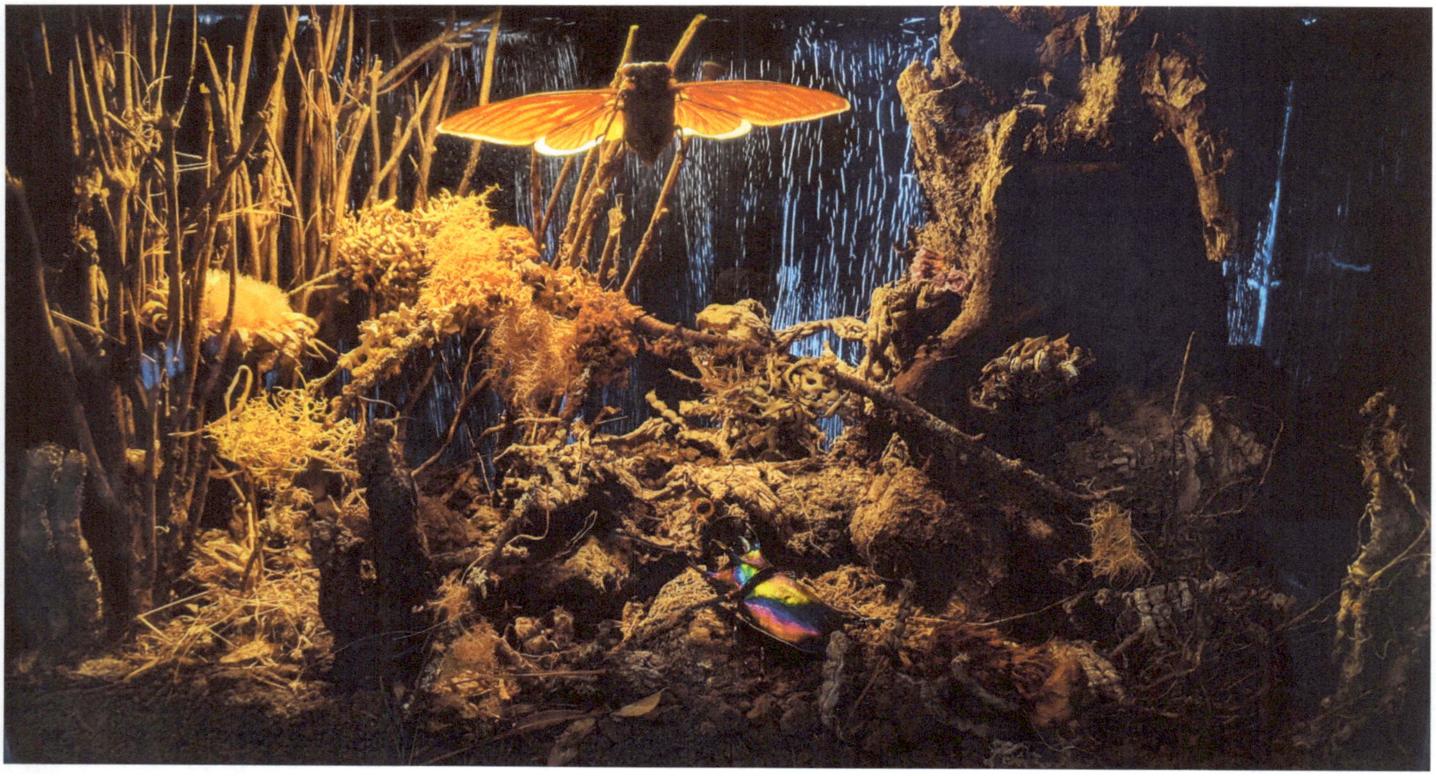

Magic Carpet

The last diorama in this terrestrial series offers some hope of rebirth. An old rug takes on new life, an the scene is presided over by a cicada with wings like the stained glass windows of a cathedral.

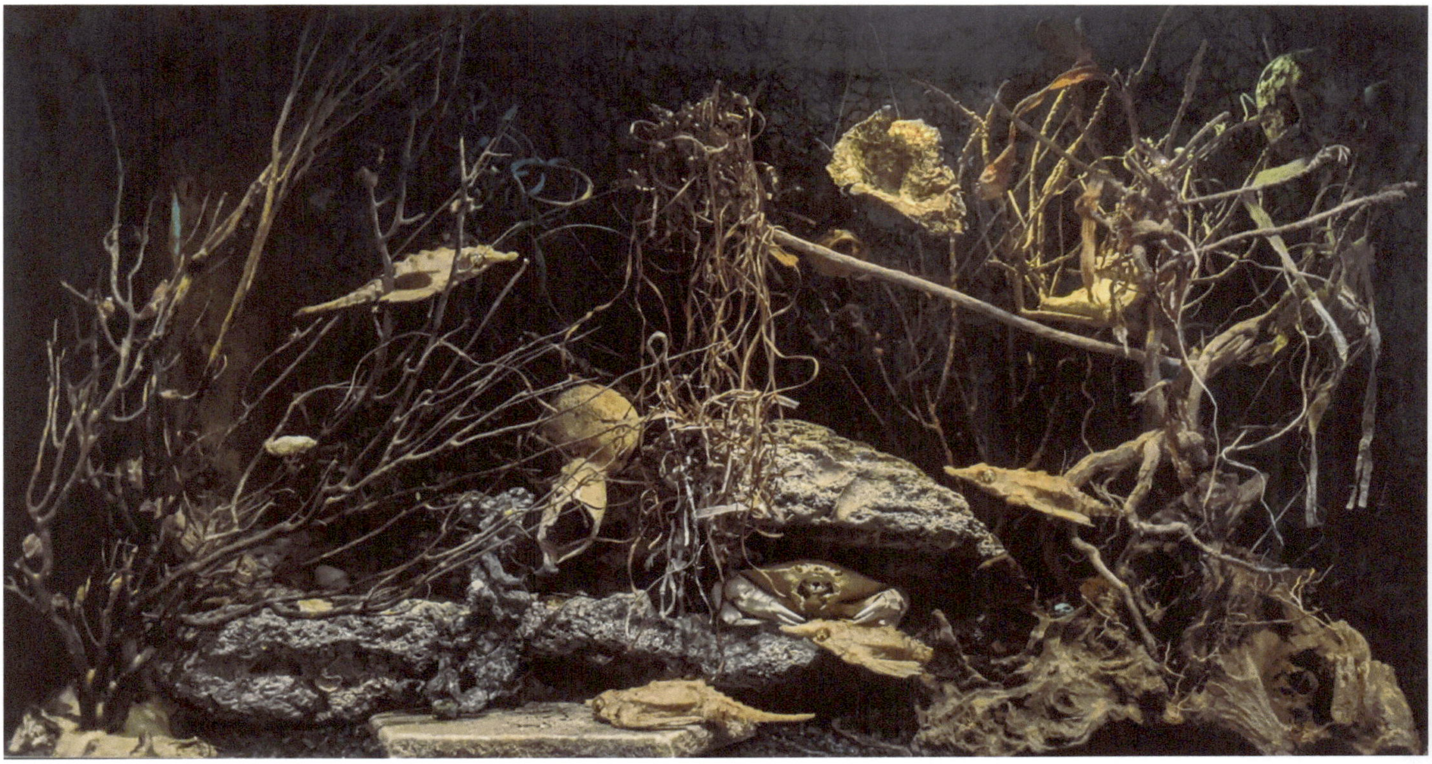

Primordial Ooze

This diorama is the first one in the Hall to have an underwater theme. Root-like tentacles emanating out of a rusty cavern hold a kelp-urn representing the mythic fountain of the primordial ooze. In an inevitable counterpoint to the creation image, a predatory tentacle-creature engulfs a hapless fish, and a small school of prehistoric reptilian bird-fish swim past the baleful gaze of a death figure.

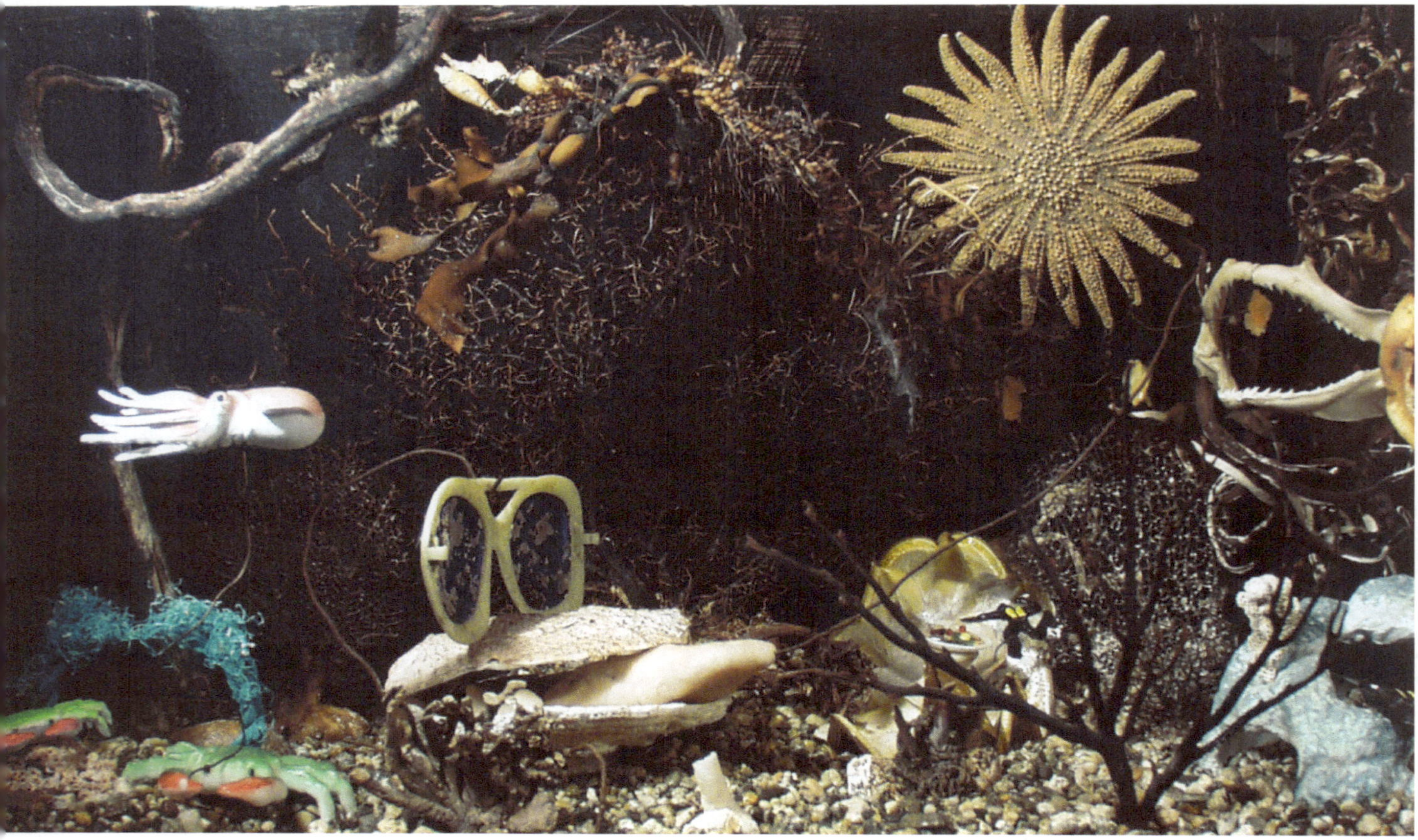

Deception

The predatory theme is continued here with an illustration of the ways in which creatures resort to temptation and deception in order to get a meal. An angler shell uses a lure at the end of its wiry tongue to lure unwary prey. An even more sophisticated mollusc creates the allusion of a yummy meal to trap a hungry diver.

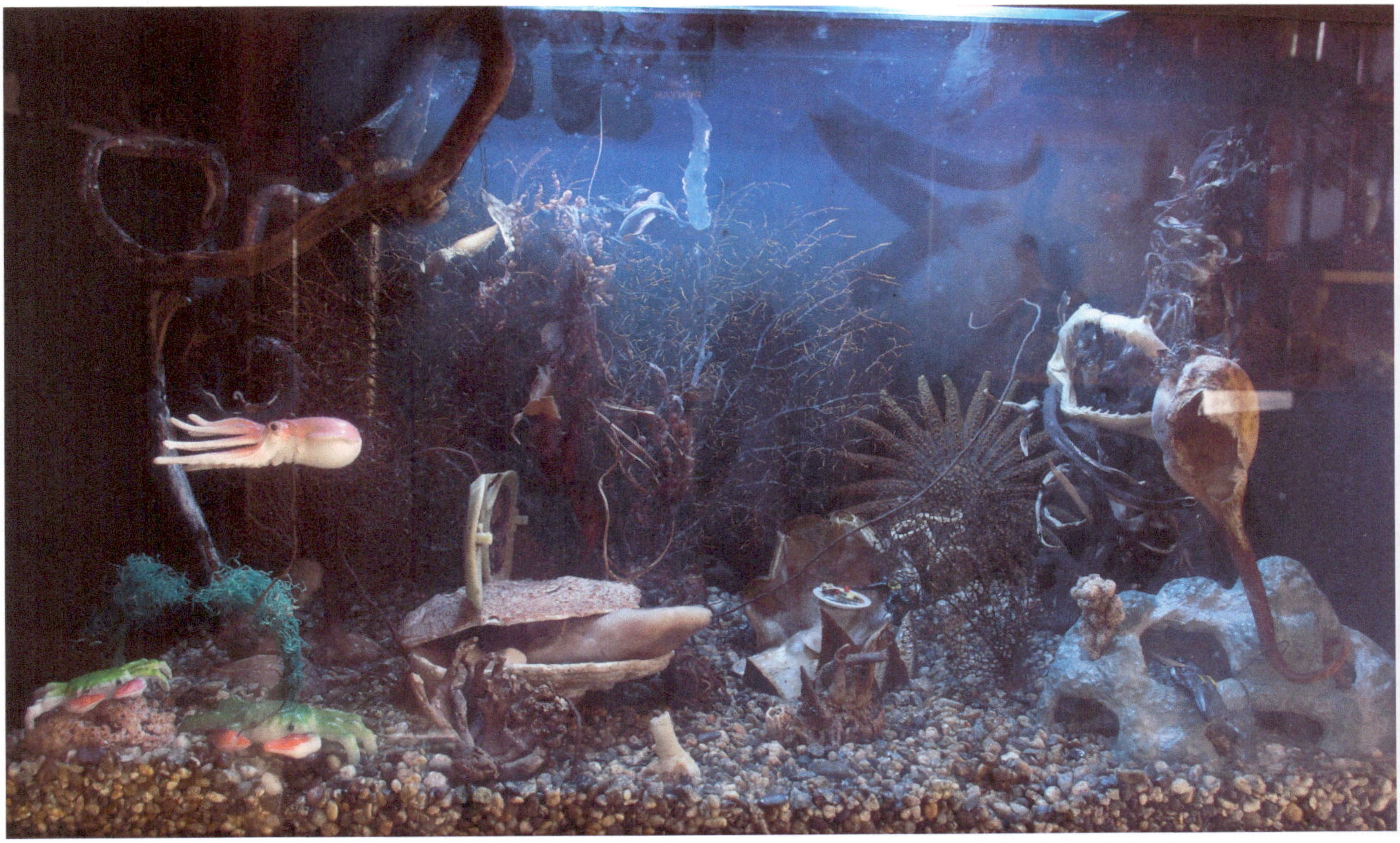

Deception - night view

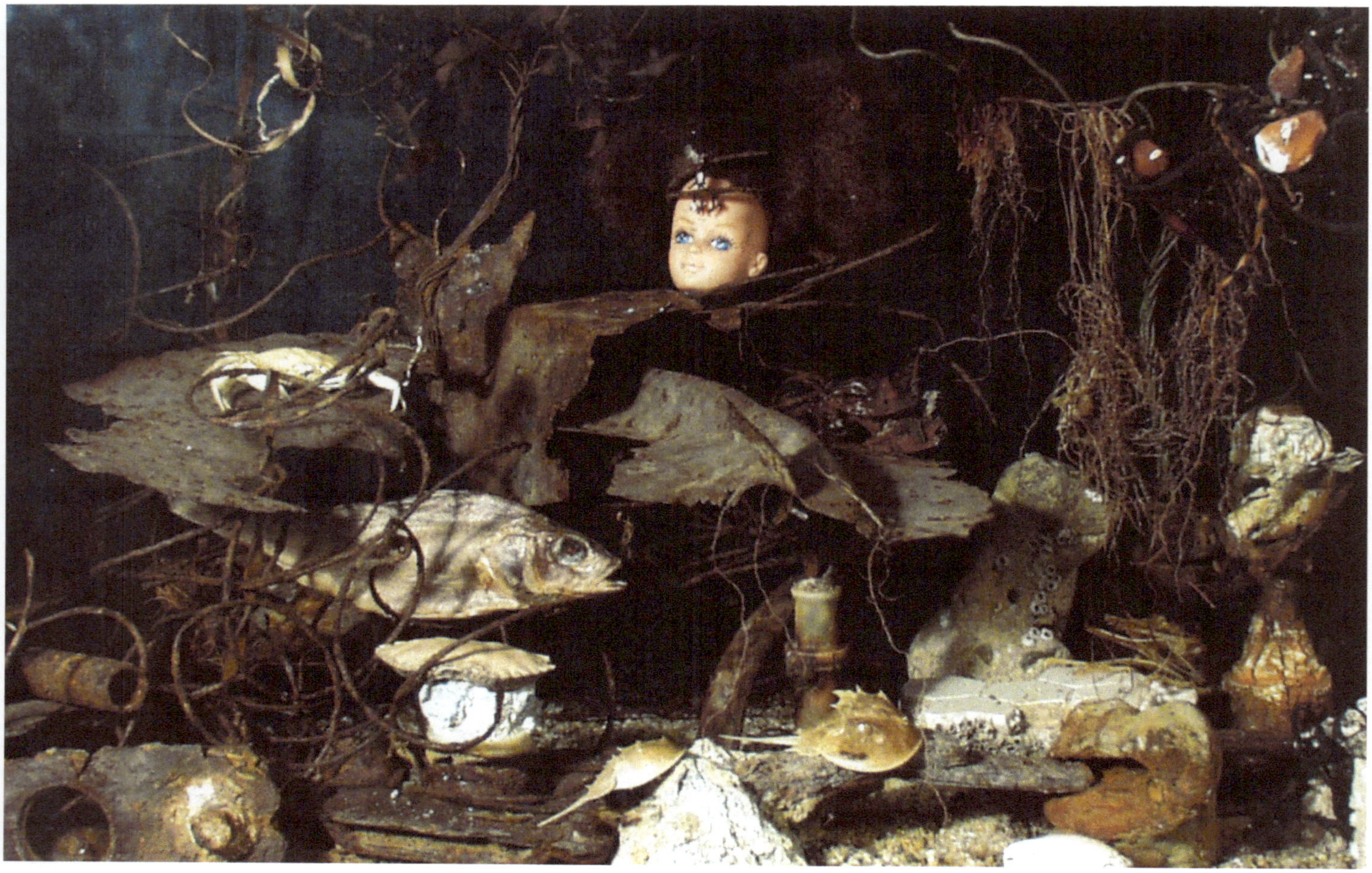

The Rusty Palace

A disembodied doll head has taken up residence in the remains of a once-glorious palace that has given way to corrosion and decay

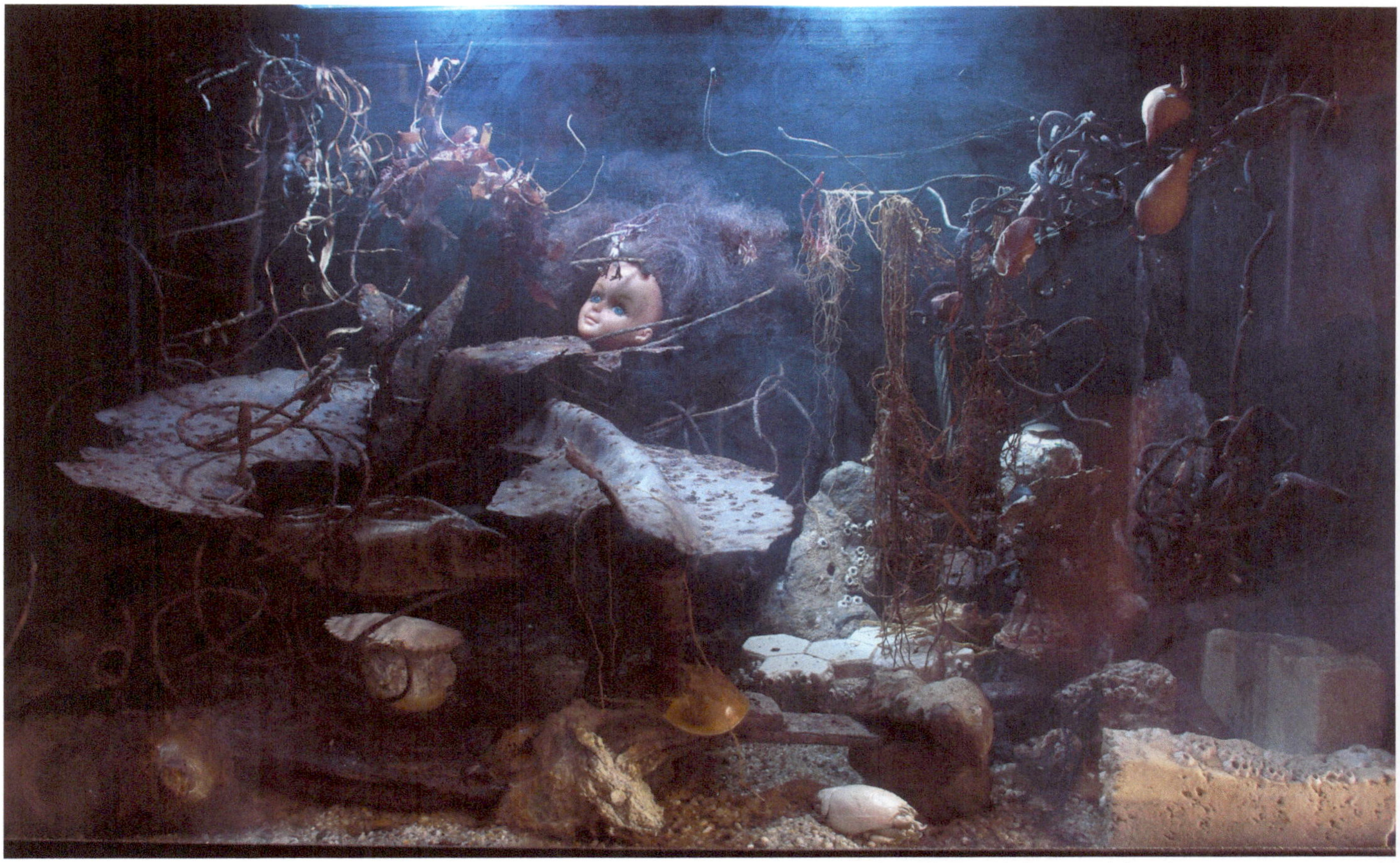

The Rusty Palace - night view

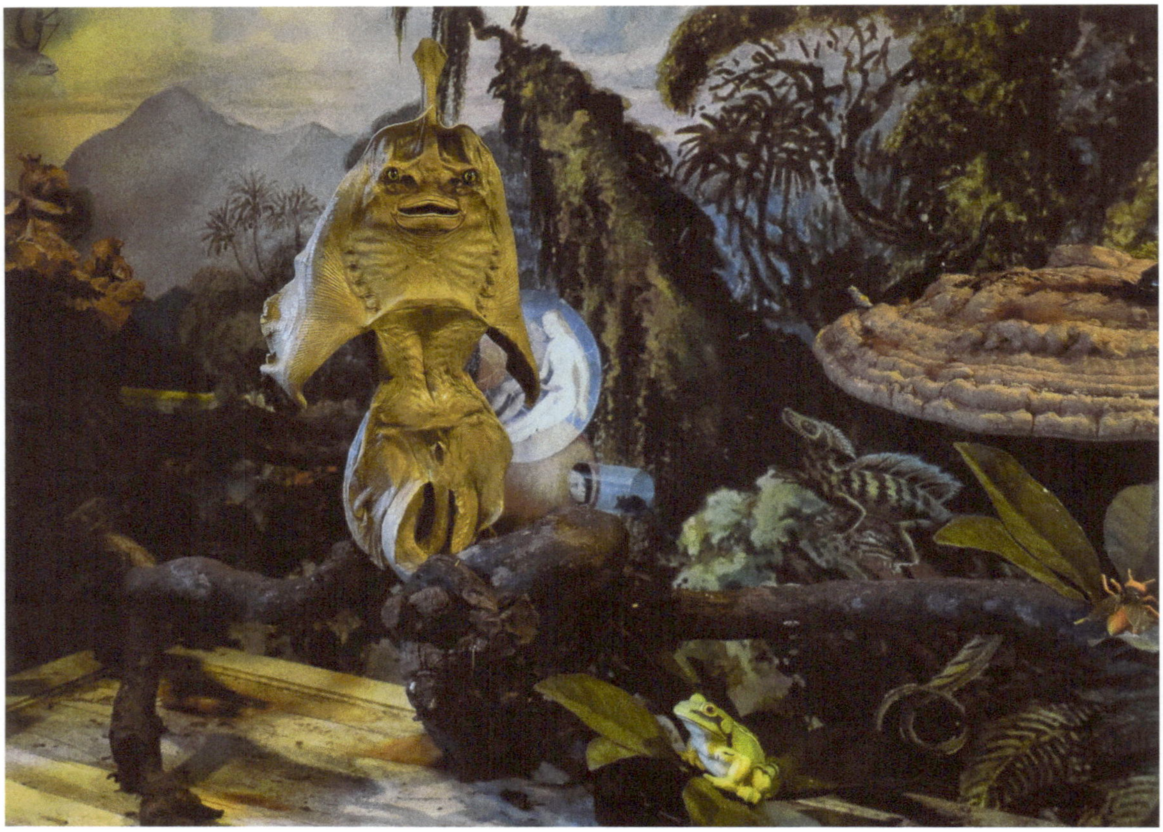

The Mermaid Lagoon

One of the museum's most popular exhibits, this large diorama recreates a typical scene in the Zymoglyphic region. Mermaids here are equally at home in the water or in the trees.

I have heard the mermaids singing, each to each.

I do not think that they will sing to me.

I have seen them riding seaward on the waves
Combing the white hair of the waves blown back
When the wind blows the water white and black.
We have lingered in the chambers of the sea
By sea-girls wreathed with seaweed red and brown
Till human voices wake us, and we drown.

—T.S. Eliot

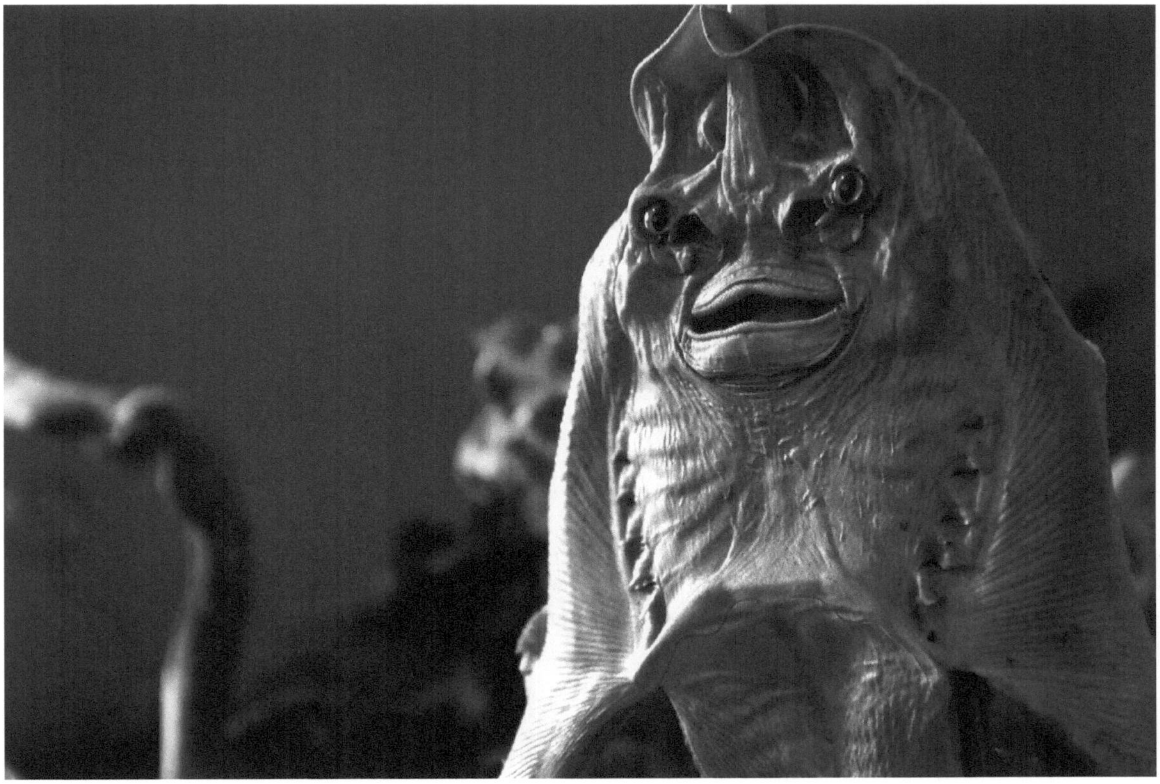

Mermaid detail

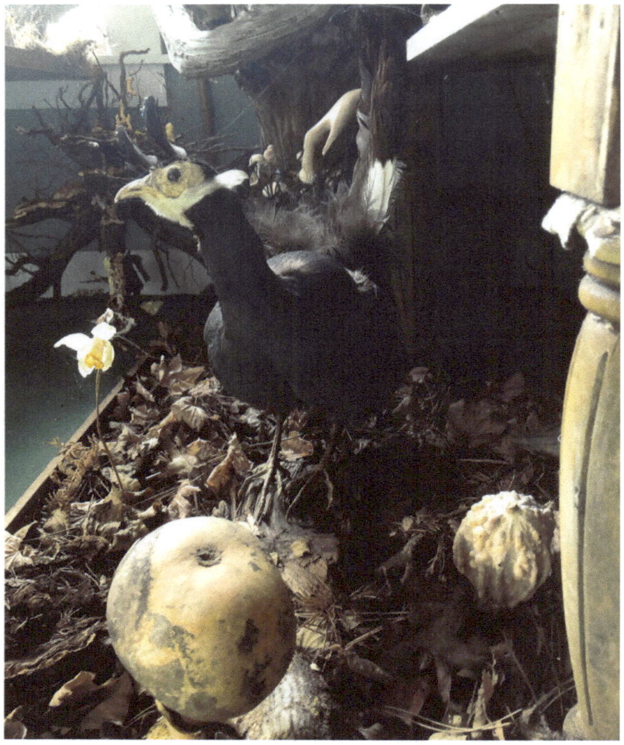
Underside view

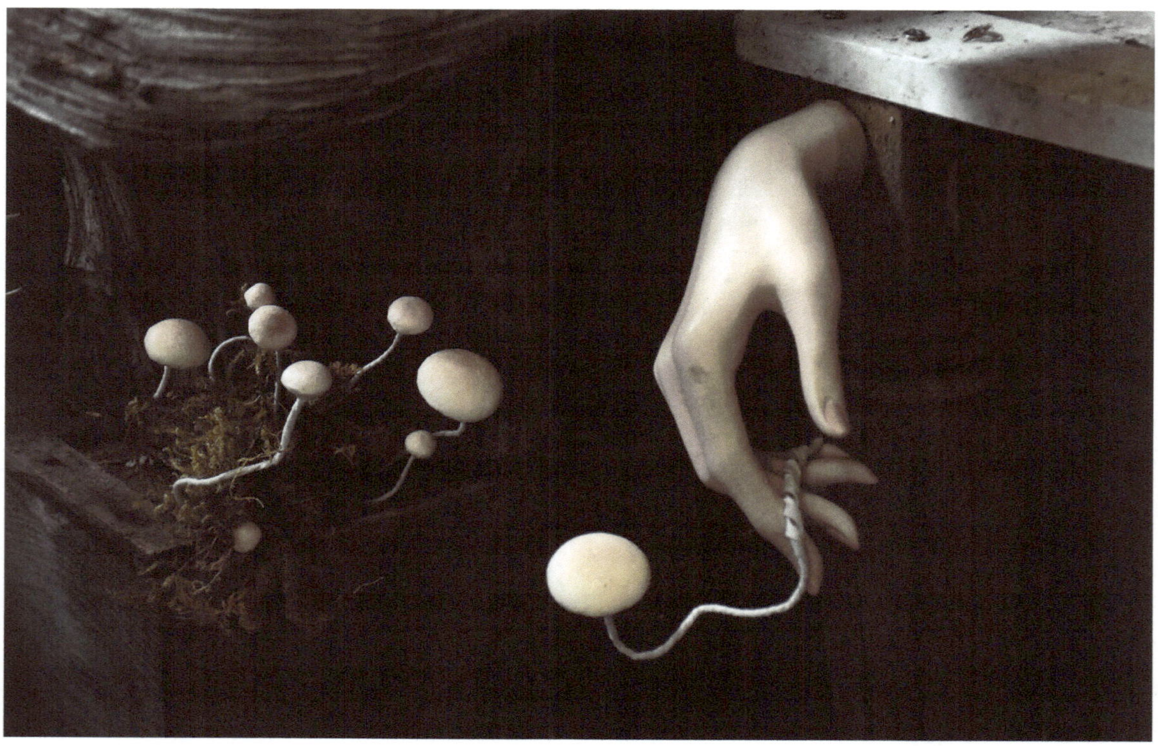
Underside detail

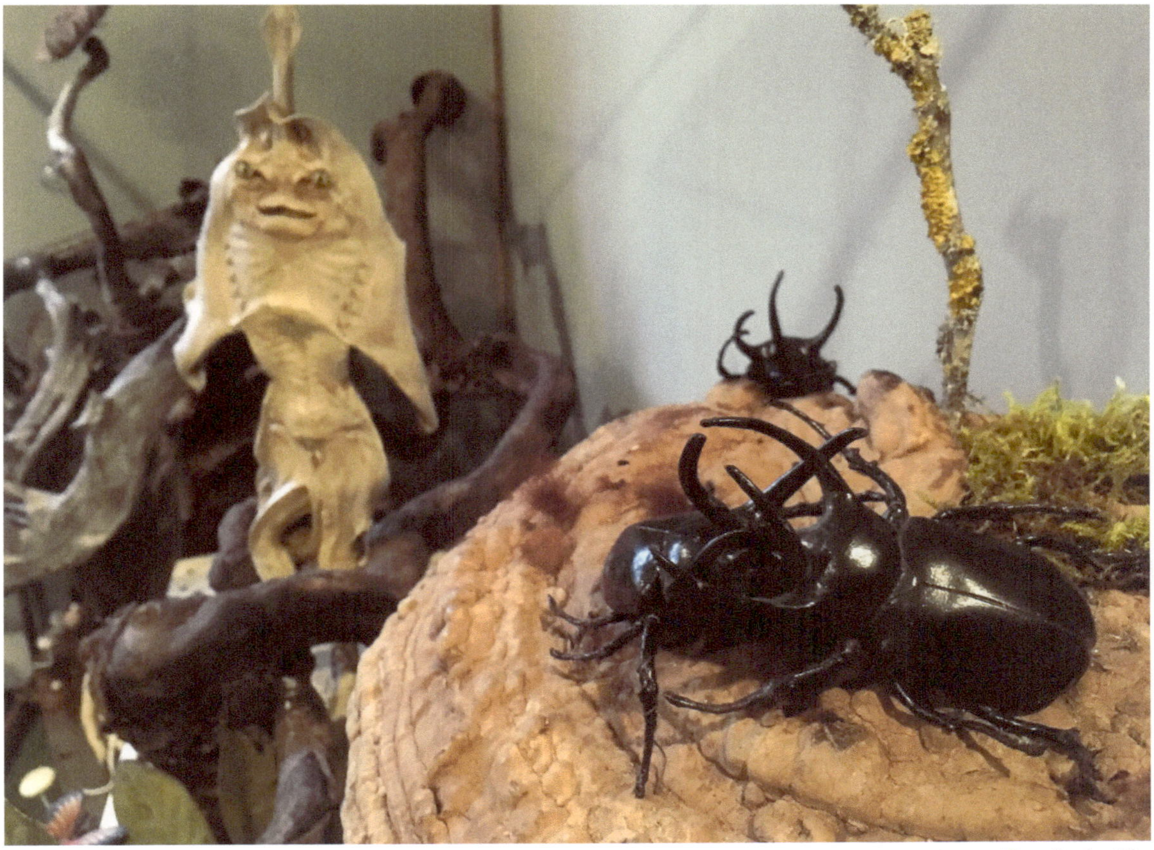

Beetle battle

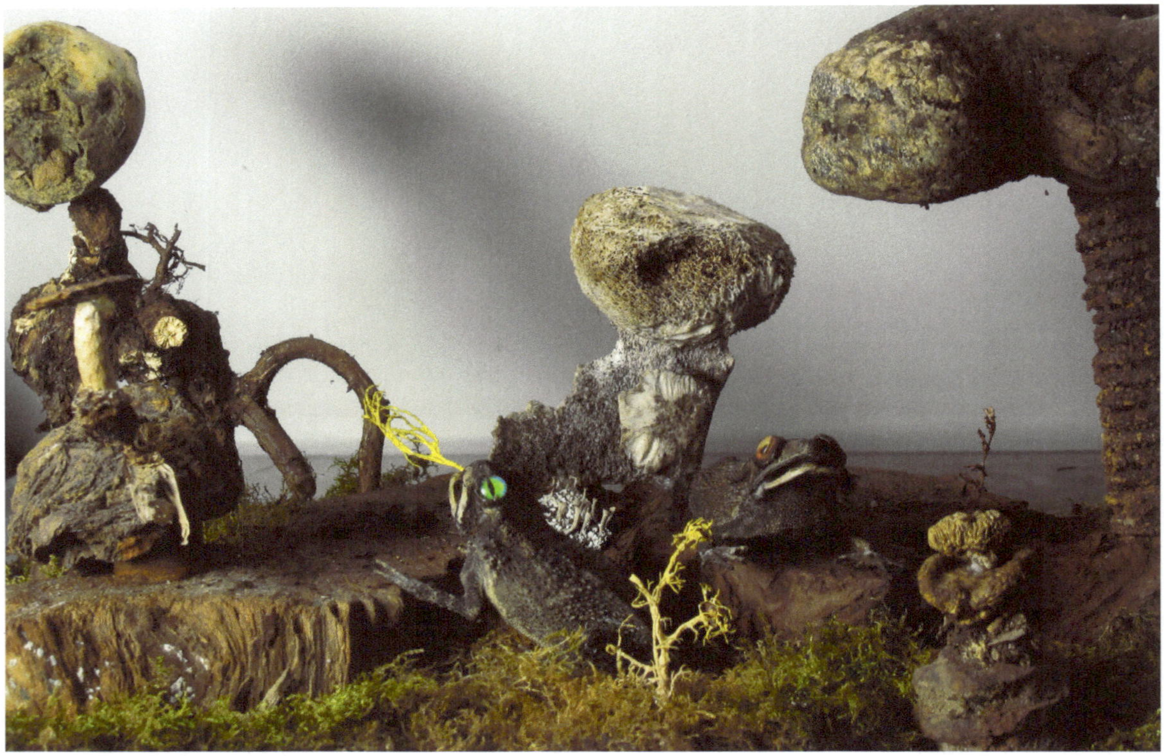

The Toads

imaginary gardens with real toads in them

—Marianne Moore

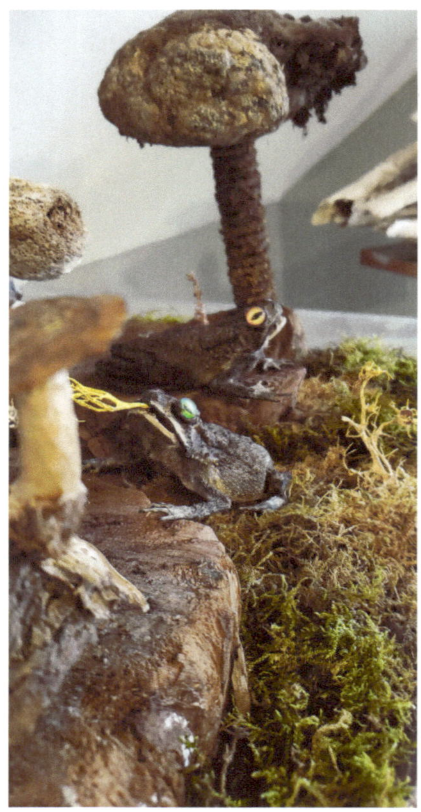

Grottoes

Grottoes are natural or artificial caverns imbued with a certain aesthetic spirit. Water seeping over limestone creates natural sculptures; crystals form. Some grottoes have springs that are thought to be home to nymphs who provide life-sustaining water as well as creative inspiration. One particularly large grotto in the region has been turned into an artists' cavern, as can be seen below.

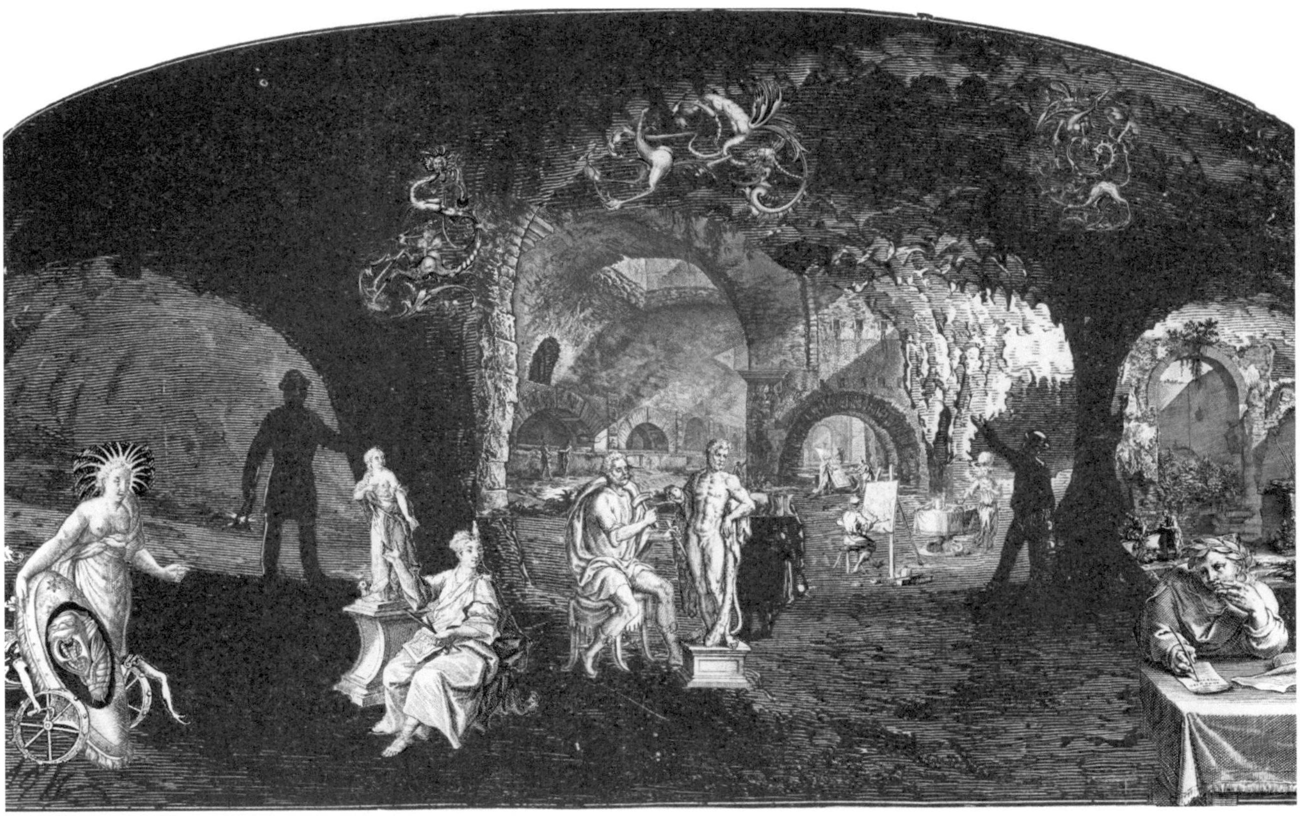

Miniature grottoes are small dioramas that capture the spirit of the grotto, using various encrustations to mimic minerals and crystals.

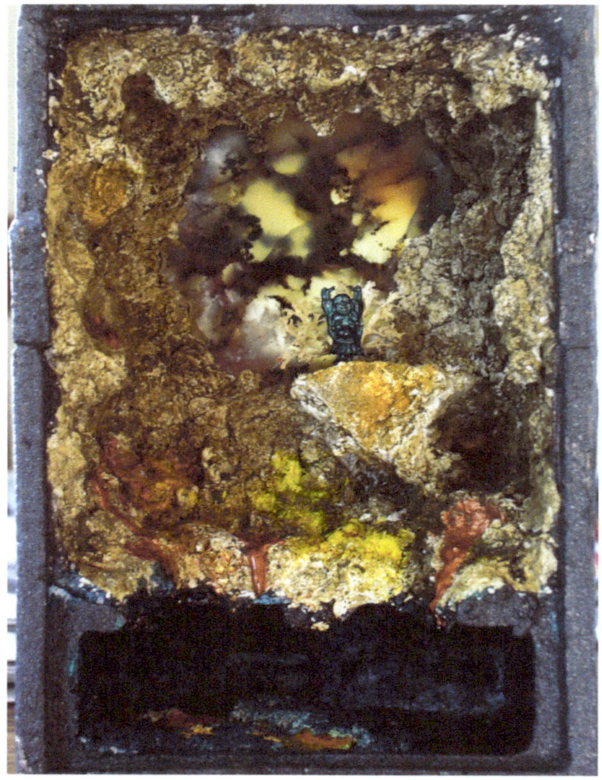

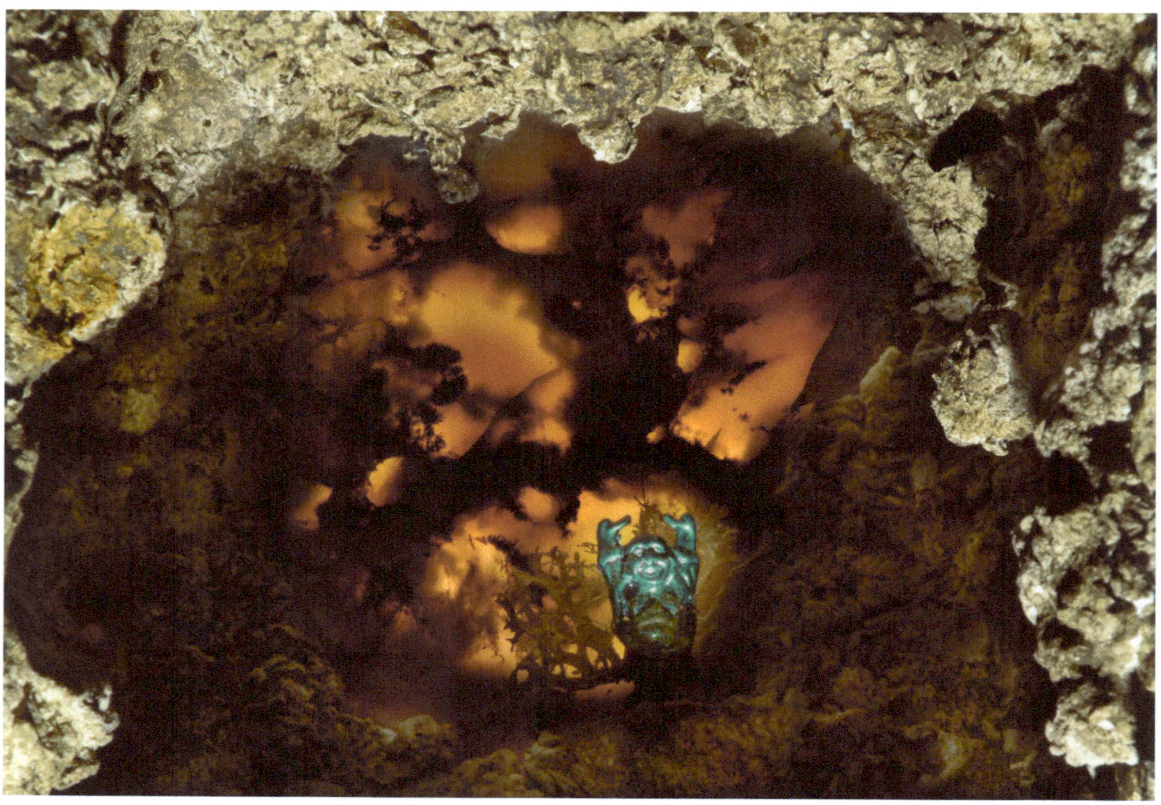

They were usually placed in windows, backlit by the Sun, to highlight the details of the agate slab that usually formed their backdrop.

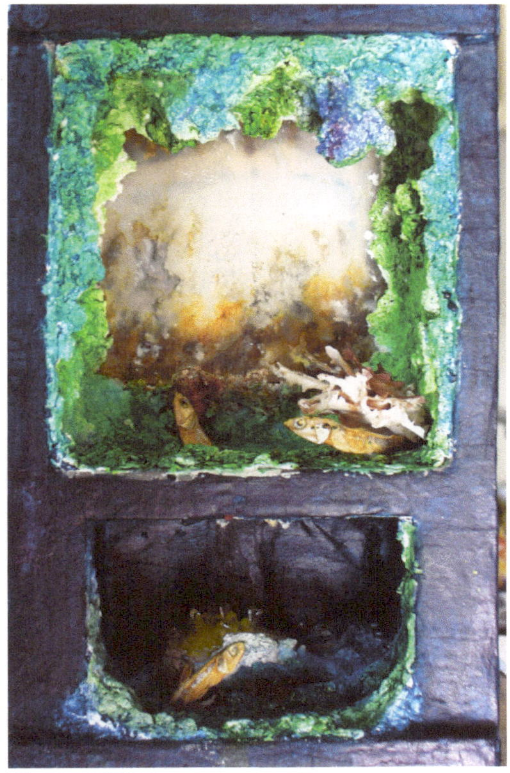

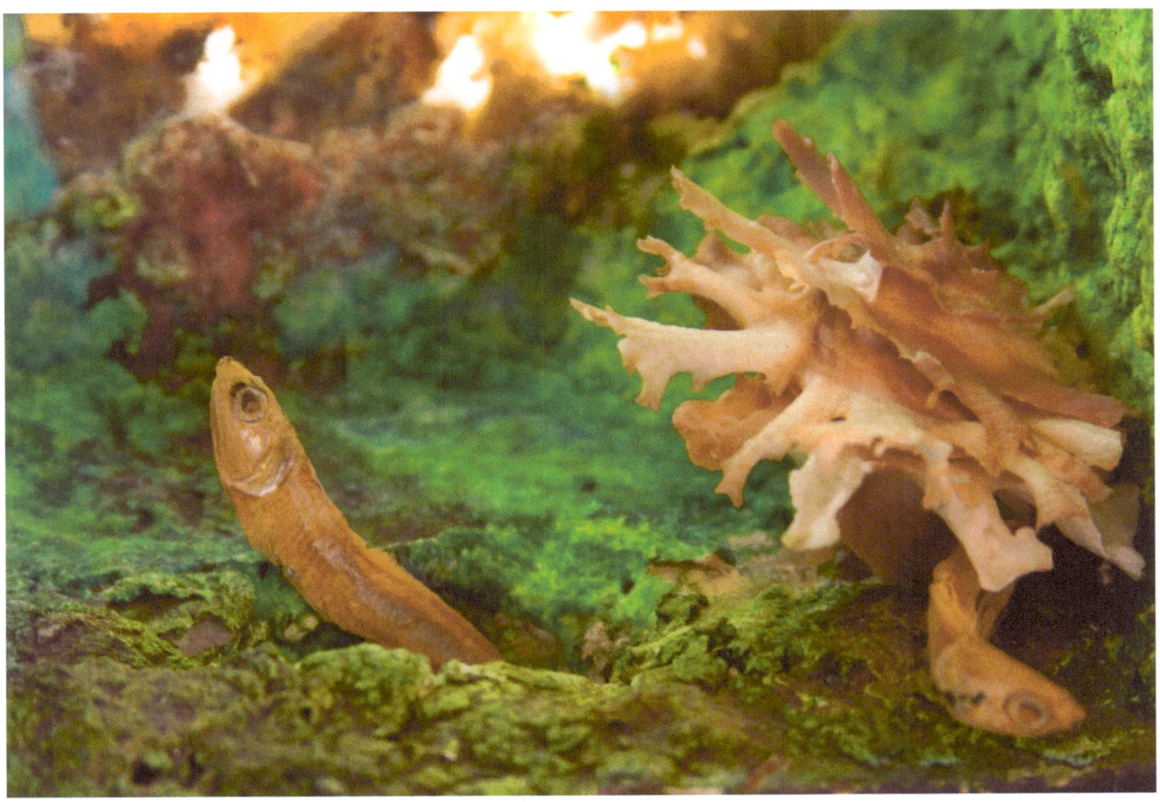

Parlor aquarium

A parlor aquarium is essentially a diorama for the home rather than for a museum. Like a live aquarium, it showcases nature's wonders while requiring little to no care. This particular model (now on display in the museum proper) is called "The Quiet Parlor of the Fishes" and was inspired by a passage from *Walden*:

> *I look down into the quiet parlor of the fishes, pervaded by a softened light as through a window of ground glass, with its bright sanded floor the same as in summer; there a perennial waveless serenity reigns as in the amber twilight sky, corresponding to the cool and even temperament of the inhabitants. Heaven is under our feet is well as over our heads.*

—H. D. Thoreau

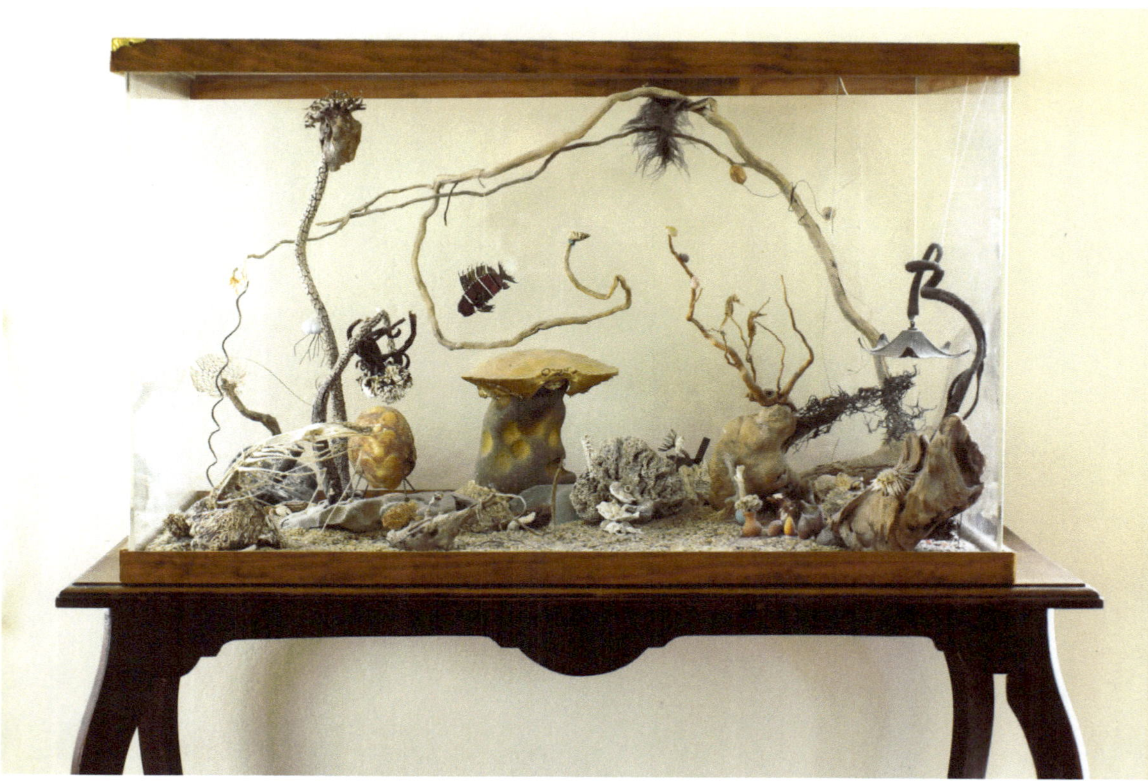

The Quiet Parlor of the Fishes

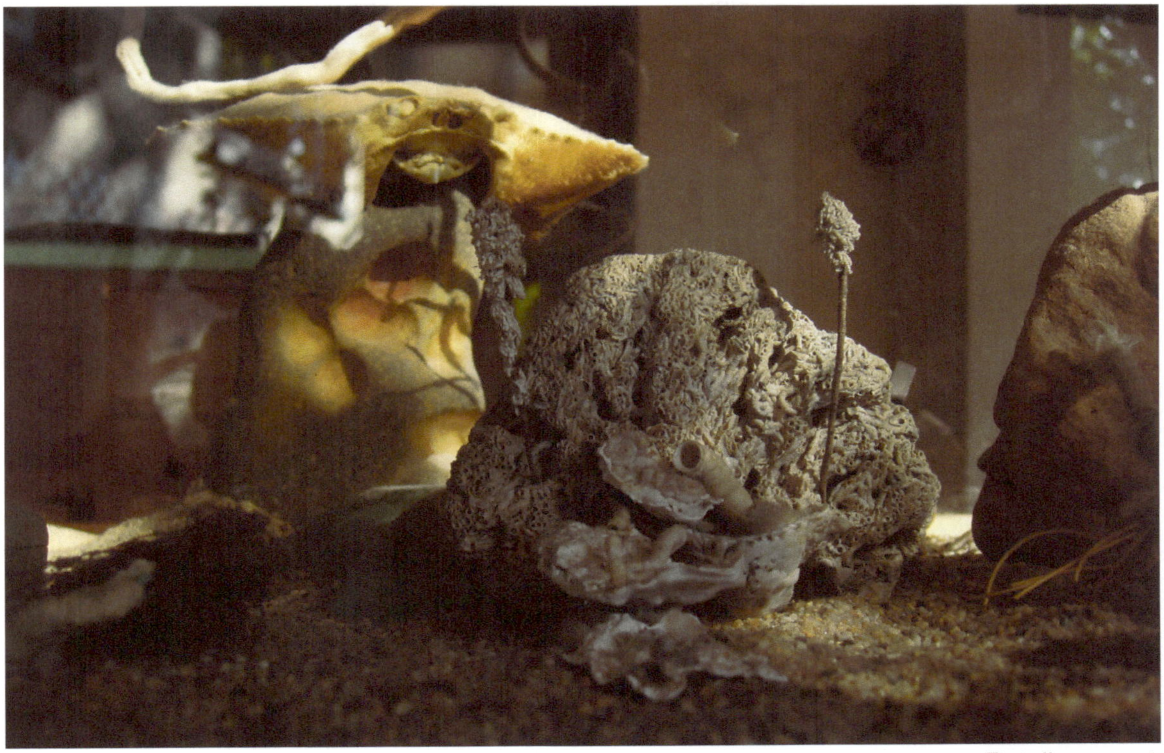

Detail - sunset

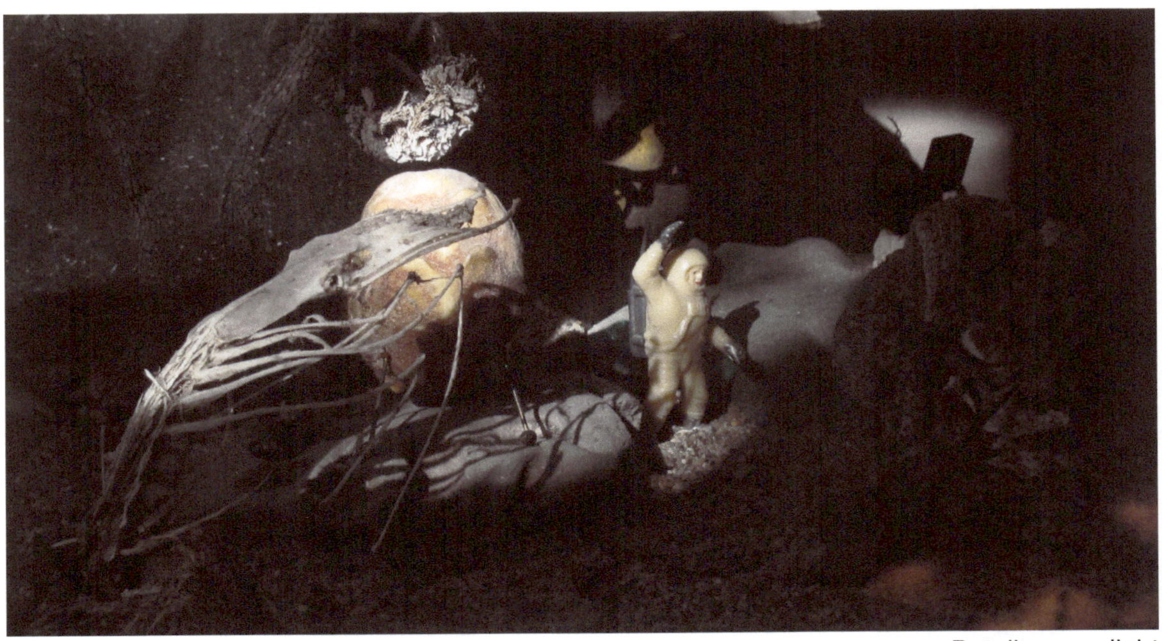

Detail - moonlight

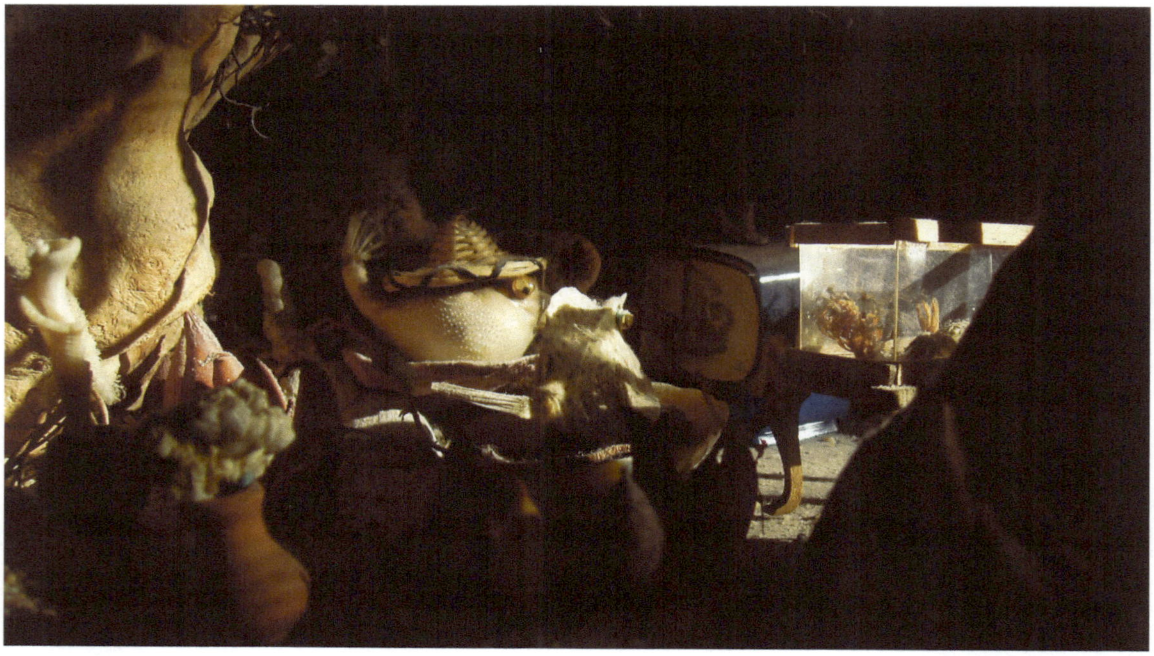

Detail - the quiet parlor

This dehydrated aquarium features its own little fishy parlor (for which it is named). The inhabitants have few furnishings, but they include a television which features the escapades of another fish in aquarium. Competing for attention, and generally winning, is their own little aquarium, which may feature an even more miniature parlor within it, so finely crafted as to be impossible to see.

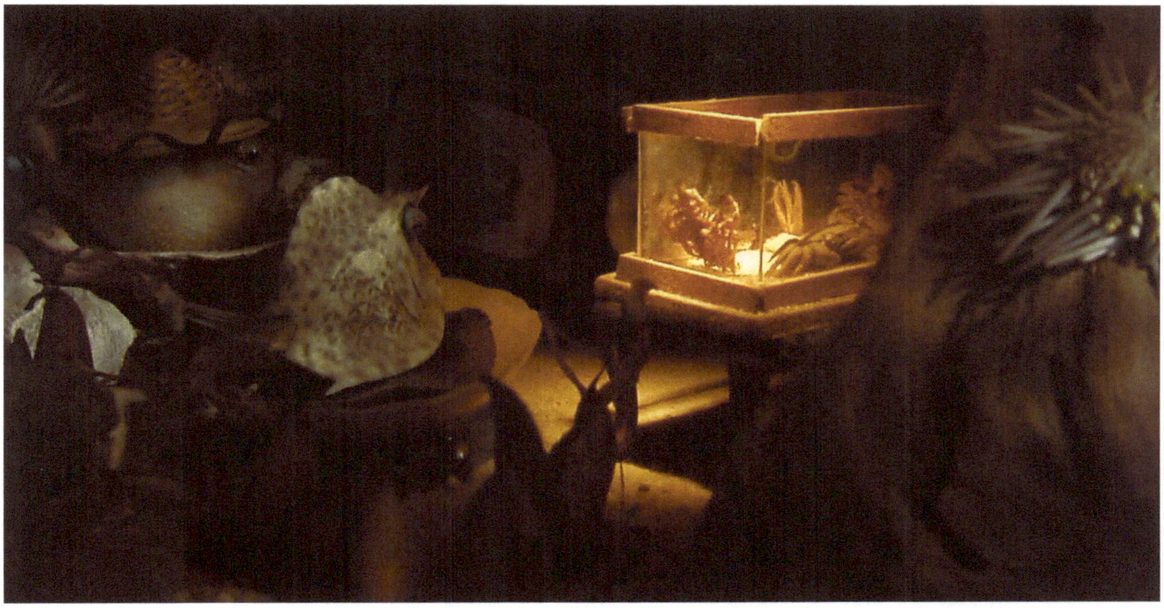

Little aquarium in the parlor inside the aquarium

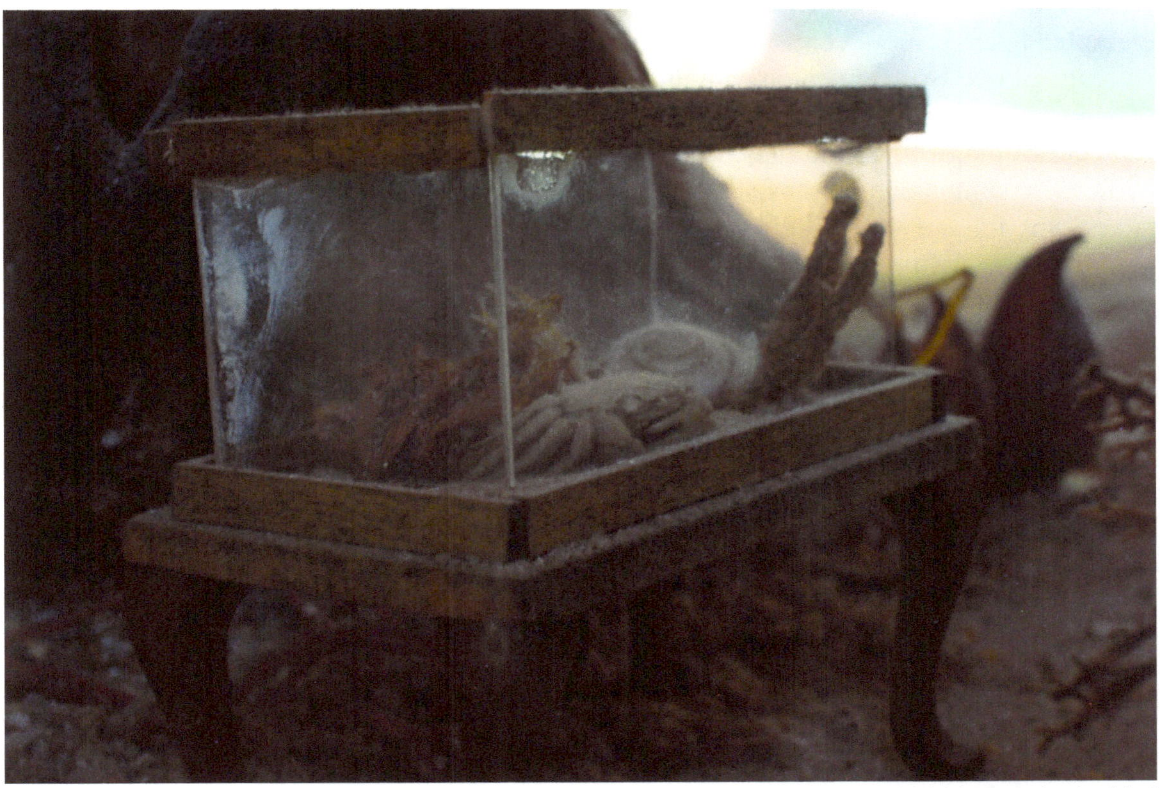

A hidden parlor inside?

Alchemy

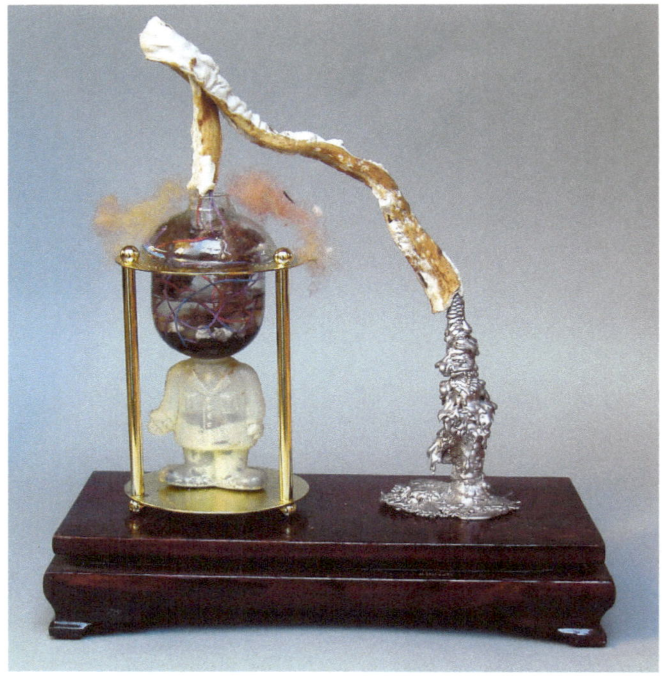

Alchemical apparatus

In the Rust Age, Zymoglyphic artisans were generally content with assembling various ritual objects from components that already had, for example, a prized patina of oxidation, or an air of rotted organic elegance. They were not concerned about finding an incorruptible philosopher's stone, preferring instead to maximize the corruption of the base metal; purity was seen a sort of bland homogeneity. The Zymoglyphic ideal was to transform something relatively pure, such as a sheet of copper, into something more complex and interesting.

In the Age of Wonder, alchemists attempted to exert more control over the various natural processes that caused objects to become imbued with a poetic meaning, the very process that gave Zymoglyphic culture its name. An apparatus such as this one could, given the right conditions, coalesce a sort of metallic sludge out of simulated thought processes and various bits of decomposing matter. The simulated thoughts are obtained by removing the head of a symbolic figurine and placing the remaining body where a fire would otherwise be burning. The space formerly filled by the head coincides with the position of a flask bulb; thus, the thoughts mingle with the decomposing matter. The resulting metal is a variant form of primordial ooze, still Zymoglyphic in style but resistant to further decay and corruption.

Alchemists sought to release "spirit in matter" through the symbolic dissolution of metal and creation of its fermentation by-products. During the Zymoglyphic Age of Wonder, alchemists focused more on metaphysical transformations, rather than chemical ones, as can be seen in this alchemical apparatus from that era.

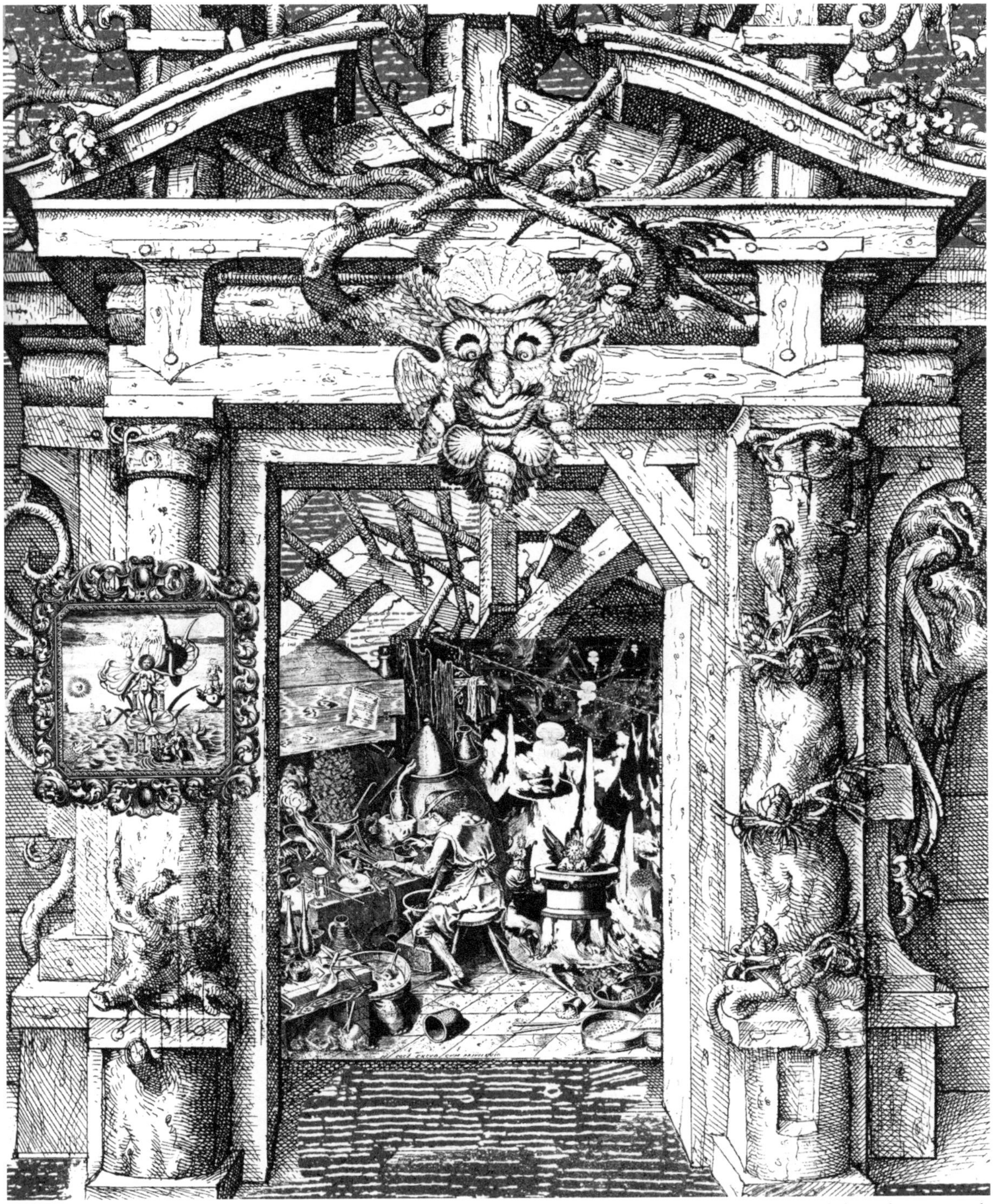

An alchemist at work

Cosmography

The blank areas on the maps and globes in the early days of the Age of Wonder were often filled in with wind cherubs, mermaids, and sea monsters. This crude orrery is an artist's conception from the Age of Wonder depicting the state of the planet at it was believed to have existed during its formative eons, known as the "Mud Age."

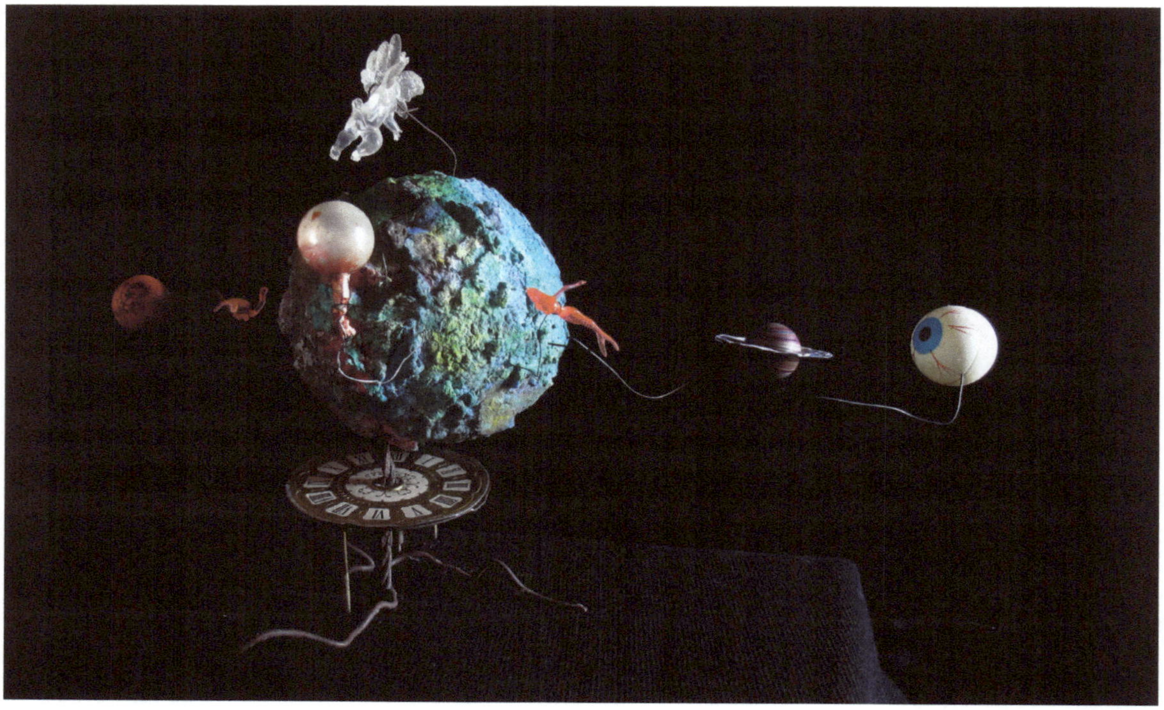

Orrery

In the old days, the sky practically swarmed with moons. It wasn't just that one big, plodding, gray moon that you see nowadays. There were speedy satellites, close ones, shiny ones, red ones. Sometimes a moon would lure a passing asteroid and keep it as a moonlet.

It was the Mud Age, after all, with that primordial ooze seeping in everywhere, continents all askew, jostling for position, each still trying to figure out where it really wanted to be. Tectonic plates piled up, eruptions all the time! Some people claimed that one of the moons looked just like a giant eyeball, always watching. It didn't help that, exactly like our one moon today, that eyeball moon was locked in orbit facing us. It never blinked. And of course for us kids it was always a treat when one of those orbiting mermaids flew over!

The sky, too, was different in those days. It was full of visions and messages, if you looked at it just right. There were angels and demons, crawly things, and those swirly galaxies were not so many light-years away as they are now. You can see the proof right there in those pictures. That's just how it was.

from "Memories of the Mud Age," Zymoglyphic Oral History Archive

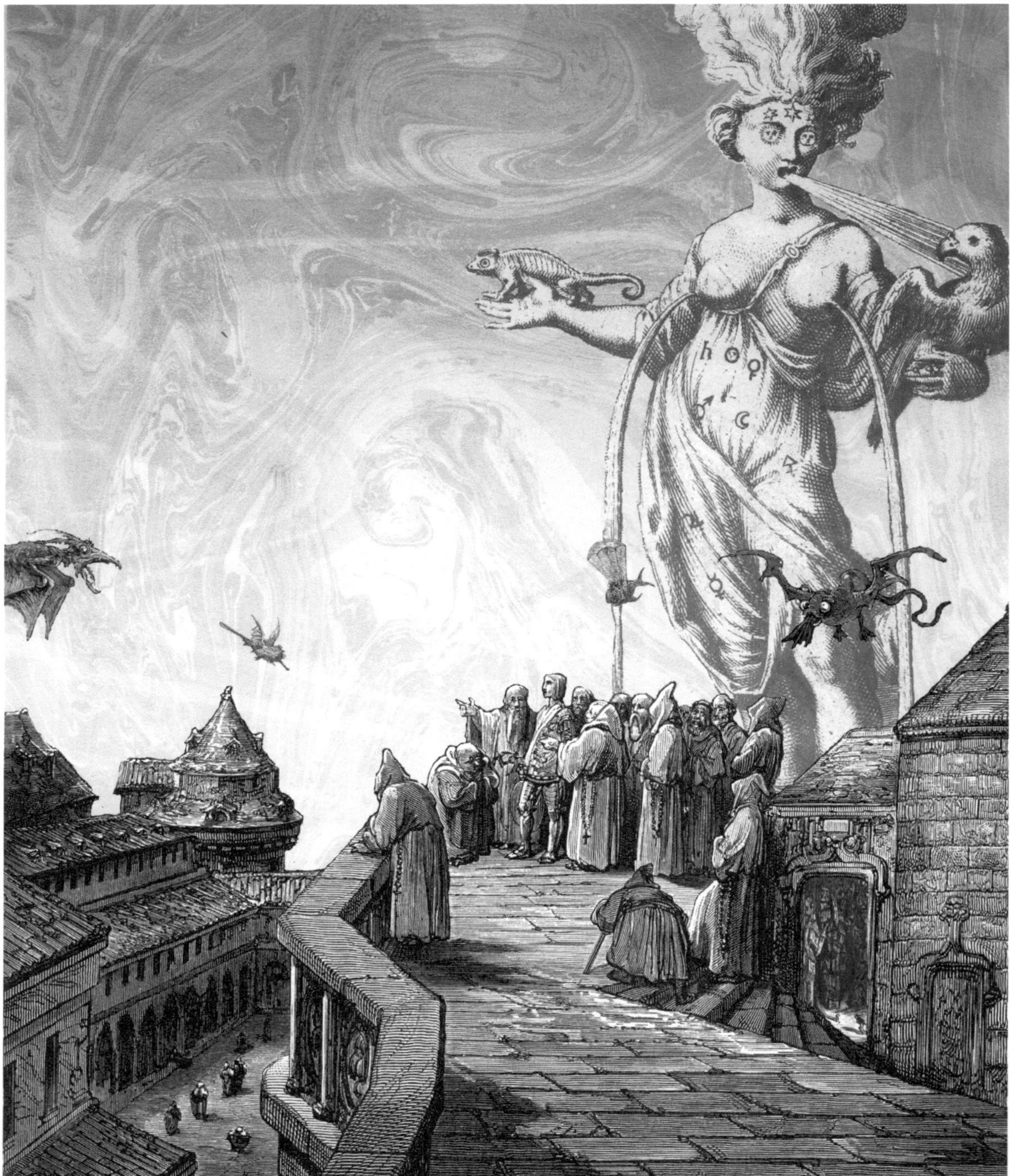

Sky apparitions

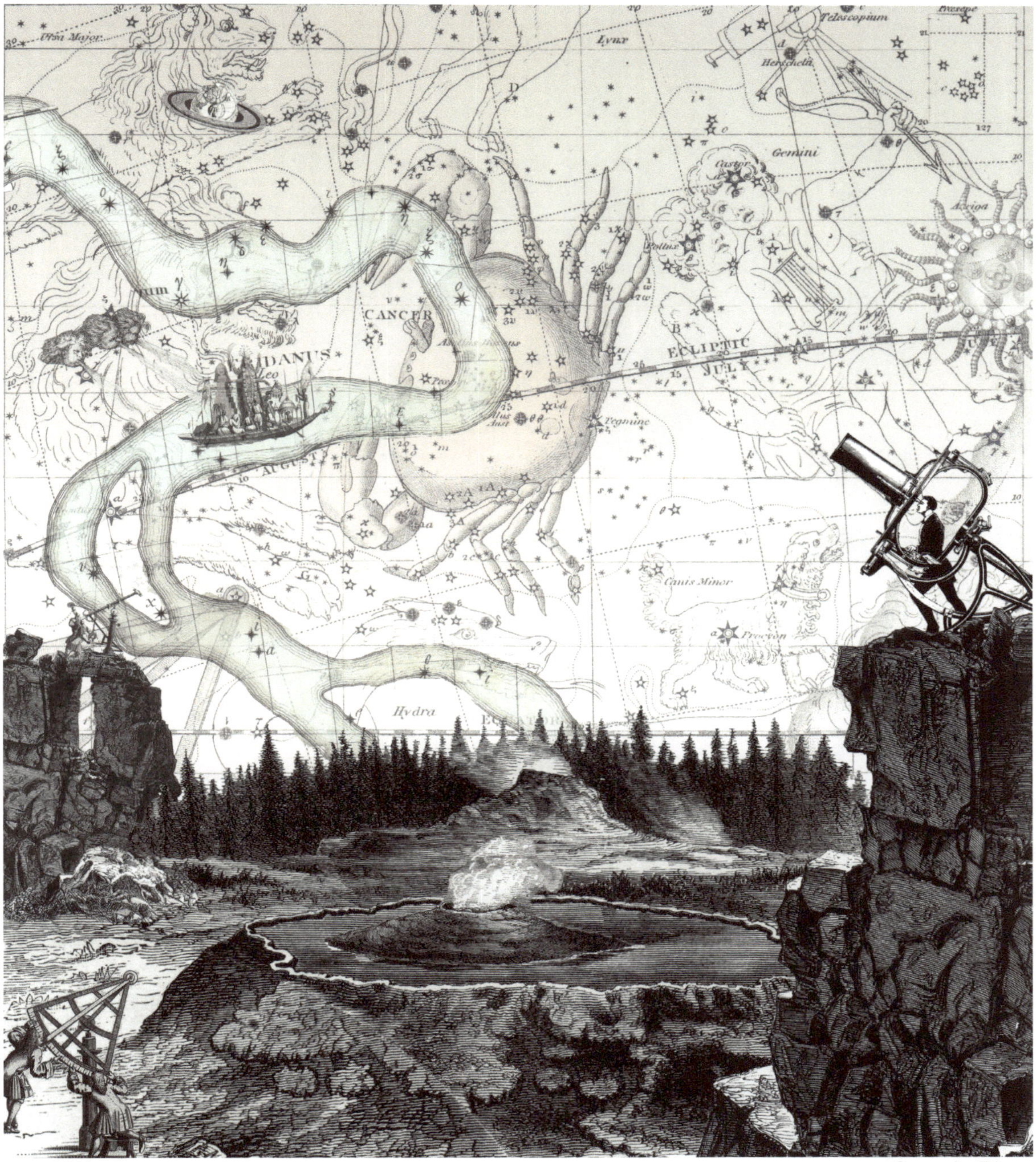

Cosmic River

THE ERA OF ORIENTAL INFLUENCE

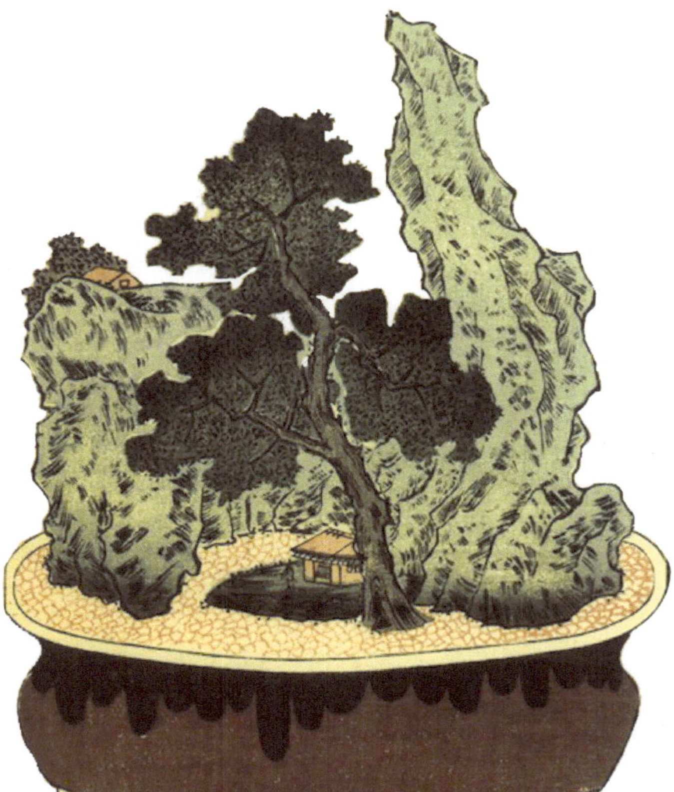

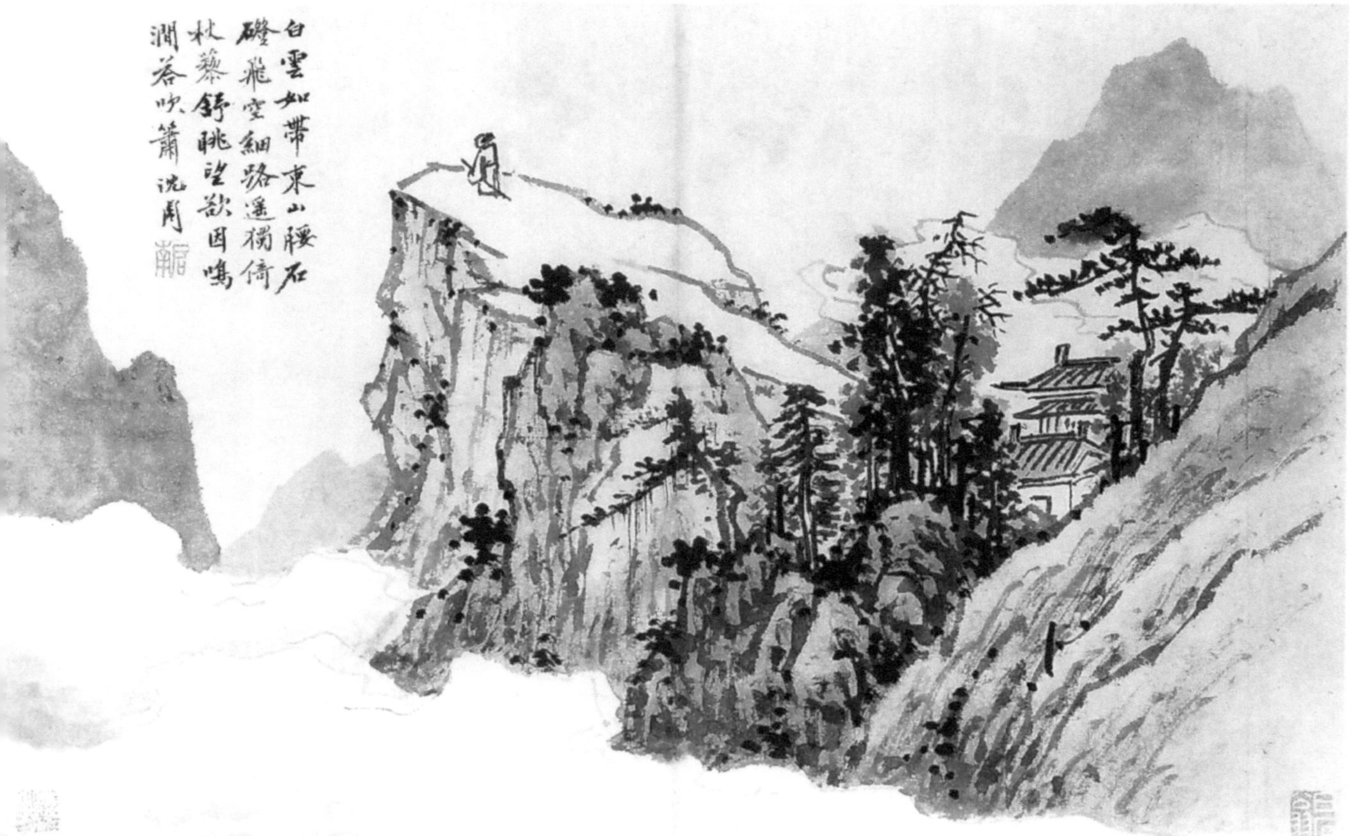

Poet on a Mountaintop by Shen Zhou (1427-1509)

The Era of Oriental Influence

During the Age of Wonder, people of the Zymoglyphic region had an opportunity to learn of and trade with other cultures in the world. Contact with philosophies and nature-based art of the fabled Orient had a profound impact and led to more streamlined aesthetic in art. Values of baroque complexity and runaway accumulation gave way to a more contemplative aesthetic, with simplified compositions and a return to the poetic effects of nature. Art was made as a meditative process, and the value of the poetically weathered surface was rediscovered.

The Literati Tradition

The artists and writers of the period were particularly inspired by the "literati" tradition of scholar-bureaucrats who worked ordinary jobs, generally in government service, then retired to pursue the arts. A multi-disciplinary approach was valued, rather than specialization; the ideal scholar would be conversant in music, painting, calligraphy, poetry, and a strategy game. Self-expression was considered more important than craft—that was left to professional artists who were considered merely technically competent. Some literati were hermits but most stayed home to study and learn from nature. They collected gnarled wood, picture stones, and other enigmatic bits of nature for learned contemplation, valuing the ordinary instead of the miraculous.

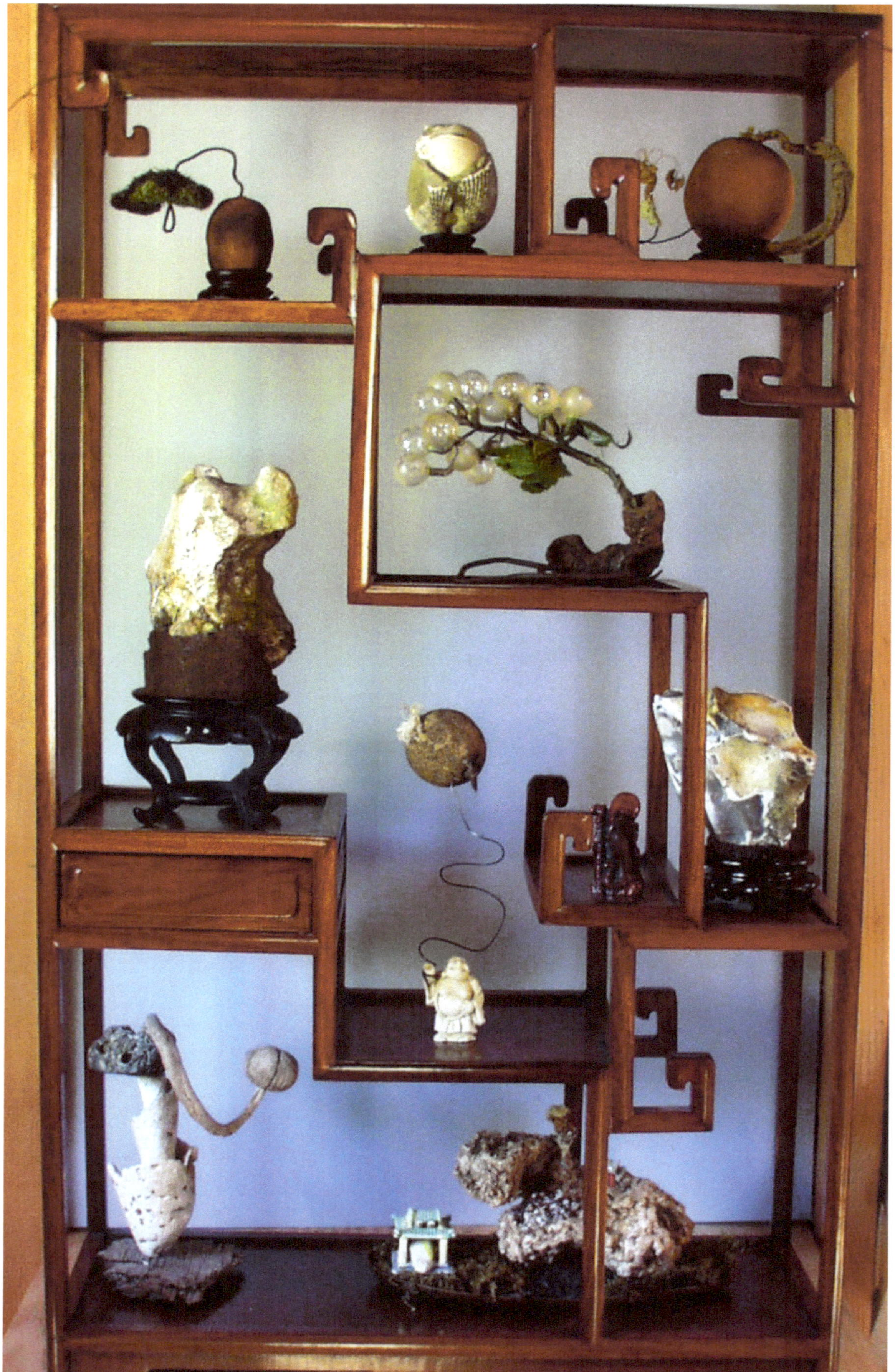

Curio stands

As the ideals of the literati tradition took hold in the Zymoglyphic region, gathering enigmatic natural objects led to making simple assemblages from them. The results were displayed in asymmetric shelves such as the one shown on the opposite page.

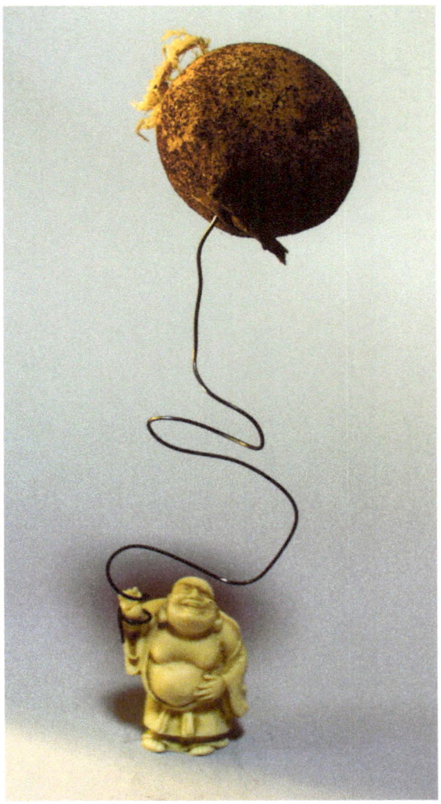

The Happy Monk is a recurring theme during this era. He is depicted here carrying a bag full of inflatable universes, bubbles in the space-time continuum that expand.

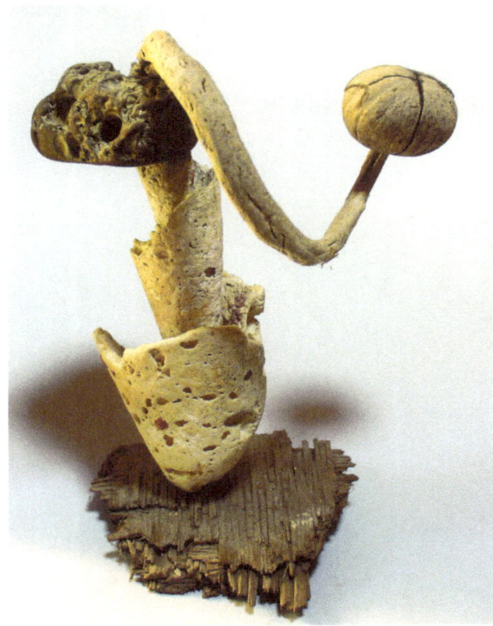

A precariously balanced arrangement of seaworn detritus.

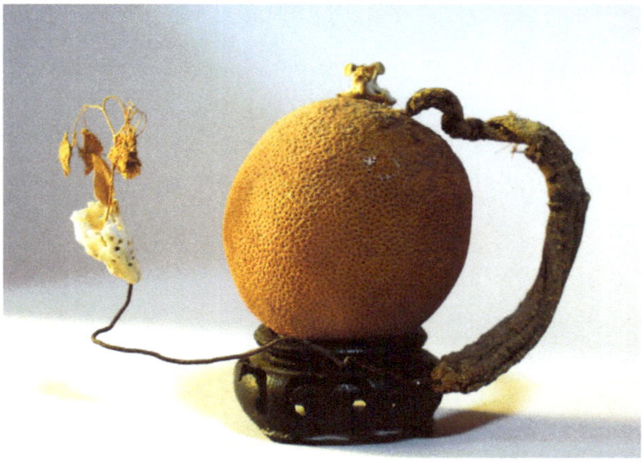

A traditional dried fruit and vegetable arrangement, this one based on an orange and a carrot

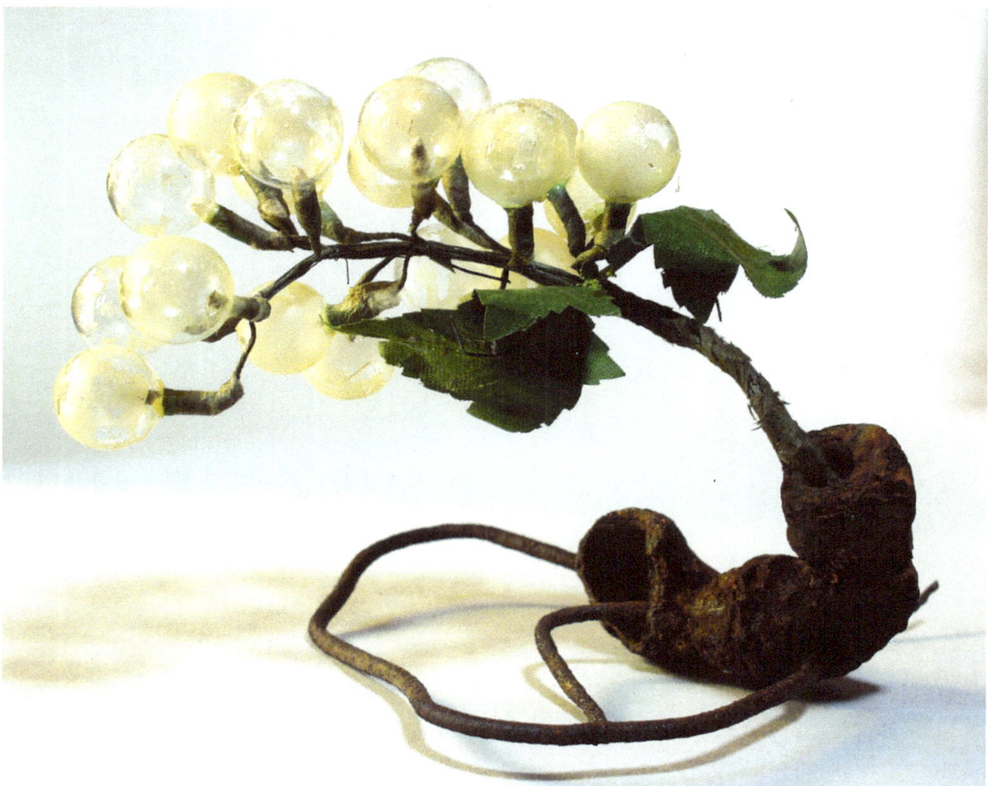

A cut piece of bubble plant, native to the Zymoglyphic region, in a simple arrangement

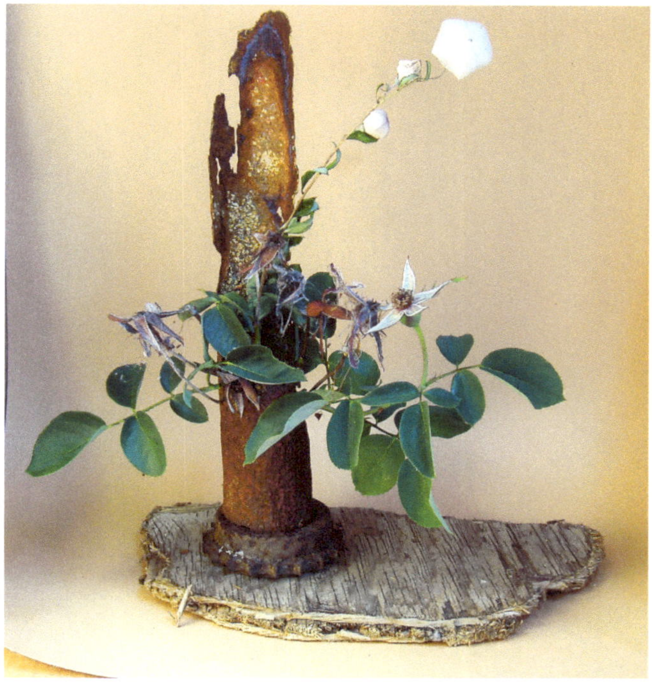

An arrangement of flowers and rust

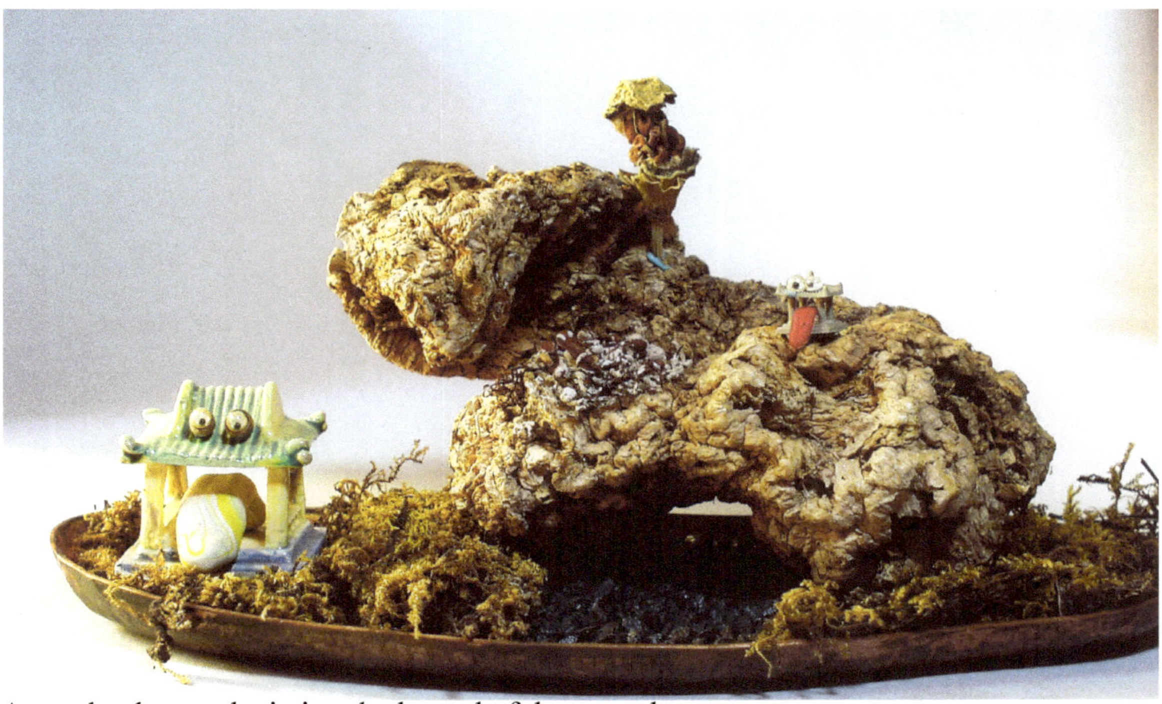

A tray landscape depicting the legend of the crazy houses

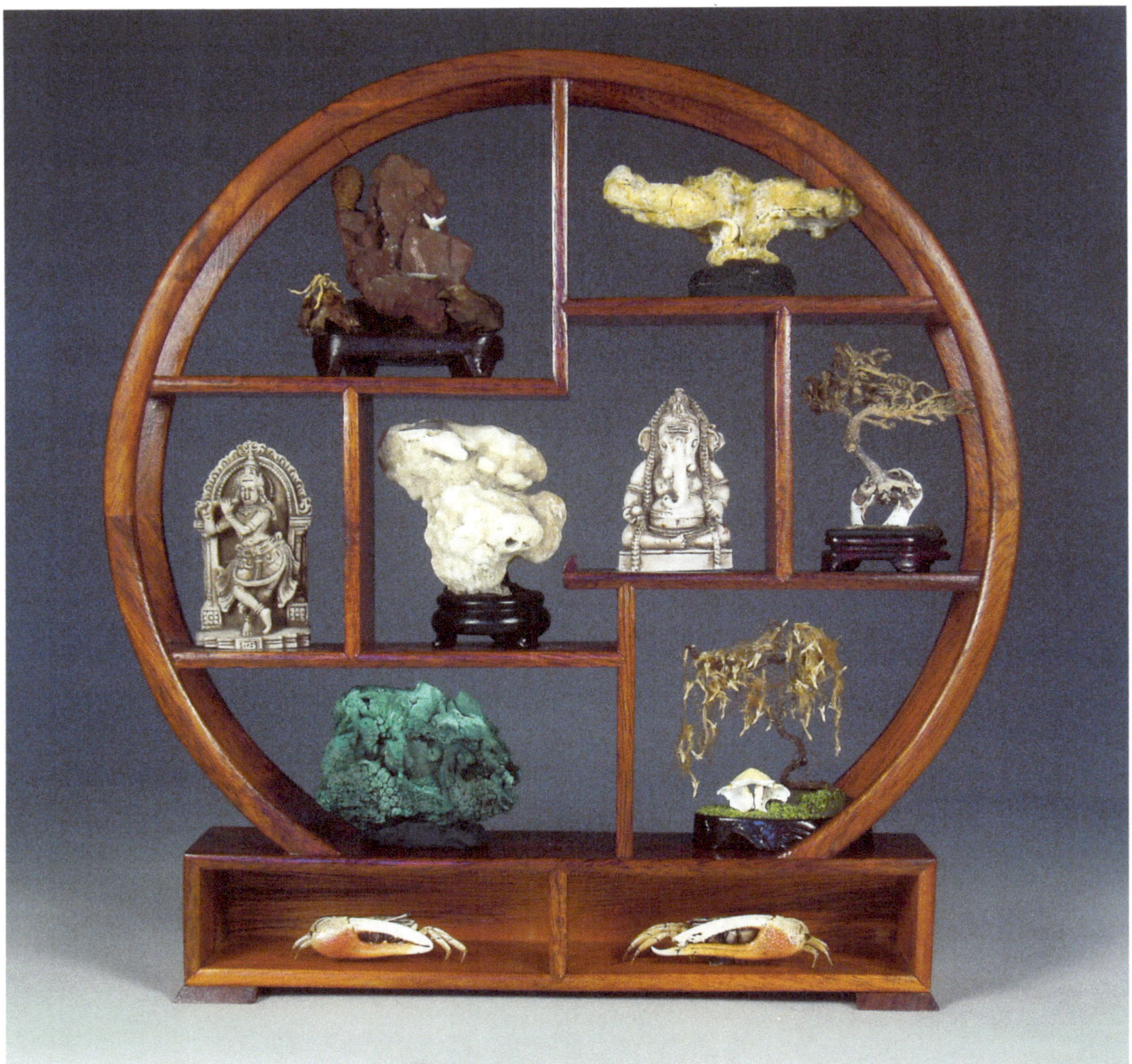

Small curio stand with miniature trees

MINIATURE TREES

During the Age of Wonder, elaborate dioramas were popular. In this era, a simplified form of diorama emerged, constructed around a single tree. These are not literal trees, but arrangements of organic material that capture the sweep, rough aesthetic, graceful curves and spirit of a tree.

The **curved-trunk style** depicts a venerable, stately tree under which philosophers may gather, or a hermit seek refuge. The **clinging-to-rock style** evokes a windswept tree hanging on to a precipitous cliff.

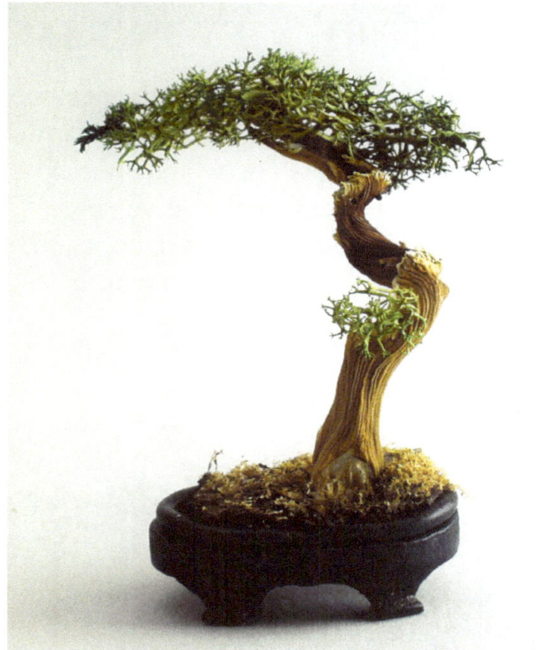

Curved-trunk style

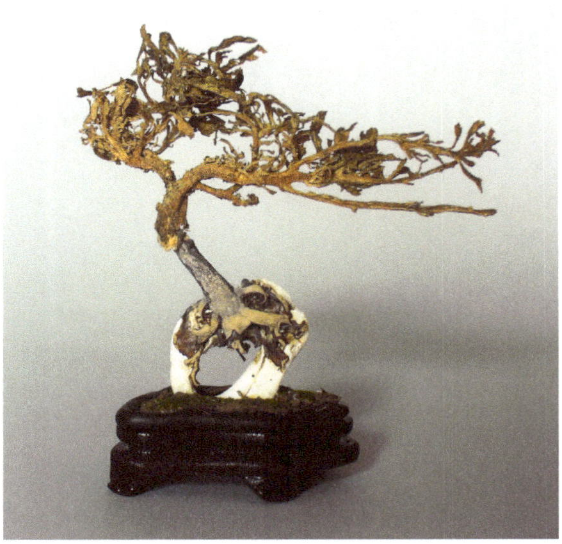

Clinging-to-rock style

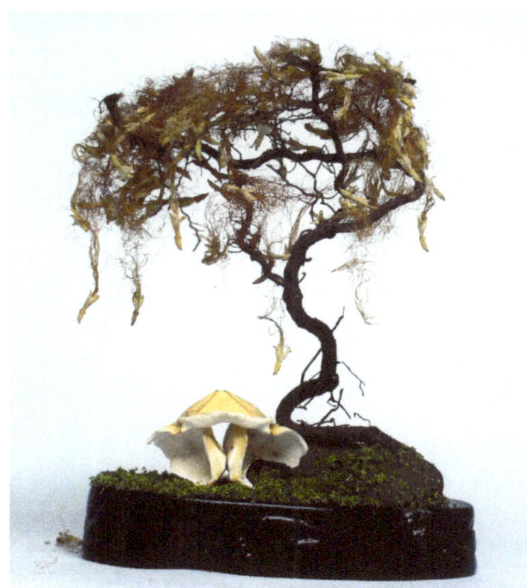

Curved-trunk style with hermit shelter

Miniature viewing stones

During the Era of Oriental Influence, the need to identify and classify rocks, or collect them for rarity or provenance, gave way to valuing stones simply on their evident aesthetic qualities. A stone would simply be placed on a stand for contemplation. The stone was often given an evocative name. The object did not even need to be a stone; it could be a piece of sea-worn shell, coral, or weathered wood. Objects with complex holes, indicating "worlds within worlds" were especially prized.

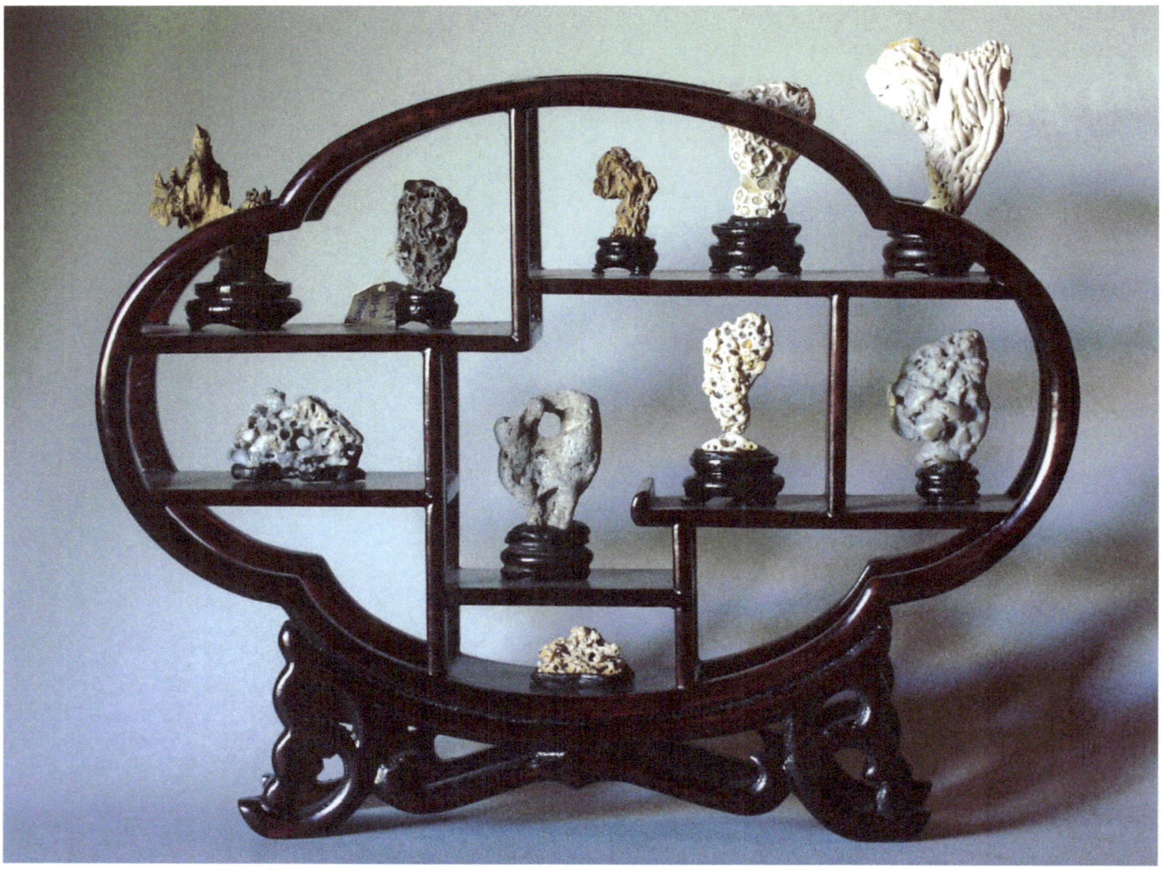

Miniature viewing stone display

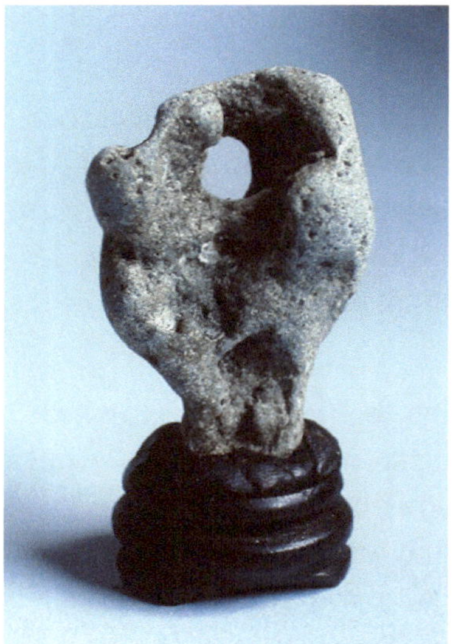

Window Stone

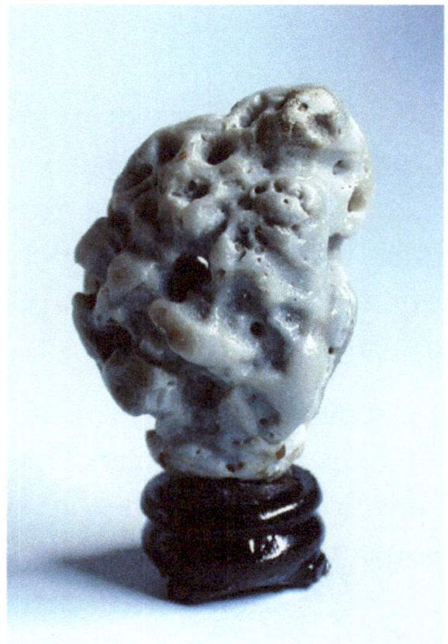

Storm Cloud

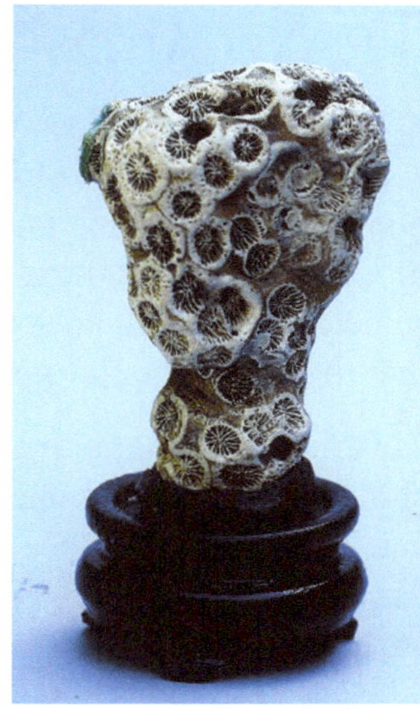

Stars-in-Stone

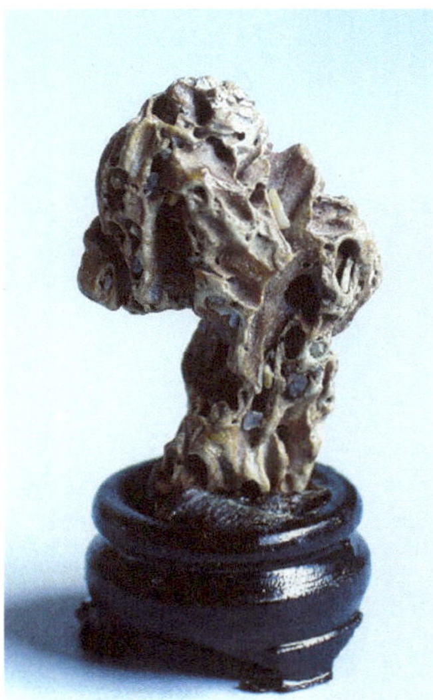

Shelter Stone

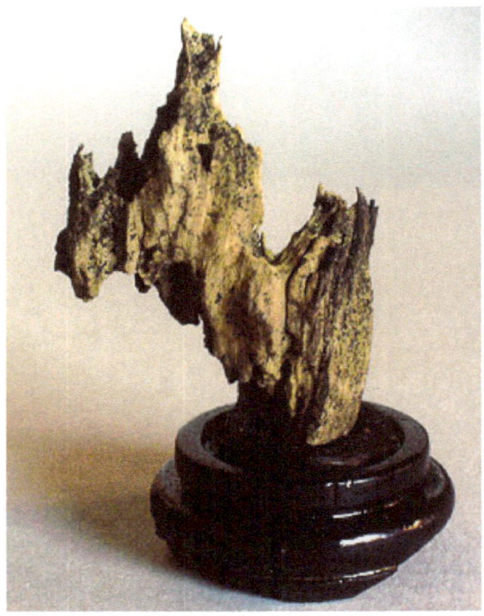

Jagged Mountain

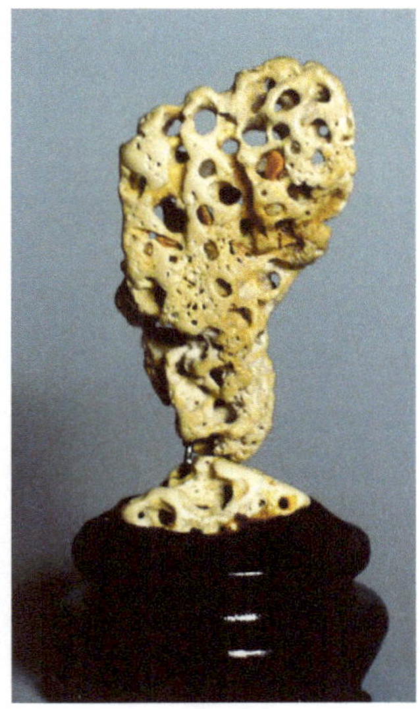

Net-for-Pebbles

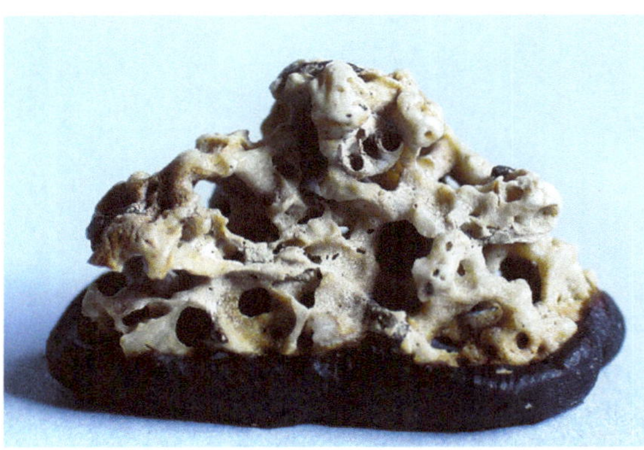

Caves-in-Mountains

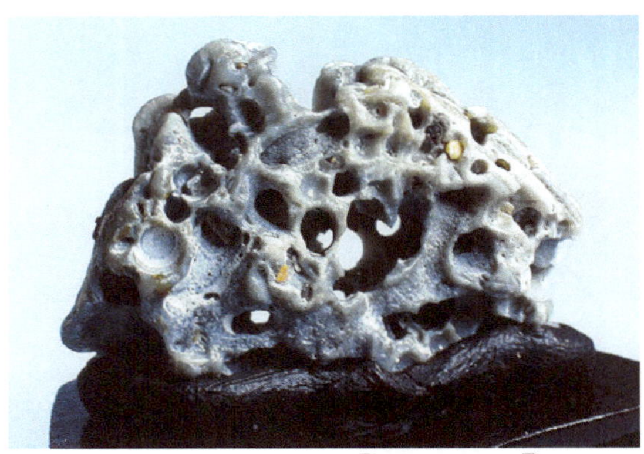

Dangerous Passage

TRAY LANDSCAPES

Sand tray landscapes were one of the earliest forms of self-expression to be developed during the Era of Oriental Influence. The process begins with a collection at hand of a number of interesting and evocative objects. Next, a frame is selected, usually in the form of an oddly-shaped tray, and filled with sand. The objects to be put into the landscape are selected and arranged seemingly at random, but actually in response to unconscious urges that may be difficult to put into words.

This method is popular in that it requires no technical skills, just the willingness to work spontaneously. The sand makes it easy to change arrangements, so one's conscious mind can just sit back and see what develops. A piece is considered finished when the objects have not been rearranged for some period of time. The piece may or may not inspire a story to accompany it.

The creation of a sand tray landscape is a meditative process that enables the artist to arrange interesting objects in a spontaneous way that can bring to life innermost worlds.

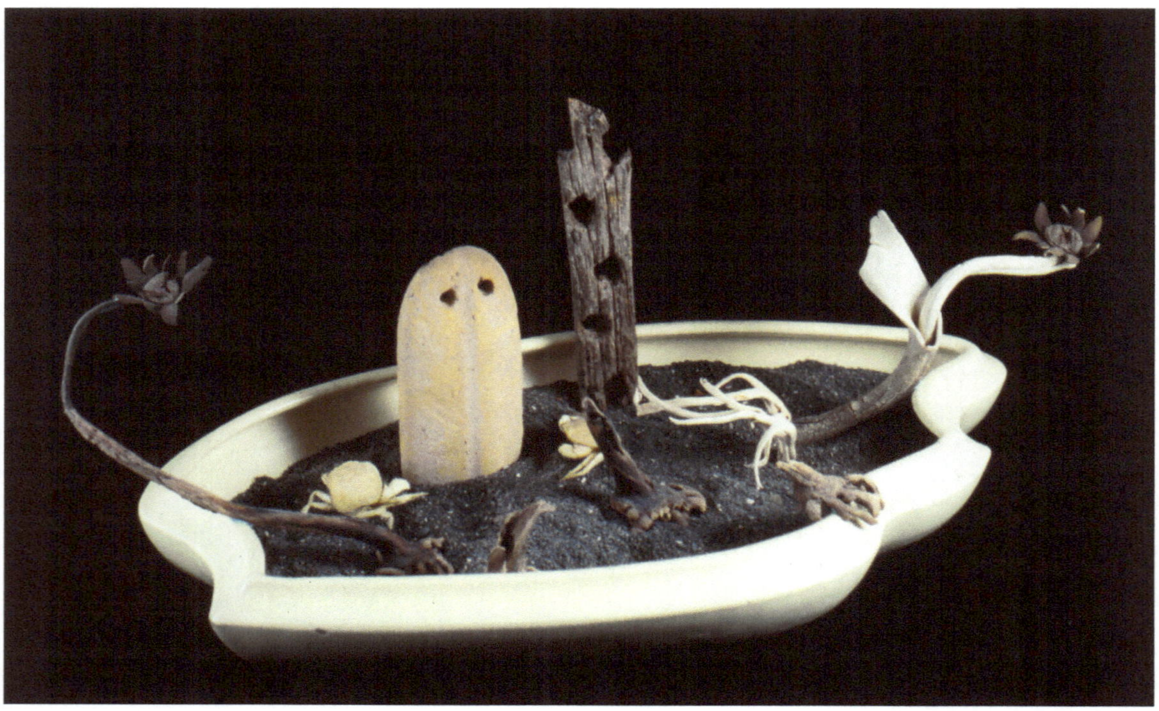

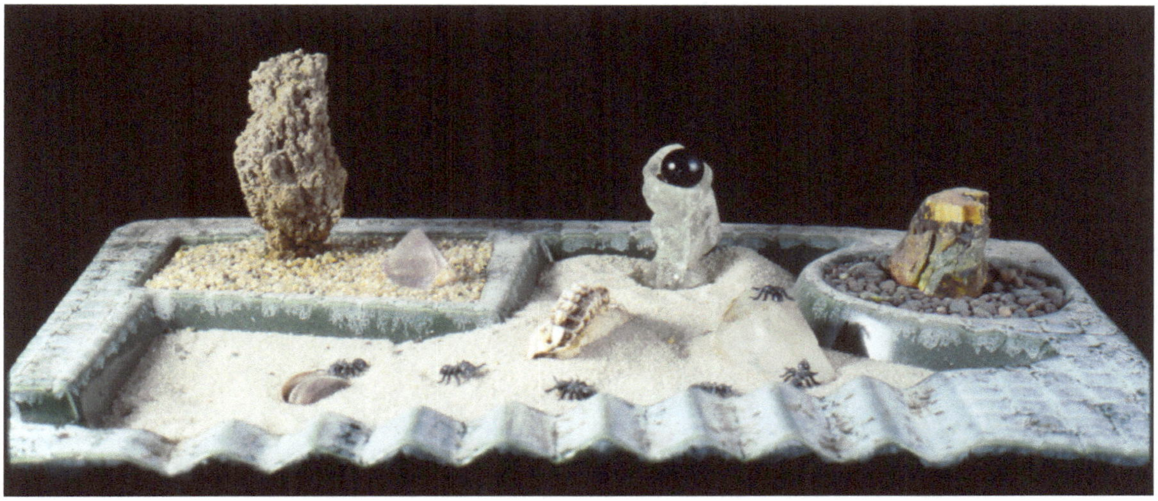

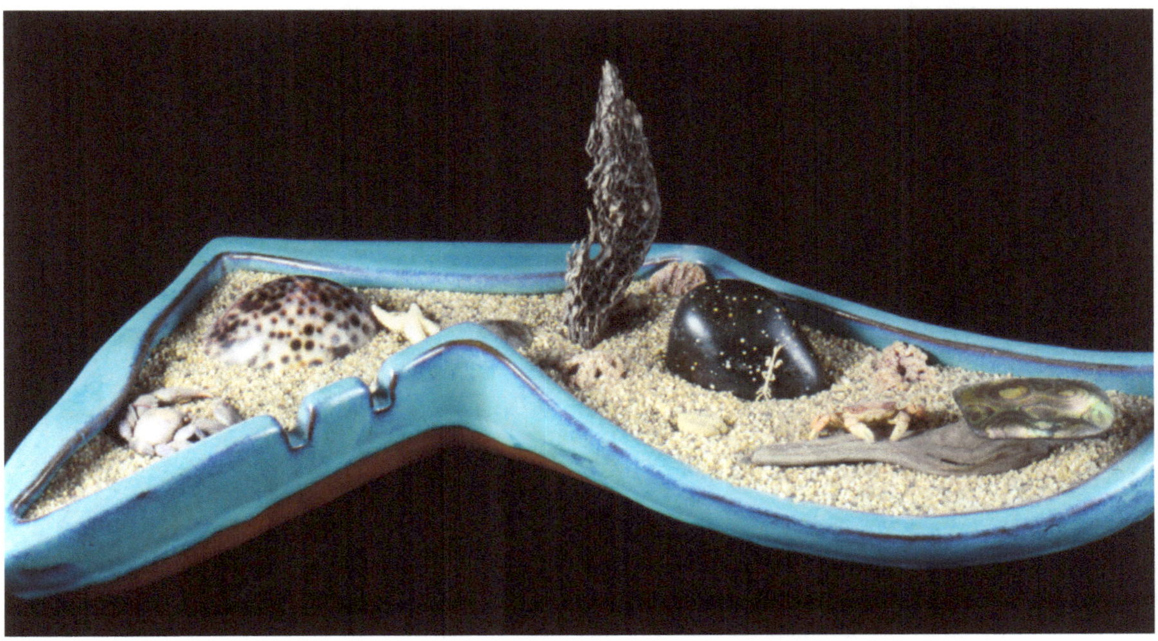

The Garden of the Four Monks

The museum's front garden is dedicated to the legend of the four Zymoglyphic monks, a tale from the Era of Oriental Influence. An ancient tradition holds that enlightenment can be sought in the study of nature and natural forces, especially decay and oxidation. According to the tale, each of four monks set out to seek enlightenment, but, as is so often the case, different schools of thought prevailed.

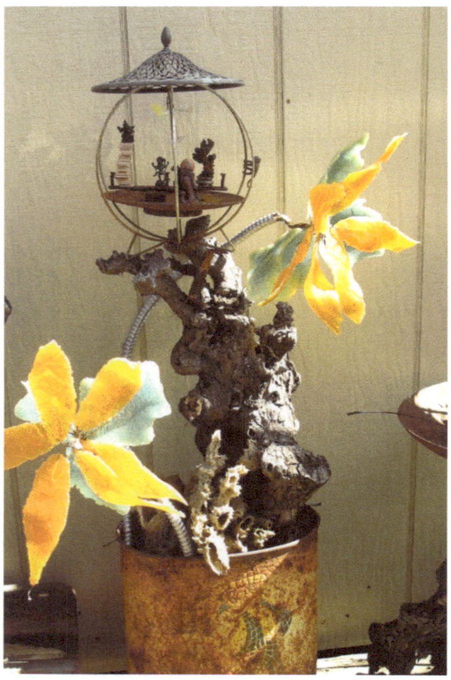

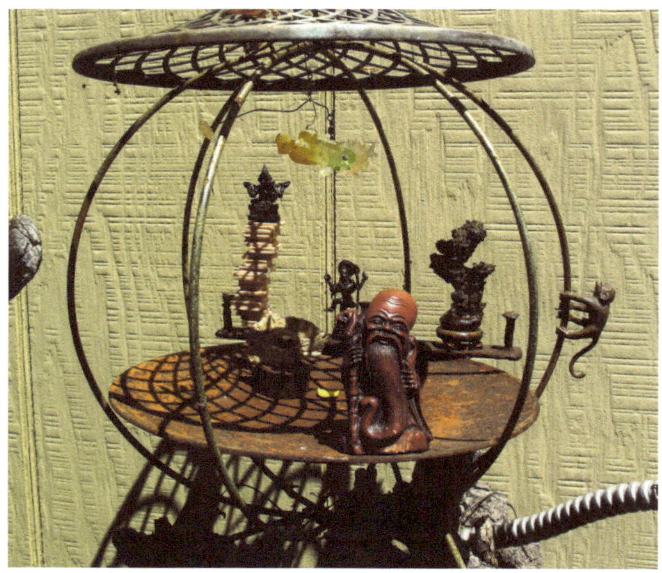

The **Scholar Monk** maintains a well-stocked library, surrounding himself with the writings of the great minds and kindred souls of the ages. He studies and reflects on them, compiles, analyzes, and synthesizes his research. He collects art and significant objects for inspiration (a favorite viewing stone, a copper nodule, is currently on display). He has staked out a breezy top-floor aerie in one of the garden plants, and installed a mobile that makes the wind visible. A little monkey comes to visit sometimes to remind him to get his nose out of his books and reconnect with nature.

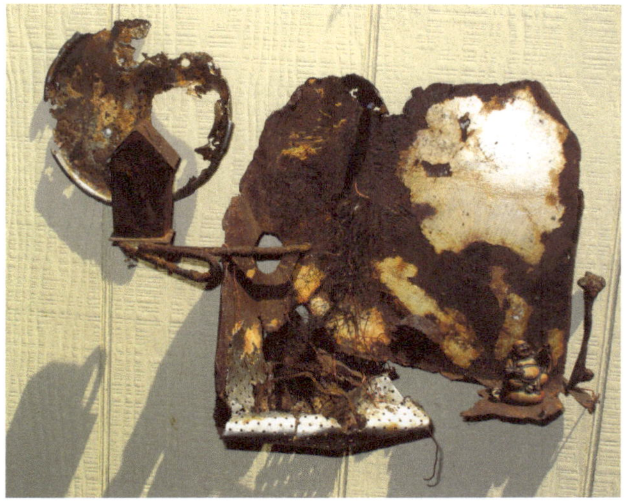

The **Rust Monk** is less interested than the Scholar Monk in what other people have said and done. He wants to find his own unique way, unencumbered by the past, listening to an inner voice. He seeks enlightenment from his creative expression, to express things that cannot be said in words. He has collected a number of rusty objects and assembled them to create a complex living environment. His creation floats above the garden, not rooted in any part of it.

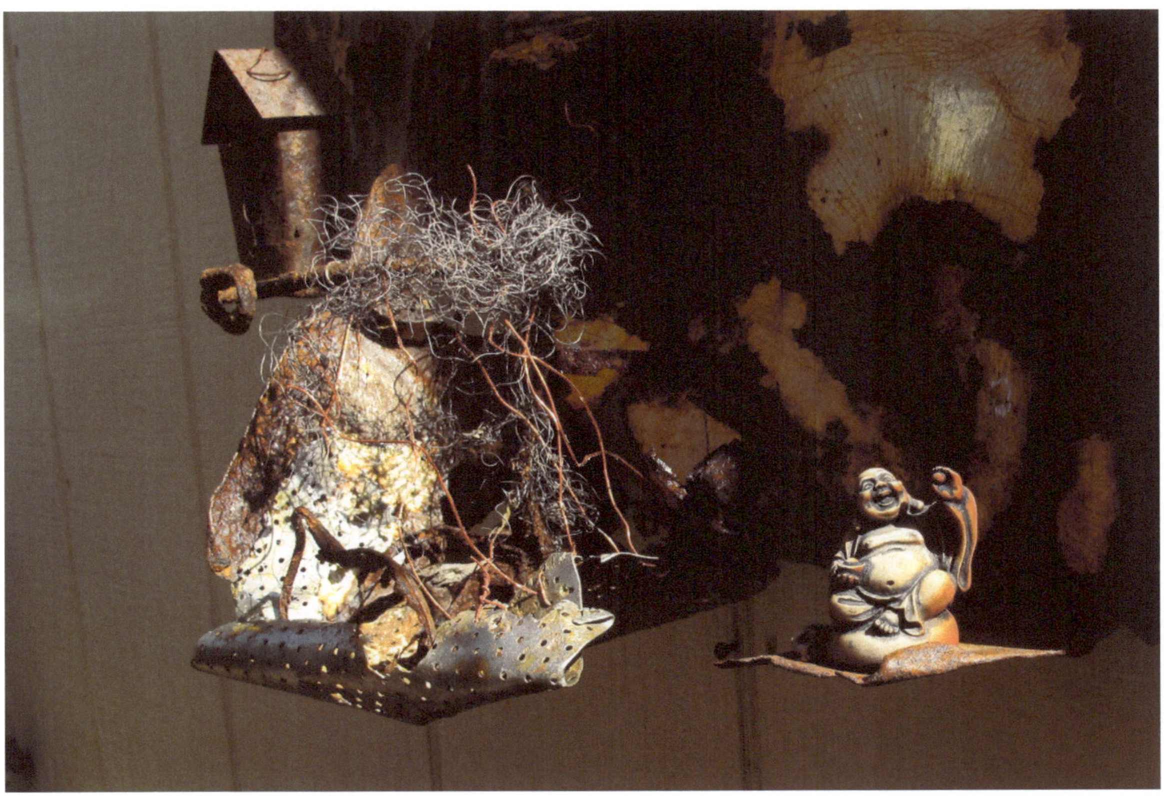

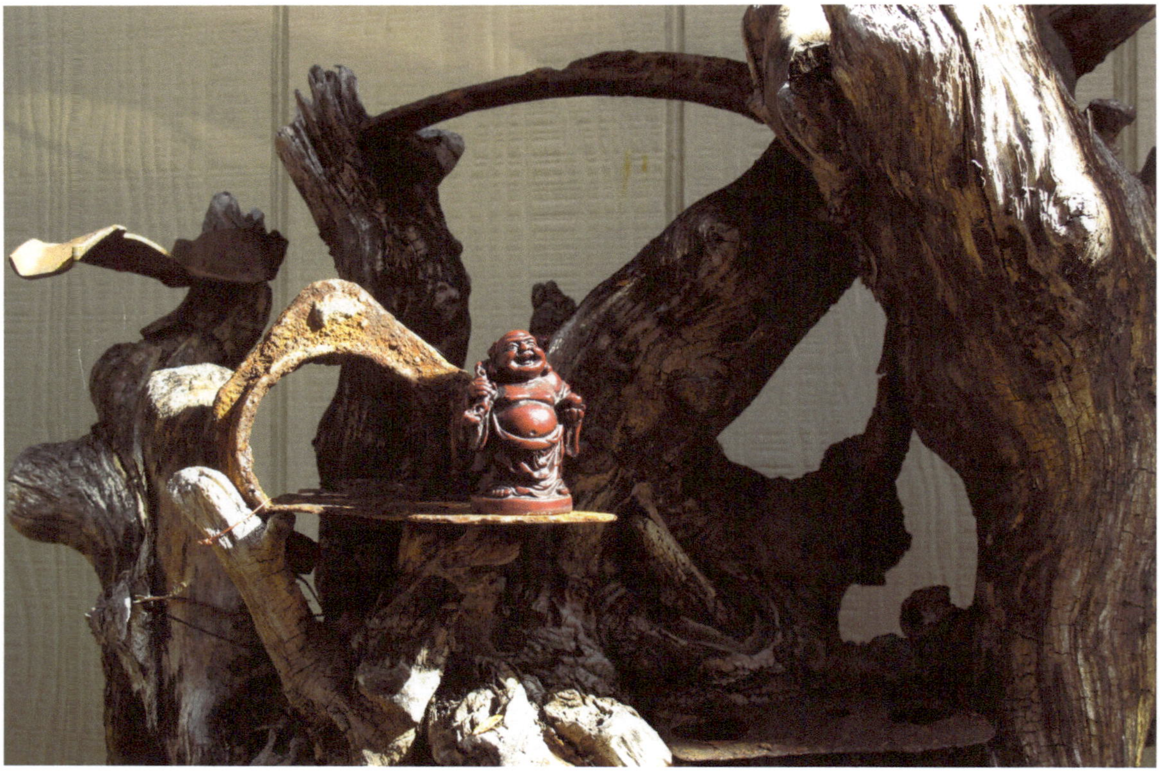

The **Wandering Monk** has decided to rid himself of the distractions of possessions, collections, books, and art, no matter how pure or ennobling they may be. He has kept only a bag full of necessities and set off to wander in the wilderness, savoring the freedom of the adventure, to see what nature and rust can teach him. In the twists and turns of the thick branches of an ancient stumpy tree, he has found a rusty viewpoint from which to view the passing scene and get some perspective on the world.

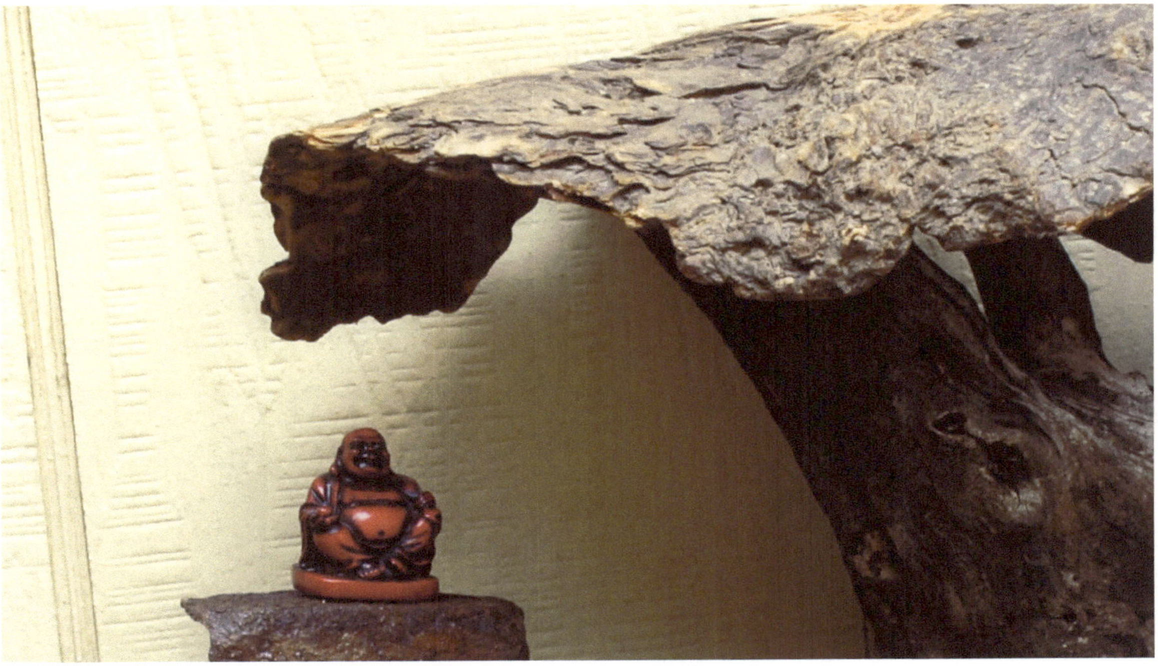

The **Shelter Monk** is a hermit. Like the Wandering Monk, he has cast away his possessions, but he is content with a simple place to sit in quiet, inward contemplation, sheltered from the buffeting environment. He believes that each part of the universe contains the whole and one need only stay in one place and fully experience it to attain the sought-after enlightenment. It is not necessary to go from one place to another. He has found his spot on a flap of rust, under a wide natural shelter, and he plans to stay there.

Each monk personifies a different philosophy. The Rust Monk transforms what he finds into art, making decay into something valuable, hoping that the art will resonate with others and live on as part of a chain of inspiration. Similarly, the Scholar Monk seeks to leave as his legacy knowledge gathered and arranged, new connections made in the web of knowledge, collecting objects and arranging them. The Wandering Monk hopes to be remembered in tales of picaresque adventure, descriptions of the world as he found and experienced it, in all its differences and similarities. The Shelter Monk cares for none of these, since, in the end, all will be rotted, and forgotten, decomposed into its original molecules, those molecules recycled into something else entirely, until the Sun expands to vaporize the Earth, and the very atoms themselves cease their motion.

As it turns out, there is in fact another monk, the **Fifth Monk**. Like the Shelter Monk, he prefers to stay in one place, hiding in his rusty cave, spending his time listening to cosmic drivel on his homemade antenna, allegedly not seeking enlightenment at all. He has become transfixed by the incessant babble of the infosphere, vapid entertainment, titillation, and interesting factoids. However, he does seem to be enjoying himself. He is often represented, as shown here, as having a number of small planets that revolve around him.

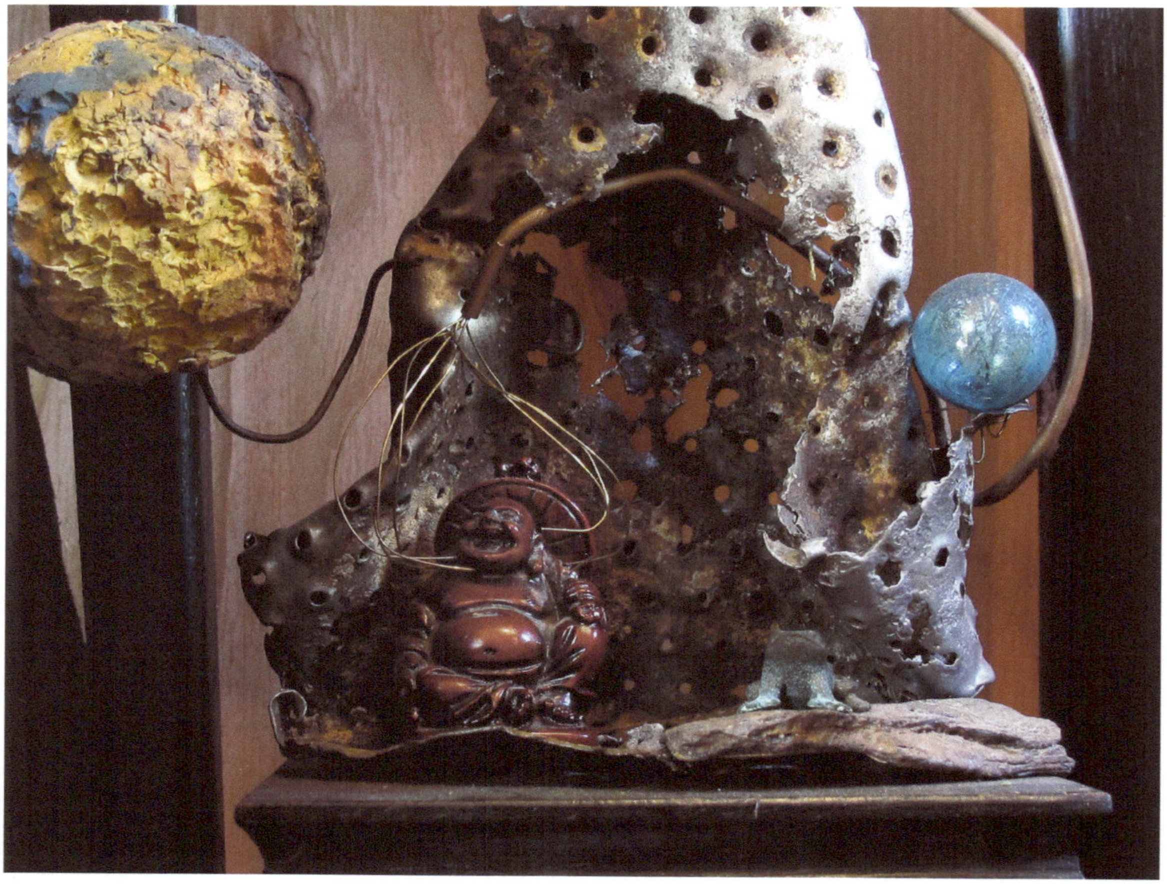

Fifth Monk - detail view

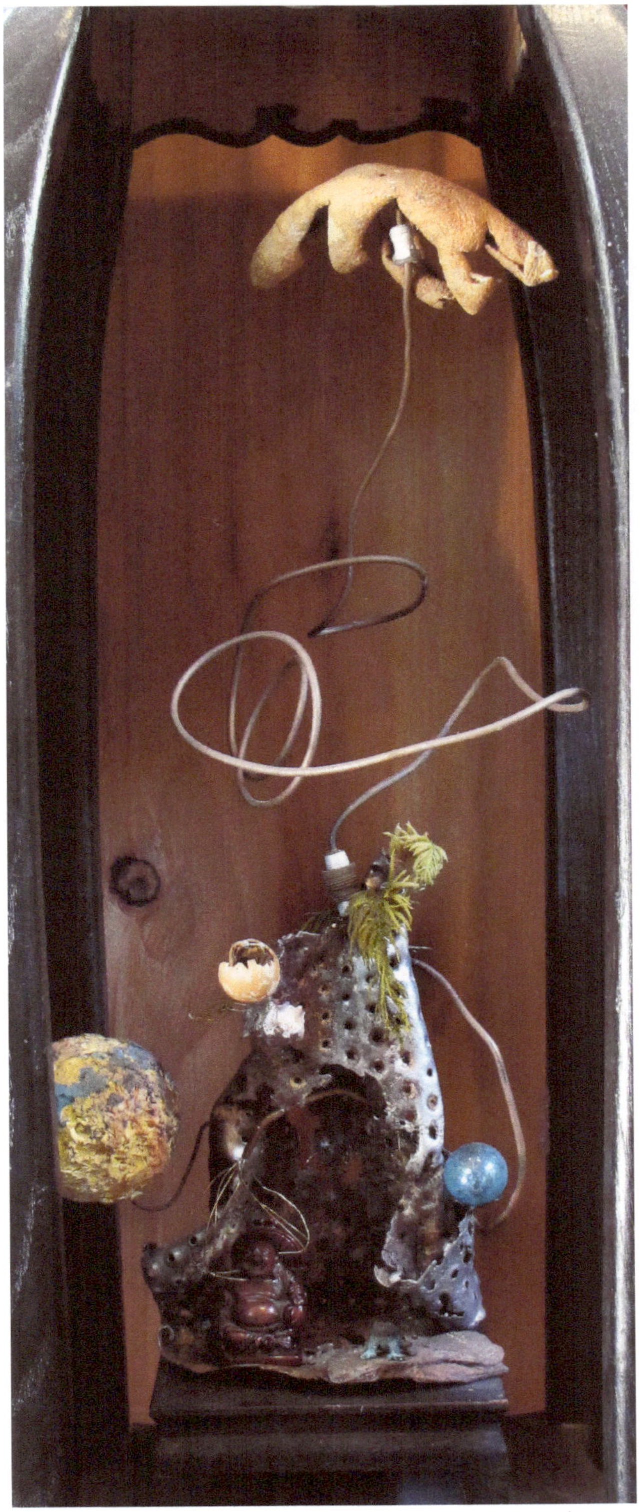

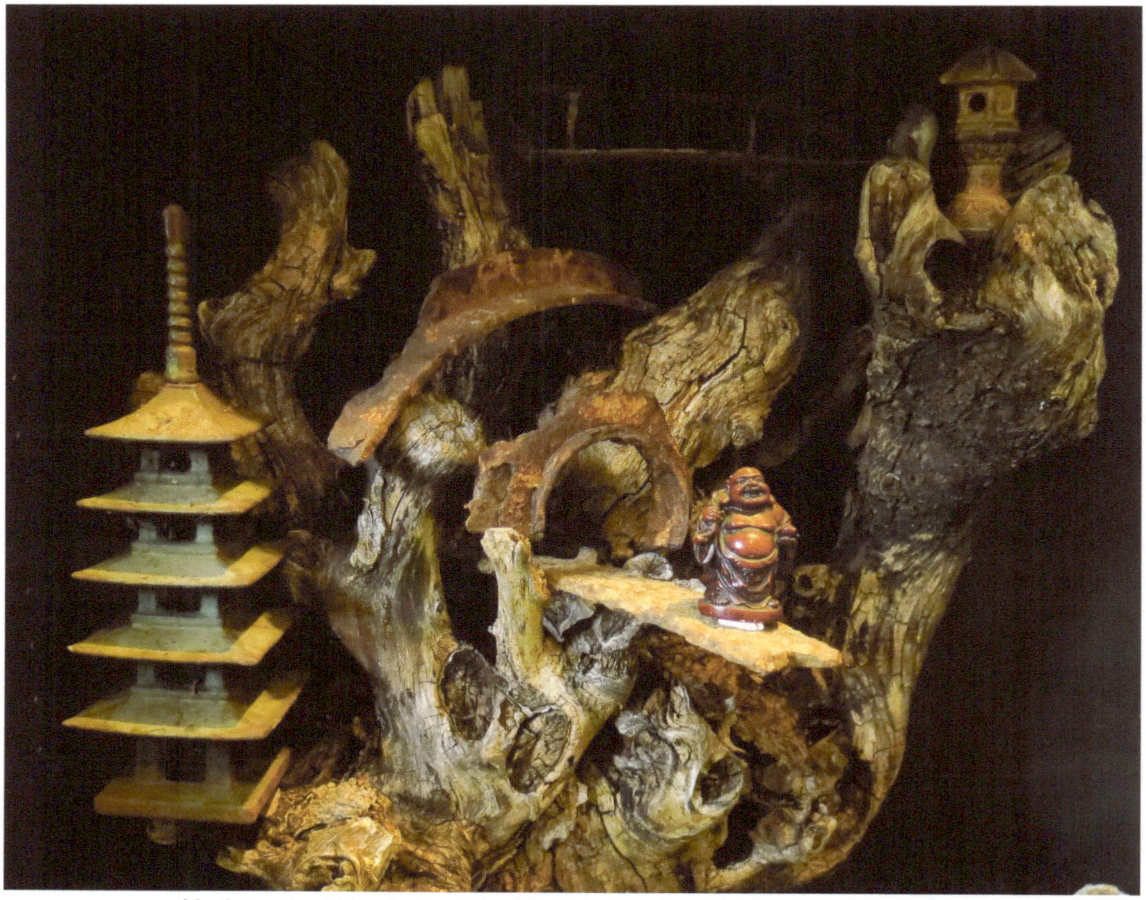

Update: the Wandering Monk builds his dream home after all and enjoys the view'

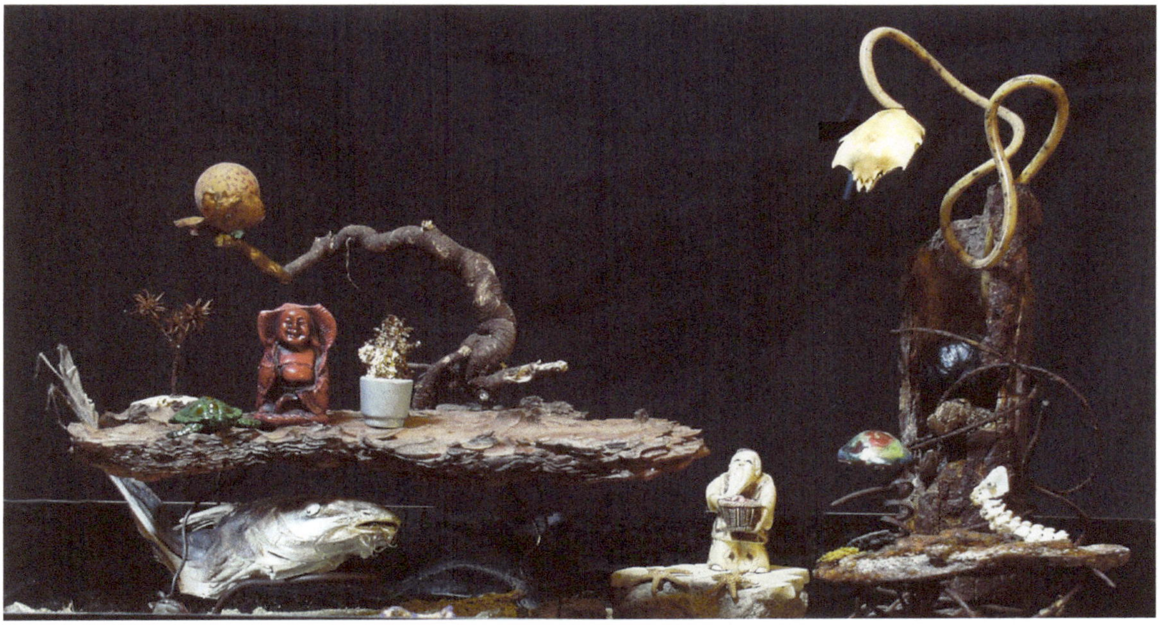

Desert Meditation

The desert monk presides over a realm that he has willed into being and is quite pleased with the results.

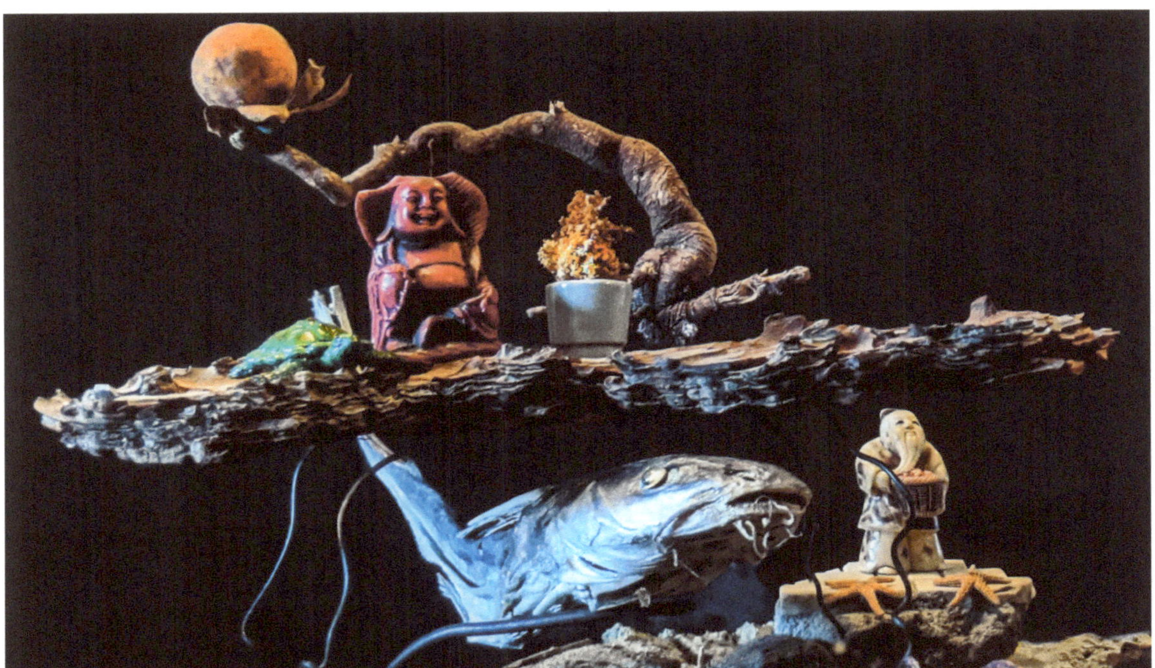

Desert Meditation - detail view

The Modern Age

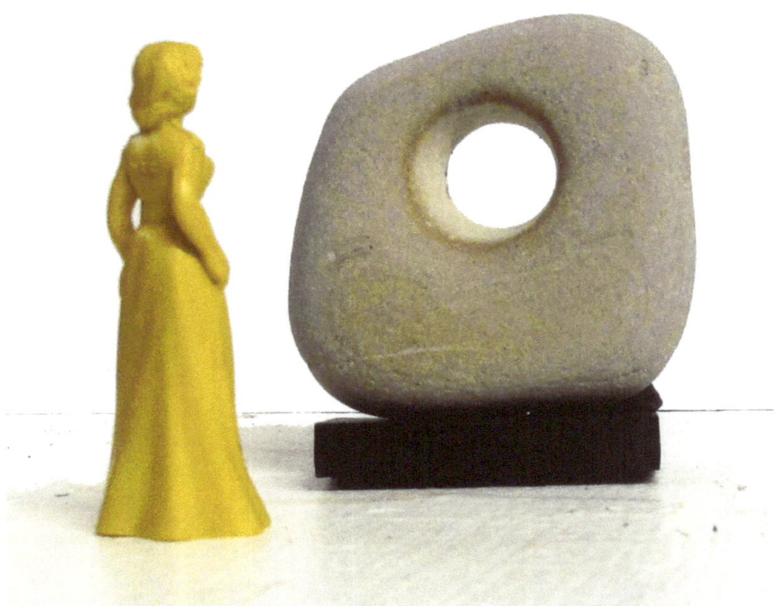

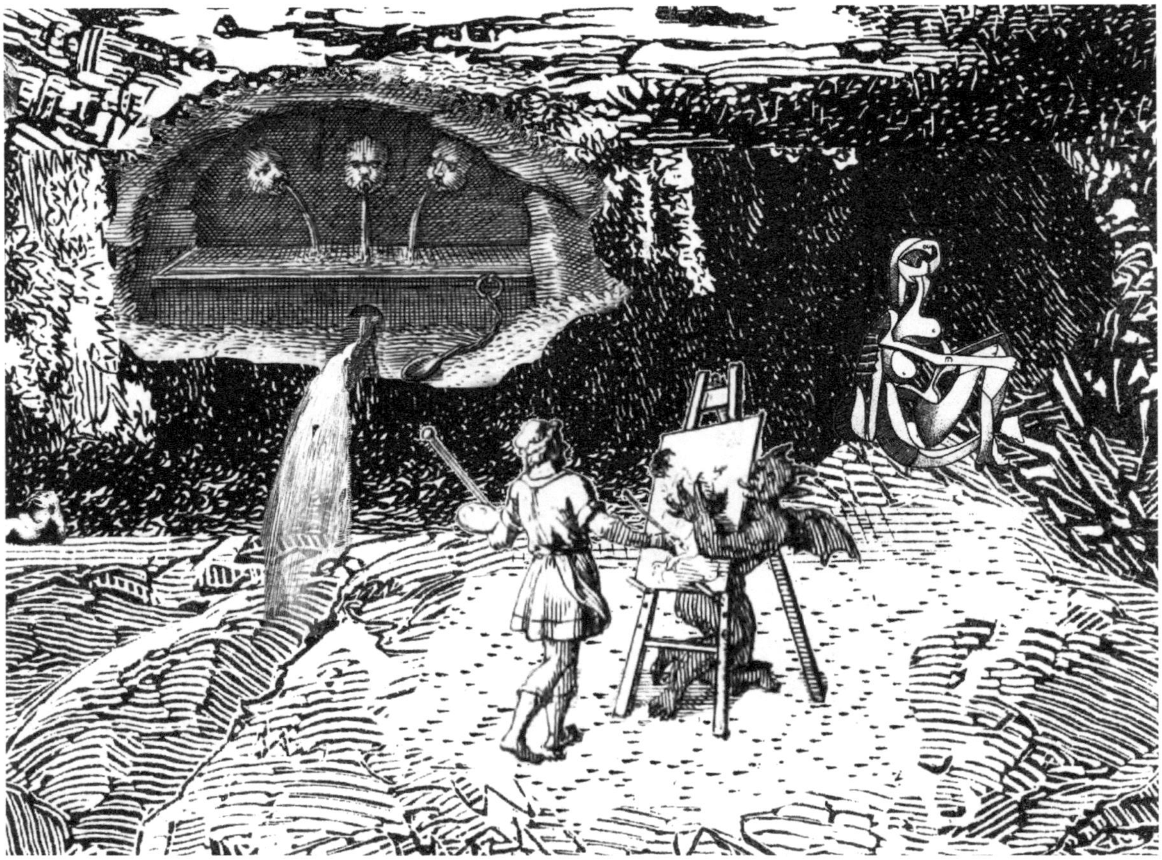

The Modern Age

Like any region in the world, the art and culture of the Zymoglyphic region has been heavily influenced stylistically and philosophically by the modernist trends of the 20th century. The development of "assemblage" as an art genre legitimized practices that date back centuries, and “surrealism” provided a theoretical basis for creating art intuitively and trying to find its meaning and purpose later.

In the Modern Age, Zymoglyphic art becomes more formalized and self-referential, more about art itself than serving a specific function in cultural life as it did in the Rust Age. We see a succession of art movements as each new trend pushes aside the old, establishing itself as the latest thing before becoming outdated itself. Each new style or medium, however, is inevitably a recasting of traditional forms. The curiosity cabinets and dioramas of the Age of Wonder reappear in modern form as shoebox art galleries. Readymades, Natural Modernism, and Ephemeral Abstraction all draw on the tradition of viewing stones, and the Biomorphic Abstractionists use the new material of acrylic paints to visualize the traditional notion of the primordial ooze.

Schools and styles

Readymades

One of the primal acts of modern art was to present castoff objects as ready-made art, appreciated for its aesthetic qualities rather than its former practical use . This act served to widen the realm of what could be considered "art." As art in general pivoted from representation of the world to abstract exploration of forms and textures, Zymoglyphic artists scoured the woods and beaches for small objects that resembled abstract sculptures, popularizing the term "Things That Look Like Art" or TTLLA. Once such objects were found and selected, they were carefully positioned and mounted in the manner of the miniature viewing stones that were so popular during the Era of Oriental Influence. In these two examples, a similar composition is found in piece of driftwood and a discarded bit of electrical wiring.

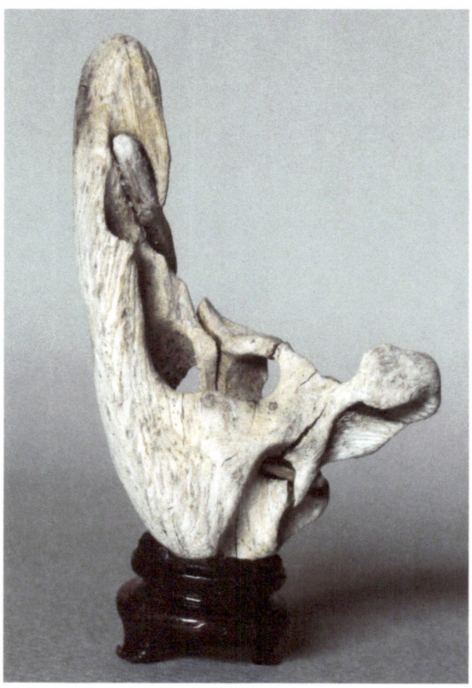

Driftwood viewing "stone"

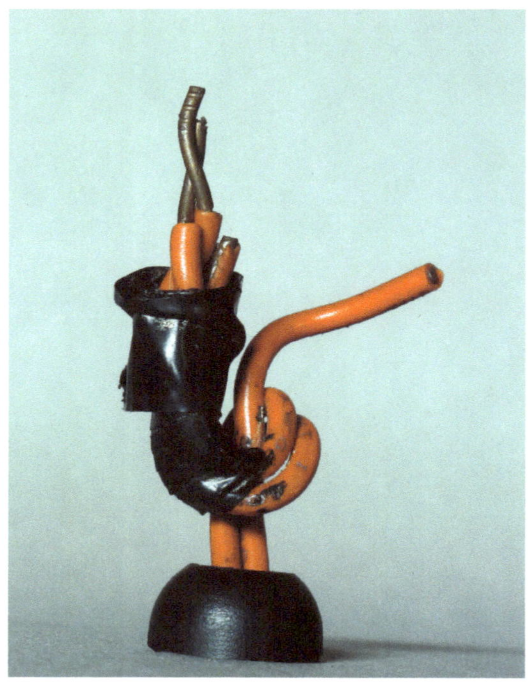

Untitled (Wire)

Natural Modernism

The sculptures shown here are a collaboration among a boring clam, the sea, and a human eye and hand to select and arrange the results. The clam in question is known as a piddock. It is more torpedo-shaped than clam-shaped and has the ability to rasp its way into rock using the ridges on its shell and a rotating motion. It uses the holes it creates for protection. When the rock is broken up by erosion (often aided by the weakening of the rock by the clam holes themselves), the resulting fragments are worn smooth by wave action and cast up on the shore.

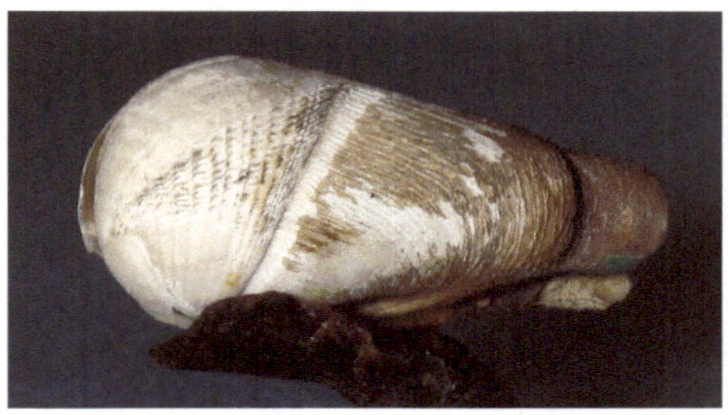

Piddock clam

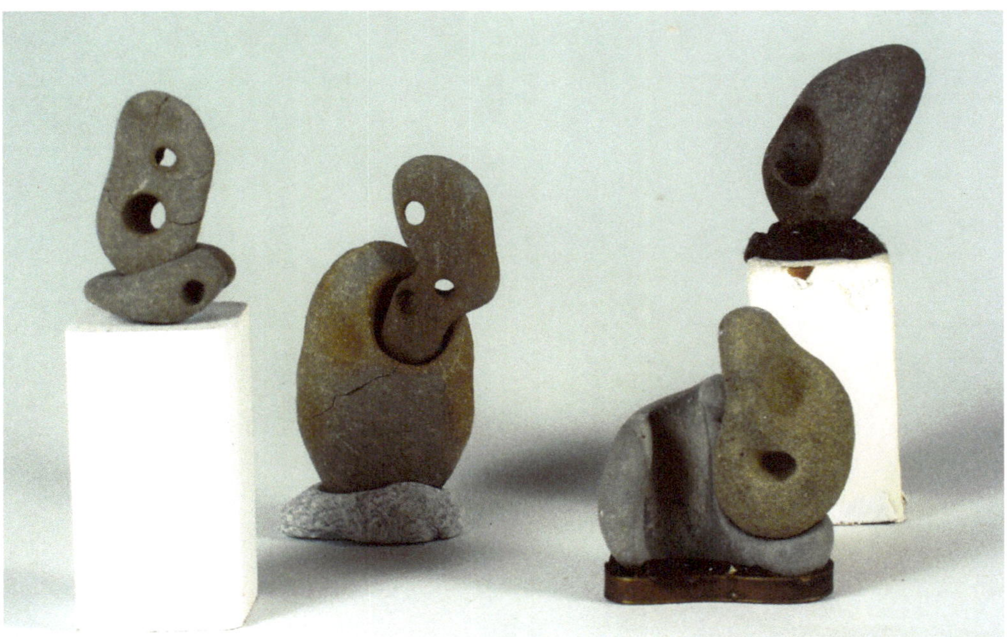

Adherents of Natural Modernism scoured the shorelines for this particular type of Readymade. It resembles a cartoonish stereotype of modern sculpture—a blobby shape with holes in it, usually mounted on a blocky white plinth. Shown below is the popular Natural Modernism exhibit in the Zymoglyphic Art of the Modern Age gallery.

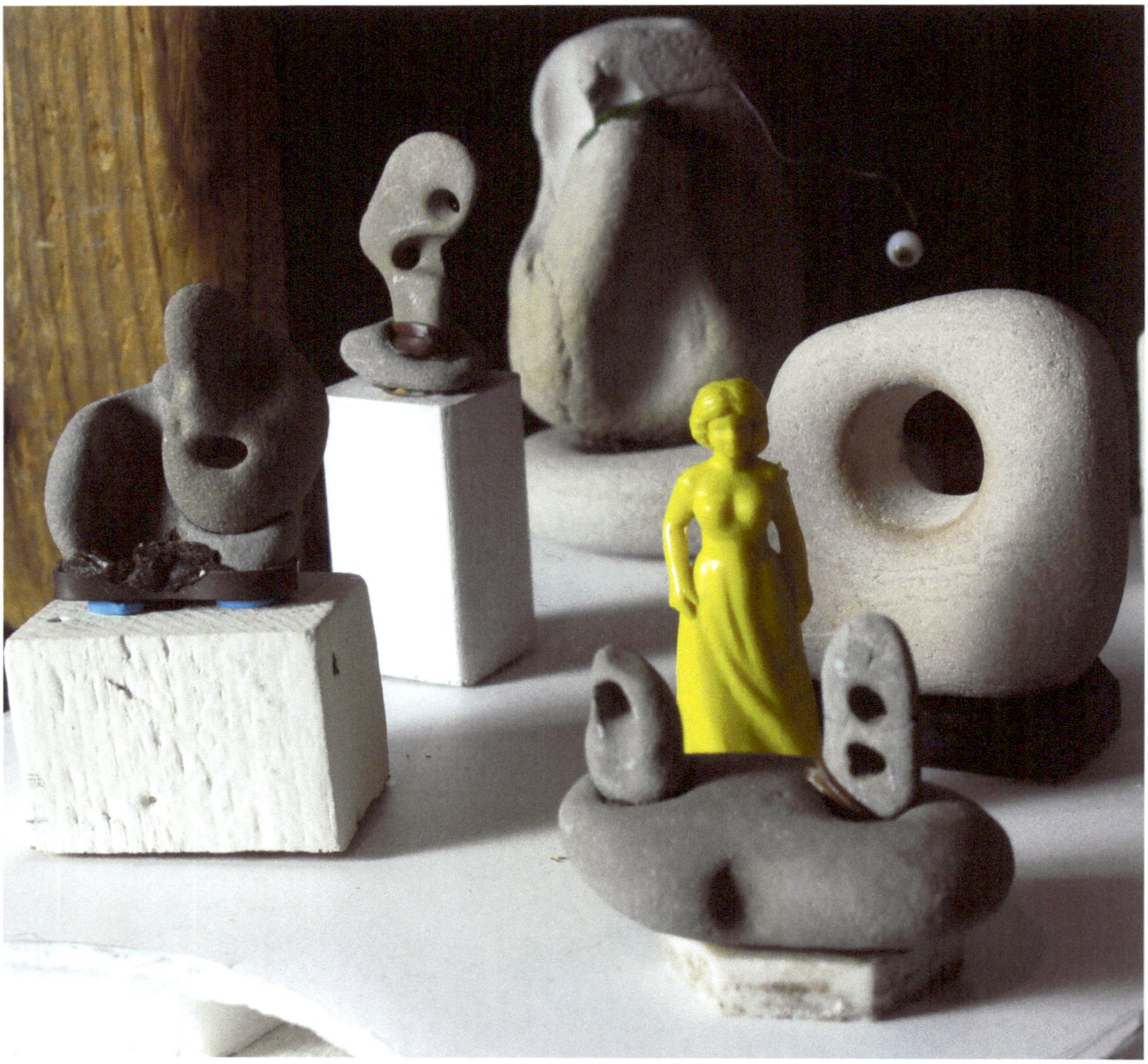

School of Ephemeral Abstraction

In contrast to the solidity of Natural Modernism, this popular school created airy "cloud sculptures" based on natural windblown assemblages of string, hair, feathers, bits of leaves and other detritus. They are found, picked up, and mounted with wire on bases as ethereal counterpart of viewing stones. The messy, weathered, delicate materials are reminiscent of those used in Rust Age artifacts.

This school split into two factions. The Pure Way group believed that only naturally occurring groupings may be used. As with viewing stones, human intervention was limited to selection and positioning, although a certain amount of "fluffing" was allowed. The Neo-Constructionists, on the other hand, took inspiration from nature, but assembled the sculpture from various artificial materials, such as wool, wire, and selected detritus to create a result that is in the spirit of the original found sculptures, but which would not actually be found in nature.

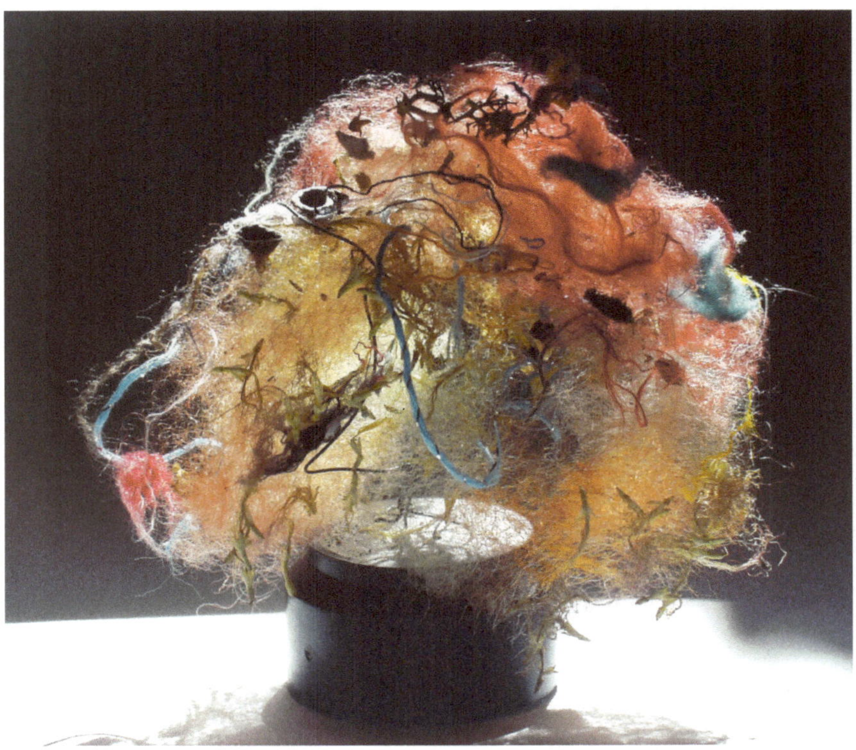

Cosmic Ruminance (dyed wool, debris)

Pure Way

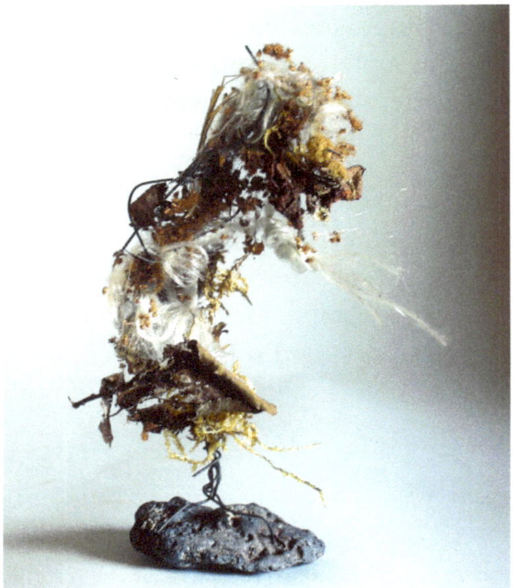

Untitled #1

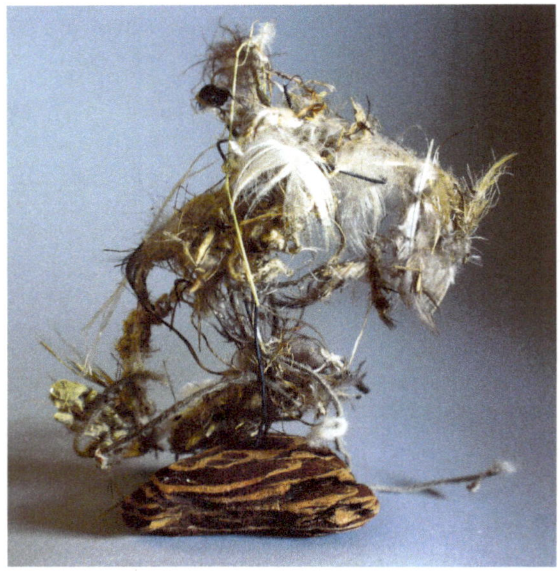

Untitled #2

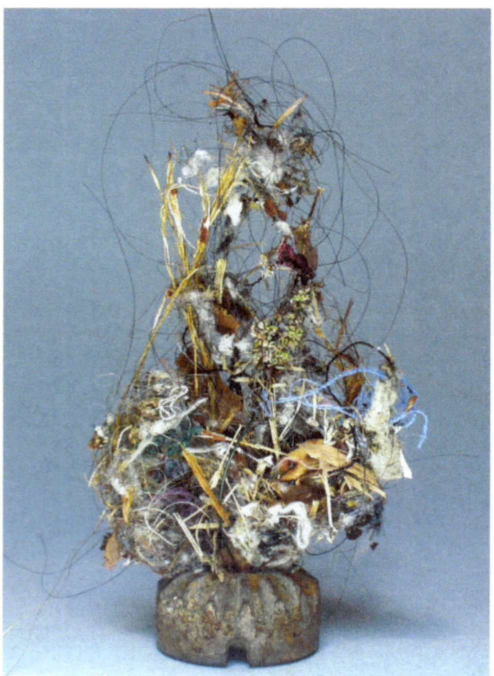

Untitled #3

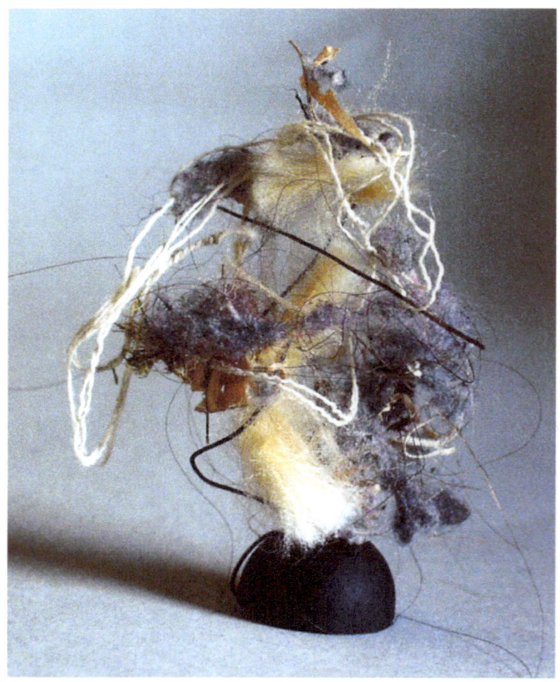

Untitled #4

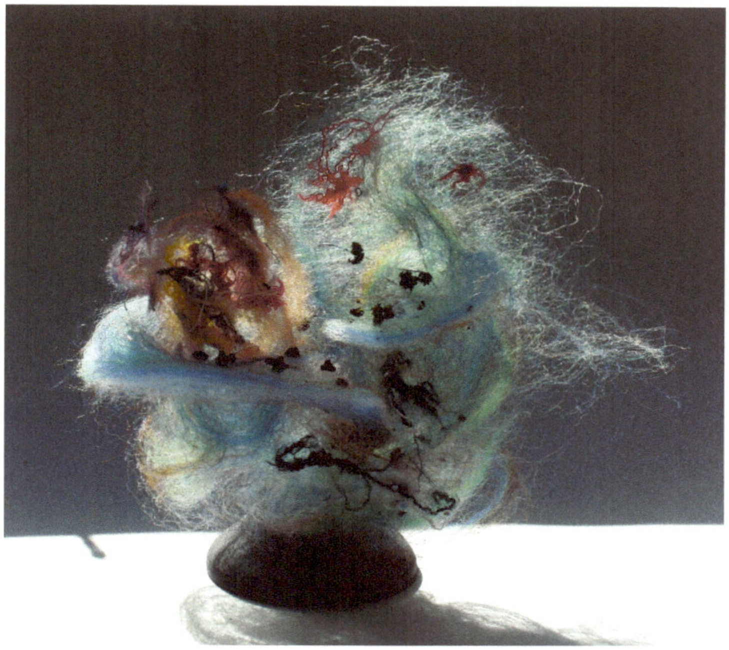

Vortex (dyed wool, detritus)

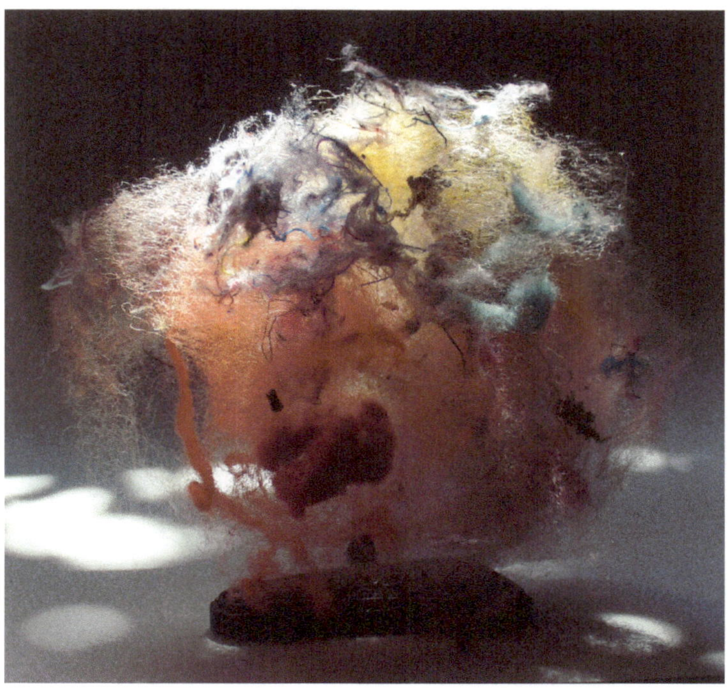

Primordial Cloud (dyed wool, dryer lint, assorted debris)

SCHOOL OF BIOMORPHIC ABSTRACTION

Biomorphic Abstractionists rejected the found object approach in favor of spontaneous application of color and form on a blank surface. They worked with minimal planning and relied on chance and natural processes such as pigment deposition to determine the content of a painting.

Acrylic painting combines modern materials with ancient themes. It is fed at its roots by the traditional collaboration with nature, in this case physical rather than biological. No brushes are used; pigments are mixed with water, spread on a board, and allowed to deposit while the board is gently rocked. Chance diffusion and particle deposition determine the detail of the pattern through the dispersal of the pigment. The resulting patterns are reminiscent of the natural dendrites found in old picture stones of the Rust Age.

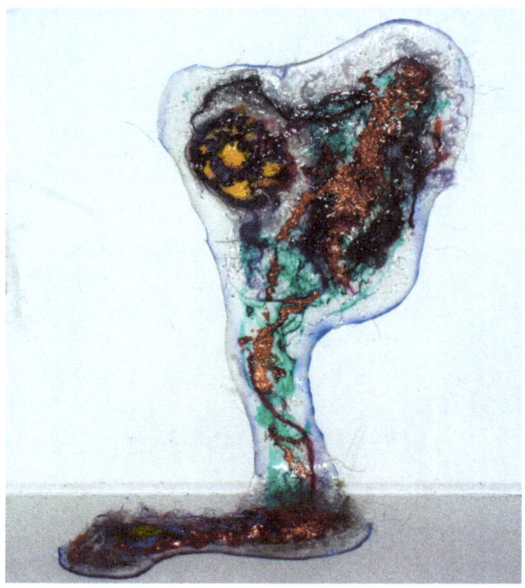

Advocates of the amoeboid style_eliminated the support medium altogether, seeking to capture the essence of the primordial ooze in the modern medium of pure plastic. Other artists of the school created miniatures; their work is featured in a special shoebox gallery (p. 186).

The following pages are from the series "Up from the Primordial Ooze," depicting an evolutionary cycle, starting from a swirling mass of waves and metallic blobs, proceeding through various alchemical transformations, to something closely resembling a landscape.

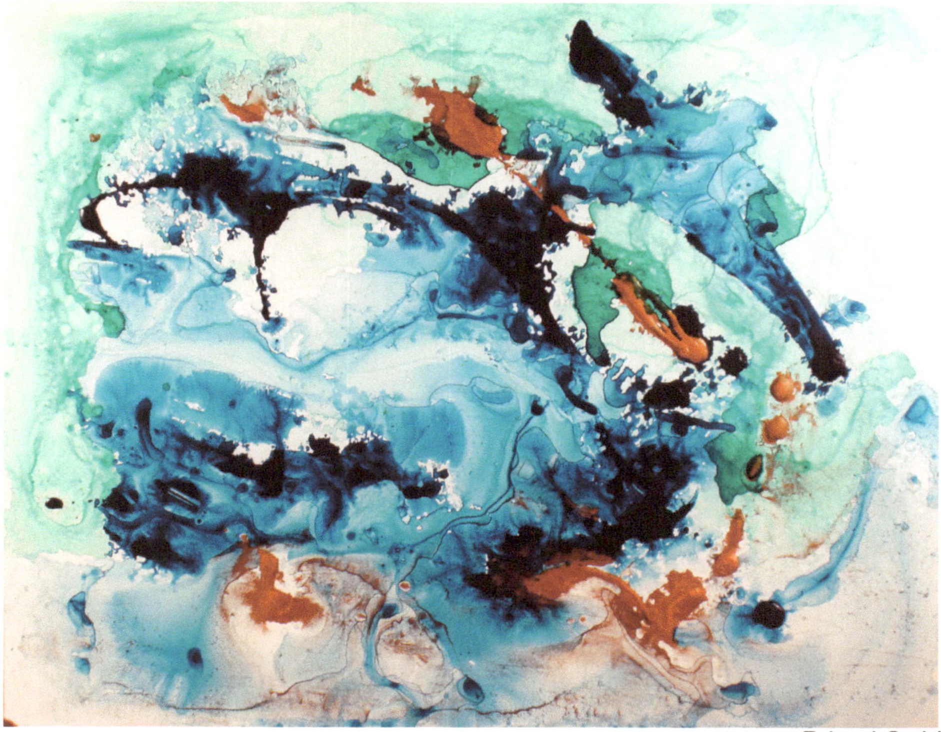

Primal Swirl

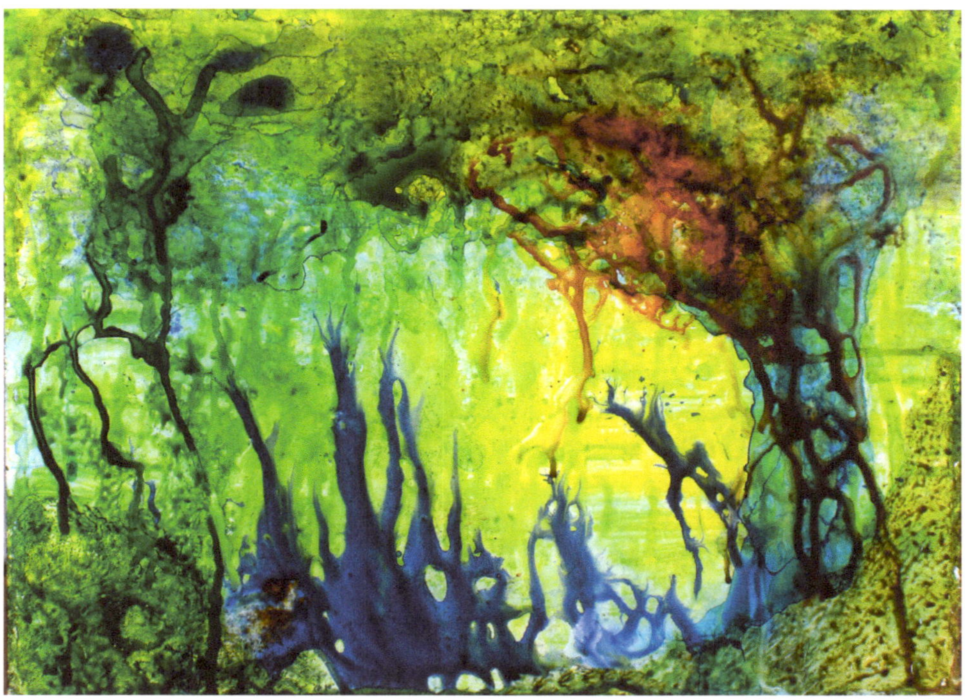

Undersea Growth

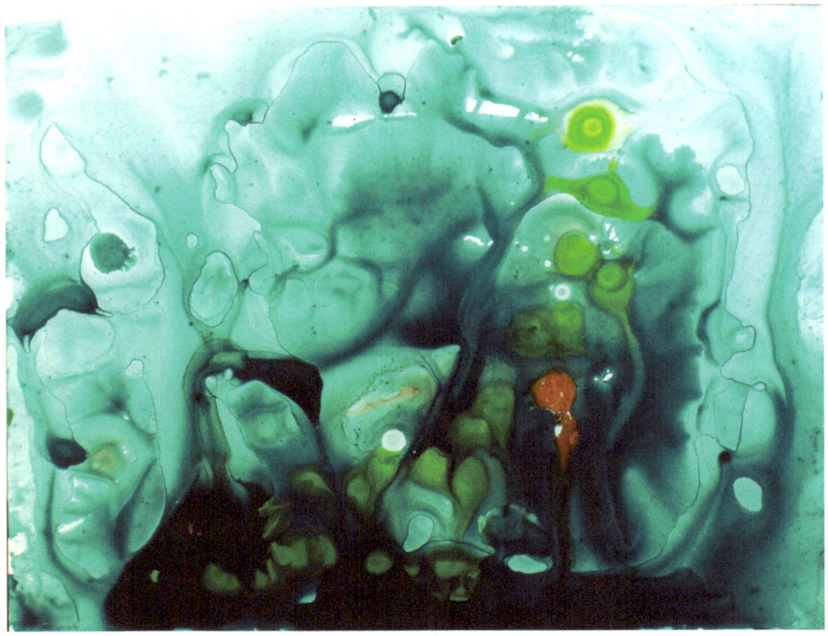

Creative Fermentation

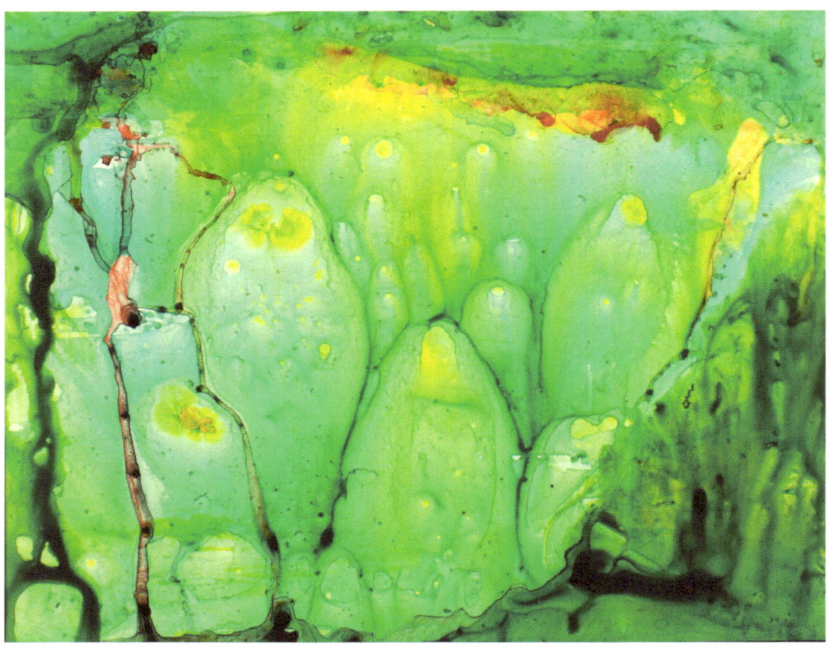

Lights in the Sea

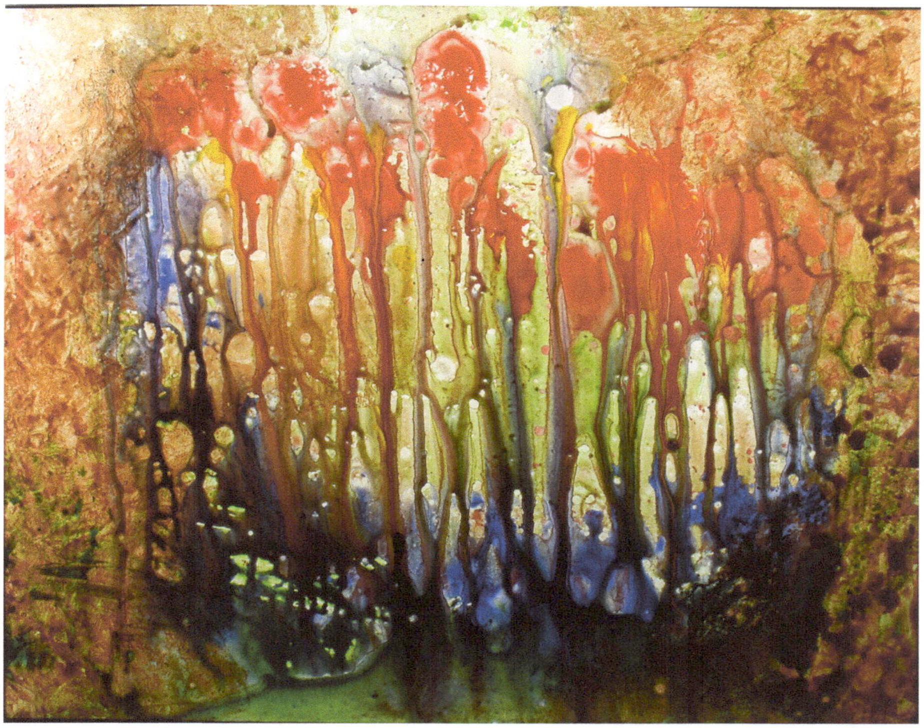

The Flowering of Color

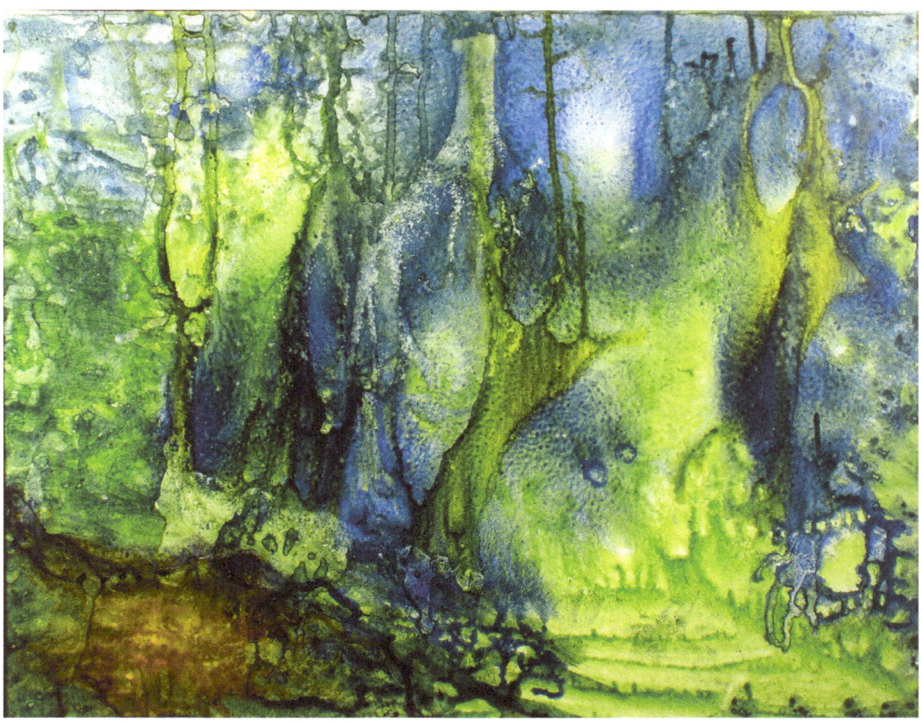

Lights in the Forest

Plein air sketches

A popular pastime in the late Age of Wonder and early Modern Age was for citizens of all types to fan out across the countryside, find a good vantage point, set up easels, and sketch away. Since wonders abounded, they often did not have to go far to find suitable subject matter. The sketches are just that—quick, spontaneous, strokes, capturing the essence of a scene, sometimes with a bit of color added.

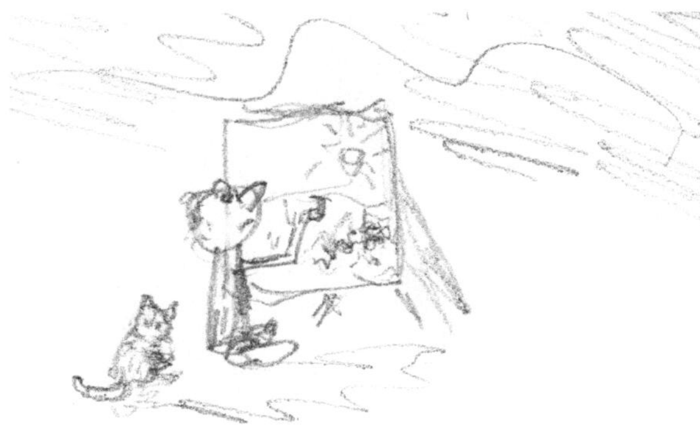

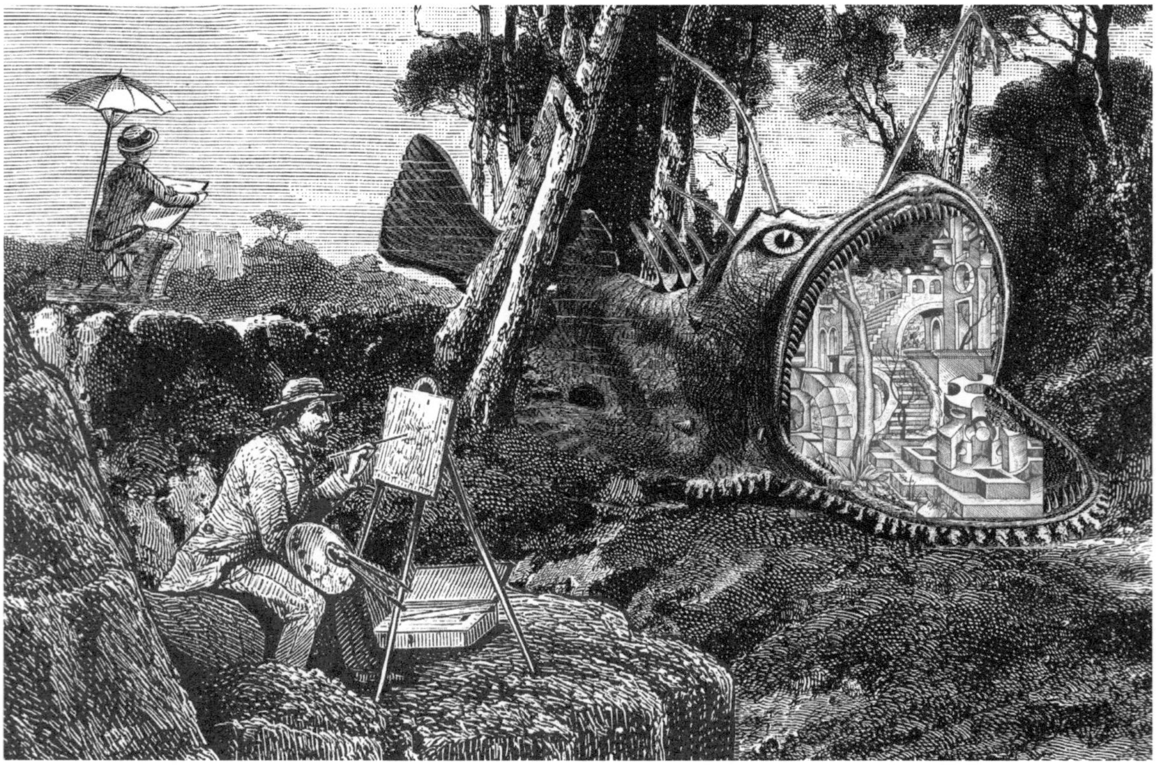

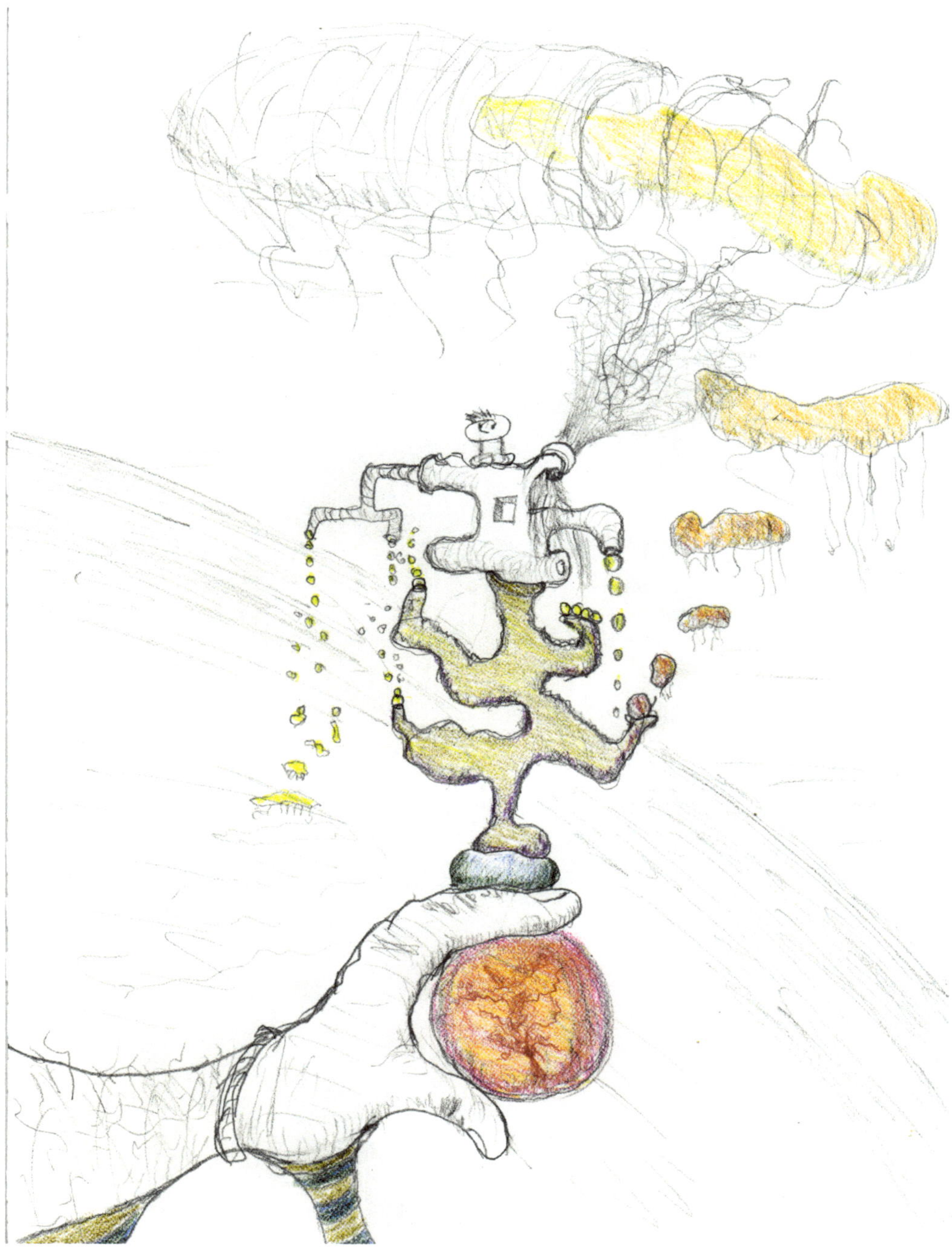

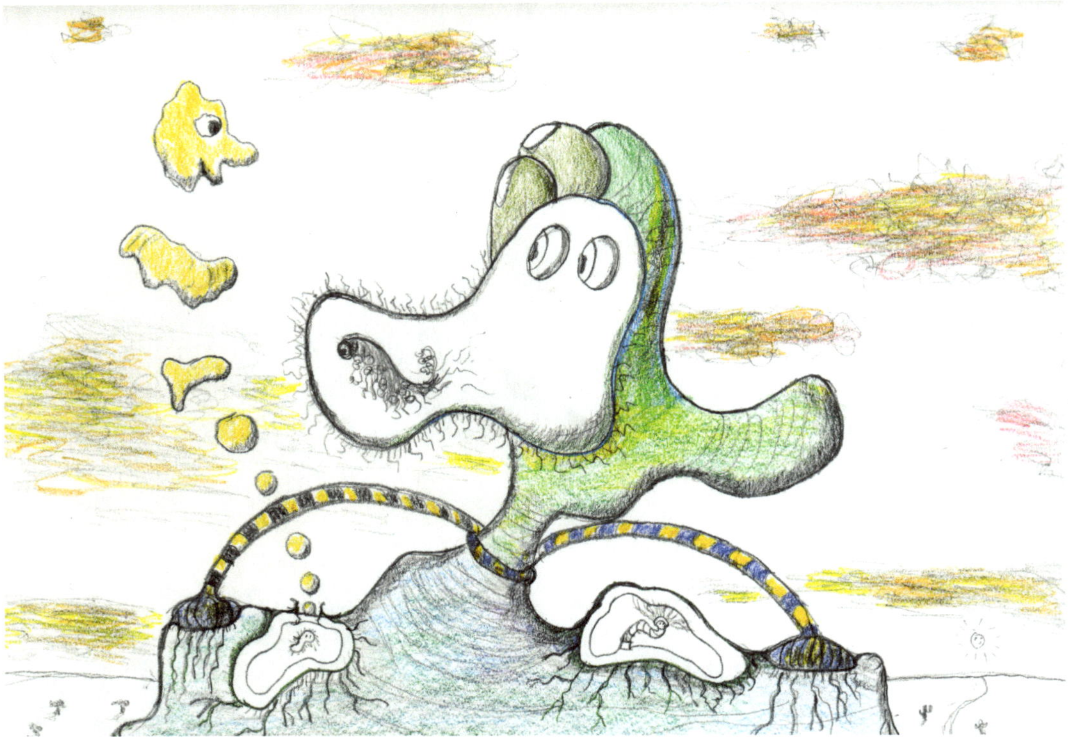

What's That??

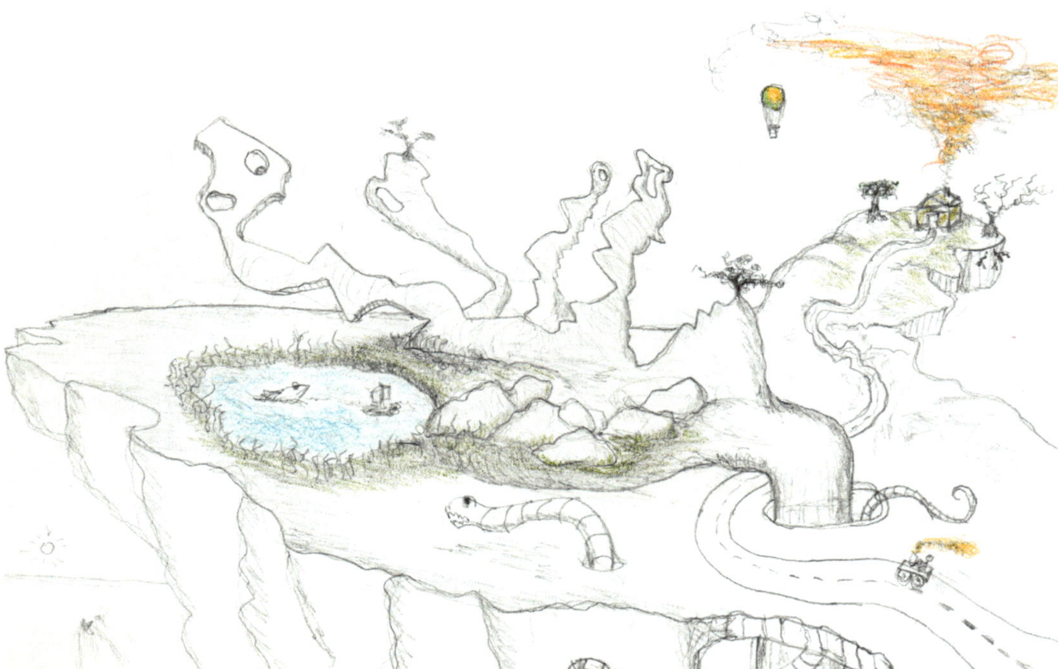

To Home and Hearth

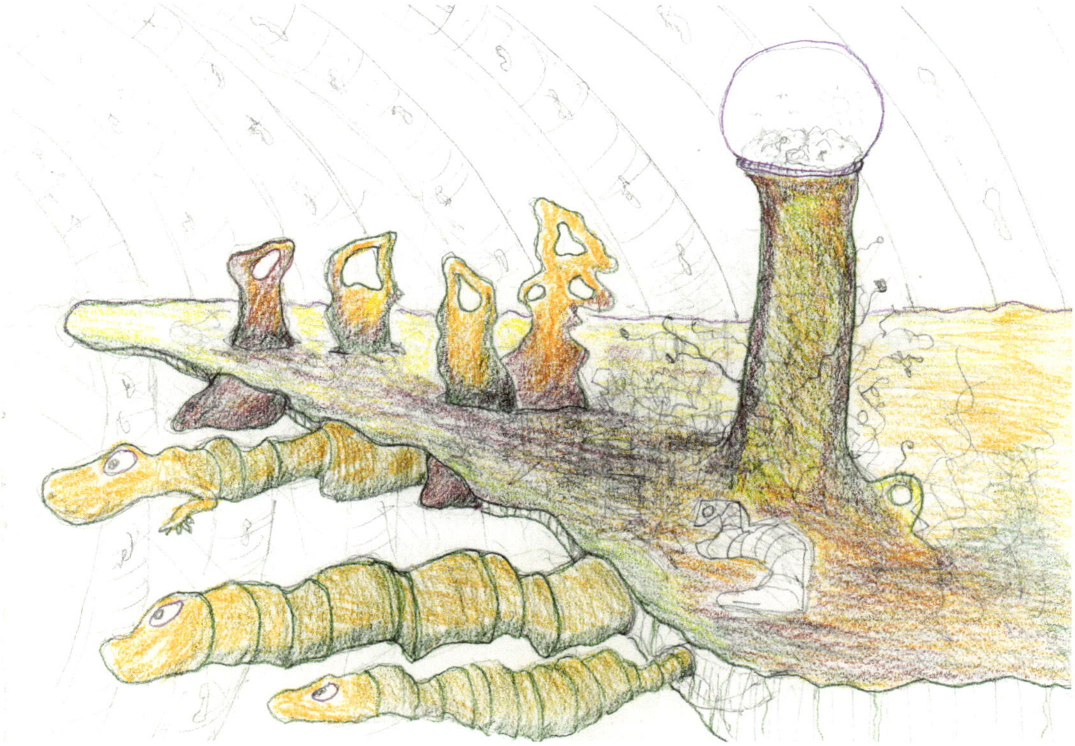

Pushing Ahead into the Unknown

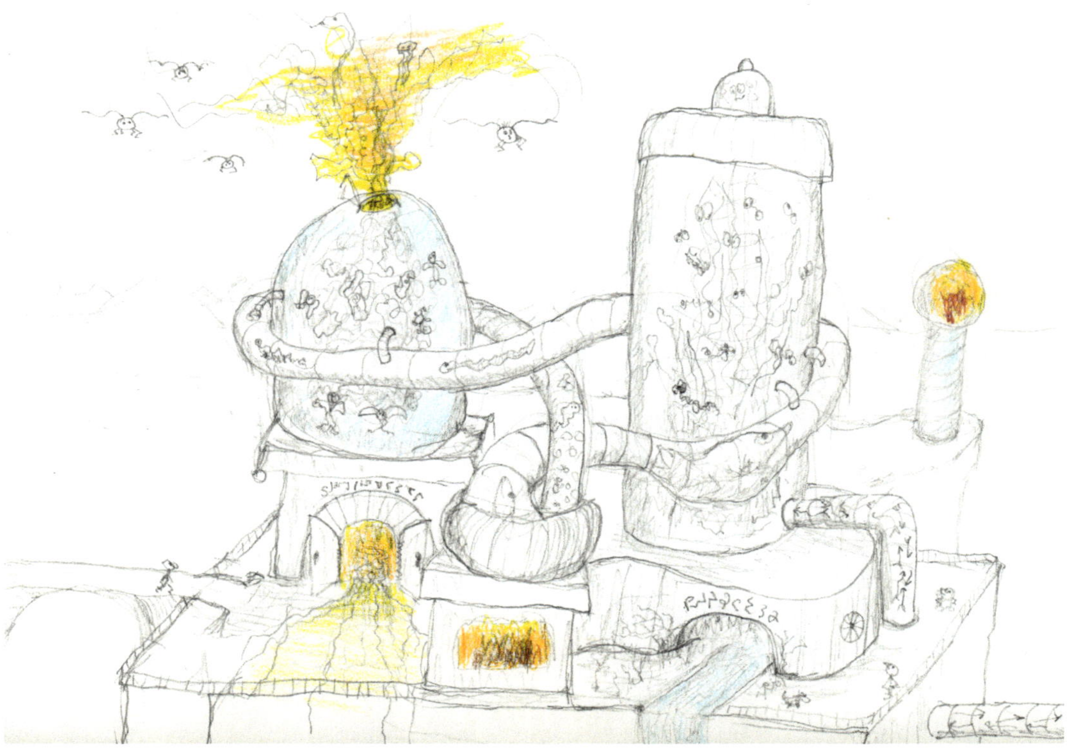

The Evolutionary Incubator

The Shoebox Museum

The Shoebox Museum was a miniature museum within the Zymoglyphic Museum. It consisted of a number of galleries of small works and artifacts, with each gallery contained in a shoebox.

These galleries are modern versions of the Age of Wonder's curiosity cabinets. Where the curiosity cabinets are complex and chaotic, the shoebox galleries were more orderly, with objects carefully labeled. Such spaces served both as little islands of order in the chaotic jumble of the larger museum, and to keep modernizing influences, such as formality and abstraction, quarantined.

The shoebox galleries also trace their descent from dioramas. While the dioramas have an emphasis on narrative, with characters acting out a story, the shoebox galleries are more formal spaces, with the only characters being the visitors to the museum. Their only function is to ponder whatever is on display (and perhaps each other).

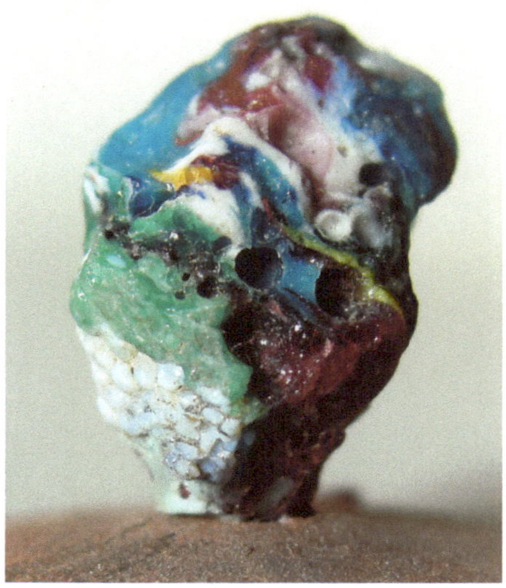

The **Rainbow Jewel from Another Planet** is one of the museum's earliest acquisitions, believed at one time (or at least hoped) to be an artifact from a distant solar system, perhaps originally a multifaceted jewel, melted and distorted like a meteorite in the last stage of its unimaginably long journey.

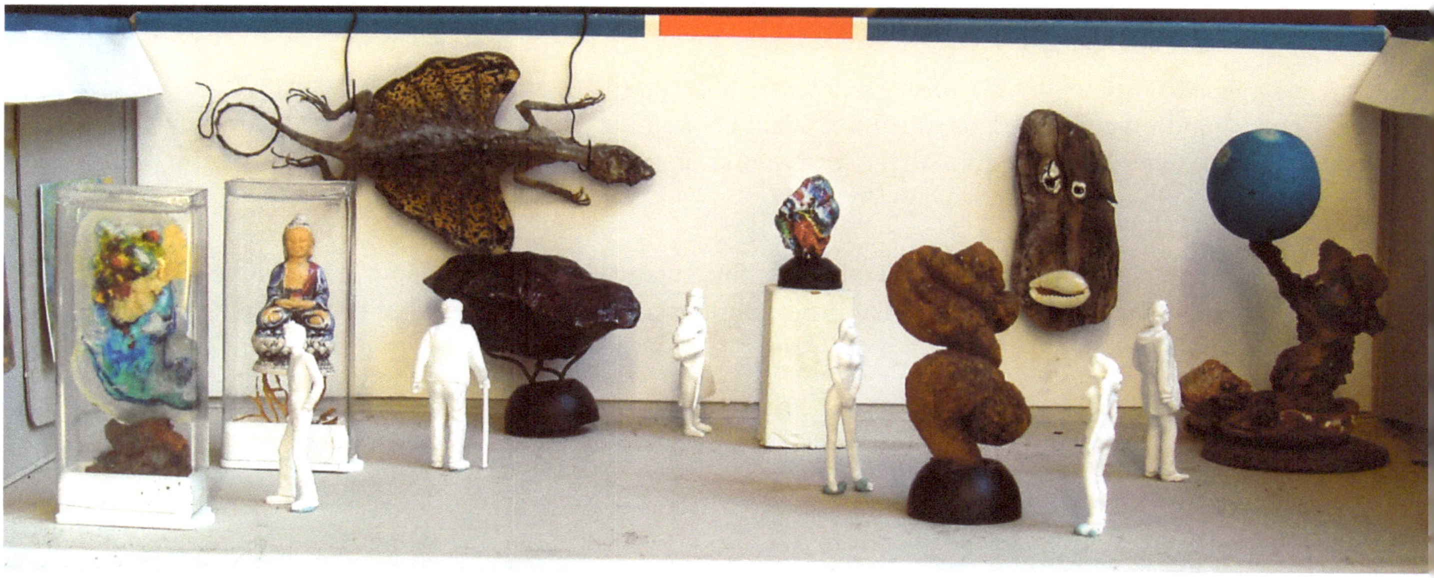

Shoebox Wunderkammer

The first shoebox gallery was stocked with wondrous and significant objects and artifacts.

From left to right:

Colorful chunk of primordial ooze from the Mud Age
Levitating monk from the Era of Oriental Influence
Mounted dragon (Draco volans)
4.5 billion year-old meteorite from the formation of the solar system
The Rainbow Jewel from Another Plant (see facing page)
Dinosaur coprolite, mounted in the style of a viewing stone
Miniature shaman's mask from the Rust Age
Mounted globe from the Age of Wonder, when the world was believed to be primarily covered in water and dotted with archipelagos

Shoebox Art Gallery #1

As the Age of Wonder progressed, specialized collections replaced the eclectic Wunderkammern. The was the first shoebox gallery devoted solely to miniature modern art. Its architecture followed a minimalist aesthetic, with a single "peep-hole" and with no apparent way for visitors to enter.

The gallery displayed a collection of miniature art from various sources. The pieces are generally untitled. The gallery is no longer extant and the photographs here are the only records of its existence.

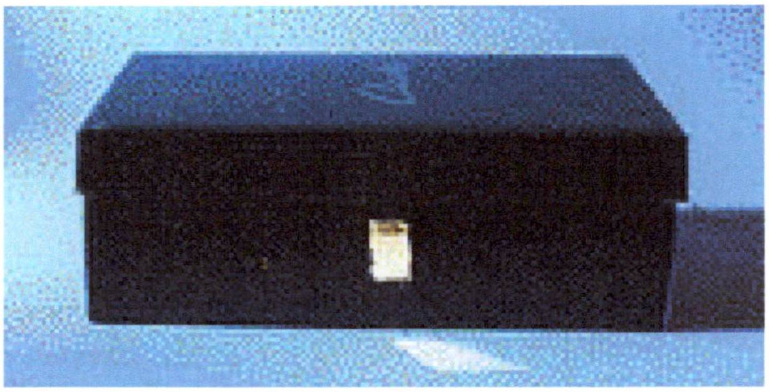

Exterior view

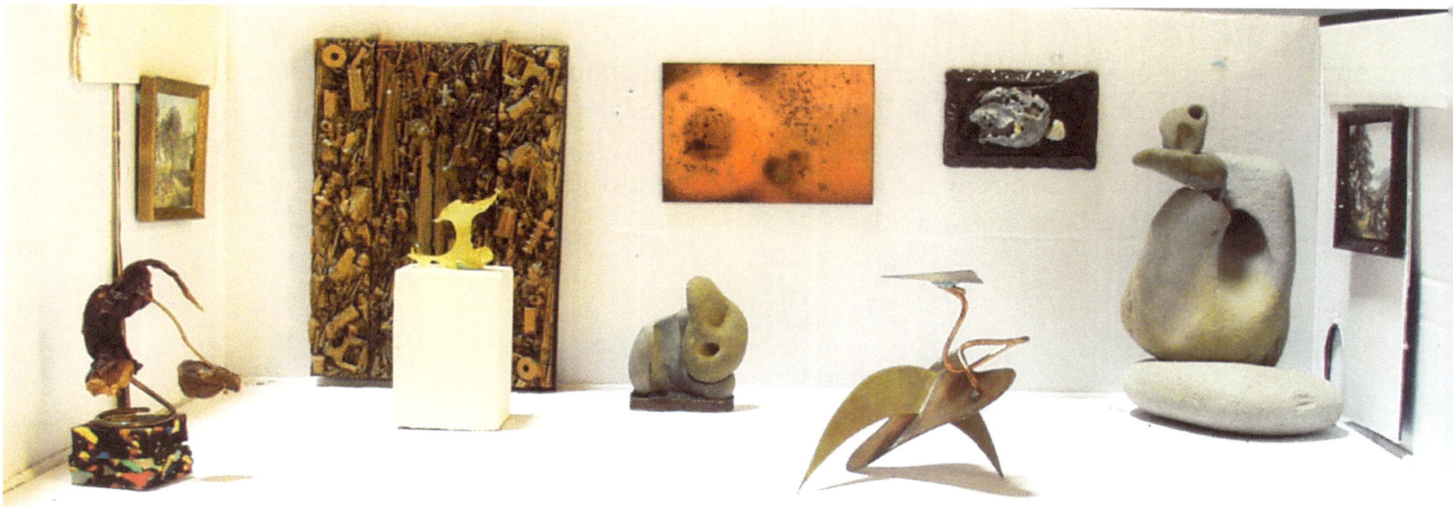

Interior view, left to right:

- Assemblage (dried pepper, wire, carpet padding)
- Dollhouse landscape
- Model railroad garbage car contents
- Readymade on pedestal (glue)
- Natural Modernist sculpture
- Readymade (weathered copper plate)
- *Aspiration* (silver, copper, brass)
- Framed assemblage (shell, wax)
- Natural Modernist sculpture
- Dollhouse landscape

Shoebox Art Gallery #2

In the second shoebox gallery, a controversial attempt was made to apply more advanced architectural principles. The gallery has been designed so as to "open up" the basic shoebox form, breaking away from the basic box form and integrate the inside and the outside. An entranceway for visitors has been added, the visitors admitted, and a few of the works have been given titles.

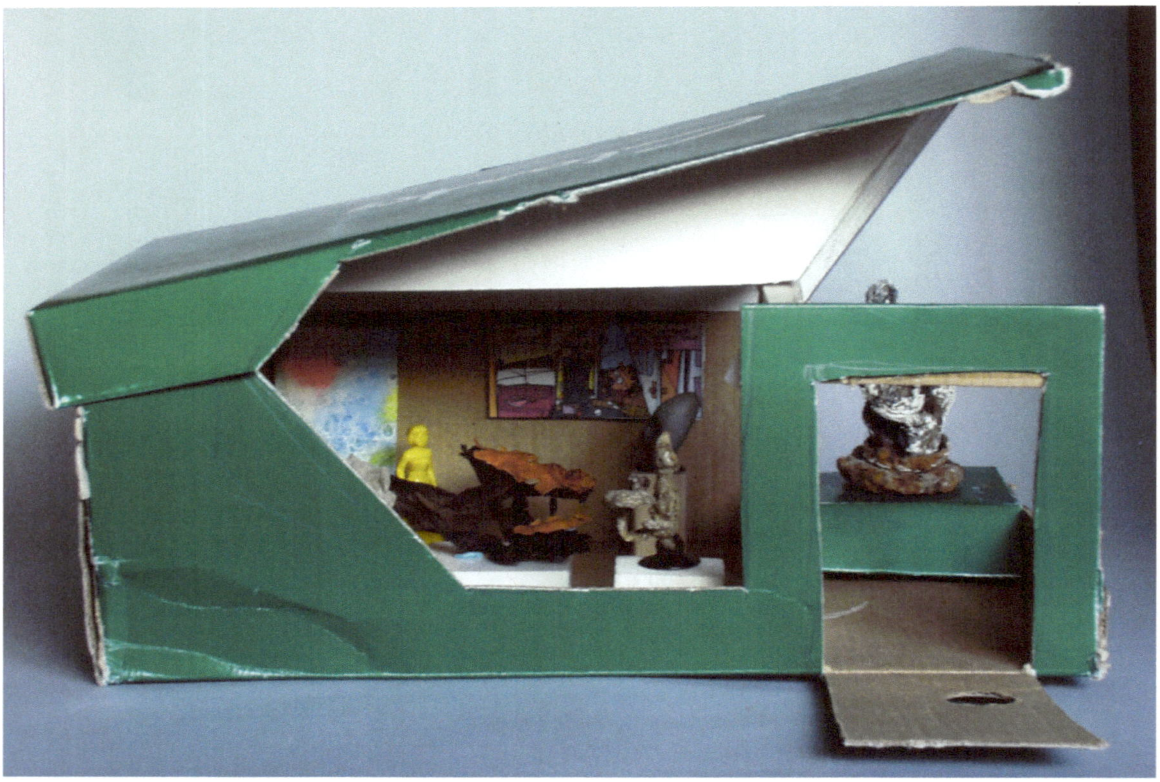

Exterior view

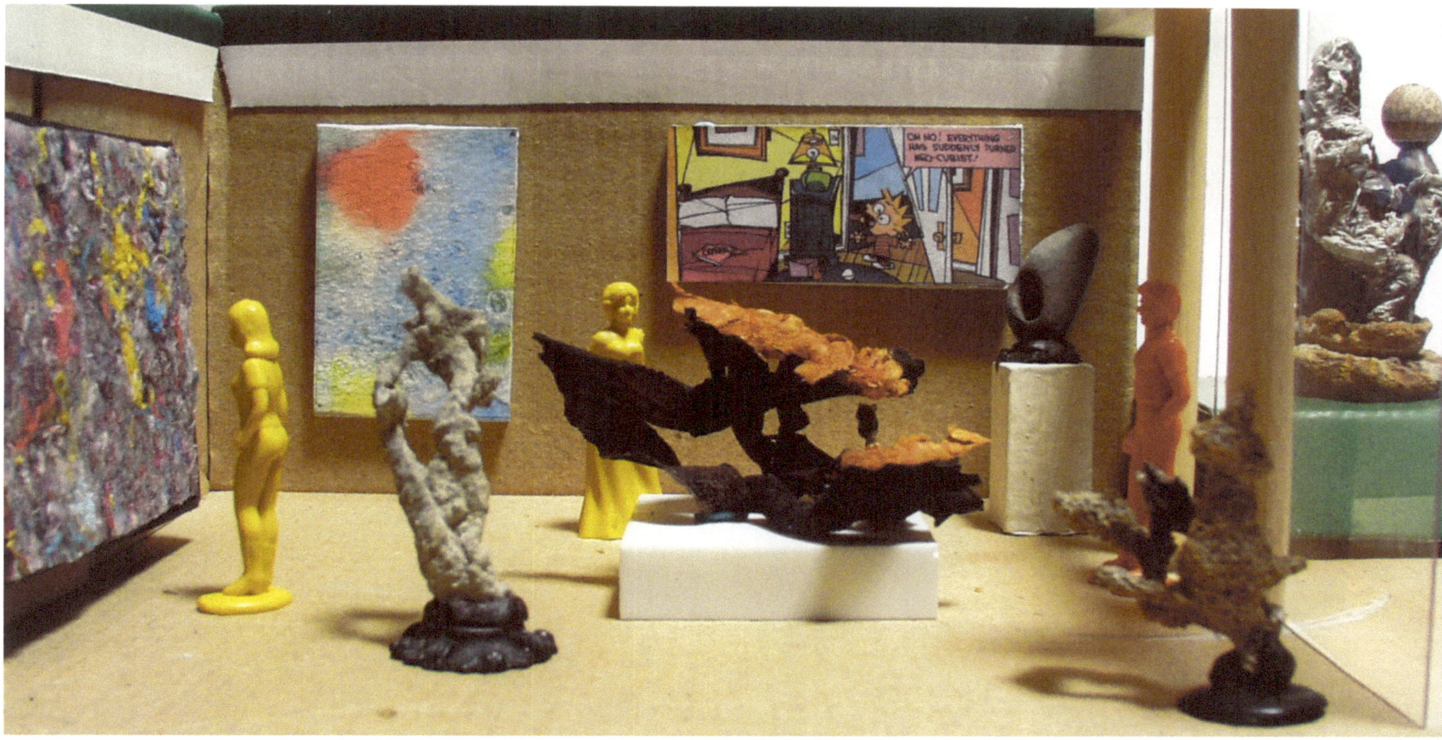

Interior view, from left to right:

String Theory (carpet padding)
Untitled watercolor
Readymade (dried mud)
Assemblage (banana peel, magnolia leaf)
Oh no... (cartoon; see p. 192)
Natural Modernist sculpture
Readymade (sea sponge)
Composition/Decomposition (melted plastic, bead, wax, rusty washers)

Shoebox Art Gallery #3

The architecture of the third shoebox gallery returns to the classic box form, augmented by some outdoor landscaping. It features miniature work by the Biomorphic Abstraction school. The two objects with sculptural qualities harken back to the Rust Age fascination with copper from the earth and intriguing objects from the sea. This gallery tended to attract a rather unconventional clientele.

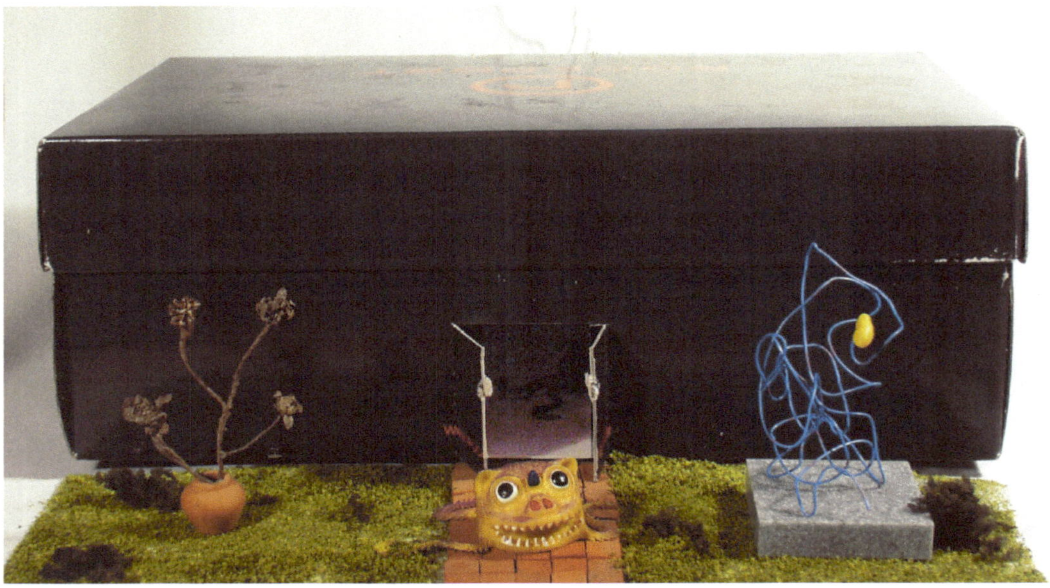

Exterior view

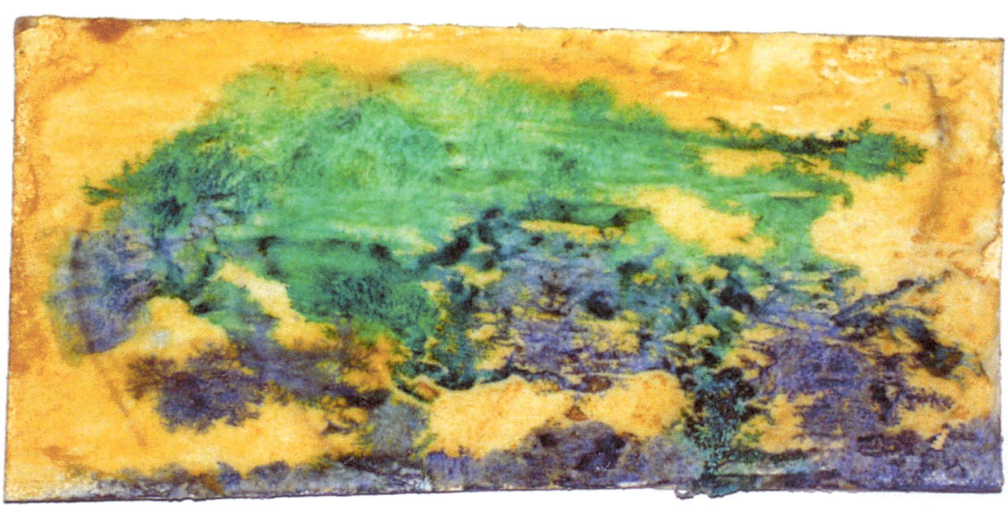

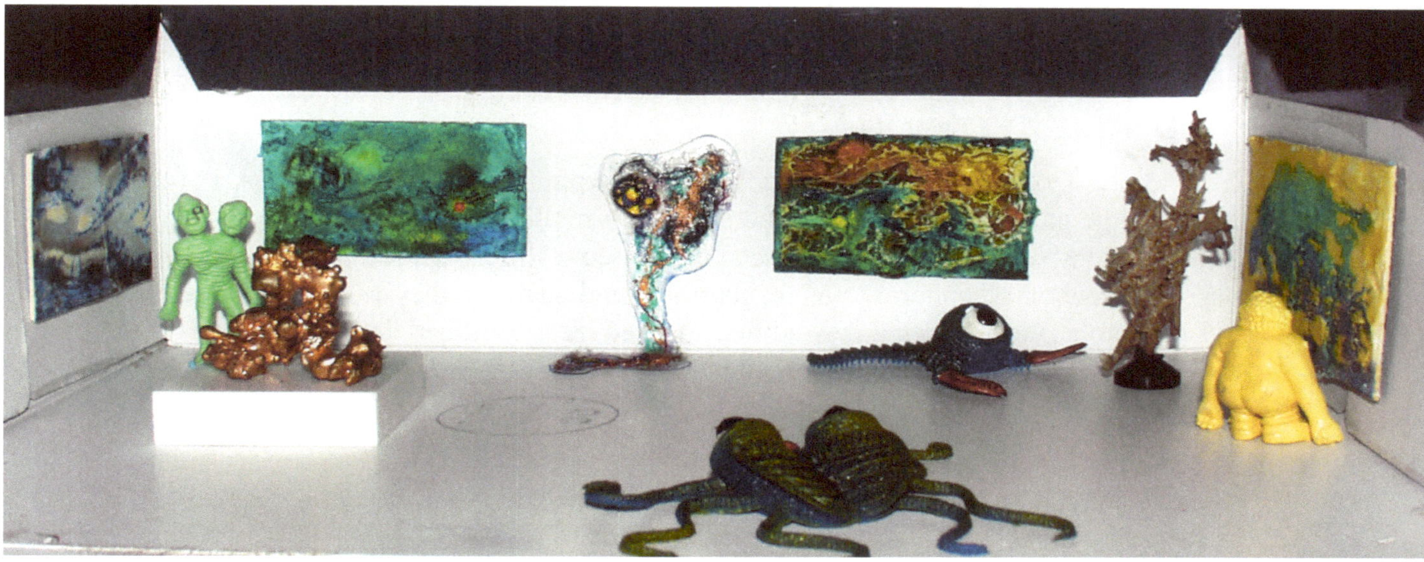

Interior view, from left to right:

- Picture stone image (see p. 19)
- Readymade (copper nodule)
- Acrylic on cardboard (right)
- Acrylic amoeba (see p. 172)
- Acrylic on cardboard (below)
- Readymade (seaweed holdfast)
- Acrylic on cardboard (facing page)

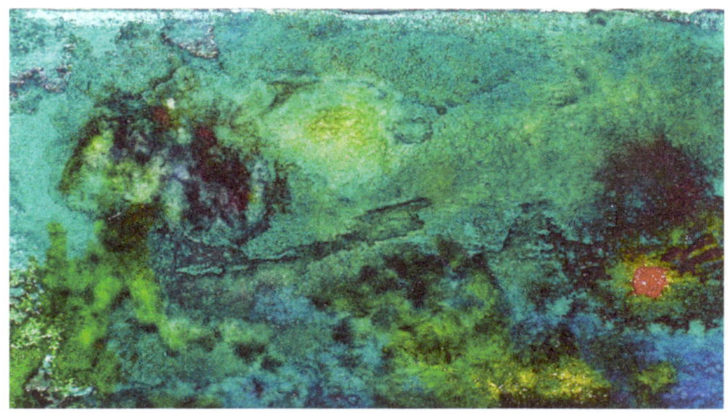

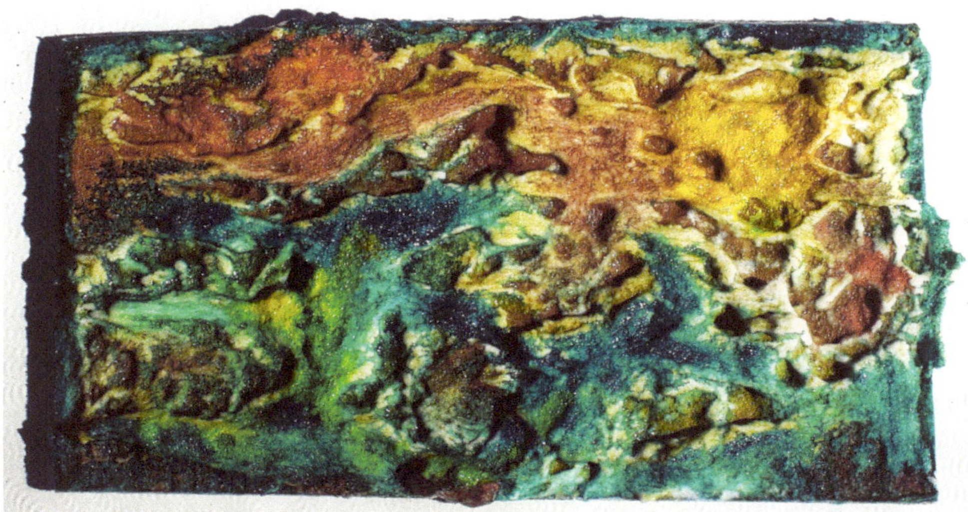

Miniature art gallery

Modernist Version

In 2013, the Zymoglyphic Museum unveiled its gleaming new Zymoglyphic Art of the Modern Age gallery to consolidate and display its smaller modern art holdings. This miniature temple of modernism replaced the museum's ramshackle and increasingly decrepit shoebox art galleries, which, charming and quaint as they were, had proved unsustainable. Visitors to the new edifice admired its streamlined design, compact dimensions (ideal for an overpopulated world), and elegant use of recycled materials. The museum also features a cantilevered rooftop sculpture garden.

The gallery's siting, tucked under an eave in the interior of the museum, and its small size enabled the architect to open up the traditional box building structure. Walls and roof are present only when necessary to support the art.

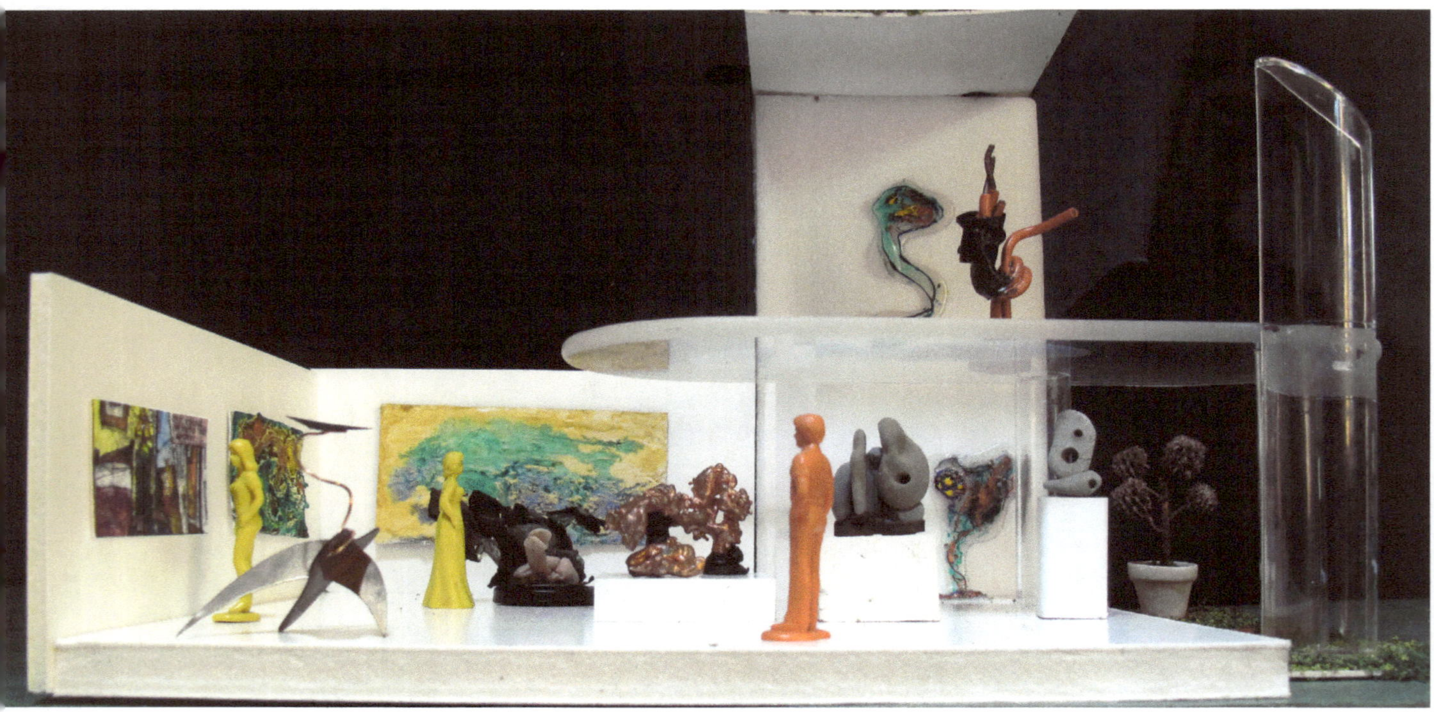

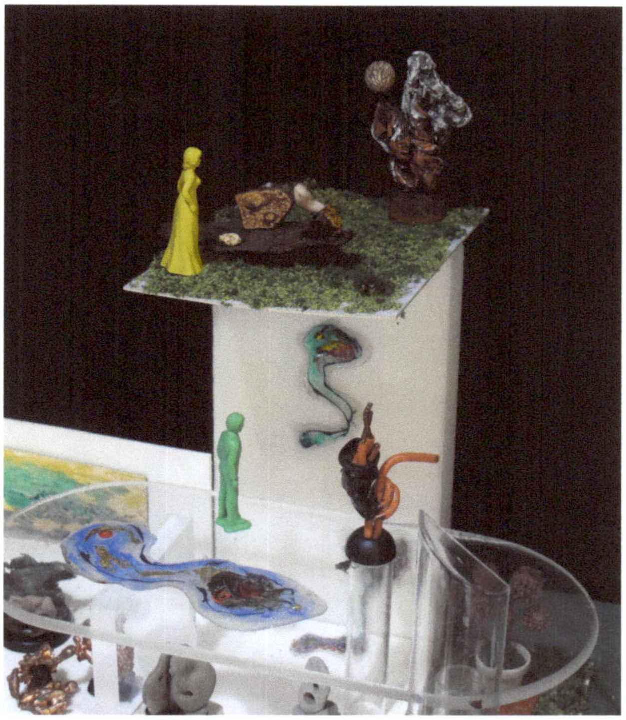

Modern Age gallery - elevated view

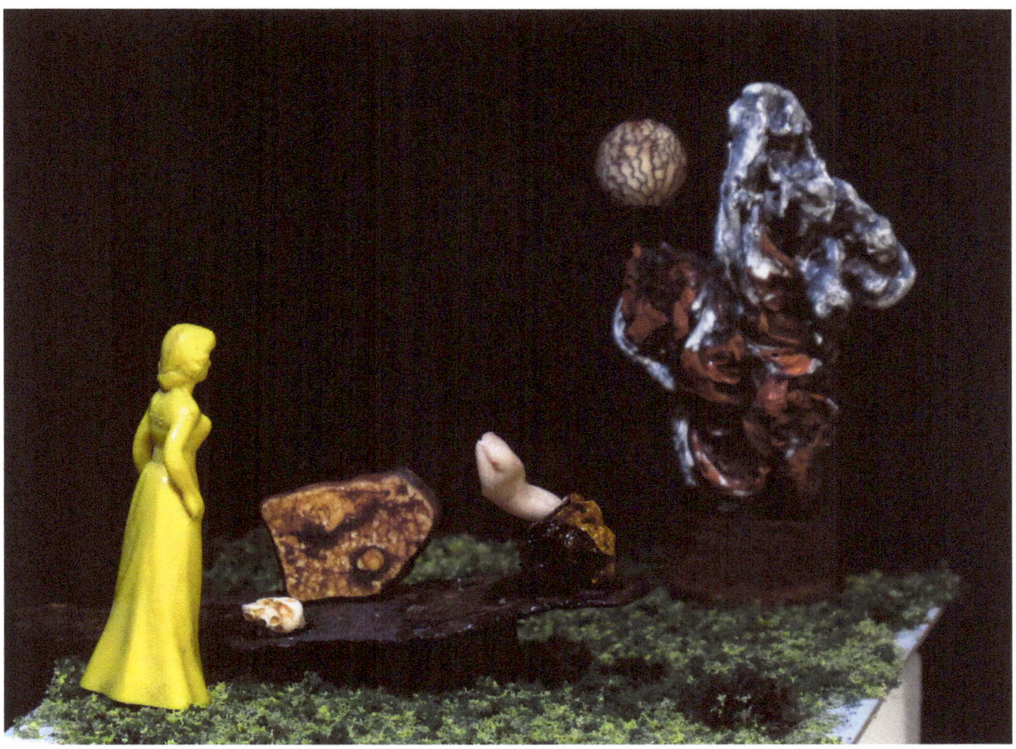

Modern Age gallery - rooftop garden

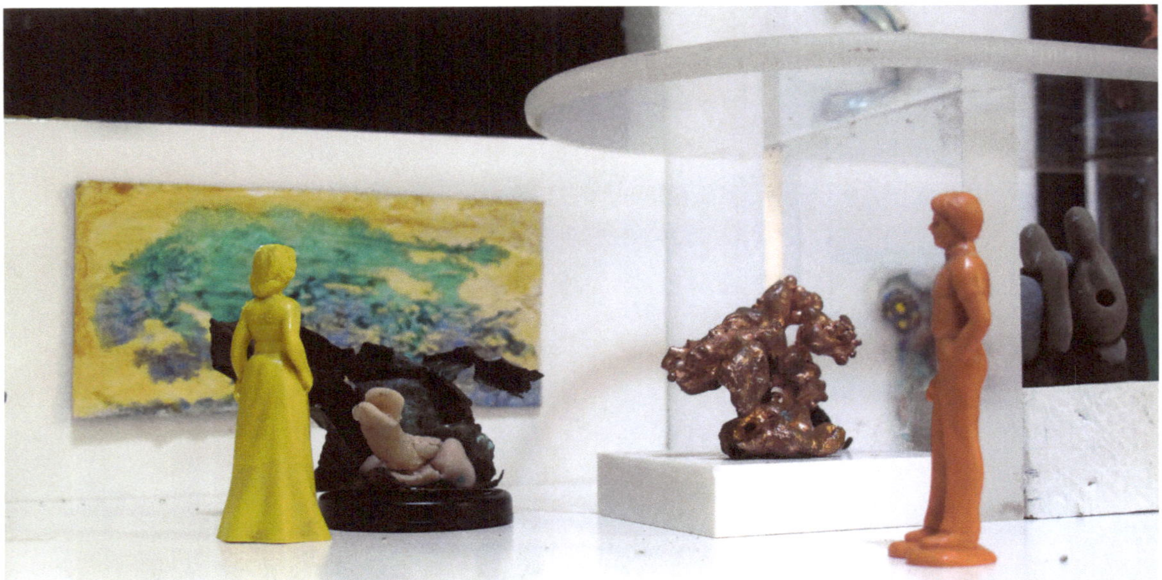

Gallery detail featuring *Hey!* (left)

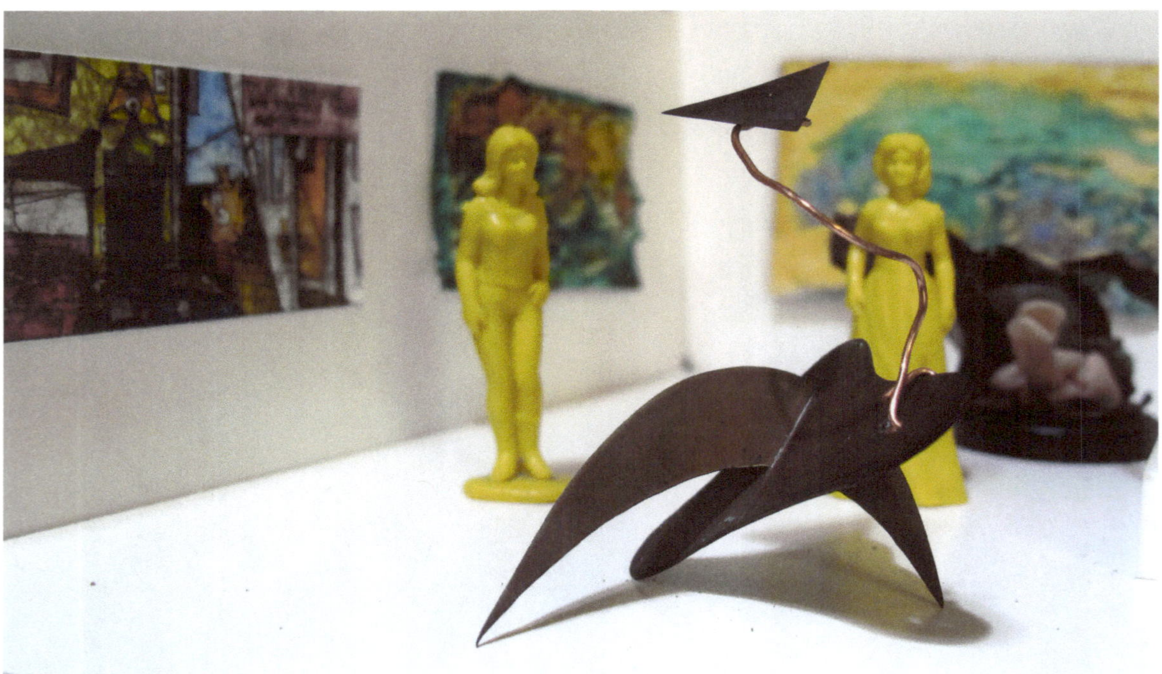

Gallery detail featuring *Aspiration*

Post-modern version

Nothing in the modern age is so constant as change itself. No sooner had the modernist ethic been proclaimed as the beacon of progress and plastic than its space age design became unfashionable and dated. In this latest incarnation, the gallery is housed in a two-story repurposed industrial space. The open fourth wall and the entranceway accommodate viewers large and small.

In addition to the major schools, the gallery shows a number of works by independent artists who rebelled against the notion of being limited to specific precepts of a style. They include (see facing page) *Hey!* (an art work that cries out for attention) and *Aspiration*. The latter was an early attempt to express the streamlined aesthetic and technological optimism of the Atomic Age, now a retro curiosity.

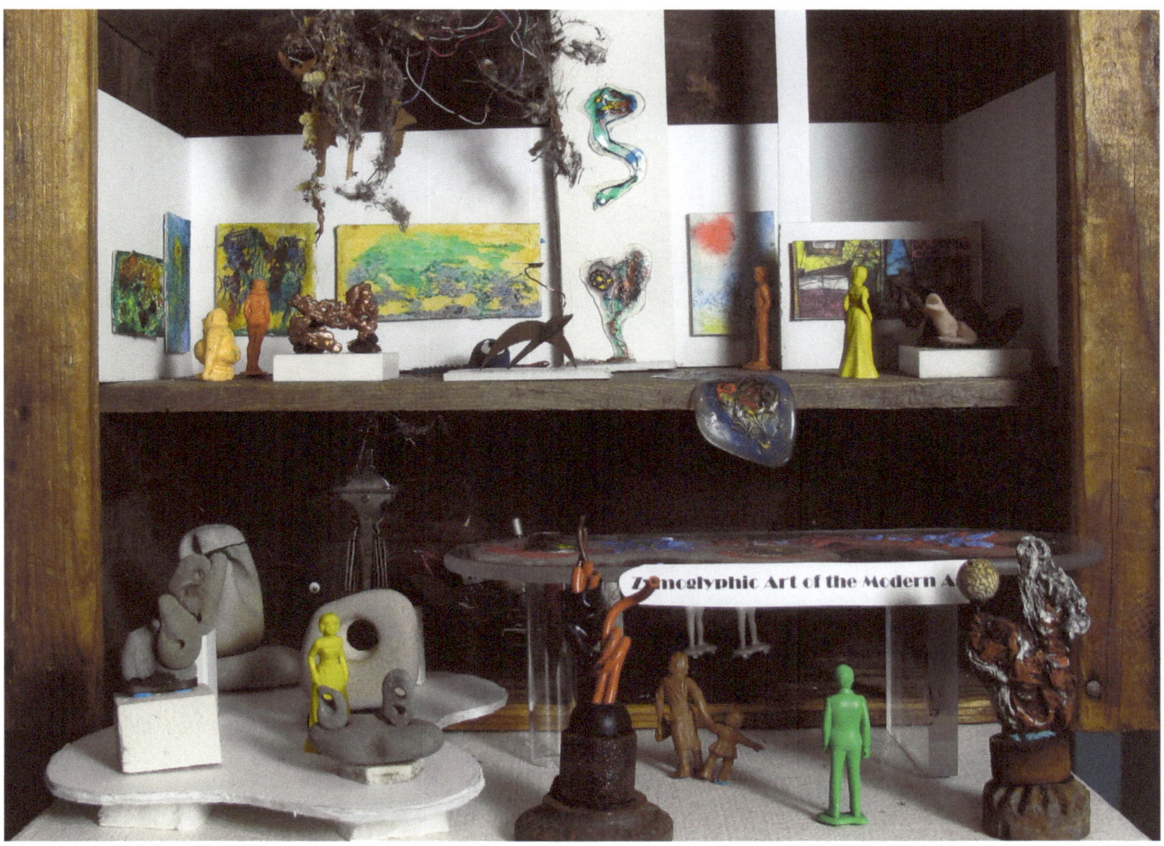

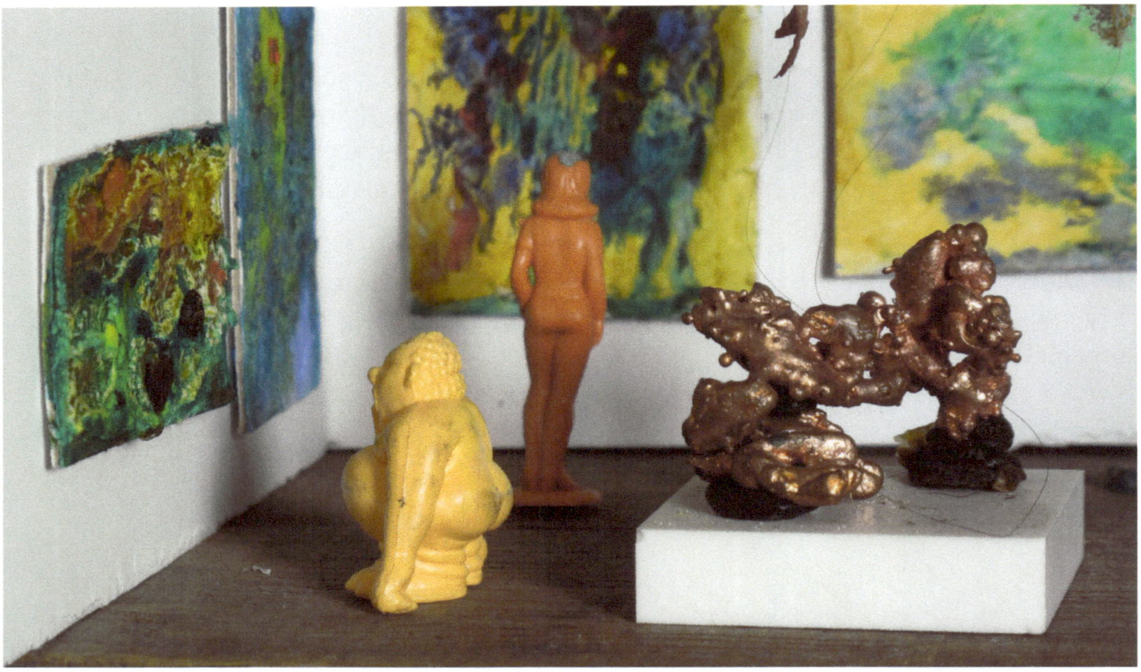

Copulae (right foreground)

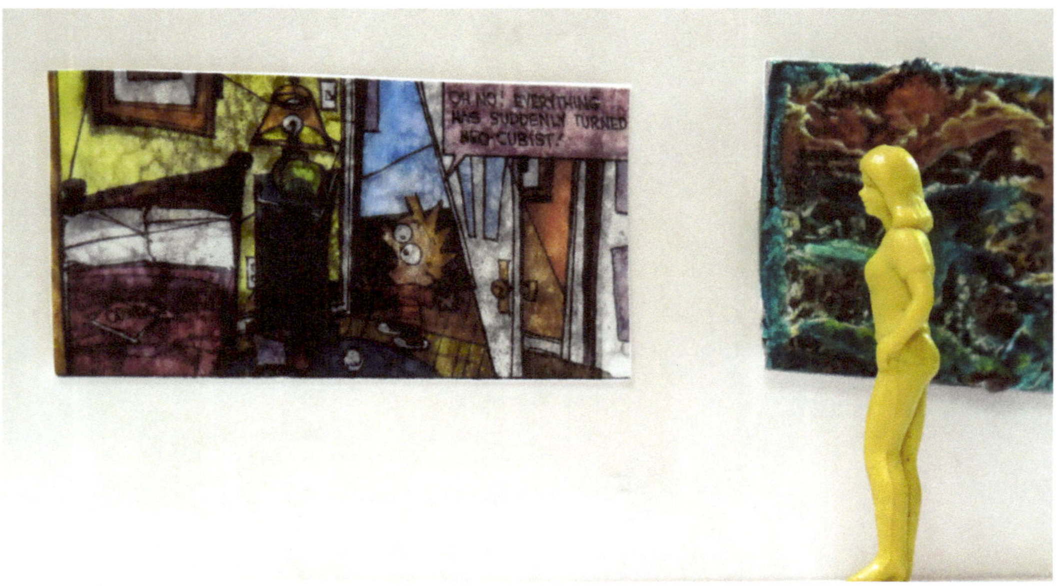

Oh no! Everything has suddenly turned Neo-cubist! (left)

Copulae is a readymade consisting of two found copper nodules onto which a sexual image may be projected. This pair was formerly a single nodule which broke into two pieces.

Oh No! Everything Has Suddenly Turned Neo-Cubist! is a water-damaged found cartoon. It is redolent with references to Cubism, Pop Art, and Postmodernist appropriation and self-referentiality, in addition to the traditional zymoglyphic values of found art and decay.

Out of Service is a partly obscured, basement-banished, depressive counterpart to *Aspiration* in the main gallery (previous page). This work symbolizes the decay and obsolescence of technology as the Modern Age cycles back the Rust Age.

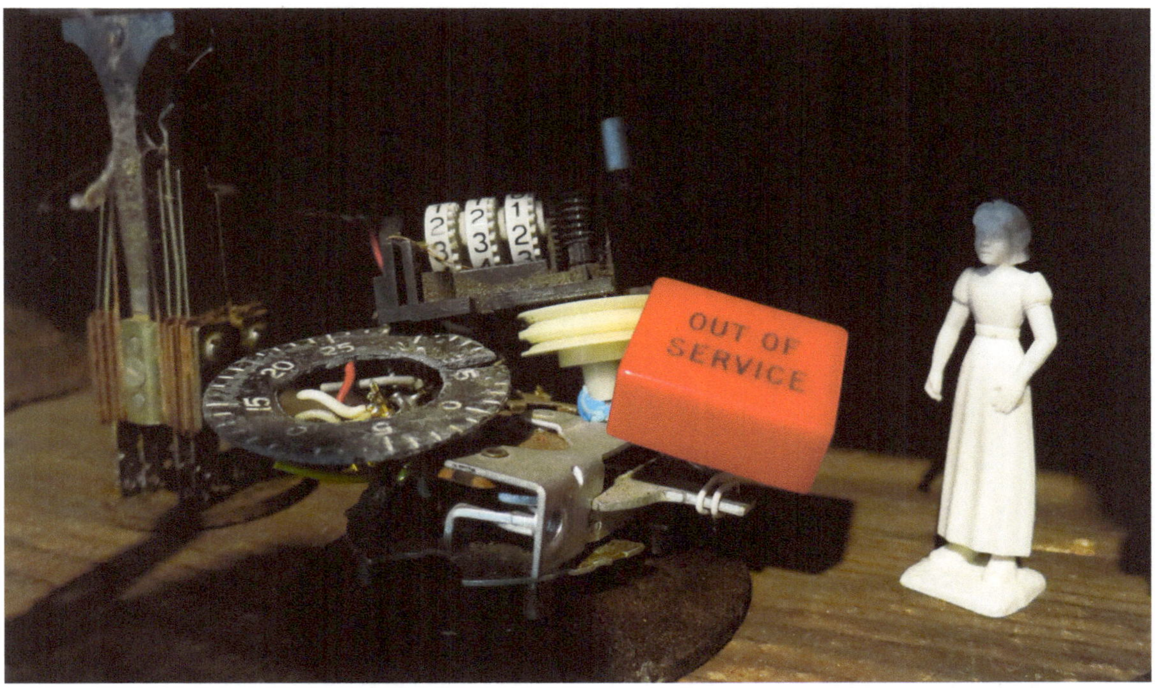

Out of Service

Dreamhouse diorama

Zymoglyphic dioramas are usually constructed in fish tanks or vitrines; this one uses an old display case to show a modern couple connecting to their "roots" in a most literal sense.

In the Modern Age, dream interpretation focused on the psychology of the unconscious instead of portents and omens. This dream-model is based on a common motif in which one discovers additional, previously unknown rooms or floors in one's home or other otherwise familiar building. A couple inhabits their tastefully furnished (by Zymoglyphic standards) habitation on the top floor, playing a ball game that will lead them down through the lower, previously unknown, levels of the house, past ancient remains, extinct fauna, wild electrical wiring, roots, fungus, and finally into to a mossy cavern containing a wellspring of genitalia

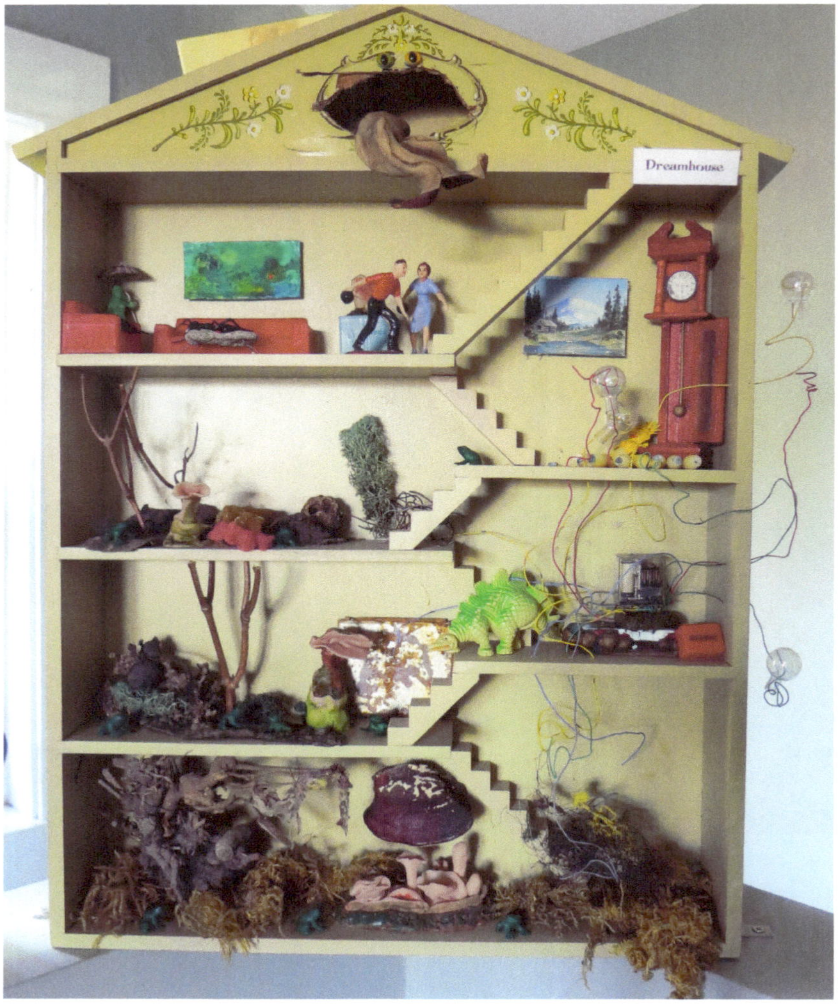

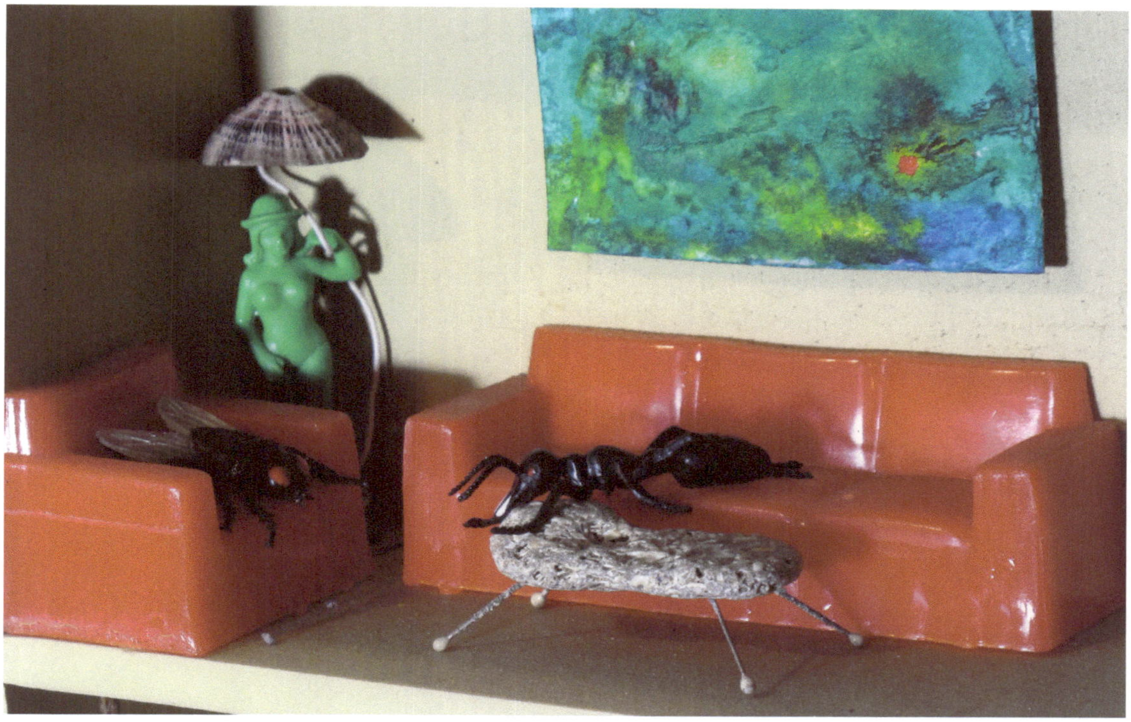

Dreamhouse - detail

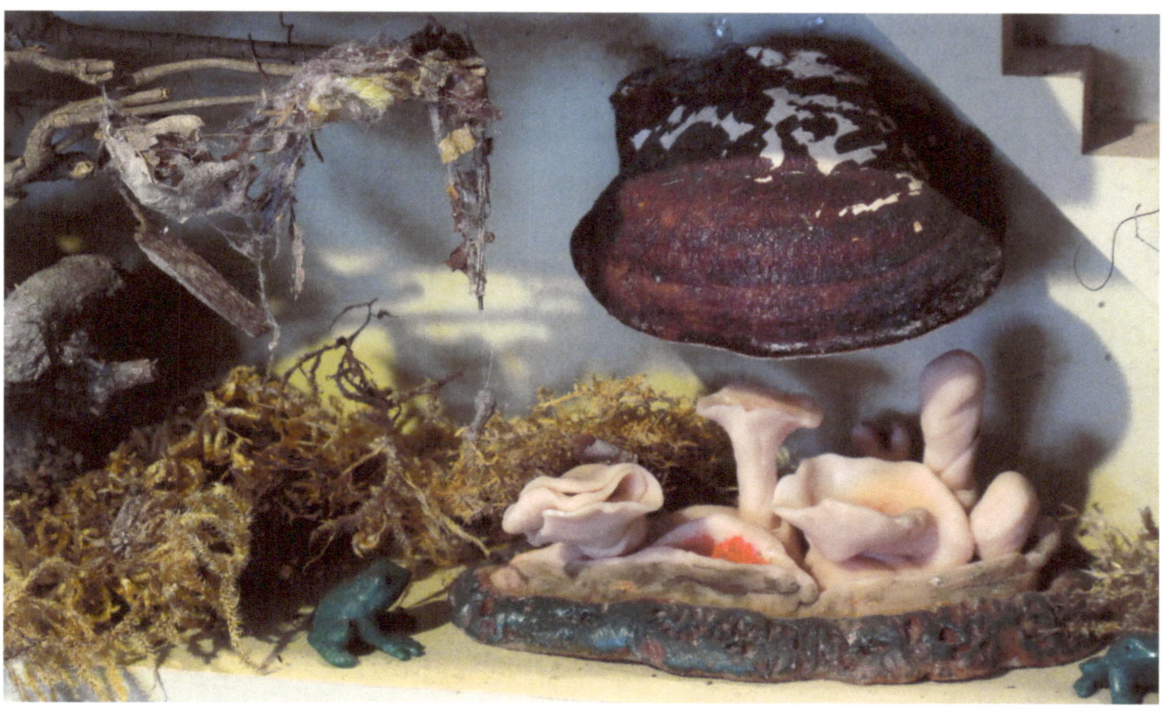

Dreamhouse - detail

The Zymoglyphic Postal Service

The Zymoglyphic Postal Service (ZyPS) is charged with two responsibilities:

- Issuance of official postage stamps for the Zymoglyphic region
- Design and printing of postcards for sale in the museum shop

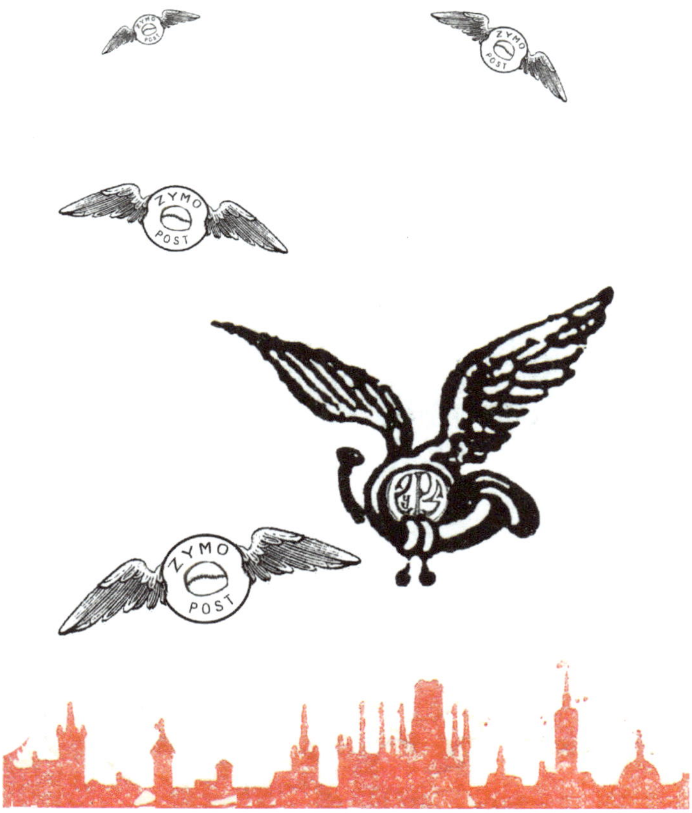

Flock of cancellations

Postage stamps

In 2012, ZyPS authorized itself to issue official postage stamps. The original authorization was based on the museum's claim to be the last territorial remnant of the once-proudly-independent Zymoglyphic region, thus qualifying the museum for "micronation" status, and thereby entitled to all the trappings of a sovereign entity.

These stamps are classified as a "local post," similar those issued by island territories for postal use within the island and to the mainland. The ZyPS postage stamps are valid only for carriage from the museum itself to a US postal receptacle. USPS-approved postage must also be present on one's correspondence to enable it to continue its journey onward through the surrounding territory of the United States and beyond.

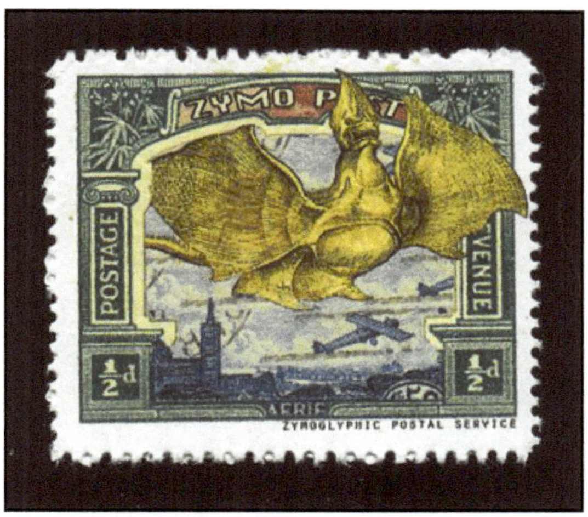

This is issue #1 of the Zymoglyphic Postal Service, a definitive airmail stamp. It features a leatherwing, one of the mysterious flying creatures endemic to the Zymoglyphic region. In this image it seems to dominate the airspace above the region's busy capital city.

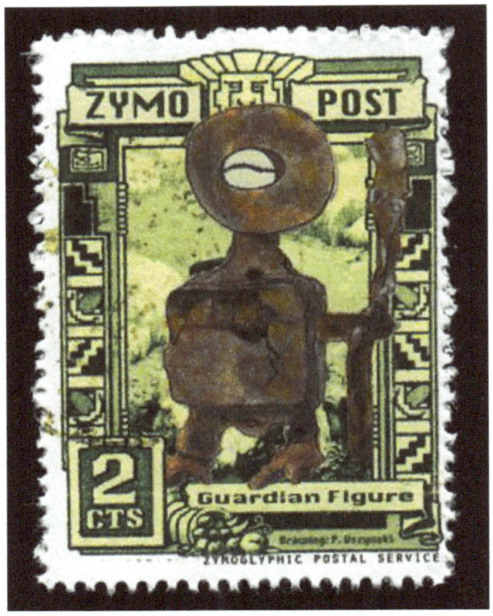

A commemorative stamp honoring the museum's iconic Guardian Figure, representing Rust Age ceremonial artifacts, combined with Latin American Art Deco elements.

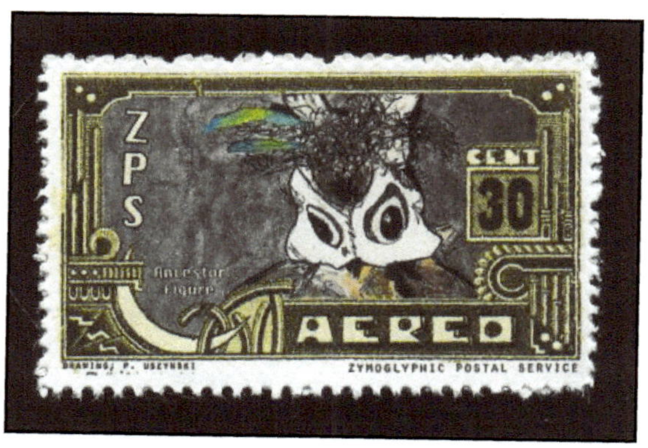

A similarly-themed stamp featuring the museum's brooding Ancestor Figure, another artifact from the Rust Age, in Art Deco style.

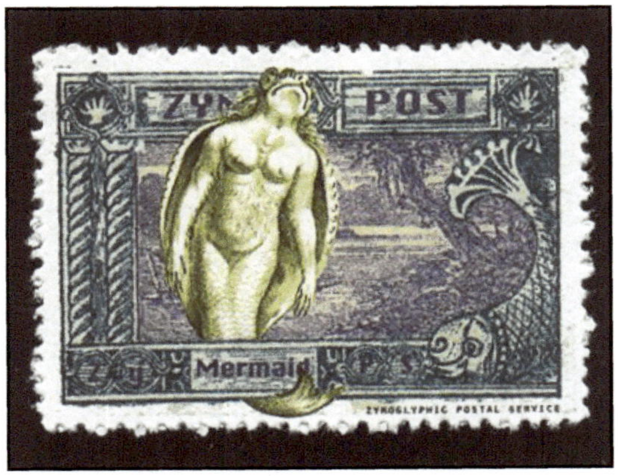

The wide, placid rivers of the Zymoglyphic lowlands once teemed with aquatic humanoids. This commemorative stamp pays tribute to these doughty chimeras as evolutionary pioneers.

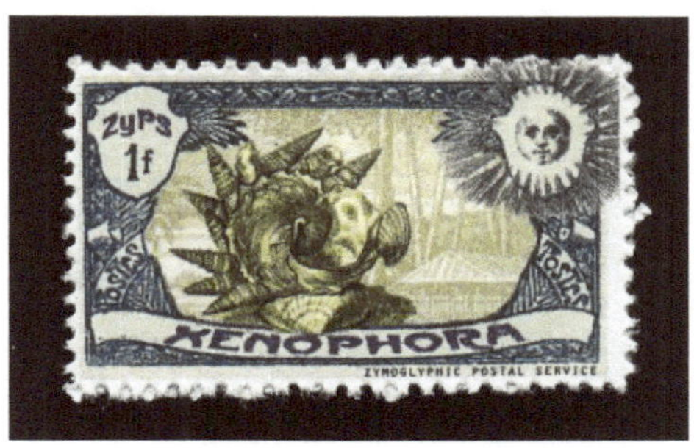

A commemorative stamp celebrating the museum's collection of "carrier shells" (genus Xenophora). These "assemblage artists of the deep" add shells, stones, and detritus to their shells as they grow.

Postcards

ZyPS has been issuing occasional postcards for the museum for more than a century, keeping in step with current styles. A dozen different postcards are currently available in the museum shop (and nowhere else).

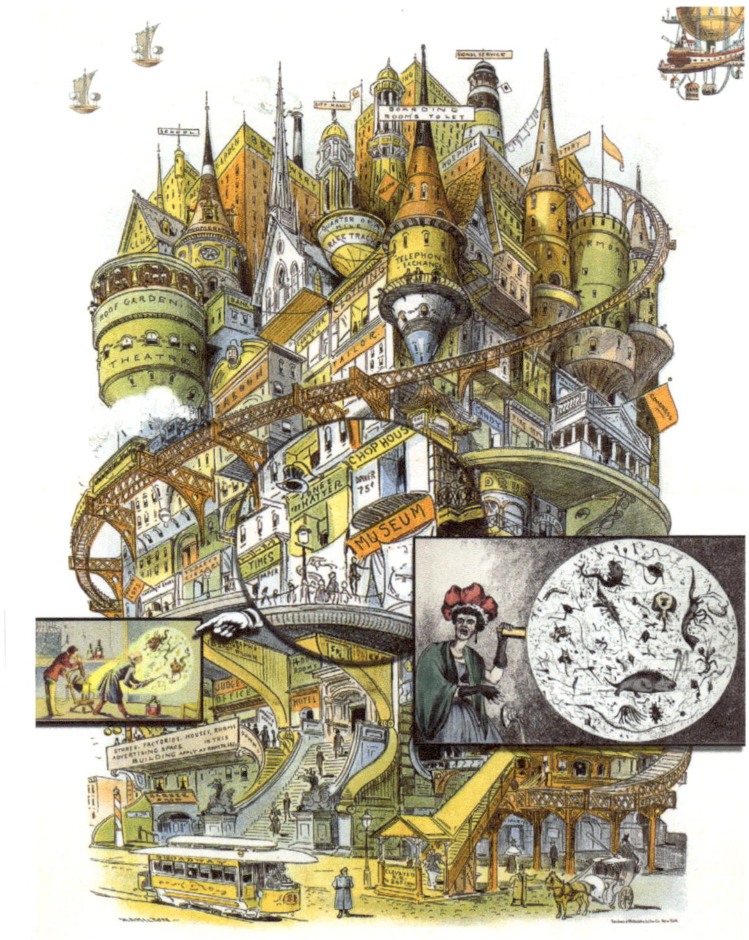

The Zymoglyphic Museum was a tenant in this fanciful structure during the decadent era that ended the Age of Wonder. Its controversial "Treasures from the Mud Age" exhibition shocked museum patrons with intimate revelations from the "primordial ooze," reminding them of their humble origins.

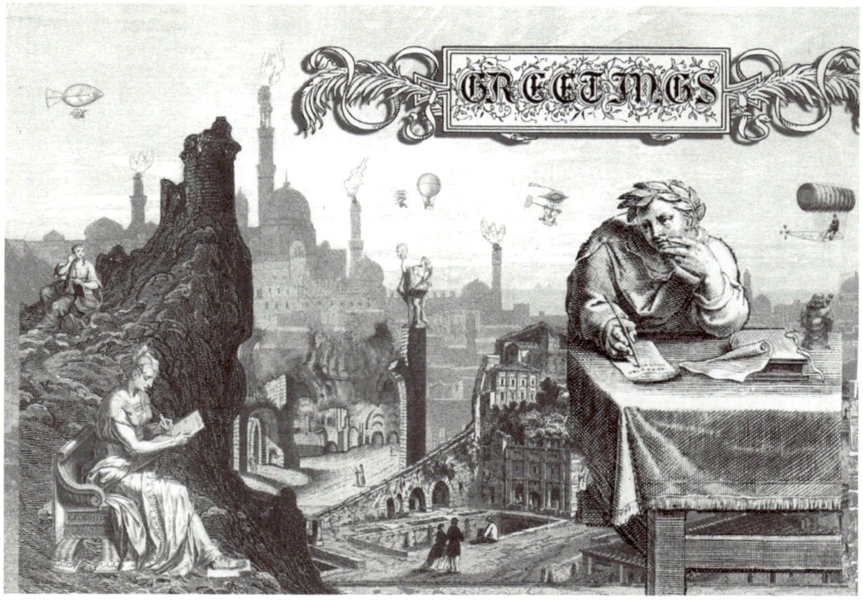

A card from the Age of Wonder showing a trio of writers trying to capture succinctly their experiences in the Zymoglyphic region's capital city and their feelings for one another and make it all fit into the allotted postcard space.

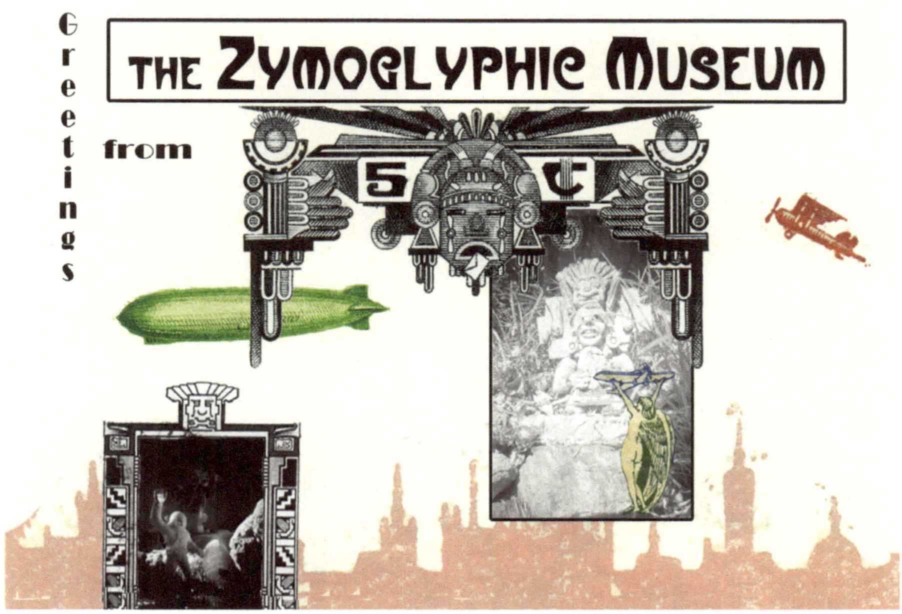

This Modern Age card shows Art Deco and Art Nouveau influence, referencing postage stamp design of the early 20th century. Art Deco was itself influenced both by indigenous Aztec design and the streamlined aesthetic of the machine age.

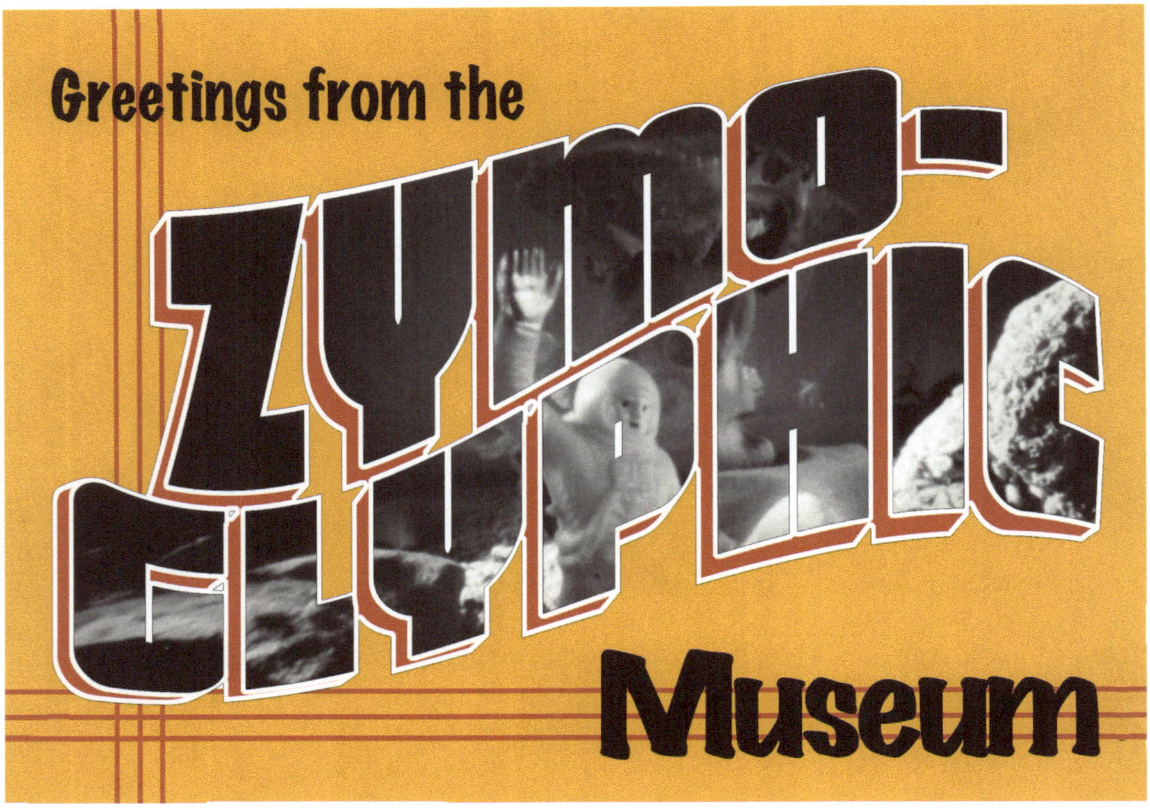

The large-letter motif for postcards became popular in the 1930s and 1940s, with scenes from the visited site visible inside the letters.

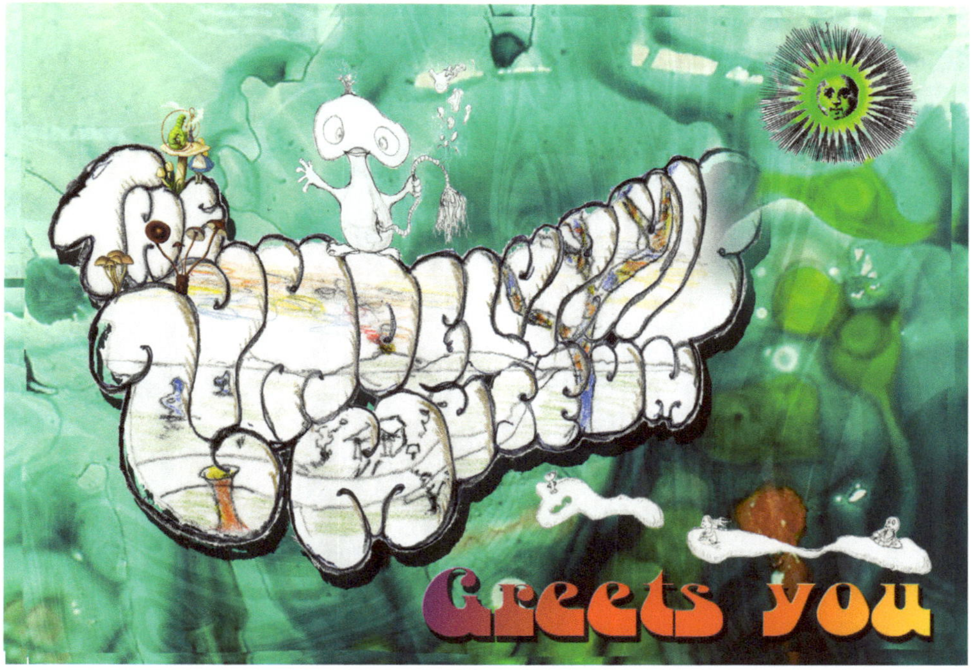

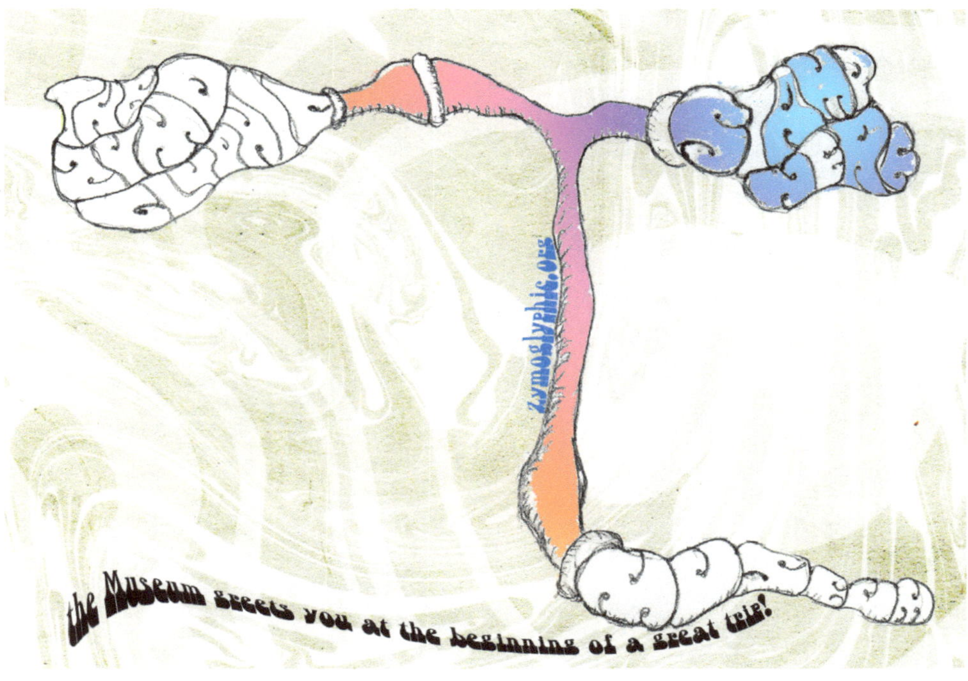

Postcard influenced by the psychedelic style of the 1960s. In a twist of roles, the museum greets you and wishes you a pleasant trip.

End Note

All art, artifacts, cover art, illustrations, photographs, and book design by the author except as noted herein.

Photo credits
p. 59, p. 61, p. 115 (bottom), p. 123, & p. 124 (lower) Dazzling Vastness
p. 79, p. 88, & p. 113 (bottom) Mark Sobell
p. 81 Meesh Rheault Miller
p. 101 (bottom) Ed Bierman via Wikimedia Commons
p. 107, p. 110, p. 111, p. 112, p. 114 & p. 122 Judith Hoffman
p. 113, p. 115, p. 119, & p. 121 Kathryn Gritt
p. 115, p. 117, & p. 161 (bottom) Terra Fenderson, Discordian Researcher
p. 125 Mark Stewart
p. 126 (bottom) Amy Eir Stocky
p. 129 (bottom) James Gouldthorpe

Art credits
Additional cover art by Taylor Perris, Camille Carpenter, and Pierre Uszynski
Jenny Haniver on p. 40 by Sarina Brewer
Primordial couple on p. 53 collaboration with Judith Hoffman
End-of-Days clock on p. 72 by Judith Hoffman
Winged lizard on p. 92 by Edward Parente
Mousealope on p. 92 by Jeanie M
Things in jars on p. 93 by Tinplate Studios
Postcard on p. 202 by Judith Hoffman

Quote sources
Jason Squamata on p. 5 from *Hotel Zymoglyphic* (2019)
Virginia Woolf on p. 88 from *Orlando* (1928)
T.S. Eliot on p. 107 and p. 122 from "The Love Song of J. Alfred Prufrock" (1917)
Loren Eisely on p. 106 from *The Firmament of Time* (1960)
Marianne Moore on p. 126 from "Poetry" (1924)

Illustrations
Pterodactyl illustration on p. 98 from signage at the American Museum of Natural History, New York City
Illustration on p. 33 by Alphonse-Marie-Adolphe de Neuville for the Hetzel edition of Jules Verne's *Twenty Thousand Leagues Under the Sea* (1869)
Section title on p. 141 by Karen Koshgarian

Publications from the Zymoglyphic Museum Press

The Zymoglyphic Anthology (2019)

An assemblage of documents by and about the museum, including historic documents, essays, fiction, poetry, and visual art

Hotel Zymoglyphic by Jason Squamata (2019)

Illustrated poem cycle inspired by a visit to the Zymoglyphic region

Views of the Zymoglyphic Region (2010)

Scenes of daily life in the cities, mountain villages, woods, and jungles of the region as seen during the Age of Wonder

Sketches of the Zymoglyphic Region (2010)

A vision of the Zymoglyphic region channeled through the medium of spontaneous drawing

Pamphlets and Booklets

The Zymoglyphic Manifesto
Creating and Curating Your Own Personal Museum
The Positively Unknown: A Kid's Guide to the Zymoglyphic Museum
by Alex Gaston
The Literary Guestbook

For more information, visit:

zymoglyphic.org/pubs.html

CPSIA information can be obtained
at www.ICGtesting.com
Printed in the USA
LVHW071818041120
670721LV00013B/57